Y0-CBF-171

FOR MARY W
FROM John W

WITH ALL THAT
LOVE OVER ALL
THOSE YEARS —

Chronicles

FORSAN

MEMINISSE

♡

Hoxton House, 1989

CHRONICLES

of the Episcopal High School
in Virginia
1839–1989

John White

WILLIAM L. BAUHAN, PUBLISHER
Dublin, New Hampshire

Copyright © 1989 Trustees of the Episcopal High School in Virginia.
All rights reserved.

Library of Congress Cataloging-in-Publication Data:

White, John, 1911–
    Chronicles of the Episcopal High School in Virginia, 1839–1989 / by
John White.
        p.   cm.
    Includes bibliographical references.
    ISBN 0–87233–100–8
    1. Episcopal High School (Alexandria, Va.)—History.   I. Title.
LD7501.A4494W47   1989
373.755'296—dc20   89–39957
                                                                          CIP

Designed by David Robinson. Composed in Linotron Sabon by
TCI, Chicopee, Massachusetts, and printed and bound at Thomson-
Shore, Inc., Dexter, Michigan.

ABOUT THE PICTURES: Many of the pictures in this book have been
copied from old issues of *Whispers,* dating back to Number One,
1903. The originals may exist somewhere, perhaps in the as-yet-
uncharted *terra incognita* of our archives, but they could not be
found. That is why these re-reproductions may be fuzzy. Too bad.
Sorry. (Will somebody, some day, *please* untangle those archives?)

This book is dedicated to all those
who have brought something to this school,
left something, and taken something away.

Acknowledgments

A great many people helped to make this book, more than can be named here. Certain ones, however, were so especially generous with memories, suggestions and criticisms that I cannot let them go unrecorded. They are:

Peter James Lee, Bishop of the Diocese of Virginia; former EHS Headmasters Dick Thomsen and Young Flick Hoxton and present Head Sandy Ainslie; Diane Albosta; Ed Alvey; Jane Baun; Roberta Biery; Anne Bingham; Harry Blackiston; Bill Boothe; John Stewart Bryan, III; Patrick Henry Callaway; Eddie Craig; V Dabney; Dick Daniel; Cooper Dawson; David Dougherty; John Dukes; Leigh Dunlap; Warren Harvey; Dorothy Hayes; Ernest Helfenstein; Sherrill Houghton; Bob Howard; Fraser Hubbard; David Hughey; Tom Hummel; Chester King; Lester Kinsolving; John and Janet Lawrence; John McCain; Nelson McDaniel; Lynn Magruder; Flip Morris; Ann Morse; Jim Parton; Al Phillips; Alice Pickman; Alice Mary Pierce; Dan Proctor; Ed Rice; Justin Slate; George Period Thompson; Richard Tidwell; Peggy Tompkins; Dick Yarborough.

Thanks of a more professional sort go to Grace Forbes, fearless and fruitful editor; Phyllis Kerr, visionary/pragmatic artist; Bill Bauhan, far-beyond-the-call-of-duty publisher, and to "Zephyr," my IBM-AT computer.

Of course, the book would not be, would not exist at all, without the reminiscences of scores of Old Boys. I am inexpressibly grateful to them. They are not listed here; their names appear throughout, and so do their faces.

Finally, we should all thank, with all our hearts, those far-sighted men of God who, distressed by the "unorganized and desultory" education available to the boys of the Episcopal Diocese of Virginia a century and a half ago, founded the school whose history this is.

Contents

Foreword   xiii

Introduction by J.S. Bryan III   xvii

I. HISTORY

1. In the Beginning, 1839–1861   3
2. The War, 1861–1866   27
3. De Profundis, 1866–1870   53
4. Old Bar, 1870–1913   61
5. Old Flick Old Flick, 1913–1947   90
6. Between the Wars, by Dick Daniel   133
7. Modern Times, 1947–1989   186

II. HIGHLIGHTS

Activities   227

Alexandria   227

Animals   230

Awards   232

Bell   232

Bun   234

Characters   236

Colleges   238

Cubicles   240

Curriculum   242

Customs   245

Demerits   250

Discipline   256
Egypt   260
Faculty   263
Food   267
Fruits (One)   269
Fruits (Two)   277
Ghosts   283
Girls   285
Honor   287
Howard   293
Latin   296
Legends   297
Malaprops   299
Miracles   300
Miscellanea   301
Misspellings   302
Mysteries   303
Names   304
Nicknames   305
Nobility   309
Numbers   312
Others   312
Plant   317
Poetry   320
Publications   321
Rat   327
Rogues   333
Sports   333
Transport   346
Vivant et Mulieres . . .   350
Washington   354
Addenda   355

Homecoming Thoughts by Todd Waters   361
Lauds   364
Epilogue   365
Bibliography   367
Index   369

List of Illustrations

Hoxton House	*Frontispiece*
Seals of Diocese of Virginia, Seminary, EHS	6
Principal Pendleton, 1839	9
Charter members of Pithonian Society, 1840	12
Letter of Worthington Johnson, Jr., 1840	14
Principal Dalrymple, 1845	17
"The visit of Poe," 1847	19
Principal McGuire, 1852	24
Civil War balloon	29
Ironclads *Monitor* and *Virginia* fighting at close range	30
T. Berry Brazelton	33
Roberdeau Wheat, Randolph Fairfax	36
Lieutenant Robert E. Lee, 1831	45
Lincoln, April, 1865	50
Russell Boyd, Robert Bunn, Lewis Johnston	52
Arlington House, then and now	55
Principal Gardner, 1866	58
Movement of center of population, 1790–1980	63
Principal Blackford, 1870	65
Colonel Llewellyn Hoxton	69
Ad for School, 1872	70
Athletic Day program, 1877	72
Invitation to Field Day, 1894	79
The Chapel, circa 1895, and Blackford Hall, 1900	82
Invitation to Commencement, 1913	86
Old Bar's plaque	88
Principal Hoxton, 1913	94
"The Old Guard"	97
V Dabney	99

Lloyd's station, 1912   101
The School library today   101
Ben Baker   103
Extract from School catalog, 1917   104
Company A, Company B, 1918   106
Charles Wertenbaker   107
A Rat's expenses, 1918   109
Richard H. Fawcett, '11, as "Ideal Soldier," 1918   110
Joe Harrison   111
Trains, Alexandria, 1927   112
Instructions for monitors, 1924   114
Skin Lane, Harry Blackiston, Aldie Dudley   116
Platt Okie, Bob Quin, Conway Moncure   119
Roy Mason, Llewellyn Thomas, Jim Meem, 1931   120
E.P. Wroth, Bill Hanson, J. Bryan, III   122
OldFlick by his father's picture and sword, 1938   124
Two Flicks, 1920, and five Blackford sons, 1939   124
The School at war, 1942   126
Norborne Berkeley, A.B. Kinsolving II, C.J. Churchman   127
The rifle team, 1943   128
Choir, 1944   130
Waiters, 1944   131
Dick Daniel   134
Reflection in lake, 1906   136
The School from the air, 1933   136
Automobile, vintage 1911   143
Joseph Bryan (1856–61)   149
Joseph Bryan's great-grandson, John Stewart Bryan III   149
Joseph Bryan Library, 1943   149
Centennial Hall   153
Blackford Hall, c. 1910   153
Red Duer, Jim Meem, Roy Mason, 1931   163
Rusty Anderson, Bo Mueller, Dean Smith, 1989   163
Jarvis Todd Baker gets a letter   171
Monitors, 1924, among them Stump Philbrick   176
Monitors, 1925, among them Billy Clay   177
Monitors, 1933, among them John Cay   181
Principal Williams, 1947   192
Young Dick Williams   193
Headmaster Thomsen, 1951   194
Last Principal, first Headmaster, 1951   197
Charley Tompkins, 1938   197
Patrick Henry Callaway, any time   197

Dick Thomsen, Pearce Connerat, Cotten Alston   198
John Pinder, DeCourcy Orrick   200
Young Flick as Head Monitor, 1935   202
Young Flick as Headmaster, 1967   203
William Bee Ravenel, 1968   205
Regi Burns   206
Dane Snowden   207
John McCain   210
Ryvers Wright, Lance Koonce, Sandy Ainslie   215
Headmaster Ainslie, 1981   217
Seniors walk in Washington, 1989   219
Commemorative Tree: Blanchard Randall and John S. Morton   219
Callaway Chapel, 1988   220
Banner on Hoxton House greets Russian visitors, 1989   222
Bill Goodwin   230
Eugene Geer   231
The bell   233
Stuart Taylor   235
Vic Donaldson's ad, 1919   235
Bun Donaldson's store, c. 1925   236
Littleton Wickham   237
Cooper Dawson, Bill Shiers   238
"In dorm," 1914, and 1979: Hughes and Lowman   241
Exercises in math and Latin of Ewing Lawson, 1896   243
Chris Wollak '84 writing four columns   251
One-fifth of four columns written by Alex Bounds, '89   251
Matt Quarles, Bill French, Clarence Gaines   253
Jack Mizell, Dick Tucker   258
Cigarettes in *Whispers* 1910, 1921   260
Egypt, 1946   262
The "New Old Guard," 1989   263
Faculty, 1906   264
Faculty, 1985   265
Newton D. Baker cartooned, Kenneth Royall, 1911   273
Steve Ailes and Bo Callaway   273
Richard Bales's "Elegy for a Master" (Robert Latham)   275
Bob Latham and Dick Bales   276
Alex Jones   276
"Whom? Meem?"   280
Joe Crow Hall among newspapers reading a book   282
Charles McCandlish, H.T. (Joe Crow) Hall   282
"Gardy-loo!"   282
Old Bar Blackford's mother, Mary   283

Pretty girl (not smoking), *Whispers* 1904   286
Harry Flippin, Hunter Faulconer, 1925   286
Hunter Faulconer, Harry Flippin, 1926   286
The honor pledge   290
Harry Klinefelter   292
How Howard House became Hoxton House: 1839, 1878 . . .   294
. . . 1893, 1940, now   295
Hollis Hand, Lester Kinsolving, A.L. Kinsolving   301
Big Tuie Kinsolving, 1948   307
Arms of Fairfax and Percy and castle of Helfenstein   310
"Instant knightification," 1929   311
Outside the Seminary Chapel   315
General Samuel Cooper   316
Map of the School grounds   318
Architect's dream—School, 1913   319
Pendleton Hall   320
Front pages of 1888 *Chronicle*, 1891 *Lightning Bug*   323
Down through the years with the *Chronicle*   324
First *Whispers*, 1903, cover of *Daemon*, 1983   325
Sports trophies, 1926   334
Football team, 1901   335
Then and now: football teams of 1894, 1988   337
Lance Mangham   338
First basketball team, 1913   341
Ben Baker jumps for the King of England   341
Ticket to Washington baseball game, 1920   342
Cotten Alston as Cotten Alston sees him   343
Vinny Giles wins British Amateur, 1975   344
Our carriages: 1894, 1910   347
Our carriage today   348
Tennant Bryan   349
Mary Landon Jett   353
Bill Boothe   356
Shack, in 1916 *Whispers,* which was dedicated to him   359
Todd Waters   363

Foreword

WHAT HAPPENS when one is given the daunting task of writing the 150-year history of his school?

How can one do rounded justice to the extraordinary chronicle of a twice-named, twice-extinguished, twice-reincarnated, oft-dishevelled, magnificent institution?

Students of Proust translate his *A la Recherche du Temps Perdu* as "Remembrance of Things Past" rather than the more precise "Search for the Lost Time." I have actual remembrance of some things of the Episcopal High School past; I was there from 1926 to 1930. But all of the times before, and most of them since, have been lost to me.

In search of our *temps perdu* I have gone down five paths:

1. *The Histories.* There are two existing histories of EHS. *The Story of a Southern School,* by Arthur Barksdale Kinsolving, traces our career from founding to 1922. Dr. Kinsolving, EHS 1878–81, taught here in 1883–84, then completed the Seminary course in two years and was Rector of St. Paul's, Baltimore, for nearly forty years.

The High School, by Richard Pardee Williams, recapitulates that earlier work and carries the story on to 1964. Mr. Williams, EHS 1901–04, taught here from 1908 until his retirement in 1958, and was Principal from 1947 until 1951.

Together these two superb books constitute a chronicle far above my poor power to add or detract: *sine quibus nihil*—"without which nothing"—without them this present effort simply could not be.

A third record, of a unique sort, has also proved valuable beyond rubies as a source. It is a comprehensive, minutely detailed, fascinating memoir of life on the Hill between the two World Wars written by a man who lived and photographically remembers that life, Dick Daniel (1925–32), son of our late master-historian John Moncure ("Dreamy") Daniel. That astonishing record appears verbatim and almost in toto as Chapter Six of this book.

Quotations from those three primary sources are identified by initials.

2. *The Archives*. In a tiny closet-room atop Pendleton Hall are thousands of old letters, diaries, publications, account-books, catalogs, registers, announcements, invitations, memoranda, pictures—every kind of detritus that you would expect a busy multifaceted institution to generate, and a lot more:

Whence that "cord that went around the service hats worn by boys of this school in 1918–19," that L.C. Smith concert-grand steam-driven typewriter vintage 1890, that "Exercise-book of Ewing Lawson/E.H.S Coledge/The Beautiful Temple of Knowledge 1898?" How typical was that "Autograph Book of W.W. Michaux 1883" with messages like MAY EVERY HAIR OF YOUR HEAD SEEM AS A WAX CANDLE AND LIGHT YOU ON YOUR WAY TO GLORY and WITHIN THIS BOOK SO PURE AND WHITE LET NONE BUT FRIENDS PRESUME TO WRITE AND MAY EACH LINE WITH FRIENDSHIP GIVEN DIRECT THE READER'S THOUGHTS TO HEAVEN? Why that two-headed umbrella, that elliptical bicycle tire? Who won that 1905 Amateur Cup of the Washington Jockey Club—was it the dashing lad whose richly moustachioed, brownly daguerreotyped face looks out of that red velvet frame?

Here on the back of this 1913 Commencement invitation are pencilled three wonderful quotations—from Sam Johnson: "I am not so lost in lexicography as to forget that words are the daughters of earth, and that things are the sons of heaven"; from Henry Ward Beecher: "A man without mirth is like a wagon without springs," and from Anon: *Ranae exclamabant utinam ne alium regem postulavissemus*—"The frogs kept crying would that we had not asked for another king."

Christopher Marlowe spoke of "infinite riches in a little room." Infinite riches are indeed tumbled together in our little room of archives; matter for scores of books infinitely more profound than this one sleeps there.

3. *Memoirs*. Certain books (some fiction, some fact) by Old

Boys and friends of the school have been wonderfully informative. Especially valuable have been these:

Memoirs of William Nelson Pendleton, by Susan Pendleton Lee, daughter of our first Principal; *Diary of a Southern Refugee* by Judith McGuire, wife of our third Principal; *Across The Years*, by Virginius Dabney (1914–17); *Before They Were Men*, by Charles Wertenbaker (1915–19); *Those Happy Years*, by Henry C. Blackiston (1923–28); *P.S. Wilkinson*, by C.D.B. Bryan (1949–52); *Days of My Youth*, by Edward Alvey Jr. Dr. Alvey didn't attend EHS but his sister Lucile married one of our best-loved masters, Francis Edward ("Nick") Carter, and he often visited the School.

In various carefully researched articles (some, alas, unpublished) Richard P. Thomsen (1926–30, Headmaster 1951–67) has preserved many a quaint and curious volume of otherwise forgotten School lore, and "Young Flick" Hoxton (1928–35, Headmaster 1967–81) has dug deeply into our past as well. And of course no one would dream of writing about this Hill without consulting the King of it—Patrick Henry Callaway. That extraordinary phenomenon remembers just about every EHS thing that has happened since he, aged 21, first came here to teach in 1916.

4. *Memories*. All Old Boys were appealed to and many summoned up memories for this book. Those memories do it!

In a famous passage the Venerable Bede (673–735 AD) compared human life to a sparrow which flies out of the dark night into a brightly lit banquet hall "but after a short space" flies back into the darkness. Old Boys' memories brightly illuminate, for flashing moments, the dark night of our past. They make Bede's Sparrows of us all.

5. *Context*. Somebody once said that an index holds the eel of knowledge by the tail. Similarly, context, the marshalling of contemporary events, gives meaning to dates and so holds the eel of history. *Sine contextu nihil*. Each chronological chapter of this book is introduced by a summary of contemporary happenings— local, national, foreign—which were to affect, then or later, the boys of this school.

Now go, little book, back and back into the *temps perdu* of a dearly beloved school.

At one or another time nursery, wailing wall, prison, playground, laboratory, hospital, refuge, secret garden, treasure house, arena—this is and always has been a very special place.

As one of its very special children, the Reverend Arthur B. Kin-solving, II (EHS 1906–14, nephew of the ABK of the history book), declared: "This place has cradled the dreams of centuries, it has cradled more than dreams. For in this place character has been formed in the greatest battlefield of life, in the moment in the upper room of a boy's mind when he decides what he will be, a breathless moment in human destiny."

Bon voyage, schoolmates!

Forsan et haec olim meminisse juvabit, as Cap'n Dick Williams, quoting his good friend Vergil, used to say—"Perhaps one day it will be pleasant to remember even these things."

Bless the School, and bless us all.

JOHN WHITE

Introduction

"SON," my grandfather is reported to have said to my uncle at his wedding in 1938, "I hope today will be the happiest day of your life."

"No, Father," he is supposed to have replied, "the happiest day of my life was when I left the Episcopal High School."

Both uncle and grandfather are dead now, so we'll never be able to know for sure whether the story is true, or apocryphal. If true, however, its bloodline was natural. It would have started with Joseph Bryan, my great-grandfather, who was sent away from Gloucester County to the Episcopal High School in 1856, at age eleven. He continued there until the School closed in May of 1861 for the duration of the War.

In a letter to one of his brothers in 1889, after a visit to the High School, where he was a Trustee, Joseph Bryan wrote, "I was called on to speak, but the uppermost thoughts were cruel, wicked schoolmates, thrashings by the Rector, and the goodness of Mrs. McGuire (the Rector's wife). It was not an agreeable speech, though very true."

I would suspect that any boy who has attended the High School, were he capable of total recall and absolute honesty, would remember some of his sojourn there as harsh, bitter and unhappy.

On the other hand, I'd also bet he could recollect days on the Holy Hill as bright and joyous as any in his life. There were so many fields upon which to play: athletic fields, to be sure, but also the pastures and meadows of literary societies, Choir, Glee Club, *Whispers*, Grins & Grimaces, Hop Committee, waiters, Honor Committee.

Surely, one could find a realm in which to excel and about which to exult. Just as each of us served time as a "rat," so each had the opportunity to enjoy being an upperclassman; a monitor; a team, society or organization leader.

Many Old Boys, from my octogenarian father to those younger than I, had the privilege of being taught by the Old Guard: Messrs. Reade, Daniel, Carter, Shackelford, Williams, Whittle, Callaway, Tompkins and Latham. Among them, only Patrick Henry Callaway survives today. How fitting that, as the School approaches its 150th Anniversary, it can be said that Mr. Callaway has been intricately and inextricably woven into its fabric for only two years less than half its life.

In the first history of the High School, published in 1922, its author, the Reverend Arthur Barksdale Kinsolving, stated in the preface: "The School was founded eighty-three years ago by men of deep piety, high character and liberal culture. Its success has been due mainly to two things—the kind of men who have conducted it, and the type of boys who came here to be educated. Hence the tone, the standards, the individuality which have carried through from one administration to another."

Those sentiments are as manifestly true today as they were sixty-seven years ago. May the same be said 150 years hence.

Gaudeamus igitur.

JOHN STEWART BRYAN, III (1952–56)

I
HISTORY

CHAPTER 1

In the Beginning
1839–1861

It is 1839. Martin Van Buren is President of the twenty-six United States, which reach from the Atlantic coast west to Michigan, Illinois, Missouri, Arkansas and Louisiana; the geographical center of population is just south of Clarksburg, West Virginia. The new nation has about seventeen million citizens, of whom some fifteen million live in the country, two million in towns and cities.

World population is about one billion.

In 1839 the Episcopal Church adopts the Book of Common Prayer; the first workable method of making photographic prints from negatives is invented in England; the first game of baseball is played in Cooperstown, N.Y.; the first bicycle is put together in Scotland; the first Opium War between England and China begins.

Napoleon has been dead only eighteen years and it is only twenty-seven years after the War of 1812 for which he was partly responsible—our most unpopular war until Viet Nam.

We are an energetic young country, proud and brash: Congress in this year outlaws duelling in the District of Columbia. We face a bright future with unlimited confidence.

From 1839 to 1861 seven states were added to the Union; the population increased to some thirty-two million (twenty-six mil-

3

*lion rural, six million urban), and the center of population moved
to a spot near Chillicothe, Ohio.*

Ether was first used as an anesthetic in 1842 (alcohol and chloroform having been tried before).

*In 1844 Samuel F. B. Morse sent four words—"What hath God
wrought?"—over a wire from Washington to Baltimore and that
was the beginning of the telegraph. (The words were quoted from
Numbers 23:23.)*

*In 1846 there was established by Act of Congress an Institution
in Washington for the "increase and diffusion of knowledge among
men"—the Smithsonian. An Englishman, James Smithson, "natural" (as they called it then) son of the first Duke of Northumberland, had been piqued by the Royal Society's rejection of a
paper submitted by him (he was a serious scientist and the mineral
smithsonite is named for him) and he willed his fortune of slightly
over £100,000 to the United States. (He died in 1829 but our
Congress took seventeen years to decide first whether to accept
the gift of an Englishman at all and then whether the Institution
should be a museum or a library or an observatory or a girls'
school or goodness knows what.)*

*In 1846–48 we fought Mexico (independent from Spain since
1821) and won the vast area that is now California, Arizona,
Nevada, Utah, Colorado, Wyoming and parts of New Mexico
(Texas had joined the Union in 1845); in 1848 gold was discovered
in California and 100,000 Easterners had waggoned their way to
that Hispanic outpost by the time it became our thirty-first state
in 1850.*

Also in 1848 Karl Marx published the Communist Manifesto.

In 1851 Herman Melville published Moby-Dick.

In 1852 Harriet Beecher Stowe published Uncle Tom's Cabin.

*In 1854 Commodore Matthew Calbraith Perry and his gunboats
forced Japan to open her ports to foreign traders.*

In 1855 Walt Whitman published Leaves of Grass.

*In 1857 England's Thomas Hughes published one of the most
popular boys' books ever written,* Tom Brown's School Days.

*Also in 1857 the Dred Scott decision further inflamed abolitionist sentiment; in 1858 Minnesota, the last of the Northern
states to permit slavery (which all of them had allowed at one time
or another), abolished it, and in 1859 John Brown led his raid on
Harper's Ferry.*

Passionate men, North and South, talked of war.

The first practical generator of electricity had been built soon after 1830, but the enormous potential significance of that development had hardly been glimpsed by 1861. More work went into the railroads, which rolled westward to join the pony express at St. Joseph on the Missouri.

Steamships began to replace sailing vessels, and in 1859 a gas-engined car was driven ten miles, in France.

And in 1859 there appeared an extraordinary book which was to alter men's thinking as profoundly as had Copernicus' De Revolutionibus 316 years before: Charles Darwin published The Origin of Species. *Copernicus had showed that the earth is not at the center of the universe, but is one of the family of planets; Darwin showed that while man may be alone in his new world of thought, he is also a member of the animal kingdom.*

Some of us are shocked by that finding, and there are those who simply refuse to believe it.

AFTER THE REVOLUTION the Episcopal Church in the new nation was in deep trouble. It was suspect because of its ties with the Church of England, and, like all religious bodies in that time, it was virtually immobilized by post-war inertia.

Despite those obstacles—or, perhaps, fired by them, in the spirit of the earliest Christian laborers in hostile vineyards—a small group of dedicated Washington-area men, among whom was Francis Scott Key, committed themselves to the task of training a new generation of church leaders. In 1818 they formed "The Society for the Education of Pious Young Men for the Ministry of the Protestant Episcopal Church," with two instructors and fourteen students. In 1823 that Society opened the "School of Prophets," which later became "The Protestant Episcopal Theological Seminary in Virginia at Alexandria, Virginia," and within ten years graduates of the new institution had gone out to serve the Church in almost every state in the new Union.

"From its very beginning the Seminary was the object of love, veneration and esteem by the families of the Episcopal Church in Alexandria and the surrounding country," declares writer Clayton Torrence in an April, 1949, article in *Virginia Magazine*. "The Custises of Arlington House and the Lees in Alexandria . . . were ardent supporters and encouragers of the Seminary."

At first the Seminary was located at the corner of King and Washington Streets in Alexandria, but town noises proved too

Confitemini Domino *means*
"Give Thanks to the Lord."

The Cross surmounts the begin-
ning and the end, Alpha and Om-
ega. The Greek above is "And the
Word was made flesh," from
John; *below is "The faith which*
was once for all delivered to the
saints," from Jude.

The divine hand pours oil into the lamp
of knowledge resting on the Bible and
the Book of Common Prayer. (Various
EHS scapegraces have said that it was
really the hand of this or that starveling
student "reaching for the gravy boat.")
Fortiter *and* Fideliter *are quite simply*
"Bravely" and "Faithfully," but Feliciter *is more than just "Happily." Its*
root is felix, *which means fruitful, or*
productive.

distracting and in 1827 it was moved to a green and pleasant hill three miles to the west.

Then it was found that younger boys of the diocese were not being properly educated. Something more had to be done. At a diocesan meeting in 1837 the Reverend Joseph P. B. Wilmer offered this resolution:

"Whereas there is at present no institution of learning under the care of the Episcopal Church in this diocese, and Whereas the sons of our Episcopal families are too often entrusted to local and irresponsible schools, which are either sectarian in their character, or totally unorganized and desultory in their operations, therefore be it Resolved that it is highly essential to the interests of this diocese that one or more institutions be established within it of an Episcopal character." [ABK].

Once the decision to found a school was made the Church moved quickly. The Trustees of the Seminary bought, for $5,000, some eighty acres of land adjoining the seventy-acre tract of the Seminary. The site was five miles from Arlington House (the future home of Robert E. Lee), seven miles from Washington, and twelve miles from George Washington's Mount Vernon.

The tract was known as "Howard" and on it was a house, built before 1800, which had been a school from 1831 to 1834. Howard House was to be the residence of the High School's Principals from 1839 to 1951, when it was renamed Hoxton House, after the sixth Principal. For years we were called, almost interchangeably, the Episcopal High School or Howard; as late as the 1890's the School's baseball team was called the Howard Baseball Club and our football team was the Howard Athletic Club, Howard Football Association or just "the Howards."

Some people have preferred the older title. In 1906 the fourth Principal, Launcelot Minor Blackford, wrote "The name of this school has always been an incubus, having, I am sure, lost it many boys. It ought to be simply Howard High School." [RPW].

Officially, the Church linked its new school to the Seminary and called the two "The Protestant Episcopal Theological Seminary and High School in Virginia." The two institutions had a joint Board of Trustees until 1923.

From its very earliest days the school has been familiarly called "The High School," with a presumed smugness which has lifted many an eyebrow.

"But consider. The University of Virginia, founded in 1819, was the only one in the state until 1871, when Washington College, after the death of Robert E. Lee, became Washington and Lee University. And the Episcopal High School, founded in 1839, was for about thirty years the only high school in the state. Almost without exception, the early schools were called 'academies' or, if for girls, 'seminaries' or 'institutes,' until after 1870, when the public school system was firmly established, and the term 'high school' became general. Thus it is that the older alumni refer to 'the High School,' not from a sense of superiority . . . but as naturally as one refers to any other institution alone of its kind. Just so, Virginians are likely to speak of 'the Beach' and 'the University.' " [RPW].

(Similarly, it might be remarked, in the Old South when you said simply "He" you were understood to mean not the Lord or George Washington or even Bobby Jones. "He" was—drums and trumpets and hats off all!—Robert E. Lee. Not even the President of the Confederacy, Jefferson Davis, got such universal respect. Indeed, in his book *War Years with Jeb Stuart* William Blackford, brother of the fifth Principal of EHS, accused Mr. Davis of "egotistical, bull-headed obstinacy.")

The Trustees persuaded a West Point man to become Principal of their new school.

William Nelson Pendleton was born in Richmond December 26, 1809. He was one of eight children. His daughter Susan wrote a biography of him (*Memoirs of William Nelson Pendleton*) in which she says that as a boy he was "tall and well-formed . . . full of animal spirits and activity, always busy at work or at play, noisy, mischievous . . . pugnacious. . . . Notwithstanding this belligerent tendency, his bright good humor and universal kindliness made him a great favorite."

In June, 1826, this "comely, manly, ingenuous boy left his home in Virginia to begin life as a cadet at West Point." (The Military Academy, born in 1802, was only seven years older than he.) The trip from Richmond to West Point was, by our standards, horrendous.

Not a foot of railway was laid in the United States, and, except upon the large watercourses, all travel was by stage or private conveyance. Young Pendleton went by stage to the Potomac, up that river by steamboat to Washington, on to Baltimore by stage, and across the Chesapeake by boat to Frenchtown. From there to New Castle, Delaware, he again took the stage, and then a steam-

William Nelson Pendleton, Principal, 1839–44.

boat carried him up the Delaware to Trenton. Jersey was crossed by stage and canal to Amboy, from which point steamboats ran daily to New York, a city of less than 200,000 inhabitants.

That stage-boat-stage-boat-stage-boat-stage-boat journey took a week. "The youth who had never travelled forty miles from home found everything delightful."

Young Pendleton had many fellow cadets at The Point who were later to be war leaders, among them Jefferson Davis, Joseph E. Johnston, John B. Magruder, Leonidas Polk and Robert E. Lee himself. (Edgar Allan Poe was almost a West Point contemporary—he entered the Academy in 1830, but was expelled the next year for what his biographers call "numerous infractions of minor regulations.")

Pendleton was an Academy favorite and graduated fifth in his class.

After a tour of duty in South Carolina he returned to the Academy as assistant professor of mathematics and demonstrated great ability as a teacher.

He was next posted to Fort Hamilton, New York. During the winter of 1832 there were disturbing rumors that Federal troops would be sent from New York to South Carolina to deal with the threat to the Union caused by the Nullification movement. "Lieutenant Pendleton could not agree to the right of the general government to coerce any one of the states, and resolved never to draw his sword in such a cause. He therefore sent in his resignation from the Army." [RPW].

He soon found civilian employment. A new Episcopal college opened at Bristol, Pennsylvania, that fall, and made him its professor of mathematics and "natural philosophy," which in those days embraced physics, chemistry, astronomy and mechanics.

The college was poorly managed, however, and after only four years it ran out of money and had to close. Then Newark College in Delaware offered him its chair of mathematics. At first he refused, "but Newark's president . . . rushed to Bristol, sat with the Pendletons while they were packing, and declared he would not move until his offer was accepted." [RPW]. What was an unemployed teacher to do? Before he took the new job he was ordained an Episcopal deacon and the next year he was made a priest. He spent two happy years at Newark, as both professor and minister. (His health, however, was not good. According to his daughter he often bled himself with cupping-glasses and leeches and one night "a jar containing Spanish leeches was upset. The little blood-suckers crawled out and made their way into various unsuitable places. A small panic ensued.")

Then he was asked to give up the best position he had ever had to be Principal of a school that didn't even exist. As his daughter said:

The question for the young clergyman's decision was a serious one. His professorship in Delaware afforded a comfortable support for his family, and permitted him to exercise his office as parish minister usefully and acceptably in the surrounding country. To give this up and enter upon an untried field; to endeavor to build up a large public [sic] school, where great outlay was necessary, without any endowment or fund to begin with, and where the personal views and opinions of the principal were to be entirely subordinate to the vague and often visionary ideas of a miscellaneous and inexperienced board of trustees; and, above all, to relinquish for years the preaching of the Gospel [was] being urged upon him. The difficulty of deciding where he could best use his talents to the glory of God and the good of men, threw him into a violent fever, and for some months he was very ill.

By the time he regained his health he had determined to remove to Virginia and take charge of the Episcopal High School. Only the most disinterested devotion to duty and hopefulness of disposition could have influenced him to this decision.

RPW characterized the "miscellaneous and inexperienced" Trustees as "Often more devoted to things spiritual than to things temporal. They were poor businessmen."

The first session began October 15, 1839. Sessions then were ten months long, with only one winter vacation, from December 24 to January 2. There were thirty-five boys and three teachers. Tuition was $210 a year; clergymen's sons were charged $110 and poor boys nothing.

The Principal, his wife and five children were, says daughter Susan, "crowded into two small rooms." And right away, she notes, her poor father was beset with professional as well as personal problems. The Principal's worst problem, and the one which ultimately destroyed him, was financial. Susan:

"The terms on which the school was placed in his hands were difficult and unreasonable almost beyond belief. No provision was made for any endowment, present or future. *All* the expenses of the institution—furniture, scientific apparatus, salaries of teachers, food, fuel, repairs, and

Names	Residence	Time of joining
A. S. Freeman	Raleigh N.Ca	January 25, 1840
H. Harrison	Cumberland Co. Va	Ditto
Milo Mahan	Suffolk Virginia	
R. A. McGuire	Fredericksburg Va	Ditto
Robinson Miller	Norfolk Va	Ditto
R. W. Nelson	Albemarle Co. Va	" "
R. B. Nelson	Clarke Co. Va	
Robt Nelson	Hanover Co. Va	" "
John Page	Hanover Co. Va	Do
Christian M Bosley	Baltimore County	Do
Sims Walke	Norfolk Va	Do "
James Williams	Clarke Chy Va	Do "
Edmund Berkeley	London Chy Va	Do
Robert Carter	Charles City Co Va	Do "
J. Harrison	Cumberland Co Va	Do " "
Wm Howerton	Halifax Co Va	Do " "
George Morison	Fairfax Co Va	Do "
Allen D Ramsey	Independence Co Arkansas Do	
William H Talbot	Norfolk Va	Do "
Pere W Lmer	Charles county Md	Do ... county Va Mar
R. M. Threat	Chesterfield	
Francis M Whittle	Mecklenburg Chy	April 1st 1840
John R Buford	Lawrenceville Va	" "
Edwin B Jones	Do	" "
Bushrod W Kobil	Fairfax Co Va	April 8th 1840

Charter members of the Pithonian Society, 1840. Milo Mahan and John Page were teachers. It should be noted that whereas George Morison signed himself that way, with one r, School records carry him as Morrison.

the thousand things for which money is required in a large establishment—were to come out of the tuition fees. These were put at the lowest possible rate. Nor was this all. Not only was there no salary attached to the position of rector, but he was required to pay to the trustees a yearly tax of thirty dollars upon each pupil over the minimum of thirty, whether that thirty were all full-pay scholars or not."

Hard to believe? True!

"Under such terms his administration was foredoomed to financial failure. Yet heroically did this Confederate in embryo fight his battle. A fine garden provided vegetables and fruit. The farm was brought to a high state of cultivation. Cattle were bought and fattened." [ABK].

Dr. Pendleton was a thoughtful Principal as well as a determined man of God. His credo:

By professing to train up youth in the nurture and admonition of the Lord, we do not pretend to guarantee an absolute freedom from temptation; we do not flatter ourselves with any visions of an earthly paradise, wherein boys will cease to be boys and subside into lambs under the broad wings of the Gospel. On the contrary, we know too well that there are those to whom any degree of godly restraint is as gall and wormwood, who will fret and wince under any degree of restraint like colts unaccustomed to the bit.

The object of the school is to educate youth on the basis of religion; to apply the instructions of the Bible in the work of training the mind, influencing the heart and regulating the habits; to provide for boys during the critical period of middle youth and incipient manhood the safest and best superintendence, the soundest and most healthful moral influences and the most faithful Christian guidance, associated with the most useful and the most extensive course of learning practicable.

In a word, it is to make full trial of Christian education in training youth for duty and for heaven.

He was not always serious, though. Susan:

"Gentleness and firmness were combined in his government. Some of his modes of punishment had a touch of the comical. A stolen fishing expedition brought a long day's angling from an upper window. A mock duel, gotten up to terrify the challenged party, was deprived of all dignity and amusement by the principals and seconds having to stand up in the presence of the assembled school and drench each other with water."

He loved to play the game called "bandy," and often "the over-

Epis. High School, Octr. 5th, 1840

My dear Grandmama:

I arrived here on last Wenesday morning and I found very few of the boys here. I came perhaps a day or two too soon as most of the boys did not arrive here until Friday or Saturday. The students did not commence their studies until today. We now have about 80 students and Mr. Pendleton expects to have upwards of ninety. We all lodge in one room, and this room has twenty-six windows in it, all of which are thrown open during the day. There is a fine dining hall under the school room, back of which is a large room which Mr. Pendleton calls the dressing and washing room, in which he has placed large wardrobes. Water is forced into the washing room from the pump by means of an engine.

I at first was a little homesick, but now I am very much pleased both with the boys and teachers. They give us a plenty to eat and as fine bread and coffee as I ever tasted, which are the most important things to me. Mr. Pendleton is very much of a gentleman, and possesses all that affability of manners which is calculated to please the boys. He permits most of the boys to go to Alexandria whenever they wish if they ask permission. Bishop Meade preached an opening sermon to the students of the Epis. High School on last Saturday night over at the Theological Seminary which was very interesting indeed. . . I also send you some of my hair, which I forgot to leave at home, and as I have now fulfilled my promise of writing to you, I shall stop.

Your sincere and affectionate grandson,

Worthn. R. Johnson

First letter of Worthington R. Johnson, Jr. (1840–42) to his grandmother, Mrs. Eleanor Potts. "Wenesday" is Worthington's.

taxed, overworked principal [was] at the head of the throng, racing up-and-down-hill and over the fences after the ball."

Somewhat ironically, considering the desperate state of the infant school's finances, during that first session the Trustees paid for construction of a three-storey main building costing about $12,000. That building (which Susan didn't like: "ugly without and inconvenient within") added greatly to teaching efficiency and subtracted even more greatly from gracious living: the top floor was a dormitory, on the second were the chapel and school rooms, and on the first were the dining room, kitchen and bathroom; the boys had to run down two floors to wash.

Not until 1891 was that lamentable situation remedied—only for those days it wasn't lamentable, comparatively speaking: Dickens' *Nicholas Nickleby*, by coincidence published in 1839, describes conditions in an English school, the infamous Dotheboys Hall, as far worse than anything then known on this side of the ocean.

The curriculum was astonishing. "Indeed, the School was at first almost a college with a preparatory department." [RPW]. Among courses offered were mental and moral philosophy, Latin, Greek, physics, geometry, algebra, arithmetic, engineering and geography.

The first three teachers were the Reverend Milo Mahan, *classicus magister superbus*, Robert Nelson, afterwards a missionary to China, and John Page, father of the Thomas Nelson Page who became a fine writer (and was always a modest man—of himself he said "I have eyes like two fried eggs and a nose like a Bartlett pear"). Those three were more than equal to the challenge of that advanced curriculum, and word spread rapidly that there was a bright educational oasis in the arid diocesan desert. Having barely survived its first year the school suddenly found its cup running over—the second year's student enrollment soared from 35 to 101. Three more teachers were added to the faculty.

The great increase—almost triple—in the number of students didn't solve the financial problem. Tuitions, minus $30 per boy, weren't enough to pay expenses; the overflowing cup didn't hold water; there was no balm in Gilead. Dr. Pendleton was not experienced in money management and the highminded Trustees couldn't seem to focus on such grubbiness. The learned Principal kept the school running, but he began to go into debt, and so did the school itself.

The 1841–42 enrollment was 110 boys, the highest it had ever been, or would be again for forty-one years (there were 113 students during the session of 1883–84). Four of the older boys were drafted to help teach. The money strain was tearing the school apart. In 1842–43 enrollment dropped to sixty, and the next year it was down to forty-seven. The Principal owed $3000 (a large sum of money then), and the school owed $5000.

The other institution that Pendleton had helped to start had failed after four years. This one lasted only a little longer.

In July, 1844, Dr. Pendleton resigned, and the school, "under a mountain of debt and discouragement" [RPW], was closed—to everybody's regret. Says Susan: "The estimation in which he was held may be illustrated by the words of good Mrs. Monroe, the laundress: 'The Scripture is against you, Mr. Pendleton, for it says Woe unto you when all men speak well of you.' "

And the evening and the morning were the first day. . . .

Dr. Pendleton was nothing if not stubborn. After he left us he started yet another school—St. Luke's Hall in Baltimore.

That school prospered; he paid off his debt, and went back into the ministry. During the War he, the West Point graduate, rose to the rank of Brigadier General and served as Chief of Artillery of the Army of Northern Virginia. A close friend of Lee's, he conducted the great man's funeral service in 1870.

The Trustees may have been shortsighted but they were steadfast of purpose. *Seek and ye shall find.* They found another clergyman willing to try to revive the moribund school.

The Reverend Edwin A. Dalrymple, always called the Rector, was in most ways a fortunate choice. He had graduated from the Seminary in 1843, had served in two Virginia parishes, and was reckoned "at once a personality, fine scholar, enthusiastic teacher and an unrivalled disciplinarian." [ABK]. Alas, in one important way he was flawed. For "unrivalled" read "obsessive."

The school was reopened in 1845, and seventeen boys came. The Rector proved to be a better businessman than Dr. Pendleton had been; although tuition was lowered to $200, that sum was payable in advance and there was no reduction for clergymen's sons. The school still had to pay the Seminary Board of Trustees $30 per student—indeed, that intolerable and absurd impost was exacted until 1913—but Dr. Dalrymple managed by careful pennypinching to scrape by.

Edwin Augustus Dalrymple, Principal, 1845–52.

(Looking back, one has to wonder at the many Trustees who served during those seven decades: how could they, so anxious to have their school excel, have made life so miserable for its Principals?)

His goals for the School were exalted:

To make mere scholars, or exact men of business, is not the sole duty of the Christian teacher. He has much nobler ends in view. No exertions are to be spared to secure thorough education of the mind, but at the same time he is diligent to bring those entrusted to his care under the influence of religious principle. He is not only to labor to make them useful men, but so far as in him lies, he is to endeavor to make them Christian gentlemen—gentlemen as well in feelings and principles as in outward conduct and manners.

But the Rector tried too hard. He was too rigid for this sinuous world. "His very dress was magisterial, a long grey or black gown with a row of jet buttons reaching from neck to foot." [ABK]. He agreed with Solomon that to spare the rod was to spoil the child. Indeed, he felt that "neglect of the Solomonic dictum as to the use of the rod when boys stood in need of it constituted an impious violation of the divine covenant." [ABK]. He demanded flawless behavior, and to get it he imposed on the school a disciplinary code that was minutely detailed and savagely punitive.

A little book of his "petty rules for the government of the group of red-blooded American boys committed to his care" has come down to us. Here are two samples. RULE 131: "No student shall eat butter and molasses at once or at the same meal." RULE 155: "No student shall sing any negro or low song or chorus or tune in the boys' parlor or elsewhere." [ABK].

"Such puerile rules are a challenge to the law-breaking spirit of any group of normal boys," [ABK], but the normal, red-blooded American boys who broke his silly rules were soundly thrashed by the Rector, and so were many who didn't.

"One of the best remembered things about his regime was the whippings the boys got. These were administered not only for misdemeanors, but for imperfect recitations. The middle recitation room [was] a veritable chamber of horrors. One after another, especially after the primary Latin class which the Rector in his long grey cassock taught, the reluctant victims entered, and the noises which came from within were not comforting to those on the waiting list." [ABK].

The Rector, secretly called by the boys "Old Dal," was an inspiring teacher of Latin literature and an efficient, respected head of the School, and as the years went by he relaxed his severity a little. The School's reputation did not suffer. "In the year 1847, while the final exercises were going on under the trees, Edgar Allen Poe was seen standing near the rostrum. He had come out from Alexandria with a party of friends. But when he was discovered he was at once the object of universal attention and obligingly went forward and recited 'The Raven,' to the delight of all who were present." [ABK, who should have known that it was then, is now, and ever shall be, Edgar Allan Poe. *The Raven* had been published two years before; Poe was at the height of his fame. Having been widowed the previous January, the poet, weakened by bouts of alcoholism and insanity, was to survive only two years after this occasion.] A visit by a personage of such distinction suggests the high esteem in which the School was then held.

"The Visit of Poe."
An artist's conception
of the Ravenish event
of 1847 as found in
Whispers, 1939.

But something was troubling Old Dal, deeply. The worm was in the rose. Perhaps he had worked too hard—he drove himself as Principal, and taught five hours a day—but his predecessor had also worked hard at administration, and taught four courses, without cracking under the strain. Perhaps Dalrymple suffered from a broken heart: "It is said that [he] had an unsuccessful love affair early in life." [ABK]. Perhaps his disciplinary pettiness and harshness had affected his spiritual equilibrium. In any case, in 1852, when he was only thirty-four, his health gave way completely. He collapsed and had to leave the school. (He later recovered and, as Dr. Pendleton had done, started a school of his own. It became the School of Letters of the University of Maryland.)

Our next Principal, the Reverend John P. McGuire, was, like Old Dal, a graduate of the Seminary—one of the very first. He completed his courses there in 1825, two years after that institution was founded, and after graduation he was given charge of two parishes in Essex County, Virginia—St. Anne's and South Farnum—and he became known as "The Apostle of the Rappahannock." He served on our Board of Trustees from the founding of the School until 1861, so that from 1852 to 1861 he had the unique distinction of being a Trustee as well as Principal. (Apparently as a Trustee he never objected to the old invidious custom of making the school's Principal pay the Trustees $30 per boy, and—*mirabile dictu*—as Principal, when the shoe was on his other foot, he seems to have paid that iniquitous head-tax without a murmur.)

He found the school pleasingly solvent, and to keep it that way he raised the tuition from $200 to $250. (As was the custom in those days, extra courses, in modern languages, music, drawing and such-like supposed periphera, were offered "at professors' charges.")

Mr. McGuire, also called the Rector, was a more discriminating thrasher than his predecessor had been. Commented Joseph Bryan (1856–61):

In the opinion of the boys at this classical School Jupiter among the immortal gods of Olympus was a secondary character compared with the Rector of the High School. He was decisive, just and brave. There was no boy who could disregard, much less defy him, and he had to handle some pretty tough customers.

To small boys who were sent to his study for laziness and neglect of their studies, his final argument was that "a bird that can sing and won't sing must be made to sing." And after that the birds generally sang. It must be borne in mind that the old English method of training boys was in full vogue in the fifties at the High School. Bishop Meade, who was the stern administrator of scholastic justice, was the president of the board of trustees, and . . . I doubt not that he would have thought the School was on the high road to ruin unless there was ample assurance that personal chastisement was either commonly applied or always held "in terrorem." The moral suasion argument with recalcitrant boys was either ignored or very brief.

My greatest personal objection to the thrashings I received was twofold, first to being thrashed alone, and secondly to the lecture I got before the switch was applied. To be ordered down to the rector's study early in the morning, before breakfast indeed, by lamplight and there to have my misdeeds recited and my home recalled, and then to be promptly thrashed was far greater punishment than when I went with a number of my classmates who could encourage one another and find some consolation watching the victims as they were successively called from the crowd that huddled behind the stove.

The School was not a downy nest for little birds—for a good reason, according to James M. Garnett (1853–57):

In my day the boys were numbered. I was No. 59, and the teachers addressed me as such. The dormitory on the top floor was one huge room. The beds, or cots, were arranged side by side in rows about four feet apart. At six o'clock in the morning the bell rang, and the boys were given fifteen minutes to huddle into their clothes and get to the lavatory in the basement. The luckless lazy ones were deprived of their matin meal. There were no furnaces, and the wood-stove heated the room only in spots. I recall the "corn-dodgers" that warmed us outside and within. Then came an hour for recreation, and sometimes, O woeful time for us small fellows, the usher notified us that Mr. McGuire wanted to see us in his study. The chosen ones put on two or three extra jackets with sundry socks, woolen comforters, or anything for stuffing that would deaden the whack of a good tough hickory limb, for "Old Mac" struck hard. But God who tempers the wind to the shorn lamb had made him so near-sighted that he couldn't see the disparity between a round body and a pair of spindle legs.

Mr. McGuire had evidently modeled the High School after the famous English Rugby and Eton Academies. The School was divided into forms, the youngsters forming the fourth class, none over ten years of age. The English system of "fags" was carried out in a very modified way. The first form kids were the only ones subject to corporal punishment, and as it was "Old Mac's" only recreation and exercise before breakfast, he had plenty of athletics as an appetizer.

The fact of the business was, the School owed its success to its strict discipline. Most of the pupils were the sons of wealthy planters, accustomed to having their own way at home until they became a nuisance, and then were packed off to the High School where they soon had the nonsense taken out of them. Quarrels were settled in the good old English fashion by a stand-up fight, gouging, scratching and biting being barred. Everything tending to luxury, ease and self-indulgence was banished.

No money was allowed the boys, only four three-cent silver pieces a week, which were promptly spent on ginger pop and cakes. In those days there were no trashy papers, no yellow journals. The book-worms read the good old English classics: *The Alexandria Gazette,* the *National Intelligencer,* and the *Baltimore Sun* were the papers read. We read by either a sperm candle or a tallow dip.

There was a deadly feud between the E.H.S. boys in uniform and the boys of Alexandria. The minute a High School boy appeared on the streets of the old burg, the town boys would yell "Eggs, hams and sausages," and then there would be a desperate fight—much blood—bunged noses.

(James Garnett was given number 59 when he came to the School as a rat in 1853 but two years later he was number 1 and John Magruder was 59.)

It wasn't hard for town to identify gown. "In those days EHS boys wore a uniform to church, and also when away from the School, consisting of a black coat or jacket, buff vest and black trousers. On the caps were the letters *E.H.S., Va.,* with a maltese cross on the left side of the standing collar." [ABK].

More about those town-gown battles, and why they were *not,* as one of our most persistent legends maintains, responsible for EHS having Monday instead of Saturday as a holiday, may be found in the section on old customs at the end of this book.

Mr. McGuire's boys probably rejoiced in the desperate town-gown blood-lettings. "These seem to have been days of special belligerency on the part of the youths of the South. Possibly it was increased by the independence and masterfulness of life on the great plantations with many servants." [ABK].

In his astonishing book *Honor And Violence In The Old South* Bertram Wyatt-Brown elaborates on that point: "A chief objective in child-rearing was to encourage the very young to be aggressive, even ferocious. Otherwise, reasoned the traditionally-minded parent, the male child would be so severely checked and overprotected that effeminacy might ensue. Very young children learned that they were supposed to grab for things, fight on the carpet, clatter their toys about, defy parental commands, and even set upon likely visitors in friendly roughhouse."

Surprisingly, such encouragement to ferocity was not confined to male children: "Girls acted with the same freedom from restraint as boys. Their introduction to the proprieties of ladyhood came much later." Look out, townies, desperate though you may be—if those eggs, hams and sausages don't get you their sisters will!

Very soon those plantation-born high spirits were swept away by the wind, "worked off," as ABK says, "during the heroic period of the Civil War." That dark period was fast approaching.

In the fateful election of 1860 Virginia, Tennessee and Kentucky of the Southern states voted for Lincoln and now-forgotten Hannibal Hamlin, and so did Mr. McGuire. He supported "the Constitution, the union, the enforcement of law." [RPW].

But when the deadly die was cast and Virginia determined that, rather than invade her sister Southern states, she would defend them, no Virginian was ever found more ready to withstand the invasion of his state. It had always been customary for the older boys to attend the Presidential inauguration but in March, 1861, when Lincoln was inaugurated, no one went

It should be recalled that our School had only the year before been aroused to the highest degree of excitement and indignation by the John Brown raid. We had at least a dozen students from the immediate neighborhood of the scene of that outrage.

When secession began, and it became apparent that war was impending, the boys of the School organized themselves into a company and were regularly drilled by Ben White as captain. We had no guns but used smooth sticks with pegs for the hammers. [Joseph Bryan, 1856–61.]

(Two years later Sergeant Ben White was killed in the Battle of Chancellorsville. Joseph Bryan survived the War.)

On May 3, 1861, the School was closed. The Rector and his wife remained there for a few weeks but the Hill was inside Federal lines and they soon had to move. In her classic *Diary of a Southern Refugee* (which came to light unexpectedly after the War) Mrs. McGuire described those last hours in the old Howard House:

May 4, 1861: Everything is broken up, the Theological Seminary is closed, the High School dismissed. The homes all look desolate, and yet

John Peyton McGuire, Principal, 1852–61.

this beautiful country is looking more beautiful, more lovely than ever, as if to rebuke the tumult of passion and the fanaticism of man. We are left lonely indeed.

I go from room to room, looking at first one thing and then another, so full of sad associations. The closed piano, the locked bookcase, the nicely-arranged tables, the formally-placed chairs, ottomans and sofas in the parlor! Oh for some one to put them out of order! I could scarcely restrain my tears.

But the writing-desks, work-boxes, and the numberless things so familiar to my eyes! Where were they? I paused, to ask myself what it all meant. Why did we think it necessary to send off all that was dear to us from our own home?

I threw open the shutters, and the answer came at once, so mournfully! I heard distinctly the drums beating in Washington.

Though frightened by the approach of war, Mrs. McGuire was confident that her beloved South would win, and she reckoned that women could play a domestic, perhaps significant, role in achieving that victory:

May 10: We all have such entire reliance in the justice of our cause and the valor of our men, and above all, on the blessing of Heaven! We are very weak in resources, but strong in stout hearts, zeal for the cause, and enthusiastic devotion to our beloved South; and while men are making a free-will offering of their life's blood on the altar of their country, women must not be idle. We must do what we can for the comfort of our brave men. We must sew for them, knit for them, nurse the sick, keep up the faint-hearted, give them a word of encouragement. There is much for us to do, and we must do it.

The embattled hosts of the North will have the whole world from which to draw their supplies. We shall indeed be dependent on our own exertions, and great must those exertions be.

We must not admit weakness. Our soldiers do not think of weakness; they know that their hearts are strong, and their hands well skilled in the use of the rifle. Our country boys have been brought up on horseback, and hunting has ever been their holiday sport. Then why shall they feel weak? Their hearts feel strong when they think of the justice of their cause. In that is *our* hope.

We went to the Chapel on Sunday as usual, but it was grievous to see the change. . . . Tucker Conrad, one of the few students who is still here, raised the tunes; his voice seemed unusually sweet, because so sad. He was feebly supported by all who were not in tears.

(Tucker Conrad, who had gone to the School from 1855 to 1857 and was then in the Seminary, was killed seventy-two days later, at First Manassas.)

On May 24 the McGuires left the High School, forever. "The day of suspense is at an end. With a heavy heart I packed trunks and boxes, as many as our little carriage would hold. As we drove off the bright flowers we had planted seemed in full glory; every flower bed seemed to glow. In bitterness of heart I exclaimed 'Why must we leave thee, Paradise!' and for the first time my tears streamed." Inevitably one thinks of that other departure from that other lost Paradise:

> *They hand in hand with wandering steps and slow,*
> *Through Eden took their solitary way.*

The Principal and his grieving wife left the School none too soon. By the next day, "Alexandria and its environs, including, I greatly fear, our home, are in the hands of the enemy."

> *For, behold ... darkness shall cover the earth. ...*
> *—Isaiah 60:2.*

CHAPTER 2

The War
1861–1866

And they shall fight every one against his brother.
—Isaiah 19:2.

Just as we are called simply "The High School" so, in parts of the
South, it is still "The War." (Although Lincoln in his Gettysburg
address said, "Now we are engaged in a great civil war," precisely
speaking it should be called the War Between the States, not the
Civil War; it was a war between two nations, one old, one new,
each composed of united states. In the Confederacy there were
about five and a half million white people; in the Union, a total
population of almost nineteen million.)

It was the most man-killing war we have ever waged: more than
620,000 soldiers died in it—about the same number as perished
in all of our country's other wars, from the Revolution to Viet
Nam, put together. Aeschylus said "War trades men for gold."
The War traded men for men. Americans for Americans.

It was a relatively modern war in equipment, the first waged
with armored ships, railroads, trenches, wire entanglements, bal-
loons and the telegraph; but it was medieval in medicine: no one
knew what germs were, or how to prevent infections, or that
mosquitoes spread malaria and foul water caused typhoid fever.

More than twice as many men died from diseases as were killed in action.

However, enough. Just as more men died in it than in all of our other wars put together, so more has been written about The War than about all of the others put together, and, assuredly, the world would little note nor long remember anything that might be added here.

Suffice it to say that our School, like its motherland, was torn, trampled, proved, and in an excruciatingly painful way improved, by that great convulsion—and the end is not yet. But enough of that, too.

Of course, while we were killing each other some things happened in the outside world.

The country's population increased to some thirty-six million (twenty-seven million rural, nine million urban) and the center of population moved to a spot some fifty miles northeast of Cincinnati.

In 1863 a pioneer labor union, the Brotherhood of Railway Locomotives Engineers, was formed. In 1864 Louis Pasteur invented the process now called pasteurization, for wine. In 1865 Gregor Mendel announced the discoveries which were to found the science of genetics, the Atlantic cable was completed, and some Tennesseeans started the Ku Klux Klan. In 1866 Alfred Nobel invented dynamite. (The first Nobel Prizes, including one for Peace, were to be awarded in 1901.)

> *Thus we bury, one by one, the dearest,*
> *the brightest, the best. . . .*
> —Judith Brockenbrough McGuire.

SOME SEVEN HUNDRED BOYS had gone to the High School when the War came. Nineteen of them were dead before 1861, one being Robert Carter Wickham (1840–42), a surgeon in the U.S. Army who died in the Mexican War. This means that there were about 680 Old Boys at the time of Fort Sumter.

Of them, at least five hundred fought for the Confederate States of America. More than 200 were in the infantry, about 130 in the cavalry, 84 in the artillery and 10 in the Navy. (When discussing Confederate figures it is often necessary to use vague terms like

Federal balloon being filled with gas for ascent. John Bryan's whimsical vessel probably looked like this.

"at least," "more than" and "about" because Southern records of that war are woefully incomplete.)

There were also at least thirty-three staff officers, twenty-seven surgeons, six chaplains, three engineers, two Marines, one ambulance driver and one scout. Franklin Stringfellow (1858–60) scouted for General Lee. And there was a man who qualified, temporarily, as a sort of extraterrestrial scout. According to RPW and Burke Davis,

"John Randolph Bryan, EHS 1853–57, was our first military balloonist. During the Peninsula Campaign [1862], General Joseph E. Johnston determined to inspect the enemy's dispositions by aerial reconnaissance, and asked General John B. Magruder to send him a soldier familiar with the region—a quick, shrewd observer whose courage would be equal to the danger and novelty of his situation. Young Bryan volunteered without knowing the task before him. General Johnston brushed aside his plea of ignorance of balloons, and the first ascent began at once. Spies may have alerted the enemy for, as the balloon rose from behind its screen of trees, it was met by a storm of fire. No damage was done, however; Bryan made his observations and was hauled back down unscathed."

Safely back on earth, Lieutenant Bryan immediately volunteered to resign from ballooning. The General said "Absolutely not! You're the only experienced balloonist in the Confederate army."

Monitor *(foreground) and* Virginia *blaze away at each other at close range.*

The second ascent made the first seem soporific. "Just as the balloon rose, a soldier caught his foot in a coil of rope and was drawn toward the windlass. His screams brought a comrade, who cut the rope. The balloon, released from all control, shot up two miles before the hot air cooled and it began to sink." The helpless balloon drifted over Federal lines. In panic, Bryan destroyed his identification papers and all of his notes. Then he was carried out over water. He "dropped his clothing overboard, prepared to swim for his life." He finally came to earth on friendly territory—and was very nearly shot as a spy.

We also had a man killed at an historic naval event.

In March, 1862, the Federal Navy's *Monitor* fought the Confederates' *Virginia* (*née Merrimack*—the Federals had scuttled her and the Confederates had raised her and armor-plated and renamed her) in Hampton Roads, Virginia, and during that famous but inconclusive battle, the first ever between iron-clad ships, James Langhorne Tayloe (EHS 1854–55, USNA 1860) was killed in action aboard the *Virginia*'s escort vessel *Raleigh*.

Fourteen EHS Old Boys fought for the North.

Our first Principal, Dr. Pendleton, became a brigadier general and Chief of Artillery of the Army of Northern Virginia, and something of a legendary figure. According to Mrs. McGuire, "The Reverend Dr. Pendleton, now captain of artillery, commanded this gun, and whenever he ordered its discharge, he was heard to say, reverently, 'The Lord have mercy upon their souls—fire!' "

He was a close friend of Robert E. Lee and was with him at Fredericksburg in December, 1862. After that great Confederate victory he wrote a memoir in which he immortalized a saying of the General's which has become one of the best-known of all comments on war:

> So blundering was the attempt of [General Ambrose] Burnside and so easily was he beaten, notwithstanding the immensity of his force that it seemed on our side rather a skirmish than a battle, though of the enemy the slaughter was terrific. Blue figures by thousands were seen [running] with faces to the rear and hundreds of gray pursuers hastening their speed. While younger spectators near us gave expression to their feelings by shouts, clappings of hands, &c., the gratified yet considerate and amiable commander turned to myself and with beaming countenance said, "It is well war is so terrible, or we should get too fond of it."

The School also gave to the Confederacy another brigadier general—Alfred Iverson (1860–61)—14 colonels, 18 lieutenant colonels, 28 majors, 63 captains, 66 lieutenants, 28 sergeants, 8 corporals and a small army of privates.

Sixty-three of those men died. The memorial tablet in Pendleton Hall lists sixty-one but RPW found that two names which should be there are missing: another Thomas Marshall, and Robert C. Taliaferro.

He says "Fifty-three were killed or mortally wounded in action, one was hanged as a spy, four died as prisoners of war, four of sickness, and one [Thomas Marshall, a surgeon] of overwork," and he goes on to state that "It is astounding that sickness claimed so few of our Confederates."

Considering the fact that altogether in that war more than twice as many soldiers, North and South, died of disease as were killed in action, it is indeed astounding. Even if, as seems possible, the ten who were listed as dying of mortal wounds actually succumbed later to infection, the total of our men who died of disease would be fourteen, about one-third as many as the forty-three killed in action instead of more than twice as many as were KIA.

An explanation remains to be found.

Another Southern mystery surfaces when one delves into figures of The War. Confederate losses by states (dead and wounded)

were approximately thus: North Carolina—20,000; Virginia—
7,000; Mississippi—7,000, on down to Alabama—700.

QUERY: Why did neighboring North Carolina, with a population not much more than that of Virginia (about a million to about
840,000) lose nearly three times as many men? Perhaps the answer
lies in the old Carolina boast: "First at Bethel, fartherest at Gettysburg and Chickamauga, last at Appomattox." (The South won
the battle at Big Bethel, Virginia, June 10, 1861.)

Of our dead, four (at least) died at Gettysburg, July 1–3, 1863:
James Keith Marshall (1852–56), William Westwood McCreery
(1852–54), Benjamin Harrison McGuire (1855–60)—he was the
Principal's nephew—and Valentine W. Southall (1857–60). On
the last day of that terrible battle Mr. McGuire wrote "When I
think of so many shot dead upon the field or maimed for life, I
am almost ready to ask, is not this enough, even for Howard?"

Of our others who died in the War, three should be chronicled
at some length. Not because they were braver than the others, or
more worthy, but only because their lives were so very different
from each others', and from the average, and yet in a way typical.
They illustrate three of the kinds of people you might have met
in the wartime South, in our School.

> For God's sake, let us sit upon the ground and tell
> sad stories of the death of kings.
> —Richard III.

Chatham Roberdeau Wheat loved war, any war. He was big,
strong, dashing and brave—born for trouble as the sparks fly
upward. The Lord talking to Job (chapter 39, verse 25) describes
him perfectly: *He saith among the trumpets, Ha, ha! and he smel-
leth the battle afar off, the thunder of the captains, and the shouting.* He was also handsome, romantic, charmingly naïve, and—
tell it not in Gath—greedy for glory: he once said "The height of
my ambition is to lead a desperate charge."

Born in Alexandria, Virginia, April 9, 1826, the son of an Episcopal minister, his childhood must have been ordinary and boring,
in his own estimation at least, because only one memorable story
of it has come down to us.

As the writer Charles Dufour tells that story in his biography
of Wheat, *Gentle Tiger*, when Roberdeau was about twelve years
old he read in a book a passage in which the hero was mistreated.

He "wept bitterly. His mother attempted to soothe him: 'This is not a true story; it is just made up by the author.' 'Not true!' exclaimed Roberdeau, drying his tears. 'And you, a Christian mother, give your child lies to read!' Throwing his book into a corner, he could never be induced to read it again."

Very interesting! Significant? Our most distinguished expert on children, Dr. T. Berry Brazelton (EHS 1934–36), Professor of Pediatrics at Boston's Children's Hospital, makes this diagnosis:

I can't believe a twelve-year-old like Roberdeau wouldn't know a fantasy from reality, and treasure it. So I think he was just (1) getting off a negativistic response to his mother's overprotection, (2) teasing her, (3) reacting to her attempt to treat him like a baby ("It's not a true story. Don't worry"), or (4) reacting to the shame of having wept openly—any twelve-year-old would be likely to regret that. Not being induced to read it again was certainly wise. It sounded a bit boring for a twelve-year-old to swallow. But, mainly, I think he was protesting his mother's attempt to overprotect him. He showed this in his macho heroism later in life.

T. Berry Brazelton

The overprotected boy came to EHS in 1841, and hated it. He complained about the teaching, the teachers, and the other boys, and he found the restraint, in Dr. Pendleton's words, "as gall and wormwood." He begged his parents to take him out, threatening that if they didn't he might become "a blackguard and a low-lifed boy." They didn't and he didn't. He settled down and finished the year with good marks.

He went on the University of Nashville, studied law, and soon demonstrated the quick wit and easy eloquence of a born orator. He began to learn the skills of a peaceable life: "He conserved his slender funds by cutting his daily expenses 'including everything,' to less than eighty cents a day."

He would have made an excellent lawyer, but his mind was elsewhere.

When President Polk's Congress declared war on Mexico, May 13, 1846, the young lawyer smelled the battle from afar and eleven days later was in it. He was elected an assistant second lieutenant and rode with his cavalrymen to Mexico. He fought bravely at

Vera Cruz, Puente de Moreno and Cerro Gordo, nearly died of yellow fever, and rose to the rank of Captain.

That war over, he looked around for another. He soon convinced himself that Spanish-held Cuba was like "a weak woman in the power of a brutal ravisher," and in 1850 he led an unauthorized, ramshackle expedition to trounce the ravisher (and despoil him of his possessions).

En route to the island there was an unforgettable moment.

Colonel Wheat assembled his brave troops, saluted the Cuban flag, and "exclaimed 'Liberators! Behold your flag! Three cheers for the Cuban flag!' Three tremendous cheers went up, 'reverberating over the billows, and arousing the listless sharks.' " Is there, among the polytalented host of EHS Old Boys, a sharkologist to account for the mood of those languid fellows?

That invasion turned out to be the greatest Cuban fiasco until the 1961 Bay of Pigs. First the ship ran aground and all five hundred invaders had to crawl single-file across a plank to shore, a spectacle which, understandably, "eliminated all element of surprise." Then there was some shooting, in the course of which our hero was struck in the shoulder. "Your colonel is killed!," he cried, "Go on and avenge his death!" But his wound was not mortal. Indeed, it was but a flesh wound from which he immediately recovered. Never mind. There was a little more shooting and a lot of confusion and pretty soon the invasion fell apart.

After the leaders sneaked back they were arrested and tried for violation of the Neutrality Act. Colonel Wheat, however, came out of the sorry affair a hero; the charges against him were dropped and he was more popular than before.

He then in rapid succession, and with ever-rising rank, fought in guerrilla actions wherever he could find them: Mexico (twice—wounded once), Nicaragua (thrown into a river when the boiler of his steamboat blew up), Mexico again, and Italy (as a General, under Garibaldi).

When the War came he was one of the most seasoned veterans on either side. He needed to be. He signed up at once, of course, and was promptly put in command of the worst bunch of scoundrels in the western world, a company of Louisiana cutthroats scraped out of New Orleans jails and gutters and called simply "The Tigers."

Those Tigers "had a peculiar dress, and wore fezzes, which, as they lacked visors, caused their faces and eyes to be terribly sun-

burned, giving them a very fierce aspect. And fierce they were."
[ABK]. Their favorite occupations were drinking, fighting, slaugh-
tering, looting and robbing the dead. They were so horridly wild
that nobody could control them—with one exception. They respected, and obeyed, Roberdeau Wheat. They admired his easy,
patrician grace, they were reassured by his obvious familiarity with
the actualities of war, and they were moved by his flamboyant
patriotism and his rousing eloquence.

They also may have been awed by his size: he stood six feet
four inches and weighed 260 pounds.

In any case, the Tigers fought for him aggressively and effectively
at First Manassas, July 21, 1861. He was shot through the lungs
and a surgeon told him that he would die. "I don't feel like dying
yet," said the Major. "But there is no instance on record of recovery from such a wound." "Well then, I will put my case on
record," and he did. Like the heroic Sir Andrew of the Scottish
ballad who cried "I am sore hurt, but not yet slain./ I'll but lie
down and bleed awhile,/ And then I'll rise and fight again," Wheat
did just that. He lay and bled awhile and then he rose and fought
again, at Front Royal, Winchester and Port Republic.

June 27, 1862, at Gaines' Mill, Roberdeau Wheat's luck ran
out. He was shot through the head. There is a legend that as he
died he murmured "Bury me on the field, boys," but considering
the nature of his wound that seems unlikely.

For the first time his boys, the loyal Tigers, broke. One of them
wept and walked away, saying "They have killed the old Major
and I am going home. I wouldn't fight for Jesus Christ now!"
("Old"—at the age of 36! One should know that in 1826 the life
expectancy of a new-born baby boy in this country was about 38
years.)

It is tempting to suppose that as that disgusted Tiger trudged
home to New Orleans he strung together the words of what became a very popular postwar ballad:

> For I'm a good old Rebel, that's what I am
> And for this land of freedom I don't give a damn.
> I'm glad I fought against her; I only wish we'd won.
> And I don't ask no pardons for anything I've done.
>
> I hate the Constitution, the great Republic too;
> I hate the mighty eagle and the uniform of blue;
> I hate the glorious banner and all their flags and fuss;
> Those lying, thieving Yankees, I hate 'em wuss and wuss.

I won't be reconstructed, I'm better now than them;
For those dirty carpetbaggers I don't give a damn.
So I'm off to the border as soon as I can go;
I'll get me a gun and leave for Mexico.

RPW, who entertained generations of EHS boys with his tales of World War I, showed no interest in Wheat's exploits and labelled him simply "a typical soldier of fortune."

Typical? Charles Dufour called Wheat "A man born six or seven hundred years too late [who] would have been more at home in the age when knighthood was in flower." Reckless, gallant (in both senses of the word; apparently he cut a wide swath with the ladies), totally without fear, or serious purpose, as randomly bellicose as a heat-seeking missile, Wheat would have fit the mold of a mercenary Crusader, or King Arthur's wild Sir Lancelot at his most romantic and irresponsible and attractive.

A fellow officer once said to him "Wheat, I would give a thousand dollars to stand in your shoes." He immediately replied "Orderly, give the Captain my shoes."

If Roberdeau Wheat was a swashbuckling Lancelot, another High School casualty of the War was a hero of precisely the opposite disposition; he was like the saintly Sir Galahad, or Chaucer's

General Chatham
Roberdeau Wheat.

Randolph Fairfax.

"parfit gentil knight," or Ivanhoe, the chivalrous protagonist of the wartime South's favorite author. (Sir Walter Scott was universally read and appreciated, a true "best seller," throughout the South during those years.) Or perhaps he was more like the Norse god Balder, who was so high-minded and virtuous—so *good*— that the other gods rejoiced in the very sight of him.

This was the semi-legendary Randolph Fairfax.

That golden lad was as fine a flower of aristocracy as pre-War Virginia could produce. His father was Dr. Orlando Fairfax of Alexandria, son of the Reverend Bryan Fairfax, Rector of Fairfax Parish and heir to a British title. His mother was the daughter of Jefferson Cary and Virginia Randolph: she was the sister of Governor Thomas Mann Randolph, Thomas Jefferson's son-in-law, and "through his mother he had in his veins the blood of Pocahontas." [ABK]. Of all of the famed FFV's—First Families of Virginia—his was what that great Southern warrior Nathan Bedford Forrest might have called the "fustest." (It was Forrest who when asked what the secret of military success was, said "Git thar fustest with the mostest." After the War he became "Grand Wizard" of the Ku Klux Klan.)

Randolph Fairfax was as modest as a true aristocrat should be.

"One day on a steamboat on Lake Champlain, while Randolph was on a visit to his aunt, Mrs. Gouverneur Morris of New York, a gentleman attracted by his looks walked up to him and entered into conversation, asking his name. On learning it he said 'I would not like to have a name already so famous that I could add nothing to it.' Young Fairfax replied, 'It is the name of my ancestors; and if they have made it famous, I at least will try to do nothing to impair its brightness.'" [ABK].

(Roberdeau Wheat's family was also aristocratic, of course, as indeed were most of the families of EHS boys in those days. Education then was not for the masses.)

Randolph was at EHS for two years, 1857–59, and, unlike Roberdeau, he loved it. He "took honors in every class and came home laden with medals and certificates." [ABK]. But such awards did not seduce him. Again unlike Roberdeau, he cared nothing for derring-do or temporal glory.

"I fear that my worldly occupations are fast drawing my heart from God; that in my eagerness to be prepared for my School examinations, I forget the great examination which my soul must stand at the bar of God," he admonished himself in his diary,

"Oh! that I could despise the things of this world; could lay aside all my vain ambition, and have the glory and service of God as my chief ambition and desire. How little are these vain honors compared with the crown of glory!"

When the War came he left the University of Virginia and enlisted as a lowly private in the Rockbridge Artillery, a celebrated company commmanded by none other than Captain William N. Pendleton. Among his messmates in that friendly outfit were fellow EHS Old Boys David Barton (1853–56), the Packard brothers, Walter (1850–60) and Joseph (1850–58), Kinloch Nelson (1854–58) and James M. Garnett (1853–57, the letter writer of Chapter One), as well as the School's future Principal, Launcelot M. Blackford.

Private Fairfax was as good and dutiful a soldier as he had been a student. He fought in ten battles and countless skirmishes and "bore all the exacting duties of the field and bivouac with equanimity, pluck and good nature, and was one of the most popular men in the army. . . . He won the love of his comrades and their complete respect." [ABK].

On December 13, 1862, Randolph Fairfax, aged 20 years and 20 days, was killed by a shell fragment at the battle of Fredericksburg. At his side was his dear friend Charles James Kinsolving (EHS 1860–61), half-brother of ABK.

> *Bright youth passes swiftly as a thought.*
> —Theognis.

Fifteen days later General Lee took the time to write a long letter to Orlando Fairfax in which he praised the "patriotism, self-denial and manliness" of his son, and said "he has been translated to a better world, for which his purity and his piety have eminently fitted him." [ABK].

> *Integer vitae, scelerisque purus—*
> "Blameless life, free of sin"
> —Horace.

His name lives on at the School in the Fairfax Literary Society and the Randolph Fairfax Memorial Prize Medal "for Character, Conduct, and Scholarship."

Our third all-but-fabulous hero, wavering indistinctly through the mists of time, was like Hamlet's father, whose ghost still walks the earth. They caught him and they hanged him, and his loyal cousin, but they could not find his secret. We have not found it yet.

What was he looking for?

William Orton Williams was as well-born as Roberdeau Wheat or Randolph Fairfax. His family was kin to Custises, Lees, Pinckneys, Dandridges, Washingtons and other FFV's. He was the youngest child of Captain William George Williams and his wife America Pinckney Peter (geographic names were usual in America's family—she had sisters named Columbia and Britannia). America died at age forty, in 1843. Three years later Captain Williams was killed in the Mexican War, and the oldest child, Martha, nicknamed "Markie," took responsibility for her four siblings.

She wrote to her cousin Robert E. Lee, then Superintendent of the Military Academy, concerning the prospect of sending young Orton to West Point, and she got a surprising reply. In a letter dated 16 September 1853 Colonel Lee, who was, to be sure, the son of the famous Revolutionary cavalry commander Light-horse Harry Lee and had himself graduated from the Academy and served with distinction in the Mexican War, sharply criticized his own occupation.

"I advise no young man to enter the Army. The same application, the same self denial, the same endurance, in any other profession will advance him faster & farther. Nothing but an unconquerable passion for Military life would induce me to recommend the Military profession." (From an article by Clayton Torrence in the April, 1949, issue of *The Virginia Historical Magazine*.)

That letter may have been wise but it was ineffectual.

Young Orton's father had graduated from West Point and so had his older brother Lawrence, earlier in the same year in which Cousin Robert wrote; family tradition was not to be denied; after spending that year, 1853–54, at the High School, Orton worked for the Coast Guard, and in 1857 he went to West Point.

He "issued thence as 2nd Lieutenant" in March, 1861. Three months later he resigned his commission in the United States Army, and on August 15, 1861 he was mustered into the Confederate Army as a First Lieutenant. He seems to have made himself unpopular with the men, because of his hot temper and arrogant manner, but he got along with his superiors.

He served as aide to General Leonidas Polk and then as assistant chief of artillery to General Braxton Bragg.

In April, 1862, just before the battle of Shiloh, his arrogance drove him to murder. A private soldier who had saluted him once refused to salute him again; he drew his saber and stabbed the man to death.

There was an inquiry. His report, quoted in the Winter, 1970, issue of *Assembly*, the journal of the Association of West Point Graduates, is chilling. It shows the patrician attitude of the Old South at its graceful worst, with absolutely no concern for a common man who didn't recognize Divine Right: "For his ignorance, I pitied him; for his insolence, I forgave him; for his insubordination, I slew him."

Nothing came of that inquiry. The slayer went unpunished. But some time thereafter William Orton Williams changed his name, by an act of the Mississippi Legislature, to Lawrence William Orton. Why he took his older brother's given name is not known.

He served, militarily, bravely and well, and rose to the rank of Colonel.

Then there was tragedy, bizarre, dramatic, and to this day puzzling.

Here is the chronicle of that tragedy, condensed from the account of William Gilmore Beymer, who found himself haunted by it and published the story in 1912 in his book *On Hazardous Service*.

June 8, 1863, had been a "hot, murky" day. In the twilight two fine-looking men in the uniforms of Federal officers rode up to the Union headquarters tent at Fort Granger near Franklin, Tennessee.

They were "superbly mounted" and rather spectacularly covered. They were wearing "merino havelocks," those knitted cap covers with hanging flaps usually worn by soldiers of the French Foreign Legion. "Havelocks were unknown to officers and men, either North or South, except as something 'foreign,' something to be looked on askance."

Colonel John P. Baird, Commandant of the post, rose to receive them.

"They dismounted and strode forward, tall, straight, dignified. The elder and taller of the two introduced himself as Colonel Auton of the Army of the Potomac; his companion as Major Dunlop, assistant in the inspection of the Western troops, for

which business they had been sent from Washington. They had
just come from General Rosecrans at Murfreesborough. Oh yes,
they had just seen General Gordon Granger too.

"As this Colonel Auton talked he made more and more of an
impression on Colonel Baird; it was with positive regret that he
heard that they must push on to Nashville that very night."

The Commandant ordered passes made out for the two distinguished visitors. While they waited "Colonel Auton told of their
misfortune. They had lost their way from Murfreesborough.
The rebels had attacked them, had captured their servant, his
(Colonel Auton's) coat and all his money; they had been pursued
for a long distance and had finally escaped with difficulty.

"It was all very unfortunate. The distressful situation of the two
officers appealed to Colonel Baird."

The passes to Nashville were brought, but there was a mistake.
They were made out to Colonel "Orton" rather than "Auton."
(By way of an alias, Orton was using a name spelled entirely
differently from his own, but pronounced—by Southerners—exactly the same. The clerk who "misspelled" the alias actually, just
by chance, got it right.)

While the name on the passes was being changed "this handsome, dignified young officer, with his easy grace of bearing, led
Colonel Baird aside; it was most unfortunate, but—they were quite
without money. Could Colonel Baird oblige them with the loan
of one hundred dollars apiece—any sum, then—for their immediate expenses?

"Colonel Baird did not have the money, but went at once to
Colonel Van Vleck, who had been sitting smoking in incredulous
silence; of him he asked the money—when they were out of ear-
shot, that the strangers might not be embarrassed!"

Colonel Carter Van Vleck did not give Colonel Baird the money.
Instead, he reported later, "I told him that I thought the men were
not what they represented themselves to be; for, said I, the Government would not send two officers of their rank from the Potomac to inspect the Army of the Cumberland, when we already
have more inspectors than we know what to do with. I declined
to let the money go, saying that the two men who were attracting
so much attention by their havelocks were certainly spies."

Colonel Baird, "disquieted, asked awkwardly for their orders;
Colonel Auton, who seemed to have taken no offense at the request, readily handed them to him."

There were many orders, which seemed to be from high-ranking

Union officers including Major General William S. Rosecrans' Chief of Staff, Brigadier General James A. Garfield—the same James A. Garfield who was later to be President of the United States.

The Commandant was "more than satisfied; he handed the written papers back, and, it is presumed, apologized handsomely. He procured for them money—fifty dollars—gave them the corrected pass to Nashville, gave them the countersign, heartily wished them Godspeed on their journey, and watched them ride away into the night.

"And then Colonel Baird thought for the first time of forgery!"

He "tensely" told the whole story to Colonel Louis D. Watkins. "Colonel Watkins was very grave; some things looked very wrong. Colonel Baird's indecision passed: the men must be brought back."

Pursuers caught up with the two men "riding leisurely along. They readily consented to return. They did not show surprise."

They were placed under guard. Their papers were examined more carefully and seemed to be in order, but queries were sent to the officers who had supposedly signed them.

Back came the replies. Those officers knew nothing of "Colonel Auton" or "Major Dunlop." General Garfield seemed irritated: "There are no such men in this army, nor in any army, so far as we know. Why do you ask?"

The handsome visitors admitted that they were impostors.

Colonel Baird telegraphed a long report to General Garfield which ended with a question and, possibly to hide his discomfiture, a ringing declaration: "As these men don't deny their guilt, what should I do with them? My bile is stirred, and some hanging would do me good."

(As author Beymer remarks, "There *is* something almost boyish about Colonel Baird.")

General Garfield replied "The two men are no doubt spies. Call a drumhead court martial to-night and if they are found to be spies, hang them before morning, without fail."

The two were searched, and a possible reason for their novel headgear was made evident: "There was found on their hatbands, concealed by the havelocks, their names and their rank in the Confederate army."

They were really William Orton Williams and his younger cousin Walter Gibson Peter (son of George Washington Peter), Colonel and Lieutenant, Army of the C.S.A.

A drumhead court martial was held at 3 A.M. that same night: "Charges: being spies."

Williams spoke for the pair, since "Lieutenant Peter had not known the purpose, the real mission, on which he and Colonel Williams had entered the Federal lines; it is probable that he never knew. Orton had led, and he had followed."

The Colonel testified freely.

At first he confessed to being a spy, but denied that he had designs against Franklin. Subsequently he said that he was pursuing a "goal" which had to remain secret; that he had "undertaken the enterprise with his eyes open and knew what his fate must be if discovered, that the value of the prize at which he grasped fully justified the fearful hazard he had made to gain it."

The trial lasted barely an hour. After sunrise the two men were told the verdict: death.

The Colonel "acknowledged the entire justice of his sentence, and said that he had no complaint whatever to make," but he asked mercy for his cousin "on account of his youth and because he was ignorant of the objects or dangers of the mission." (Walter Peter was then twenty-one years old. Orton was twenty-four.)

Colonel Baird, having discovered that Williams was a cousin of Robert E. Lee, sent a message to General Garfield requesting that the prisoners be pardoned or at least not hanged. "They . . . prefer to be shot." But Garfield's superior, General Rosecrans, had gone to bed, leaving strict orders that he was not to be disturbed: "Pilate had washed his hands."

Colonel Baird had no choice. "He gave the order for the execution."

A scaffold was built on a wild cherry tree; "The unfortunate men embraced each other and Lieutenant Peter sobbed and said 'Oh Colonel, have we come to this!' [His cousin] at once checked him by saying 'Let us die like men.' And they did," at 9:20 in the morning of June 9.

So ended the two lives. So began the mystery which has lasted 126 years.

What was "Colonel Auton" looking for? And why didn't he tell his cousin—or did he??

When caught, the two impostors "had made no attempt to gain information . . . had no drawings of fortifications, had naught to condemn them but an intention that was never known."

Their real mission, as Colonel Van Vleck wrote later, "to this day is a most mysterious secret to us all."

Although Williams freely admitted that they were not Union officers, he first said they were spies, and then denied it.

In his June 9 report to General Garfield Colonel Baird said that the pair "after they confessed, insisted they were not spies, in the ordinary sense, and that they wanted no information about this place. Said they were going to Canada, and something about Europe; not clear. . . . Though they admitted the justice of the sentence and died like soldiers, they would not disclose their true object. Their conduct was very singular indeed; I can make nothing of it."

Their conduct was indeed singular, from the insouciant wearing of the flamboyant havelocks, through the awkward attempt to borrow money and the leisurely departure to the affable surrender and polite acceptance ("no complaint whatever") of the rope.

After all these years one can still make nothing of it.

Before he died Orton Williams wrote to his sister Markie "Do not believe that I am a spy; with my dying breath I deny the charge."

At the time there was endorsement of the justice of the execution at the highest level: W.F.G. Shanks, war correspondent of the *New York Herald*, wrote "The President has telegraphed to General Rosecrans his approval of the prompt action." But later there was doubt. In 1866 Robert E. Lee wrote an astonishing letter to his cousin Markie about the hanging of her brother. Lee's letter, cited in that April, 1949, *Virginia Historical Magazine* article, is as tantalizing as it is passionate:

"My own grief is as poignant now as on the day of its occurrence, & my blood boils at the thought of the atrocious outrage, against every manly & Christian sentiment which the Great God alone is able to forgive. I cannot trust my pen or tongue to utter my feelings. He alone can give us resignation."

Unfortunately, in that letter General Lee's reason for believing the execution to have been an "atrocious outrage" is not specified.

There seems now to be only one clue to the mystery of Orton Williams' mission, a wispy clue of the most tenuous sort: Europe.

It was generally known that during the War there were "attempts made by the agents of the United States to obtain in Ireland recruits for their army." The Confederate Secretary of State, Judah P. Benjamin, was personally concerned about the actions of "these ferocious persecuters in the destruction of this nation. . . ."

Could Orton Williams have been on some intermediate assign-

Himself, as a strikingly handsome youth—Lieutenant Lee, 1831.

ment meant to end in Ireland? (And would poor Cousin Walter, who died as bravely as did his leader, apparently without knowing why, have gone with him?)

Mystery within mystery. . . .

It seems safe to say that Lawrence William Orton *né* William Orton Williams is still, after 135 years, the most enigmatic personage ever to have attended our School.

Was he villain, hero, madman, spy, "secret agent," or extraordinarily bold deserter?

Having once been a suitor of his cousin Agnes, daughter of Robert E. Lee, who had refused to marry him, Williams fell in love with a Mrs. Hamilton, who was apparently not what she claimed to be, a respectable widow, but an adventuress of sorts. Just before his execution he'd written her a letter in which he spoke of his intention to marry her within the month—in Europe.

So it's even possible that this mysterious man was a wild romantic, willing to risk honor, patriotism, his own life and another's, in hopes of flight to foreign shores to join a woman whose charms made even mortal risks seem worth while.

Would that his knowing cousin Robert E. Lee had seen fit to elucidate.

The tragedy was shattering for the families. The Williamses had already suffered the agony peculiar to that war: division. Orton's brother Lawrence had stayed in the Union Army (from which he was dismissed in March, 1863, on trumped-up charges of being AWOL brought against him apparently because of his friendship with the out-of-favor Union General George B. McClellan), his brother-in-law John Upshur was an officer in the Union Navy, and other relations had similarly separated. That Orton and his loyal cousin Walter had been branded spies and hanged must have been almost too much to bear.

In 1864 Orton's sister Kate died, apparently of grief.

Walter Peter's mother, until her death in 1867, wrote a letter to the Secretary of War on each anniversary of the hanging, reminding him of the "crime."

After the War sister Markie herself married a Union man who was in a way the most remarkable Union man of them all.

Samuel Powhatan Carter of Tennessee graduated from the Naval Academy in 1846, one year after that institution was founded. During the War he was detailed by the Navy to special duty at the U.S. War Department and he rose simultaneously to the rank of Major General in the Army and Commander in the Navy. After 1865 he stayed in the Navy and in 1882 he was advanced to the rank of Rear Admiral on the retired list.

Thus, he became the only man in the history of this country to have been both a General and an Admiral.

At least one other EHS Old Boy served in two branches of the armed forces. According to Hardesty's *Historical and Geographical Encyclopedia* (Virginia Edition), John Tyler Waller (1860–61), grandson of President John Tyler, was "a gallant but rash young officer, successively of the Confederate Navy and Army, who sealed his devotion to the South with his life"—but there is no record of what his rank in either service was, or how he died.

It must be stressed again that records of Southern deeds and deaths in that war are lamentably incomplete.

One can only know for sure that at least five hundred EHS boys and men went into service, South or North, and sixty-three of them, perhaps more, died in it or because of it, and as Mr. McGuire wrote, "Is not this enough, even for Howard?"

In her diary Mrs. McGuire said more:

Enormous as were the wrongs done us, yet we had no desire to do the slightest wrong to even the bitterest of our enemies. We refused not to do them justice; we were not unwilling to seek for them the mercy of Heaven; to extend to them the hand of Charity; to supply their wants when captured; to attend as far as possible to their sick, and dying, and dead; and asked for nothing from them but that they would leave our borders, never to return.

We could not forget the injury done to our country. . . . The ruin of the whole South! Where are the colours dark enough for that picture! With her rightful government overturned; her territory seized by lawless hands; her system of domestic labour suddenly broken up; her estates robbed; her fields desolated; her barns destroyed by fire; her temples profaned; her once joyous homes here and there silent as death; her old men and women going with sorrow to the grave, because their gallant sons are not; her fair and fainting daughters mourning for loved ones whom they girded for the fight, and saw again never more; her widows and orphans, whom sorrow may kill, if want does not starve them; her wounded, and scarred, and crippled, and suffering, with no rest for any save in the quiet graves at home, or in the vast cemeteries, where such hosts of her slaughtered children lie.

How must we think or speak of all this? Let the coldest heart ever frozen by Northern interest or prejudice answer.

It is heartening to report that the McGuires were not destroyed by "Northern interest or prejudice."

During the War they lived in Richmond and Mr. McGuire served as Chaplain at camps and hospitals and as supply Minister for a number of churches (he didn't formally resign as Principal of EHS until early in 1866). He then moved back to Essex County and resumed his pastoral ministry. He died on Good Friday, 1869.

Of his life Dr. Kinsolving had this to say: "He bore in his heart the shafts of many sorrows. He stood for the Union and the Constitution as long as possible, and then when the passions of the people and the politicians split the nation in twain, he stood, as all true men do, with his people, and made their cause his cause. But he had served an eternal kingdom in the training of a generation of Christian youth."

The McGuires' son, John Peyton Jr., attended the School (1852–54) and later taught there while his father was the Rector, and during the dark days he served on the staff of the Confederate Naval Academy. Soon after Appomattox, in September, 1865, he started a school of his own, McGuire's University School in Richmond. Thanks mainly to two men, that school was, for seventy-seven years, a fine day school. John Peyton McGuire Jr. served as its Principal from 1865 until his death in 1906, and his son John Peyton III carried on the good work until his health failed and he had to close the school in 1942.

To this day the memory of "McGuire's" is as dear to its alumni as that of our School is to us.

PS: While this book was going to press there surfaced astonishing evidence that one of Us might have been involved in a plot to kidnap Abraham Lincoln, a bizarre plot conceived, hatched and almost brought to successful completion by a group of powerful men including John Wilkes Booth—and Confederate President Jefferson Davis! It had always been known that Benjamin Franklin Stringfellow (EHS 1858–60) was one of General Lee's best and most trusted scouts. Last Fall retired General William A. Tidwell and two collaborators published a book, *Come Retribution*, in which they make use of a wealth of old material, and some new, to demonstrate that Stringfellow *might* have played a very active role in an aborted Southern effort to end the War by capturing the Northern President and holding him hostage.

Their evidence is all circumstantial, but surprisingly cogent.

ITEM: "It can be shown that the Confederates had the knowledge and technical skill to mount an operation against President Lincoln; that they engaged in a number of activities in 1864 and 1865 that could have been related to planning such an operation; that John Wilkes Booth was in contact with known Confederate agents; and that the course of the war developed in such a way that an attack on Lincoln was a logical amendment to the original plan to capture him."

ITEM: Benjamin Franklin Stringfellow was such an agent, "probably the most trusted and effective scout in the Army of Northern Virginia." He was in close communication with Jefferson Davis, who was famed for his close supervision of intelligence and espionage operations and therefore might well have been intimately associated with any plan to kidnap Lincoln.

ITEM: "Stringfellow was not new in this field." In a letter of September 16, 1864, submitted directly to General Lee, "he proposed to kidnap Union General August Kautz." That plan came to nothing, "but Stringfellow continued to nurse a yen to capture a Union general [and] he raised his sights. On 24 February 1865 he again wrote directly to Lee, this time proposing to kidnap Grant, a formidable undertaking. The letter ended up in the hands of President Jefferson Davis. Davis had something on his mind. He called Stringfellow into his office and laid it out." The Confederate President then gave the scout "an assignment that would take him to Washington immediately."

What President Davis had on his mind we do not know, for sure, but we do know that it could not have been the kidnapping of Grant, because that General was then at City Point below Richmond.

ITEM: Stringfellow was given a good cover for his secret agent assignment in Washington: "He was to become a student of dentistry, using the name and papers of a Union soldier from Maryland who had been a prisoner in Confederate hands."

ITEM: The "student" appeared in Washington March 5, the day after Lincoln's second inauguration, and pursued his studies so diligently that a month later he was given a license to practice dentistry.

ITEM: About noon on March 17 John Wilkes Booth heard that Lincoln would attend a matinée performance of the play *Still Waters Run Deep* to be given at Campbell Hospital on the outskirts of Washington, and "The action team [Booth and five co-conspirators] planned to stop Lincoln's carriage as he returned from the play. Lincoln and his driver would be overpowered and hand-cuffed. The carriage would be used to make a dash through south-ern Maryland to the Potomac River." But instead of going to the hospital that afternoon the President went to the National Hotel. "The Campbell Hospital fiasco ended any realistic hope of cap-turing Lincoln." The action team fell apart.

ITEM: "Stringfellow was captured in Charles County, Maryland, on Sunday, 2 April, by a [Northern] patrol." Two days later he escaped.

ITEM: On Good Friday, April 14, John Wilkes Booth shot Lin-coln; a fellow-conspirator, Lewis Thornton Powell, stabbed (not fatally) Secretary of State William H. Seward; a third conspirator, George Atzerodt, "got drunk instead of carrying out his assign-ment to kill Vice-President Andrew Johnson." (Mrs. McGuire: "Lincoln is dead. His efforts to carry out his abolition theories have caused the shedding of oceans of Southern blood, and by man it now seems has his blood been shed. We may have much to fear. My native land, good-night!")

"With malice toward none," four days before malice killed him, April 15, 1865.

ITEM (FINAL): "Ultimately Stringfellow made his way to Canada, where he remained for more than a year. A reasonable explanation for this extended Canadian stay is that Stringfellow feared to come home until he felt certain his Washington assignment had not been disclosed. He need not have worried. There was no leak."

There still, after all these years, has been no leak.

There has, however, been a little light.

Come Retribution (that title comes from a cipher key used by the Confederates in 1865) makes a strong case for the involvement of our Scout in a high-level conspiracy which ended with a murder by one man. It is somewhat as though evidence more persuasive than has yet been produced should be advanced indicating that Lee Harvey Oswald was part of a conspiracy to kidnap or kill John Kennedy. But the case is not closed.

For us, Benjamin Franklin Stringfellow joins William Orton Williams in intriguing limbo.

Fortiter, Fideliter, Secrete. Secretly.

After he did whatever he did in 1864–65 Frank Stringfellow returned to the Hill, went to the Seminary, graduated in 1876 and became a minister. He served, openly, as an Army Chaplain in the Spanish-American War. And did he, after working for a whole month to get it, ever make use of that license to practice dentistry? Apparently not, although if he had he might have been quite successful.

Three EHS Old Boy/dentists comment:

"Dentistry was relatively primitive then, lots of extractions and little else. It took more strength than skill. Guys who made false teeth like those famous ones of George Washington were few and far between and I'm sure George wore his only for smiling and took them out as soon as possible; they must have hurt like the devil." [Russell Boyd, 1948–51.]

"If student Stringfellow had gone a little farther north it might have taken him a lot longer to get that license. In Baltimore there had been a regular school of dentistry, the nation's first, since 1849." [Robert Bunn, 1973–76.]

"It seems that Mr. Stringfellow was better at dentistry than at kidnapping!" [Lewis Johnston, 1937–38.]

Dick Daniel, EHS Historian-without-Portfolio whom we shall meet again in Chapter Six, has this to say about the kidnap theory:

"Booth's motive has never been satisfactorily explained. There is a legend that the motive was the hanging on February 24, 1865,

Russell Boyd   *Robert Bunn*   *Lewis Johnston*

of John Yates Beall, a close friend of Booth. The execution was for alleged spying, although Beall was a commissioned officer in the Confederate Navy. The legend further states that Booth went to Lincoln to plead for a stay of execution and was promised one.

"My interest stems from the fact that Beall was my grandmother Daniel's first cousin. And his younger brother, William, attended the High School, 1858–60, so he was an EHS classmate of Stringfellow. Although there is no irrefutable evidence that Booth and Beall knew each other, the legend persists."

Curiouser, as Alice remarked, and curiouser. . . .

CHAPTER 3

De Profundis
1866–1870

Reconstruction—and the beginning of slow healing. Twenty-five hundred years ago Aeschylus said "God, whose law it is that he who learns must suffer. And even in our sleep pain that cannot forget falls drop by drop upon the heart, and in our own despite, against our will, comes wisdom to us by the awful grace of God."

Outside of the South life went on quite busily, if not always wisely, during those years.

The population increased to forty million (twenty-nine million rural, eleven million urban) and the center of population moved closer to Cincinnati.

In 1867 Nebraska was admitted to the Union, and in the same year the United States bought Alaska from Russia for $7,200,000. (The $200,000 was to repay the Russian Ambassador for bribes paid to certain of our Senators.) That purchase was immensely unpopular at the time. People jeered at Secretary of State William Seward, who had negotiated the treaty, and called the vast new territory "Seward's Folly" or "Seward's Icebox."

Early in 1868 President Andrew Johnson, who had succeeded Lincoln, was accused of being too soft on the South, and he was impeached. He was acquitted by one vote. That November the

Union General who had won the War, Ulysses S. Grant, was elected President of the re-United States. Also in that same year the world's first professional baseball club, the Cincinnati Red Stockings, was formed, and Lousia May Alcott published Little Women.

In 1869 the Suez Canal was completed. For the first time ships could sail from the Mediterranean to the East without going all the way around Africa.

Near the School something very strange was happening. Northern soldiers were being buried around the house of the Southern leader.

Robert E. Lee's wife Mary Custis inherited the old house named "Arlington" just across the Potomac from Washington and Lee loved it more than any other place on earth. In May, 1861, Union forces occupied the house and made it a military headquarters. In 1862 Congress levied a tax of $92.07 on the property. The Lee family offered to send the money by messenger, but the tax collector arbitrarily declared that the property owner had to pay in person, and the Federal Government confiscated the estate for tax default.

In 1864 Arlington was designated a military cemetery and 200 acres around the house were appropriated for burials.

Robert E. Lee died in 1870 without having visited his house since the War began, but in 1877 his heir, George Washington Custis Lee, brought suit for recovery against the U.S. Government. Five years later the Supreme Court declared him the rightful owner of Arlington. By then sixteen thousand soldiers had been buried there. All of those bodies could not be exhumed. The Government had to pay Lee $150,000 for the property it had wrongfully seized.

Now, the Southern Commander's old home strikes the visitor as the only living presence in the City of the Dead.

THREE TIMES BEFORE, the Trustees had had difficulty finding a Principal for their struggling school. In 1866 they were faced with the severest challenge of all.

The whole South, of course, was brought low, admitted back into the Union as a starveling in rags, but threatened still more by the vengeances of bigotry than by hunger and defeat. As that very perceptive and articulate observer Julius Fleming ("Juhl")

Federal troops at Arlington during the War.
Below: "Father, forgive. . . ." Arlington today.

wrote to the *Charleston Courier,* "Slavery being now dead, we are all one again. But we are weak. Let no fabulous tales of cruelty to the freedman be received at [sic] the North. And, in looking at the black man, let us not withhold our sympathies from the white.

"Let not the fact be forgotten that through all this land the war has left its desolating marks, families robed in mourning, Davids mourning their Absaloms, and Rachels weeping for their children and refusing to be comforted because they are not, and that by one sweep the wealth of the country is taken away, and a people accustomed to wealth and ease are suddenly reduced to poverty, humiliation, and toil."

As for our Holy Hill, that poor place was like the "abomination of desolation" of *Matthew* 24:15. All during the War the School and the Seminary had served as Federal hospitals (our Chapel was used for storage of dead bodies awaiting burial) and the occupying doctors and nurses had not treated the wounds they themselves had inflicted on our buildings and grounds.

Says RPW: "These temporary tenants were little concerned with the care of the property, and when they finally departed the beautiful oaks were found hewn and the buildings defaced. Great injury ensued here.

"It was no easy assignment to find a man willing and able to undertake the task [of running the school] with the certain knowledge that the Trustees had no funds to back him. How many were considered for the post we have no way of knowing; but eventually it was offered to a young Confederate veteran of a status unique in the South at that time: he had money in the bank.

"Solvency is not always the most important qualification for success in education, but in 1866 it was vital, and EHS was fortunate in finding a young alumnus as well qualified in that area as in others."

("Vital" is *le mot juste*: "Think of $350 for a sack of flour and $40 for a gallon of molasses."—"Juhl.")

William Fowler Gardner was born in Alexandria in 1840, attended the High School for two years (1855–57), and was at the University when the War came. In the Spring of 1861 he enlisted as a private in the Old Dominion Rifles. At Second Manassas (August, 1862) he was so severely wounded that he was declared unfit for further field service. He then entered the Seminary (temporarily in Staunton, Virginia) and graduated in 1864. He returned to the Army as a chaplain and served with the 24th Virginia Infantry until the end.

He clearly had a strong sense of mission (and the money for implementation), and when he came to us in 1866 "He set to work gradually to restore and make habitable the buildings. He did this largely out of his private resources. The work he did for the School in its greatest emergency has hardly been fully recognized, for Mr. Gardner reopened and reclaimed it from the ravages and even the vandalism of war." [ABK].

Mr. Gardner took the High School in the morning of a new day after a dark night of tragic warfare, and in spite of many discouragements, and scant resources he did what God is forever doing, beginning again, getting new mornings out of old nights. Think of the conditions when that old School was reborn. In this School God began all over again. He is at it still in individuals and institutions of good learning. [Jacob Brittingham, 1869–72.]

Another Old Boy vividly describes some of the conditions prevailing on the Hill "when that old School was reborn":

I had been at a Calvinistic school in the North where conversation at table was forbidden and a joyous laugh was regarded as criminal. Then my choice fell upon the diocesan School of Virginia with the Reverend William F. Gardner at its head. Religion was with him joy and gladness, and he wore a smile of peace which seemed banished from the other school.

The School building, owing to the decay of shingles during the war, was covered now by a sort of chemical substitute. The rain came in freely in consequence and caused the plaster to fall in all three stories, so that more of it was on the floor than on the ceiling.

The recitation rooms had been used the year before for storing a crop of corn grown on the premises, and in this way hundreds of rats invaded the building. The only room in it occupied then was the chapel. This was the sleeping place of four boarders.

I have never known a higher standard of Spirituality among boys. [James R. Winchester, 1866–69, who later became Bishop of Arkansas.]

As his predecessors had done, Mr. Gardner strove mightily in the fields of the Lord. And like those valiant men who had gone

William Fowler Gardner, Principal, 1866–70.

before, ultimately he found the forces arrayed against him too powerful to overcome.

Eighteen boys came for the first year, 1866–67. During the next two years that number increased, but then attendance dropped off. The Principal's task was becoming impossible: shadows of the evening. . . .

He was too truly Christian. Too tender.

He was a great influence for good with me and all the boys who had the capacity to appreciate him. His characteristic high mindedness and gentleness, in fact an evident nobility of character was there for us to draw upon, though his lack of aggressiveness, or indisposition to make claims for himself, perhaps prevented some of the boys from appreciating him. [Archibald H. Taylor, 1867–69.]

In that gentle man's darkening evening there was one brilliant flash. "In the spring of 1869 a carriage drawn by a pair of handsome greys drew up in front of the School and the face of General Robert E. Lee was discovered within. Immediately the boys and the teachers gathered around the carriage with such cheering and manifestations of delighted admiration as only the sight of such a beloved hero could evoke.

"General Lee halted and chatted with the boys and others for fifteen minutes, then went his way, waving his hat out of the window in answer to the cheering of the boys. He had looked that day upon pillared Arlington, the home of so many bright and painful memories, for the last time." [ABK].

Finally, however, "despite heroic efforts and financial sacrifices, Mr. Gardner found the difficulties of re-establishing the School insurmountable." [RPW].

In June, 1870, that good man resigned. He accepted a call to Trinity Church in Dorsey, Maryland, and lived there until his death in 1907.

Of all of the Principals we have ever had, William Fowler Gardner, it seems, was the dearest. "No one who recalls his beautiful countenance, his gentle bearing, his unflagging interest in the School, can fail to think of him with high regard or to honor him for his courageous work of revival during the years of hardship which followed the war." [ABK].

"There is in the School Chapel a tablet with an inscription that haunts me: *Aliorum memor, immemor sui*—'Mindful of others, unmindful of self.' I can think of no one to whom it could be applied more justly than to Mr. Gardner, who never gave a thought to self, who wanted only to help where best he could.

"He took a badly run-down plant, rehabilitated it at considerable cost to himself and turned it over to the Trustees in operating condition. Our debt to Mr. Gardner has not yet been paid. Perhaps it is so great that it can never be paid." [RPW].

CHAPTER 4

Old Bar
1870–1913

There were giants in the earth in those days. . . .
—Genesis 6:4.

During these decades the population of the United States increased to some ninety-five million (fifty million rural, forty-five million urban), and the center of population moved westward, always westward, to a spot a few miles northwest of Bloomington, Indiana.

In 1870 France lost the Franco-Prussian War and Schliemann started digging at Troy. In 1871 Mrs. O'Leary's cow's fire destroyed much of Chicago and Stanley met Livingstone at Ujiji, Tanganyika. In 1873 color photographs were first developed, modern tennis was begun in England and the Remington gun company produced its first typewriters. (Mark Twain fell in love with one and learned to type at a rate of nineteen words per minute; Tom Sawyer was published in 1875.)

In 1876 Alexander Graham Bell said to his assistant "Mr. Watson, come here, I want you," and those were the first intelligible words ever spoken over the telephone; the next year England's Queen Victoria got a telephone, and was crowned Empress of India. (Ten years later the British Empire, at the apex of its might,

*celebrated the Golden Jubilee of her reign. She came to power two
years before the High School was born.)*

Also in 1877 *Thomas Edison invented the phonograph, and in
1880 he and the Englishman Sir Joseph Swan independently invented the electric light. In 1882 the Maine-born inventor Hiram
Maxim patented his machine gun. In 1883 there was built, in
Chicago, the first "skyscraper," ten storeys high.*

In January, 1887, *a blizzard raged through the northern Great
Plains for seventy-two hours, killing millions of cattle and bank-
rupting big ranchers. It effectively ended the heroic age of cattle
ranching in this country. After that ranches were smaller and more
scientifically managed. Later in that year Arthur Conan Doyle, a
Scottish physician, published* A Study in Scarlet *and Sherlock
Holmes' brilliant career was launched.*

In 1888 *George Eastman perfected the "Kodak" camera, and
the first beauty contest was held, in Belgium. In 1892 the German
Rudolf Diesel patented his internal combustion engine and U.S.
iron and steel workers struck. In 1895 the French brothers Auguste
and Louis Lumière invented a motion picture camera, sports en-
thusiasts saw the first professional football game and the first U.S.
Open golf championship, and the Viennese Dr. Sigmund Freud
began to illuminate the dark world of the subconscious with publication of* Studien über Hysterie *("Studies of Hysteria"). In 1896
the first modern Olympic Games were held, in Athens, and gold
was discovered in the Klondike. Alaska was no longer called "Seward's Folly."*

In 1898 *the French couple Pierre and Marie Curie discovered
radium. The U.S. won a quick war with Spain after which that
country ceded to us, for $20,000,000, Cuba, Puerto Rico, Guam
and the Philippines.*

In 1899 *Kipling published* Stalky and Co., *a psychically en-
grossing story of scheming lads in an English boarding school.
(The school was really Westward Ho, in Devonshire, and Kipling
was the skinny, bespectacled "Beetle.")*

*The year 1900 marked the end of the century of steam and the
beginning of the age of electricity.*

In 1901 *President McKinley was assassinated. Two years later
there were two "firsts" as portentous as they were brief: a full-
length movie,* The Great Train Robbery, *ran for twelve minutes
and Wilbur Wright flew a powered aircraft for twelve seconds.
(Samuel P. Langley, Secretary of the Smithsonian Institution, had*

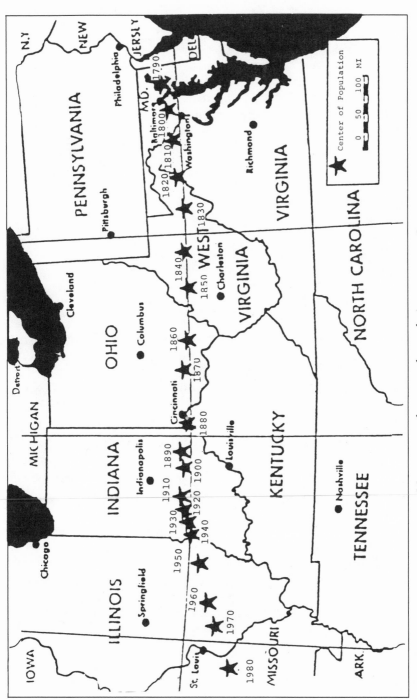

Movement of center of population, 1790–1980.

flown powered but unmanned models over the Potomac in 1896, but in 1903 the machine he had designed to carry an operator failed to fly in two tries.)

In 1905 the Japanese defeated the Russians at Port Arthur and the German-born Albert Einstein formulated his Special Theory of Relativity. His famous equation, $E = mc^2$, foreshadowed, inter alia, *the atom bomb.*

In 1907 the English Baron Baden-Powell founded the Boy Scouts. In 1909 Robert E. Peary created one of the enduring myths of the Twentieth Century by claiming (mistakenly) to have reached the North Pole, and the first commercial manufacture of Bakelite heralded the beginning of the plastics industry.

In 1911 the Norwegian Roald Amundsen reached the South Pole. In 1912 the unsinkable Titanic *sank, and five million Americans were going to the movies every day. In 1913 this country authorized the first Federal income tax, and Henry Ford started his first assembly line.*

ONCE MORE, after Mr. Gardner resigned in 1870, the Trustees were hard pressed to find a new Principal for their school.

The position seemed as untenable as the famous Siege Perilous of King Arthur's Round Table. Of our first four heads, two had been defeated by money (lack of), one by his own inner devils, and one by war.

"The High School had attained an honorable name during the thirty years since its establishment, but in 1870 the School was at a low ebb. There were but twelve boys. It needed a strong and experienced head." [ABK].

The Trustees offered the job to James M. Garnett (EHS 1853–57, the letter-writer quoted in Chapter One). He had served in the Army, afterwards worked for two years at the School as an assistant to Mr. Gardner, and was highly regarded. (Later he became President of St. John's College, Annapolis, and Professor of English at the University.) He was studying in Europe when the Trustees' invitation to head our school came. He declined.

At this low point a wonderful thing happened: a highly qualified man applied for the position!

Launcelot Minor Blackford was born in Fredericksburg in 1837, the fourth of five sons. In 1846 the family moved to Lynchburg, where his father edited *The Lynchburg Virginian.*

His mother, a Virginian, was an ardent abolitionist. It is said

Launcelot Minor Blackford, Principal, 1870–1913.

that all during the War she slept with a copy of *Uncle Tom's Cabin* under her pillow. She raised her sons to be abolitionists, but when "the dreadful die was cast" all of those sons joined the South. They made the point that they were defending their state, not slavery. Mary Blackford spent her declining years with her "best beloved son, Lanty" at the School and there is a legend that the ghost of that powerful woman still walks our halls. (Her grandson Launcelot Minor Blackford, Jr., has written a very good book about her, *Mine Eyes Have Seen the Glory*.)

Launcelot entered the University in 1855 and taught for four hours a day at a Charlottesville school while working towards an M.A. degree, which he took in 1860.

He was teaching at the Virginia Female Institute (now Stuart Hall) in Staunton when the War came. In May, 1861, his older brother William wrote to him advising him to "join the Home Guard at once. . . . be careful about protecting yourself from the ground when sleeping . . . always keep on dry clothes when you can . . . as to the duties of a soldier you can soon get them. It is all comprised in the first word of command: '*Attention.*' "

"He at once entered a camp of instruction at Charlottesville, and on September 2 [1861], Private Blackford joined the famous Rockbridge Artillery at Fairfax Station, ten miles from the school which was to be his lifework." [RPW].

"When this pale, spare youth with a face of almost feminine delicacy first joined the battery and began his duties by putting on the harness hind part before, no one would have dreamed what he was to learn in the school of war." [ABK].

He learned a lot, fast. As he reported later, "I was at first not a cheerful soldier, though never moping. After a little while, however, I got used and reconciled to the life. I felt I was just where I chose to be; that I would not change. . . . Moreover, my health and appetite were good, and I had no grievance. Above all, my heart was unreservedly and enthusiastically in the cause."

His unit fought in the bloody Virginia battles at Kernstown, Winchester, Port Republic (where all officers above his captain were killed or wounded) and Cross Keys. In October, 1862, after Second Manassas, he was assigned as secretary to a Lynchburg surgeon and in 1863 he was made clerk of the military court of General Longstreet's Corps. Late in 1864 he was returned to field duty as adjutant to his cousin, Lieutenant Colonel Richard L. Maury, of the 24th Virginia Infantry, Pickett's Division.

On April 6, 1865, he was taken prisoner at the battle of Sailor's Creek, Virginia, but after the surrender at Appomattox three days later he was paroled, and he walked home to Lynchburg.

The War turned the "pale, spare youth" into a firm, disciplined, compassionate man.

It has been pointed out more than once how profitable were these wonderful years in the Confederate Army. A student at Washington College, when General Lee was there, lamented to that great soldier the time he had lost in the Confederate Army. "Never again," was the reply, "speak of the time you lost in the Army. Those were the best years of your life."

The four years in the army constituted an incomparable post-graduate school for [the High School's] future Principal. [The experience] gave him the discipline he needed to harden, mature and broaden him. In the military court he learned wisdom in dealing with men, developed markedly his fine judicial faculty, his knowledge of character and the merits of causes.

He further learned humanity, common-sense, justice, and all these qualities showed out conspicuously when it fell to his lot to handle a corps of irrepressible boys. [ABK].

After Appomattox the battle-hardened veteran went to the Norwood School in Nelson County, Virginia. He was Associate Principal there when he heard that the Episcopal High School was looking for a Principal. Then, in his own words, "Having made up my mind to apply for the appointment, I knew that no time was to be lost and sat up all one night writing to persons of influence whom I knew to ask them to recommend me to the appointing power."

The Trustees who had struggled so often to find someone willing to head their school must have been stunned to find a qualified man not only willing but eager to take the responsibility. Quickly, with what ABK called "divinely guided sagacity," they approved the appointment of Launcelot Minor Blackford as, in his words again, "Principal of the High School at Howard, near Alexandria." And so began the longest and one of the finest epochs in the whole history of this School.

The new Principal found the School in disarray and immediately set out to restore it to physical and spiritual health and to assure that it should be "an institution of learning where youth can be thoroughly educated on Christian principles, and where their morals and habits can be preserved from the dangers of evil associations."

He acted with remarkable dispatch. To quote him again, "Considerable repairs and improvement of the premises were at once made by the Trustees and the necessary equipment purchased by myself. One of my first considerations, of course, was to get suitable assistant teachers."

And that he did.

His method was simple: "He prayed earnestly and long before the selection of each new master." [ABK]. His success was great.

One of his boys, William Holding Echols, Jr. (1875–78), said:

It was a noble spectacle, the group of gifted ex-Confederate soldiers who, when the war was over, turned, in the terrible reconstruction days, to training and educating the neglected youth of the South— often the fatherless sons of their dead comrades.

These boys were the most precious possession the nation had, and their supreme good fortune was to have teachers just come out themselves of the greatest school of efficient and disciplined manhood that one could pass through.

We were all sons of Confederate soldiers running wild in a disordered South. They hunted me down with hounds in Sand Mountain, Alabama, only ten years after Appomattox, made me put on shoes, and sent me here to this place of marvellous peace and quiet to be taught by Confederate soldiers that which was worth while in order to live one's life.

They taught us many things. They could never teach me how to spell or to learn mental arithmetic, but they did teach us two things which stand out indelibly.

The first was painted on an old board over the wooden gymnasium door: "In order that there may be a strong mind in a strong body." The important word is that Ut—in order that there may be, not for any other reason. It is like the sportsman's prayer:

> Not the quarry, but the chase,
> Not the laurel, but the race,
> Not the hazard, but the play,
> Make me, Lord, enjoy alway.

The other thing was also painted on a board and nailed over a door in the old school room. It stared us in the face every hour of every day we lived here. We knew every fly speck on its dirty face. The old Honor Pledge, it grew to be to us like the Confederate Flag, a thing to live for, to fight for, and to die for.

Mr. Ramsey, the chief engineer of the Dupont Corporation, once said to me "We like to have the Virginia boys work for us, not because they are any better prepared technically than those from other places, perhaps not even quite so well, but they will not lie to you, you cannot make them lie."

All educated people know that there is nothing in nature or in life that is immutable, it is only in man's transcendental ideal that there exists absolute stability. But there are certain of these absolute invariants upon which all of our faith and all of our hopes and happiness depend. There are other standard invariants of the school, but these two—the Creed of Sportsmanship and the Honor Code—have impressed me most indelibly and pursued me most relentlessly.

And so it goes, the same old boys in the same old place, the same old standards in charge of the same old men, the same blood of the generations that have gone before, and they builded well in the land which the Lord their God gave unto them.

("Reddy" Echols became a famous math professor at UVA.)

The first teacher recruited by the new Principal was Llewellyn Hoxton, a West Point graduate who had served with distinction during the War and risen to the rank of Colonel. He was an

Colonel Llewellyn Hoxton.

extraordinarily wise and capable man. Few of our masters have ever been so beloved.

Colonel Hoxton was a finely equipped mathematical scholar, and an admirable teacher, a perfect disciplinarian and a man who inspired in boys a deep and sustained reverence. For twenty-one years he was Mr. Blackford's chief counselor. Successive generations of boys marked him as a man of stainless honor, of singular self-control, a loving and gentle husband and father, a modest and consistent Christian.

He came to his place in the School from a conspicuously gallant career in the western army where he had fought some of the hardest battles of the war against the bravest troops under some of the ablest Federal generals.

The very embodiment of truth, honor and chivalrous fidelity to duty, in him the boys had before them a Christian knight. Who can tell the wide-reaching influence of this man upon the lives of hundreds of youths who, at their most susceptible age, came under the power of his pure and single-minded example? A true Christian soldier, ever on duty at his post, who of us can ever forget the look in those luminous, sad eyes, or escape the persuasion to a life of goodness and usefulness of his quiet, steadfast example? [ABK, who was at the School from 1878 to 1881.]

The first session began September 21, 1870, and thirty-five boys came. The new Principal had this to say:

"Of these thirty-five . . . six became clergymen and one died in course of preparation. . . . The behavior of the boys this session was nothing to brag of, though only one was expelled, and some of the best I ever had were included in their number.

WASHINGTONIAN.

LEESBURG, LOUDOUN COUNTY, VA.

SATURDAY, AUGUST 3, 1872.

EPISCOPAL HIGH SCOOL OF VIRGINIA, NEAR ALEXAN-DRIA.—The 29th Annual Session of this SCHOOL FOR BOYS opens SEPTEMBER 25, 1872. TERMS: $330 per year. Catalogue, with particulars, sent on application to

L. M. BLACKFORD, M. A.,

Principal, Alexandria, Va.

aug 3-2m

Hide not thy light under a bushel.

"We had only one dormitory floor and each bed, though enclosed within calico partitions, was double. All ablutions were made in the lavatory on the ground floor. Old fashioned desks, with detached chairs, were used in the school room; fairly comfortable for the boys but distracting to the master in charge from the noise they occasioned.

"We had prayers before breakfast then and all recitations before dinner." [In the South at that time, and in many rural places still, "dinner" was the noonday meal.]

Two memorable things happened in that first session. On October 12 Robert E. Lee died, and his friend, our first Principal, Dr. Pendleton, conducted the funeral service at Washington College, the institution of which the General had been head for five "immortal years" [ABK] after the War and which was to become Washington and Lee University. And on some unspecified day that other great man, the former President of the Confederacy, Jefferson Davis, visited a friend of Mr. Blackford's near the School and the entire student body was invited to pay respects.

Mr. Blackford: "For the first and last time in my experience a half-holiday as a mark of respect to anyone was given and the visit made. No one who was present will ever forget the mingled dignity and sweetness with which our late illustrious chief received his young countrymen."

That first session inaugurated, "quietly and unobtrusively, an administration that took a school struggling for its very existence and in forty-three years pushed it to the front rank of the secondary schools of the nation." [RPW]. For "an administration" read "Launcelot Minor Blackford and the like-minded men he gathered around him."

I arrived in the autumn of 1872. I came over incredibly bad roads in a little, springless wagon drawn by a black mule that my father had been permitted to bring home with him from Appomattox. I was only thirteen years old. In a short time I found that the man upon whom I could rely most was the Principal of the school: one of the great men of Virginia and of this country. [R. Walton Moore, 1872–77, who also became a great man of this country—a superb diplomat.]

One of the new Principal's first official acts was to form a literary society. The old School had always had such a society, the Pithonian, named perhaps for Peitho, the mythical personification of Persuasion usually portrayed with Aphrodite, the Goddess of

Episcopal High School of Virginia.

Athletic Day----Session 1877--78.

Saturday, ~~November~~ 10th, 1877.

MANAGERS:	JUDGES:
ARTHUR A. SNYDER, *of Georgetown, D. C.*	Col. WM. W. BLACKFORD, *of Washington, D. C.*
BRICE W. GOLDSBOROUGH, *of Maryland.*	Rev. WM. M. DAME, *of Alexandria.*
WILLIAM W. GORDON, *Jr., of Alabama.*	Capt. ALEX. INNIS, *of Fairfax.*

SCHEDULE.

1. *THROWING THE BALL*.........PRIZE: *A Ball and two Bats.*
   COMPETITORS: Echols, Goldsborough, W. W. Gordon, jr., S. B. Garnett, Herndon, F. H. Larned, jr., Powell, Shepherd.

2. *WRESTLING MATCH*.........PRIZE: *A Box of Tools, 24 pieces.*
   COMPETITORS: Cowen, W. W. Gordon, jr., A. A. Snyder.

3. *JUNIOR HURDLE RACE*.........PRIZE: *A Game Bag, Powder Flask and Shot Pouch.*
   COMPETITORS: Blackford, Carson, P. Gordon, E. H. Hopkins, Rhett, Spencer, Terrett.

4. *RUNNING LONG JUMP*.........PRIZE: *A pair of Boxing Gloves.*
   COMPETITORS: Cornwall, S. B. Garnett, P. Gordon, W. W. Gordon, jr., Lockwood, Shepherd, Spencer, Wilson.

5. *FLAT RACE, 440 yards, handicapped*.........PRIZE: *A fine Pocket Book.*
   COMPETITORS: Baltzell, Carson, Cowen, J. Garnett, S. B. Garnett, Goldsborough, Heyward, Meredith, W. K. Miller, Powell, Rhett, Shepherd, Terrett, J. W. Wheat, Wickham.

6. *RUNNING HIGH JUMP*.........PRIZE: *A horseman's Pocket Knife.*
   COMPETITORS: Echols, F. H. Larned, jr., Lockwood, Shepherd, Wilson.

7. *THREE LEGGED RACE, 100 yards*.........PRIZE: *Two Pocket Knives.*
   COMPETITORS: Amblet and Cornwall, Carson and Fleming, S. B. Garnett and Goldsborough, Glenn and Hubbard, P. Gordon and Spencer, Lewis and Wierman, Lockwood and Shepherd, Meredith and Wickham, W. K. Miller and Wilson, J. C. Wheat and Powell.

8. *RUNNING HOP, SKIP AND JUMP*.........PRIZE: *A fine double Shot Belt.*
   COMPETITORS: W. W. Gordon, jr., Lewis, Shepherd, Spencer.

9. *FLAT RACE, 100 yards*........PRIZE: *A pair of Maple Clubs.*
   COMPETITORS: J. C. Calhoun, Cornwall, Cowen, W. W. Gordon, jr., Minor, Wilson.

10. *POTATO RACE, 60 yards*.........PRIZE: *A fine Shot Pouch and Powder Flask.*
    COMPETITORS: Baltzell, Blackford, Branch, Carson, Cowen, E. H. Hopkins, Hyer, Jemison, Meredith, Minor, Powell, Shepherd, A. A. Snyder, Walton, J. C. Wheat, Wickham, Wierman, Wilson, F. J. Winston.

11. *SENIOR HURDLE RACE, 6 hurdles in 140 yards*.........PRIZE: *A pair of Acme Club Skates.*
    COMPETITORS: W. W. Gordon, jr., Lewis, Lockwood, J. W. Wheat, Wilson.

12. *FLAT RACE, 1 mile, handicapped*.........PRIZE: *A pair of Rosewood Clubs.*
    COMPETITORS: Baltzell, J. C. Calhoun, Carson, J. Garnett, Heyward, J. D. Hopkins, Lewis, Meredith, Powell, Terrett, J. C. Wheat, J. W. Wheat, Wickham, Wierman, C. G. Waller.

13. *CONSOLATION RACE, 300 yards, open only to those who have engaged in one or more of the preceding contests and have taken no prize*.........PRIZE: *An English Game Bag.*

NON SINE PULVERE.

Non Sine Pulvere—"*Not Without Toil*"—*was the Athletic Day motto.*

Love. That society was started by the noted classics teacher Milo Mahan on December 7, 1839, and it had flourished until 1861. (Sample debate topics: "If a puppy dog's tail curls up so tightly that it lifts the dog's hind legs from the ground, is it a quadruped or a biped?", "Resolved, that Anarchy is justifiable.") But the society had not been revived when the School reopened in 1866.

In October, 1870, the Principal proposed that a successor to the Pithonian be created, and "The boys asked me to suggest names. I submitted Randolph Fairfax and Philip Sidney and, greatly to my satisfaction, they chose the former." (He was referring to Sir Philip Sidney, the Elizabethan poet, statesman and soldier.) So, without any fuss, our first post-War literary society made our most saintly War casualty our first eponymous hero.

Four years later another such society was founded. It was named for the Principal himself. There has always been a legend that the Blackford Literary Society was begun six years after the Fairfax, and indeed Mr. Blackford himself once wrote "There was but one literary society, the Fairfax, until 1876." But that legend (and Mr. Blackford) is (was) wrong.

The proof: RPW found this 1884 letter from Old Boy E. Wickham Byrd (1874–77) to Mr. Blackford:

> I see by your catalogue of last year that the Blackford Society is said to have been founded December, 1876. I beg to make a correction here. The Blackford Society was founded December, 1874, and was named after you. . . . I had the honor to be one of the founders in 1874. In 1875 the Society fell to the ground, and in 1876 was re-founded by some of the old members, myself among the number.

Chronologicoliterosociophiles take note.

Our third Literary Society, the Wilmer, was named for the Right Reverend Joseph P.B. Wilmer, one of our founding fathers, and begun in 1911. It is for boys who are less than fifteen years old when the school year begins.

Mr. Blackford's respect for language rivalled that of the famed sixth-century Latin scholar Priscian, *arbiter grammaticus* of the Middle Ages. Once when a doctor examining him pronounced the word "abdomen" with the accent on the first syllable the Principal winced and murmured "Doctor, please—ab*do*men." Stiff upper lip?—nothing so banal: "I deem it treason to repine." Told that a baseball player had flied to center field, he corrected "flied" to "flew."

He took a keen interest in the intellectual activities of his boys and was in no doubt that those activities should be carefully and firmly directed. Said he, "This allowing boys to choose what they shall study is one of the latest and worst fruits of what I consider the parent of many ills of democracy. I have no sympathy with it." (What would he have thought of the infamous "permissiveness" in education that disgraced this country in the 1920's and again in the sixties?)

He also took thought for his charges' spiritual welfare:

"Wednesdays and Sundays alike they had a brief chapel service before breakfast; on Sundays there was also morning prayer and a sermon in the Seminary chapel at 11, Bible class for the whole School at 4, and evening prayers at 7:30, with a sermon by the School's chaplain once a month. The lessons at the evening service were read by the monitors, serving in rotation and wearing white ties. There was always grace before meals and, after supper, a short Bible reading and prayer.

"Dr. Blackford also introduced one service at which attendance was entirely voluntary: the half-hour Friday night meetings, between supper and study hall, conducted by students from the Seminary in conjunction with the School chaplain. No boy could fail to benefit." [RPW].

He started our Honor System, and our practice of delegating some authority to students called monitors.

As early as 1877, possibly before, he formed a choir to lead the singing in the Seminary Chapel on Sunday mornings, and in 1878 he reported to the Trustees that "We have gotten up a Missionary Society, the object of which is (1) to raise money for Missionary and other beneficent work, and (2) to diffuse information in regard to such work, to increase interest in it and in every way practicable to advance it."

That Society, as every Old Boy knows, has flourished like the green bay tree. In the 112 years since its founding it has provided leadership and support for many charitable causes and in 1963 it "adopted" a nine-year-old Greek orphan girl.

After attending to things spiritual—the gathering together of an outstanding group of teachers dedicated, like himself, to the proposition that in matters of educational guidance all men and boys are not created equal, and to the provision of services designed to nourish the boys' souls—Mr. Blackford turned his attention to things temporal: comfort, health, and healthy recreation.

The two one-storey two-room wings connected by arcades to

the Principal's residence were, in the 1870's, supplanted by two-storey houses for masters, and in 1882 each of those houses was enlarged to five rooms and a front porch. In 1874 a small frame hall was put up south of the main building for the Blackford Literary Society (the Fairfax was housed in another small hall to the north).

Meanwhile, a cry was heard across the land, "Let there be sports!"

And sports there were.

It seems that the School had had no organized athletics before the War. It was not customary for schools here or abroad, with the exception of a few like England's Eton, to support competitive athletic teams, or even organized exercise classes, in those days. From 1866 to 1870 EHS boys played the popular new game of baseball, and that was all.

Dr. Blackford changed that.

In one of his first letters to the Trustees he wrote: "The play-room formerly known as the boys' parlour, in rear of the school building, was . . . demolished by the enemy during the war, and has never been rebuilt. . . . A playroom, in a separate building, for cold and wet weather, is absolutely necessary for the proper conduct and discipline of the institution, and the comfort and well-being of pupils." In another letter he said:

One floor only (on which are the schoolroom, the recitation rooms and the teachers' rooms) is, the occasions of eating, dressing and sleeping excepted, allowed the boys. Imagine this place the sole abode of even forty boys on a rainy afternoon after study hours, and you perceive the difficulty—I had almost said the impossibility—of repressing noise and making the school-room what it is intended to be, a place of quiet employment or recreation.

Imagine too the confusion in which, under such circumstances, the unfortunate assistant teachers must live. And then, even if by the strong arm of authority the boys are kept quiet, how unnatural, even cruel, such a constraint the whole 24 hours through, and so it must be in bad weather. Would not their health too suffer?

If there was a room to romp in, all disorder in the school-room out of study hours could be, as it ought to be, effectually repressed; otherwise, it cannot.

Those impassioned pleas must have pierced the other-worldly contemplations of the Trustees. A new play-room was soon decreed. And of course that new play-room was the forerunner, or progenitor, of our modern magnificent gymnasiums, indoor athletic buildings and playing fields.

Mr. Blackford started track at the School the year after he came. By good fortune we know the exact day. On December 19, 1871, he staged what he called "Prize Foot Races," along the Leesburg Turnpike near its intersection with Braddock Road. The next November a 700-yard "Steeple Chase," with three classes of contestants, was held, and from those modest beginnings a full-fledged track and field program soon developed.

The year 1877 brought us our first gymnasium. Mr. Blackford described it thus (his money figures will make twentieth century builders weep): "I may state in round numbers the cost of the building at $730 and the equipment at $220. A fine voladore, placed outside, costs $50 more. The building is 60 by 35 ft. and about 18 ft. to the eaves, open to the ridgepole inside." (What was a "voladore"? That researcher-of-lost-words Dick Thomsen thinks it may have been a set of "flying rings.")

Baseball, as has been mentioned above, had been popular at the School in the years immediately after the War, and Mr. Blackford encouraged that sport. Football sprang up almost by itself in the early seventies and also quickly became popular. In March, 1878, Mr. B. wrote "Football has been quite the rage," and the next October he "ordered a Rugby football for $7 and a book of rules for ten cents. The boys furnished their own uniforms and continued to do so for some years." [RPW].

In the first issue of *The Monthly Chronicle*, November, 1888, there is a stirring paean which makes "Foot Ball" the sport, literarily, of Kings: "We read of Foot Ball in the days of King Arthur. . . ."

(When the semi-legendary Arthur, King of the Britons, lived—apparently in the sixth century—games often ended in death, and a thousand years later the English diplomat-scholar Sir Thomas Elyot complained that football was "nothyng but beastely fury and extreme violence, whereof procedeth hurt." For more about more recent and less violent football, including the rest of that *Chronicle* rhapsody, read the section on Sports.)

The ninth issue of *The Monthly Chronicle*, July, 1889, described in suitably stately terms the celebration of the School's first fifty years. Some sixty-five Old Boys came back to the Hill for special ceremonies including speeches by distinguished persons.

The Reverend Joseph Packard, who had been a friend of Bishop Meade and a sort of Godfather to the School, gently characterized the second principal, Mr. Dalrymple, as one "whose discipline was not of a paternal character but modeled more after the precepts of Solomon than would make it popular in this enlightened day, which is wiser than Solomon."

The *Chronicle* editors did not see fit to comment on that exaltation of the super-Solomonic enlightenment of the year 1889.

The Reverend Cornelius Walker said that on his first night at the School, October 17, 1840, he "had seen one boy tickle the ear of another and heard him quote the words, *Homo natus est titillari*." (Translation: "Man is born to be tickled"—but what Roman philosophized thus? Dr. Walker didn't say, knowing that his hearers probably knew, as, probably, fifty years later, did Cap'n Dick Williams. But we don't. Too bad. Somebody deserves credit for a very happy titillation.)

Dr. Walker also spoke of an "under master" who must have been an interesting mentor: Henry B. Bartow was "an intense Yankee, a dyspeptic, a man of many absurd remedies for his own ailments. . . ."

The Right Reverend Leighton Coleman, Bishop of Delaware, said "The completion of fifty years of the School's life calls especially for an expression of thankfulness to Almighty God for the many blessings he has vouchsafed it during a period not altogether devoid of perils and anxieties." (Understatement!)

It was decided to memorialize the anniversary by building a gate at the main entrance. The *Chronicle* editor summed up the ceremonies eloquently: "So much sad happiness one does not meet with often. . . ."

During those early years Mr. Blackford helped to introduce to the School games other than baseball and football.

Tennis and lacrosse seem to have begun about the same time as football. The 1882–83 catalogue is the first to mention a "Tennis Club" and the 1884–85 catalogue lists a "La Crosse Club." For some reason lacrosse was dropped after only one year, however. It does not reappear in the catalogue until 1963.

Finally, the busy Principal considered the problem of shelter. In 1870 there had been few improvements in the buildings of the School from the year of its founding until the War, and none afterwards, except for some emergency repairs of Federal ravages. But the new Principal was determined that his charges should not continue to live like soldiers in barracks, or worse: consider those "hundreds of rats" of James Winchester's letter. (Perhaps a change in his own life made Mr. B. more aware of matters of comfort. In 1884 he married Eliza Chew Ambler.)

The Principal appealed repeatedly to the Trustees for help in improving the living and working conditions, in vain. At last, in 1890, he sent them this despairing letter which tells us a great deal about living conditions in the School as well as about the relation between him and the Trustees:

More than once in recent years I have asked . . . for an additional building here for instruction in physical sciences and for Commencement purposes. I did not request this because such a building (important as it unquestionably is) was in my judgment the improvement the most needed but because it was the only one which I then thought it possible to secure.

I desire to lay before the Board (1) the reasons why I think material modification of the accommodations here indispensable and (2) a few words as to the kind of change should be made.

In the last ten years the number of applications for admission has declined more than is known to you; the reason being the increasing dissatisfaction with our accommodations. The public to whom we look for support is growing more and more discontented with an arrangement which requires boys to sleep on the third floor and come down to the first floor for their morning toilet in a common lavatory; and which makes no provision for separate rooms after several years' residence. The public—our public—may be all wrong about this; it may be best for their boys to continue to rough it as others quite as good have done for more than half a century; it may be best for the older boys to have no extraordinary privileges—but if this public refuses to think so and for the want of the advantages in question gradually withdraws its support, what are we going to do about it?

From uncertainty as to the amount it may be proposed by the Board to raise, I forbear to state now in detail my views of the improvements required. A hundred thousand dollars would be none too much, though one-half or one-third of that sum could be advantageously used.

We are cramped for room on all sides. We need a larger chapel and dining room, more room for the work of instruction, better bathing facilities, more lodging places for servants, a Commencement Hall; but above all, improved accommodations for students. Each boy should have a separate apartment, say 6 by 8 feet, with bed, washstand, press and chair, and dress there in the morning; not generally having access to the room during the day, but performing his ablutions before meals in a lavatory as now.

For the monitors—say twenty percent of the whole number—there

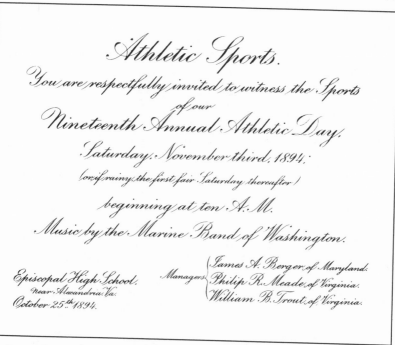

Athletic Sports.

You are respectfully invited to witness the Sports
of our
Nineteenth Annual Athletic Day,
Saturday, November third, 1894,
(or, if rainy, the first fair Saturday thereafter)
beginning at ten A. M.
Music by the Marine Band of Washington.

Episcopal High School,   *Managers* { *James A. Berger, of Maryland.*
near Alexandria, Va.   *Philip R. Meade, of Virginia.*
October 25th 1894.   *William B. Trout, of Virginia.*

Formal invitation to a Field Day, 1894. The Marine Band also played during our long, long Commencements.

should be regular rooms to be occupied by two; but none such for the boys generally should be thought of. Bad as the room system is anywhere, it would be here, in the neighborhood of large towns, equally inconsistent with the preservation of proper discipline and of sound morals, and cannot be too strongly deprecated.

That letter is fascinating. It shows that Mr. Blackford, although devoted as the next principal to the English schools' notoriously Spartan ways, felt keenly the winds of American change and was willing to bend to them. It was perhaps the first time that the principal of a major American preparatory school had dared to challenge the ancient British tradition of austere-to-the-point-of-sadistic treatment of boarding school boys.

That one gesture was not the herald of a wider rebellion by Mr. B. against the British school model, however. He continued to go to England in the summers, as he always had done, mainly to observe the practices of those English principals whose conduct of their schools was modeled after that of the famous "Arnold of

Rugby." Dr. Thomas Arnold, father of the poet-critic Matthew Arnold, was principal of Rugby School from 1828 until his death in 1842. It was he who formulated the credo which for our school as for many others became Holy Writ: a boys' school should aim to turn out "first Christians, then gentlemen, and then scholars. My object will be, if possible, to form Christian men, for Christian boys I can scarcely hope to make." That lofty aim, Dr. Arnold believed, could not be achieved by soft handling.

ABK notes that Mr. Blackford "spoke more often of the ideals of a gentleman than of a Christian; yet the type he had in view was not an English gentleman of the period of Charles II or the Georges, but a Christian gentleman of the type of Randolph Fairfax or General Lee." (Conan Doyle, whose Sherlock Holmes stories began coming out in 1889, listed "three tests of a gentleman: firstly, his attitude of protection and chivalry to women; secondly, his courteous behavior to people of lower social status than himself; and, thirdly, his rectitude in financial matters." Nowadays a gentleman is reckoned to be any man who can wear, without looking self-conscious about it, a three-piece suit.)

The Principal's letter to the Board of Trustees proved tremendously effective.

RPW states that "The improvements Dr. Blackford sought were made during the summer of 1891 and added to the efficiency of the plant and the comfort of all." A fourth floor was added to the main building, this and the third floor each having a master's room and forty bunks or cubicles for boarders. Three bathrooms were added to the west end of the first and second floors, along with sinks at the end of the dormitory floors. From those sinks the boys filled their water buckets and carried them to the washstands in their cubicles. They became clean so as (almost) *no fuller on earth could white them.* Says RPW, "All bathing was done during study hall. Boys were assigned to bathing squads, six boys to a squad, three squads to an evening. Thus every boy was assured of a hot bath at least once a week. There is no record of a boy's not leaving the schoolroom with his squad, though the opportunity to take a bath was frequently foregone."

In addition to those improvements the School received, in 1893, its first sizeable gift: Mrs. Emma Coleman Liggett, widow of Hiram Shaw Liggett (1874–76), gave us a much-needed hall for commencement exercises, lectures, readings, concerts, plays and other such activities. Liggett Hall served faithfully for more than half a century. Now it has been turned into two apartments, for teachers.

Soon after the happy consequences of the Principal's extraordinary letter there was trouble, however. In 1895 certain Trustees decided to play a more direct part in managing the School. They introduced a system whereby the Principal, instead of having total charge of all School affairs, would yield control over matters of boarding, lodging and some other material concerns to two administrators, a steward and a financial officer, under superintendence of a Board of Trustees committee.

The Principal objected violently. Always articulate, he wrote "How could I be responsible to parents for their boys in all respects with the boarding, lodging, care of the sick, etc, in other hands?" Most of the Old Boys supported him, and "Fortunately for [his] peace of mind and for EHS, the radical Trustees eventually saw the folly of what they had advocated; Dr. Blackford remained in sole charge of the School." [RPW].

After that triumph, the oft-embattled Principal took the lid off of another long-simmering grievance. From the beginning of his tenure he had had a curious financial arrangement with the Trustees: he leased the School from them. He did not pay them cash, but provided a stipulated number of scholarships for sons of clergymen and other worthy, needy boys. He received as his salary half of the net proceeds and the other half went to the Trustees.

In 1898 Mr. Blackford reported to the owners *re* their leasing contract: "The serious drawback to the working of the arrangement thus far is, of course, the small income from the School. . . . This income on the one hand yields to the Trustees an amount adequate to the proper repairs and improvement of the premises, and on the other hand a net return to myself utterly insufficient for my support. Last session it was exactly $274.42. This year it may reach $700."

Where then was any kind of guild or union or even unwritten equity? In 1898 Mr. B. had been the hardest-working and most effective of principals for twenty-eight years. Exactly how the Trustees responded to his declaration is not recorded, but "Thereafter, with some fluctuations, the net increased [until] the session of 1906–07 brought for the School and Dr. Blackford $4,457.98 each, their best year financially since he assumed charge." [RPW].

Poets call the 1890's "the Mauve Decade," suggesting a complacent era, but for the Episcopal High School of that time no

The Old Chapel, c. 1895. Front Row: *C. F. Englehardt, E. V. Valz, V. H. Browne, F. S.R. Brown, M. Earhart, R. Fleet, C. R. McCulloch, ———?, R. N. Dame.* Second Row: *H. B. M. Watkins, G. W. Dame, A. G. Randolph, O. H. Johnson, D. B. Tennant, J. Hayes, W. H. Buck, J. W. Price, G. H. Dortch, B. W. Waters.* Back Row: *E. W. Robertson, J. H. Kunkel, W. P. Dame, R. C. Wilson, R. A. Walke, W. C. W. Yen, D. I. White, Jr., J. C. Armistead, C. P. Macgill, W. H. Randolph, F. S. Perry.*

Blackford Hall, 1900.

description could be further from the mark. Vigorous, active, growing by leaps and bounds, our School was transformed from an institution whose very survival was sometimes in doubt into the splendid, sturdy and distinguished Alma Mater we see today.

All of us owe an enormous debt to the vision, determination and spirit of Launcelot Minor Blackford.

As the new century began Mr. Blackford had every reason to look forward with pride and confidence. His School was flourishing and he, the very soul of it, was admired and respected and even, *privatim*, cherished.

Like all proper larger-than-life figures he held fiercer-than-fact views. He was especially positive on matters Southern.

Once Mr. Williams was asked if Mr. B. was perhaps unreconstructed. The answer was unequivocal: "Unreconstructed? He felt the Revolution was a mistake." Commenting on "Sherman, Sheridan and their ilk," the old Confederate said "I thank God I can bear malice for life." And when he saw a statue of Sherman in front of the Treasury building in Washington he said to Mr. Daniel "John, I will pay your expenses to cross the river and blow that up!" His opinion of the Gettysburg Address? "A masterpiece of commonplaces."

Altogether, Mr. B. was, in that good old Southern patois, "something else."

We pupils called him "Old Bar." We did not know the origin of the nickname, but it took on a kind of sanctity as the years advanced and we came to appreciate, more and more, what sort of man he was.

"Old Bar": One explanation is that he once let his beard go untrimmed for so long a time that the boys saw a resemblance to Uncle Remus' "Brer Bar." Another is that it derived from his effective reading about Bar-Jesus in *Acts* 13. The boys even referred to him as "Bar-Jesus" until he asked them to stop it, as sacrilegious; then they began to call him "Old Bar."

But my favorite explanation, and the most plausible, I think, is that, in the presence of a witness, he refused the evidence of his own senses in order to accept a boy's denial of guilt. The witness, aware of Christ's words to Simon Peter, who had just acknowledged Jesus as the Son of God: "Blessed art thou, Simon Bar-jona: for flesh and blood hath not revealed it unto thee, but my Father which is in heaven," the witness, I say, began to refer to Mr. Blackford as "Old Bar-jona," which later was shortened to "Old Bar." [RPW, who was at the School from 1901 to 1904.]

Joel Chandler Harris' *Uncle Remus* stories of Georgia Negro folklore began appearing in 1880 and were enormously popular. The Bar-Jesus of *Acts* was a "false prophet. . . . full of all subtilty, and all mischief [who] withstood" the Apostles Paul and Barnabas and was by them made blind "for a season."

However he got his nickname, "Old Bar" was "greatly beloved but never feared by the boys." [ABK]. And his outstanding work was recognized by his peers. In 1904 Washington and Lee made him a Doctor of Laws, and he was twice elected to Phi Beta Kappa, first by the parent chapter at William and Mary and later by the chapter at the University.

Then the School itself was honored. A third Very Distinguished Person visited the Holy Hill. It will be remembered that in 1847 Edgar Allan Poe had come out and read *The Raven*, and in 1869 the boys had cheered Robert E. Lee. In 1908, according to ABK, "Quentin Roosevelt was very young, only ten or eleven years old, when he was here [at EHS] in 1908–9. He was modest, hated publicity, was impulsive but full of magnetism. One day he went home to the White House without leave. His father, the President, questioned him as to this when he found him at the table, and on being told that he had come off without permission, made the boy leave the table at once and return to the School." (Apparently it never occurred to Bully Teddy to collude with his son against the authority of the great "Old Bar.")

"The President and Mrs. Roosevelt visited the School on Athletic Day, 1908, and he made a speech to the boys."

Ten years later that modest, impulsive lad, a World War I pilot, was killed when his plane was shot down behind the German lines at a place very special to him. When he was eleven years old he had visited the city of Rheims. There he had seen an aerial race, and been so excited by it that he had written a glowing account to his friend Ambler Blackford, one of the Principal's sons. It may well have been the sight of this contest that inspired him to join the Air Corps. Quentin Roosevelt flew to his death in an air battle only twenty miles from Rheims.

Dr. Blackford's last years at his beloved School were deservedly tranquil. Some faint savor of that gentle, innocent *temps perdu* lingers in Edward Alvey's memories of one of his trips to visit his sister and her husband, longtime EHS teacher Francis E. ("Nick") Carter:

A train trip in 1910 was an impressive undertaking, especially for an eight-year-old traveling alone. My name and address had been written on a card and pinned to the lapel of a coat. My railroad ticket was in an envelope securely pinned to the inside coat pocket.

Before the train stopped completely I spotted Frank and Lucile waiting for me on the platform. Frank's buggy at the time was a stylish vehicle known as a "runabout." Its gleaming black body provided a striking contrast with its bright yellow wheels. It was sometimes called a "pony runabout," although typically a spirited horse was harnessed to it.

The three-and-a-half mile drive in the open buggy was an exhilarating experience. First, there was the long climb up Shooters Hill. Then the road, now King Street, leveled out, and we sped along at a brisk pace.

The autumn air was crisp and cold in the late afternoon, and we were glad to have the buggy robes tucked closely about us. It was a thrill to see the school in the distance as we turned into the grounds and began the long, gentle ascent to the main buildings. The steam-heated rooms in Blackford Hall felt good.

The evening meal in the dining hall was always an impressive occasion, for it concluded with a brief devotional service. Mr. Hoxton read a short passage from the Bible. Then there was his prayer, which always concluded with the words, "God protect you from the dangers and perils of the night." I was always a little apprehensive as we went back through the darkness to the rooms in Blackford Hall.

Days passed happily with the activities of the school. Afternoons were devoted to athletics. There was either football practice or, frequently, a game. Runners circled the track. In the gym there were workouts. All contributed to a keen appetite for supper and a restful night's sleep.

A high point was a trip to Washington. Unlike most schools, E.H.S. had its weekday holiday on Monday instead of Saturday so that the boys would not have to prepare for the next day's classes on Sunday evening.

We were up early Monday morning. By eight we were on our way down the long driveway. Upon reaching Alexandria we drove at once to the livery stable, where Frank left the horse to be unharnessed and housed until our return from Washington. We watched the fast trolley come down King Street to Washington Avenue.

The eight-mile trip to Washington took about forty-five minutes. Our trolley crossed the Fourteenth Street bridge into Washington and ended its journey at Eleventh Street and Pennsylvania Avenue. From there it was only a short walk to Woodward and Lothrop, on F Street, where we shopped and looked.

Lunch was at Brownley's, a popular candy store famous for its chocolates. Then we continued to Chase's Theatre, later known as Keith's Theatre, where vaudeville acts of high quality drew large and appreciative audiences. The show was excellent. Many Washingtonians attended regularly. Woodrow Wilson, burdened with the cares of the presidency during World War I, often occupied his favorite box seat.

The trip back to Alexandria seemed short.

As a footnote it should be added that the school soon built a cottage for the Carters. Many old boys recall their Sunday evening visits to the Carter cottage, where they enjoyed the cake and chocolate caramels my sister used to make.

Tranquil, pleasant, delightful times; as Wordsworth paeaned (in a very different context),

> *Bliss was it in that dawn to be alive,*
> *But to be young was very heaven!*

Dr. Blackford had indeed builded well. The instrument which he had fashioned was the best of its kind. The stone which the War and its ravages had rejected had become the head of the corner. And a serene corner it was.

In our current catalogue his extraordinary professional achievement is eloquently assessed:

Dr. L. M. Blackford, Principal, requests the pleasure of your company at the Commencement Exercises of the Episcopal High School of Virginia, near Alexandria, at 10.30 A. M. Thursday June 12th 1913
Liggett Hall

Old Bar's last official act.

"Dr. Blackford was a traditional academician, an ambitious administrator, and a bold innovator who established at Episcopal everything from a modern academic curriculum to an interscholastic athletic program, from the buildings that form the nucleus of the present-day school to the routine that is still the foundation of much of Episcopal's tradition today."

Then, having fought the good fight, run the good race, Old Bar walked into the cool of the evening, when man's work is done.

The end came gently.

In the summer of 1909 as he was returning from his accustomed trip to England to study his fellow principals' management of their public schools he suffered a slight stroke.

"The ship's doctor was both capable and attentive; he accompanied Dr. Blackford back to New York on the voyage, and indeed all the way to the High School." [RPW].

The School was ready for such an emergency. Archibald Robinson Hoxton, son of Colonel Llewellyn Hoxton, the Associate Principal who had died in 1891, was appointed to the post his father had held. Old Bar, relieved of most of the administrative chores, enjoyed an Indian summer that lasted four years.

In June, 1913, admired, honored and loved, he retired.

In that year's volume of the School's annual, *Whispers*, there appeared this dedication:

To Launcelot Minor Blackford, M.A., L.L.D., who for forty-three years, as Head Master of this School, has, by precept and example, taught his pupils that cleverness without goodness is not to be desired; that material prosperity is not what makes a man truly rich, that the smallest man in any community is the most selfish man; and that character, based on Christian ideals, is the greatest asset any man can possess. . . .

A year later, May 23, 1914, he went quietly to his rest. *And all the trumpets sounded on the other side.*

He was buried in a little cemetery beside the main road which led then from Alexandria to the School, with this inscription, from *II Timothy*, on the stone which marked his grave:

> *The servant of the Lord must not strive,*
> *but be gentle unto all men, apt to teach, patient.*

Dr. Blackford served as Principal of our School for forty-three years, a long time, but not the longest. The record for length of

✝

IN·MEMORY

OF

LAUNCELOT·MINOR·BLACKFORD·M·A·LLD

Beloved·Principal·of·this·School·from·1870·to·1913

Born·in·Fredericksburg·Va·Feb·23·1837·Died·May·23·1914

CHRISTIAN   SOLDIER   TEACHER

A·Power·in·the·Lives·of·many·his·Influence·is·undying

The·Lord·is·the·Strength·of·my·Life

Erected·in·1914·by·his·old·Boys

service as head of a major American preparatory school was set by Frank Boyden. He presided over Deerfield Academy from 1902 to 1968. Second-longest tenure was registered by the Reverend Endicott Peabody, who founded Groton in 1884 and led it until 1940.

Old Bar was not the only literarily inclined member of his family. Two of his brothers wrote books. William, the one who had counselled him to keep his clothes dry, wrote a memoir, *War Years with Jeb Stuart*, that is at once informative, trenchant, tragic and funny. Samples:

"Napoleon, I believe, once said that a dog-fight might bring on a battle, and [so it was] that the Battle of Gettysburg was brought on upon that spot by shoes." Some barefooted Southern soldiers heard that there were shoes in Gettysburg stores, "marched towards the place to get them," met Union outposts, and. . . .

"These mortar shells were the most disgusting, low-lived things imaginable; there was not a particle of the sense of honor about them; they would go rolling about and prying into the most private places in a sneaking sort of way."

"A fresh battlefield is a painfully interesting sight, though a terrible one. Human nature confronted with death and stripped of all disguise is here presented in the noble calmness of the hero or the abject grovelling of the coward."

The wartime correspondence of another brother, Charles, has been preserved in the book *Letters From Lee's Army*. Like the others of his family Charles was a keen observer and an articulate, sardonic commentator. Writing to his mother from an encampment near Fairfax July 10, 1861, he said:

The ball will open on this line in a few days, if not hours. Of that you can tell more than I can. I really know less of what is going on in other parts of the army than you do. Of course it is right to keep everything as dark as possible, even from our own men; no other way would keep our designs a secret from the enemy. As it is they learn a vast amount.

Just as I wrote the last line a wagon passed by with four women in it belonging to Col. Wheat's 'Louisiana Tigers,' all dressed up as men. I presume they are vivandieres from New Orleans. They are disgusting-looking creatures who have followed the camp.

The ball did indeed open on that line in a few days. The first battle of Bull Run took place at nearby Manassas on July 21. Vivandieres were women who followed European armies and sold many things not always including themselves; our gallant Colonel Wheat would probably not have permitted anyone except his Tigers to call those four "disgusting."

To paraphrase a famous ditty, "Blackford is Blackford and Wheat is Wheat/ And never the twain shall meet." (Rudyard Kipling was born December 30, 1865.)

Or should that ending be "And ever the twain did meet, almost, at the Episcopal High School"?

CHAPTER 5

Old Flick Old Flick
1913–1947

During this third-of-a-century the country's population increased to some one hundred and forty-five million (sixty million rural, eighty-five million urban—the 1920 census showed 51% of the people living in cities and towns of more than 2500). The center of population moved to a spot about five miles northeast of the little town of Louisville, Illinois.

In 1913 there was war in the Balkans; the first Charlie Chaplin movies were shown; in Paris, the first playing of Stravinsky's Rite of Spring, *as overpowering as Homer's loud-roaring sea, caused a riot.*

In 1914 two new books delighted American youngsters: Booth Tarkington's Penrod *and Edgar Rice Burroughs'* Tarzan of the Apes. *Robert Goddard started experimenting with rockets; the Panama Canal was opened, and, on June 28, Archduke Franz Ferdinand of Austria and his wife were assassinated in Sarajevo, Yugoslavia. That was the beginning of World War I.*

In 1915 a German submarine sank the U.S. passenger ship Lusitania. *In 1916 the "Dixieland Jass Band" (yes—"jass") brought the new sound north to Chicago, and more than one million cars and trucks were sold in this country, at an average price of $600.*

In 1917 *the United States declared war on Germany, and,* mirabile dictu, *an Old Boy had a great deal to do with that declaration. Newton Diehl Baker (EHS* 1887–89) *was President Wilson's Secretary of War from* 1916 *to* 1921.

Also in 1917 *Charlie Chaplin's movies made him more than a million dollars.*

In 1918 *the influenza epidemic which had ravaged Europe reached this country. By the time it ended, some ten months later, about* 500,000 *Americans had died of the disease. World-wide, that epidemic took more than twenty-two million lives. (The bubonic plague or "Black Death" of the fourteenth century killed perhaps twenty-five million people, but it lasted twenty years.)*

The Armistice was signed November 11, 1918. *In Russia, the civil war between the Reds and the Whites began.*

In 1919 *the Eighteenth Amendment was ratified, "prohibiting the manufacture, sale, import, or export of liquor." The bribing of eight men on the Chicago White Sox baseball team created the country's first major sports scandal. The "Black Sox" lost the World Series to the Cincinnati Reds,* 5 *games to* 3.

In 1920 *the Boston Red Sox sold a promising young player named Babe Ruth to the New York Yankees for* $125,000.

In 1922 *Secretary of the Interior Albert B. Fall leased, without competitive bidding, the Teapot Dome oil reserves in Wyoming and California. In* 1924 *he was indicted for accepting bribes. He was tried and retried and found guilty; in* 1931 *he became our first Cabinet Secretary to be sent to jail. The unexpected death of President Harding in* 1923 *has been ascribed by quite a few historians to suicide. It may be that the President couldn't face the impending disgrace.*

In 1925 *Tennessee school teacher John T. Scopes broke a state law forbidding the teaching of the theory of evolution and the ensuing "Monkey Trial" created a furor. Scopes was convicted and fined* $100. *Crossword puzzles became the rage.*

On May 20–21, 1927, *Charles Lindbergh flew his monoplane* The Spirit of St. Louis *from New York to Paris:* 3,600 *miles in* 33½ *hours.*

The first talking picture, Al Jolson's Jazz Singer, *was released in* 1927, *and the first movie in colors, a mélange of bright-hued objects including goldfish, flowers and pretty girls, was shown the next year.*

On Tuesday, October 29, 1929, *the stock market crashed. In a matter of days about fifty billion dollars (paper value) disappeared. In a matter of months the Great Depression began.*

In 1933 President Franklin Roosevelt launched his New Deal and Adolf Hitler was appointed Chancellor of Germany.

In 1935 FDR signed the Social Security Act and Hitler repudiated the Versailles Treaty. Italy invaded Abyssinia.

In 1936 Italy "annexed" Abyssinia; Mussolini and Hitler proclaimed the Rome-Berlin axis, the Spanish Civil War began, and King Edward VIII of England abdicated, to be with "the woman I love." Margaret Mitchell published Gone With The Wind. *(One of our Old Boys, the diplomat R. Walton Moore, knew Margaret Mitchell: "She told me that nearly every reviewer compared* Gone With The Wind *with* Uncle Tom's Cabin, *stressing the fact that the pictures given in the two books [of the pre-War relations between masters and slaves] were entirely different.")*

In 1937 German bombers annihilated the defenseless Basque town of Guernica. Picasso's painting of that carnage has been called the most terrible of all evocations of war. In that same year the Nazis opened their concentration camp at Buchenwald, and the British tried to "appease" Hitler. Invading Japanese seized the Chinese capital city of Beijing (then, of course, Peking). The zeppelin Hindenburg *exploded on landing at a New Jersey airport, an event which like the rocket* Challenger *disaster five decades later was described live over the air and shocked the nation at the very time it was happening. That radio report has never been forgotten.*

On October 30, 1938, radio outdid itself with Orson Welles' broadcast of H. G. Wells' The War of the Worlds. *Many people believed that Martians were landing and panicked. In 1939 European orders for arms helped to speed our recovery from Depression.*

On September 1, 1939, World War II began in Europe, and on December 7, 1941, Japanese planes bombed Pearl Harbor and we declared war on that country. It is not generally remembered now, but we did not declare war on Germany. Hitler waited four days and then, infuriated by FDR's taunts, on December 11 he declared war on us. (If he hadn't, he might have won his war in Europe. FDR and the interventionists might not have been able to overcome isolationist resistance to our joining the Allies.)

In 1944 Allied troops landed in France. In April, 1945, representatives of fifty nations, including the Soviet Union, met in San

Francisco and chartered the United Nations. (Eleanor Roosevelt said at the time that it was a pity that we couldn't paint the Russians green so that always in dealing with them we would remember that "they are different.") Later in 1945 the war ended, first in the West (May 7), then, after we dropped atom bombs on Hiroshima and Nagasaki (August 6 and 9), in the East (September 2). With those bombings the Nuclear Age began.

During that war penicillin and sulfanilamide saved countless Allied lives. Those antibiotics had been discovered in the 1920's but were not marketed in this country until 1944; Hitler's armies did not have them.

In 1947 Bell Laboratory scientists invented the transistor. On June 24 of that year the first "flying saucers" were reported, in the skies over Mount Rainier.

FLICK HOXTON was born on the Hill June 28, 1875. He entered the School at the age of eleven and studied here for nine years, demonstrating marked ability in mathematics, Latin and Greek. He demonstrated even more ability in athletics, becoming one of our all-time best football and baseball players, and an expert gymnast.

In 1895 he went to the University and although he weighed ("even with my mouth full of shot") only 137 pounds he starred in athletics there as he had done here, as football quarterback and baseball shortstop. He interrupted his University work for two years, 1897–99, to help the School by teaching and coaching.

Upon his return to Charlottesville he served as head coach of both football and baseball, and after an outstanding athletic career as player-coach, graduated in 1901.

The next September he came back to the School for good, and took on familiar responsibilities. He was appointed head of the Department of Mathematics, the post which his father had held from 1870 until his death in 1891.

He also coached. His 1901 football team was the first to play Woodberry Forest, and that game (which we won, 54–0) started one of the longest unbroken school football rivalries in the country.

In 1909 he was made Associate Principal, and after Old Bar retired in 1913 the Trustees, for the first time in the seventy-four-year life of the School, had no trouble finding a new Principal.

"Flick" Hoxton's nickname was "inherited by him for some unknown reason from a red-haired playmate known as 'Flicker' "

Archibald Robinson Hoxton, Principal, 1913–47.

[RPW] and it fitted him perfectly. He was quick, brisk, deft. He could, and often, to the gratification of the boys in his math classes, did, break a stick of chalk on the blackboard and then catch every one of the pieces before they hit the floor. He was the hero of three (at least) sports legends:

1. On the University football team he was running with the ball when he saw two Yale players closing in; he tossed the ball in the air, stiff-armed both would-be tacklers, caught the ball and ran on for a touchdown.

2. On the baseball team he made a triple play against Princeton —all by himself. (Actually, this legend has been authenticated: he was playing third—Princeton had the bases loaded with no outs —the batter hit a hot line drive down the third base line—he caught it: OUT ONE—he touched third base before the runner heading for home could get back: OUT TWO—he ran down the runner who had left second for third: OUT THREE. Final score: UVA 10, Princeton 6. Year: 1897.)

3. He habitually knocked home-runs into his grandmother's cellar (she would open the cellar door before the game began).

Such stories did nothing to lower the respect amounting almost to awe with which he was regarded by his boys, most of whom knew from startled experience that the saga describing his throwing dexterity was not exaggerated at all. How often it happened: some poor uninitiate sat in math class in the very back row secretly (he thought) reading a letter held low and *zip*—a piece of chalk unhanded that letter! He was the Holy Hill's William Tell.

He called boys "Old Tom" or "Old Dick" or "Old Harry" and when he was pleased, repeatedly and rapidly, "OldTomOldTom," so they called him "OldFlickOldFlick"—*sotto* of course *voce*.

Like Robbie Burns, he was quick to learn and wise to know.

No sooner had he become Associate Principal in 1909 than he decided that the School needed money. He strongly urged action. The Trustees appointed him a committee of one. "Mr. Hoxton at once visited Washington, Baltimore, Philadelphia, New York, Richmond, Norfolk and Charleston . . . and turned over to the Trustees about $30,000." [ABK].

With that flying start the Trustees had no trouble floating a bond issue of $85,000, and for the first time the School had some money of its own. In 1913 the old main building was renovated, and in the next year two new dormitories were built, Alumni Hall to the south of the main building and Memorial Hall to the north.

Also in 1913 the School received two large gifts.

The two Misses Stewart of "Brook Hill," near Richmond, with their sister Mrs. George W. Peterkin, wife of the Bishop of West Virginia (EHS 1856–58), gave us the Stewart Gymnasium, in memory of their father and uncle. For three-quarters of a century now the UT SIT MENS SANA IN CORPORE SANO of that imposing structure has been the most visible (and intimidating?) of all of our Latin exhortations.

Two sisters from Washington, Mrs. B. H. Buckingham and Miss I. C. Freeman, gave an athletic field, named for the new Principal. Activities *pro corpore sano* too farflung for the Stewart Gymnasium expanded onto Hoxton Field.

OldFlickOldFlick also at once demonstrated a talent for carrying on Old Bar's practice of getting good teachers and making them better by seasoning.

It has been said that kindergarten and grammar school teachers should be surrogate parents, high school teachers models, and college teachers teachers. The High School has always been fortunate in securing and holding masters who with wisdom mellowed by time have been the best of models as well as teachers, and, often enough, surrogate parents.

When Old Flick retired after thirty-four years as Principal he left the School six masters who had been here when he came: Willoughby Reade, nicknamed "Wiley Boley," who had signed on in 1893; John Moncure ("Dreamy") Daniel, EHS 1899–1902, signed on in 1905; Grigsby Cave ("Shack") Shackelford, 1906; Francis Edward ("Nick") Carter, EHS 1899–1902, 1906; Richard Pardee ("Cap'n Dick") Williams, EHS 1901–04, 1908; Robert Llewellyn ("Twit" or "Herr") Whittle, EHS 1903–06, 1910. By the time the last of those amiable veterans had presided over his last class ("Herr," 1965) they had, amongst them all, racked up the astonishing total of 293 teahing years. That worked out to an average of 48.8333 + years, of instructing, guiding and being models for shall we say approximately 293 × 200 = 58,600 boys. BUT—since Old Flick himself taught for some fifteen years before he became Principal and continued to teach thereafter, those figures should be adjusted upward: total teaching time—342 years; average per teacher—48.857 + years; total number of boys taught—68,400.

(Patrick Henry Callaway, who seems to most living alumni as ancient and indestructible as the fabled bristlecone pine, came here to teach after Old Flick had been P for three years.)

"The Old Guard."

Mr. Hoxton did indeed get off to a very strong start. The School was in excellent health, and so was the world around it.

Or so it seemed. . . .

It is hard, now, to believe it, but in those years just before 1914 many thoughtful people were convinced that there would never be another war. They thought that finally, after all of the aeons of boasting and marching and killing and glorifying that killing, rulers had at last realized that war was too terrible to be unleashed ever again.

> O, God, *when others speak against some man,*
> *however small, let me speak kindly of him,*
> *or not at all.*
> —Thomas Rutherfoord Goodwin, 1914–20.

For such innocents Sarajevo came like a thief in the night. Or like Dr. Jekyll's Mr. Hyde.

Even before battle was joined, hearts broke.

Afterwards, there was, for a long time, incredulity and despair.

Our Old Boy Secretary of War, Newton D. Baker, called that war "the most significant event in the history of mankind since the Flood." [ABK]. At our School the impact was not felt at once. Old Bar's Indian summer hung, as the Irish say, honey-heavy over the Hill. The Carters didn't scare little Edward Alvey with stories of what the terrible Huns were doing.

Virginius Dabney, who became one of the South's best authors and the Pulitzer Prize-winning editor of the Richmond *Times-Dispatch,* entered the School just three months after Sarajevo, and wars and rumors of wars were the farthest things from his young mind:

It was the afternoon of September 14, 1914, and my father and I were walking the three miles from Alexandria. A three-mile walk was nothing unusual in those days, but it did seem slightly bizarre for us to be making our initial appearance in this fashion at Episcopal High. I do not recall that I was particularly apprehensive, although I was aware that I would probably be homesick, like virtually all the other "rats," or first-year boys.

En route to the school we passed through what was known as Mud-town, a collection of squalid shacks. The school grounds were surrounded on three sides by open fields, and on the other by the Virginia Theological Seminary. The facilities were distinctly Spartan.

Prior to 1914 the boys were breaking ice on their buckets in the morning.

The dormitories actually had hot and cold running water, showers and "electric lights throughout," as stated in the school's catalog. Yet the living quarters were decidedly austere.

V Dabney

Each boy had what was really a stall, with a green curtain hanging across the entrance. The stall was about six feet wide, and there was a bed, a small rush-bottom chair with no arms and a wooden press for clothes. The stall had a window in one end, but no electric light and no desk. The only light at night was in the ceiling of the long corridor on which the bunks faced. It was hoped that the boys would use these quarters for sleeping purposes only, and would stay out of them in the afternoons when classes were not being held. Athletic, literary or other activities were supposed to engage their attention each day after school. Everybody had to attend study hall at night.

The school trustees and administrators were not being parsimonious in providing these limited facilities. They simply did not have the money to do more. Tuition for each of my three years was $400. Despite this low figure, lack of funds almost prevented me from enrolling for the session of 1914–15. It was only because my father got an increase in salary at the last minute that he was able to send me off to school.

But if the living quarters and recreational facilities at E.H.S. in 1914 were somewhat primitive by latter-day standards, they were almost luxurious compared with those available to the boys before the Civil War. In that era, furthermore, the rod was not spared, either for misbehavior or unsatisfactory recitations.

As a rat, I was required every morning to wake up Allison Palmer, an older boy in a neighboring stall, with the following salutation: "Hi thee up, m'lord, it is time to arise. Seven-fifteen is tolled by the morning belfry." Every boy had to be in his place in the dining room at the stroke of seven-thirty, more or less fully dressed. There was hot competition to see who could stay in bed longest and still make it to breakfast without getting "stuck" demerits for being late. Fabulously fast times, some of them in seconds rather than minutes, were recorded.

Everybody complained loudly about the food, as is seemingly inevitable at all boarding schools. We paraded around the grounds on Saturday nights singing "Proc, Proc, Proc, the boys are starving," a heartfelt appeal addressed to the proctor, George C. Stuart, who was responsible for supplying the food. There was undoubted monotony in the menus; you knew that you would get scrambled eggs for breakfast every Tuesday and hot dogs for lunch every Wednesday.

A none-too-inspiring variety of molasses known as "treacle," pronounced "trickle," was served at all three meals the year-round, and was not conducive to gastronomic joy. There was a simple dessert each day, and the term for it was "boss." The chief form of gambling around the institution was to bet a "week's boss" or "two weeks' boss" on this or that. A favorite bet was whether the progeny of any teacher's pregnant wife would be a boy or a girl. I won two weeks' boss when I bet that Mrs. Hoxton's second child would be a boy.

The origin of the term boss is lost in the mists of antiquity. It was used at Locust Dale Academy in Madison County during the 1870's, when my father-in-law was a student there.

My allowance during my first year at school was twenty-five cents a week, which was less than most boys received. (It went up to $2.00 a month in my senior year.) I kept a diary and recorded my expenditures. "Went to the store and spent .10" occurs several times. Such an outlay was a momentous event. The store was owned by "Vic" Donaldson, and was a couple of hundred yards beyond the athletic field. An individual whom everybody called "Bun," Vic's brother, was in charge. Vic also operated wagons and buses, the latter being available to boys going to Washington or Alexandria. He was commonly regarded by the boys as little short of a highway robber, probably with no justification whatever.

I could go to the store occasionally and spend five or ten cents, but transportation on the bus to the Washington trolley stop was out of the question. I always walked the two miles to the suburban station at Lloyd's.

When I went to Washington with one or more friends, it was almost always for such raucous diversions as a vaudeville show at Keith's or a visit to the zoo. There was also the Gayety, which was considered quite risqué.

In my second and third years I was somewhat more affluent, and was able to attend an occasional baseball game of the Washington Senators. I saw Ty Cobb try to steal third base with a Detroit base runner already on the bag and almost get back to second. The play was so close that Ty protested vehemently, so vehemently, in fact, that he was thrown out of the game by the umpire.

The Confederate tradition was strong at Episcopal High, since most of the boys were from the South. Robert E. Lee was therefore one of

One way to get to Washington, 1912.

The big, beautiful library today. Why so empty? "The boys are too busy to read."

their idols, but in the annual polls taken to decide the school's favorite historical character, Lee sometimes lost to Cleopatra.

For no now-known reason Cleopatra continued to rival Lee in the School popularity polls until at least 1927. 'Twas not, however, ever thus. In the *EHS Annual* of 1892 it is recorded that in the poll of that year the winner was Grover Cleveland, and "George Washington voted for himself."

We had no library at the school, and I confess, to my genuine embarrassment, that it never occurred to me that we needed one. [The School's spacious, comfortable, fully-computerized library/media center now contains almost 25,000 books, magazines, etc.]

Dances [were] held several times a year. The steps were of a conventional nature, such as waltzes and two-steps. [There were also dance steps called] "fox trot and the horse trot, the crab step and the kangaroo dip, the camel walk and the fish walk, the chicken scratch and the lame duck" not to mention "the snake, the grizzly bear and the bunny hug."

It should be remarked that no sooner had our observant young man arrived on the Hill than he himself came under observation:

My long and unusual first name attracted immediate attention. The result was that I was instructed by various older boys to add other names, so as to make my cognomen even more impressive. Thus I ended up with Virginius Theopidus Sempronius George Washington Jim Jeffries Abraham Lincoln Hannibal Artaxerxes Dabney. It got to be a regular ritual: "Boy, what's your name?" and I would reel off "Virginius Theopidus Sempronius. . . ."

Had he been asked (which he was not) he could have explained that the long and unusual first name was his for a perfectly good reason: "I was named for my grandfather, Virginius Dabney, who in turn was named for the state of Virginia." Our School has always been blessed with boys bearing bizarre first, middle and/ or last names, and almost always those names have undergone sea-changes into even richer and stranger nicknames. Virginius Theopidus Sempronius etc. Dabney got so topheavy with classic coinages that he finally wound up being called just V—without even a period.

A contemporary of V Dabney, Ben Baker (1916–19), has similar recollections, in which the events overseas played little part:

I went to the High School in September 1916 and was one of three graduates (there were very few because of rigid requirements the details of which I forget) in June 1919. I well remember my first day, arranging my bunk next to the bunk of a gorgeously built monitor who shouted "Rat, what are you going to do in athletics? I am [or will be, I forget] captain of the track team," he said.

B. Baker, Jr.

I was a scrawny kid but in desperation I replied that I too would try for track but under my voice I swore I'd beat that guy if it killed me and I did a year later. Little did he know what an influence he had on my subsequent career of running for the High School, the U. of Virginia and eventually Oxford where I ran against the hero of *Chariots of Fire*.

My closest friends and those I most admired were Sellman Hall, Dick Carrington, John Staige Davis, V Dabney, "Boota" deButts, Johnson McGuire. "Toofie" Hall was the superb head monitor and a great athlete. He stood about 5–10 and weighed a scant 165 and played guard on the football team, I think for five years at EHS and five at Virginia. I think I am correct that in those ten years he played 60 minutes of every game.

I don't recall a bad teacher. Mr. Hoxton made early math seem simple. He took great pride (I'm sure) in using a long piece of chalk, writing with his characteristic athletic quickness, breaking the chalk and catching the broken piece before it hit the floor. The class clapped!

Grigsby Shackelford was my favorite teacher. He was superb at making mathematics really alive.

Mr. Hoxton to the vast majority of us was a beloved Principal. He would greet the student (most of the school) as "Old Jack" or "Old Tom" indicating that the student was in his good graces. If the student wasn't, it would just be "Will" or "Dick." He kept a watchful eye over us all. We all knew that he had made a triple play unassisted for Virginia's baseball team against Princeton.

Young Flick, the subsequent distinguished Principal, was born while

I was in school. There was widespread betting of bosses (our only accepted gambling) on whether the new baby would be a boy or a girl. I lost!

This was the time of the great flu epidemic. Those who do not recall this cannot imagine the catastrophe this was. There were a few cases at the school as I recall but Mr. Hoxton wisely decided to close the school and send us all home for I forget how long. There were lots of military units in the vicinity and I well recall going to the station in Alexandria and seeing almost endless rows of coffins awaiting RR transportation.

Chariots of Fire was a lovely 1981 movie about the 1924 Olympics. When Ben Baker was a Rhodes Scholar he ran against the Englishman Harold Abrahams, who won the 100-meter dash in those Olympics with a time of 10.6 seconds. BB was invited to compete in those 1924 Games but declined. Mr. Daniel's wife Margaret died in the flu epidemic and the School was closed from October 4 to October 29, 1919.

Except for the flu, those were evidently halcyon days.

Military events abroad were not going unnoticed, however. "In June 1916 the Prize Composition was on 'Preparedness.' It was by Homer L. Ferguson, whose father from his shipyards along the James played a leading role in building ships to take the place of those Germany was sinking." [ABK].

That summer some twenty-five Old Boys and four masters attended training camps. The next September came news that Cuthbert Corbett Buckle (1906–10), Lieutenant in the English Army, had been killed in France. "By November, 1917, there were [about] eighty-two E.H.S. boys and masters in the service of their country." [ABK].

Life at the School was affected but not disrupted. Ben Baker:

EXTRACT FROM CATALOGUE OF THE EPISCOPAL HIGH SCHOOL
NOVEMBER 1, 1917

MILITARY TRAINING

IT IS NOT THE INTENTION OF THE AUTHORITIES OF THE SCHOOL TO TURN IT INTO A MILITARY SCHOOL, BUT THERE WILL BE MILITARY WORK WITH DRILL UNDER COMPETENT INSTRUCTORS. A VERY SATISFACTORY BEGINNING IN THIS LINE WAS MADE DURING THE PAST SESSION.

THE COST OF THE NECESSARY EQUIPMENT WILL NOT EXCEED TEN DOLLARS. THIS EQUIPMENT SHOULD BE PURCHASED AFTER ARRIVAL AT THE SCHOOL AND AFTER THE DETAILS OF THE MILITARY FEATURE HAVE BEEN WORKED OUT.

After the U.S. got into WWI we had military drill; I forget about
the uniforms but we had 'em; I do remember the wrap leggings; they
would come loose on the particularly clumsy boys and the drill would
have to stop while the leggings were rewrapped.

Ben Baker's friend V Dabney, the future newspaperman, was a
little more concerned:

The declaration of war on Germany by the United States Congress
in April, 1917, caused a stir in the school, but in view of the long
period of rising tension between President Woodrow Wilson and the
German Government it had been more or less expected. We had followed the course of the war in Europe on the school bulletin board
for years.

John M. ("Dreamy") Daniel, who taught history and government,
put pins in the map to show the movements of the armies. In the
spring of 1917 we did some elementary drilling.

It is fantastic to recall that such persons as David Starr Jordan, then
president of Stanford University, and Norman Angell, the British author, were saying shortly before World War I that such cataclysms
were no longer thinkable. Jordan declared that "great international
wars are practically at an end," while Angell told all and sundry that
"far from these great nations being ready to fly at each other's
throats, nothing will induce them to take the immense risks of using
their preposterous military instruments if they can possibly avoid it."

For the youngest boys *Götterdämmerung* came on little cat feet:

EHS was in part military for the first time since the Civil War. Daily
drills with battalion inspection every Friday. Although listed in B Co. I
was too small to carry a regulation rifle so was "issued" a facsimile of
one to carry.

As a very young and shy homesick boy I looked forward to Sunday
evenings when the married Masters would have open house. Their
wives served cookies and beverages and did their best to comfort the
younger boys and we would compare notes on which ones served the
best goodies. The school also had wonderful matrons who were comforting to new boys. I especially recall Miss Jett and Miss Stoney.

I was in awe and afraid of Mr. Hoxton when a small boy but as I
matured I grew to admire and respect him. He always carried a walking stick with which occasionally and surprisingly he would good
naturedly flick one's backside.

I wonder if the school still conducts a Field Day for students. As a
14-year-old I hero worshipped Willing Brown, who won the baseball

Company A, 1918. . . .

. . . and Company B.

throw: over 100 yards. [Harry "Stump" Philbrick, 1918–24. Philbrick is among the 1924 monitors pictured in Ch. 6.]

No, Stump, the School does not have Field Days any more, alas. They were fun. They became track meets between Blackford and Fairfax Literary Societies, with an intra-society meet for Wilmer, and the last recorded one was held in the Spring of 1927. Willing Brown's baseball throw may still be the EHS record, depending on how far "over 100 yards" it was. An earlier EHS boy, James C. Greenway (1890–95), went from here to Andover and "broke the records at Andover by throwing a baseball 363 feet and 3 inches." [ABK]. That record-breaker became a distinguished doctor, and gave the School the Greenway Fields and the flagpole as memorials to his four brothers Addison (1885–89), Gilbert (1888–92), John 1887–90) and William (1894–96).

The peaceful tenor of the School, in which sporting events provided the principal excitement, was not to last. In his lightly fictionalized novel about EHS, *Before They Were Men*, Charles Wertenbaker describes life at "Blackford" (EHS) in wartime:

Charles Wertenbaker

When Blackford Academy opened for its seventy-ninth session on the third Thursday in September, 1918, things were different somehow. Most of the older masters were still there, the school had its usual enrollment of a hundred and seventy-eight more or less untamed young men, but things were different.

It might have been the absence of Mr. Wilson and Mr. Cox, who were now in France, or it might have been the news that Mr. Seymour, who had taught at Blackford for eight years, was dead somewhere around Château-Thierry; maybe it was the consignment of old rifles lent by the War Department, or maybe it was just the restless look in the eyes of older boys, who were supposed to have a steadying influence on the younger ones—anyway, things were different.

Blackford was now an official R.O.T.C. unit, registered with the War Department. An outfitter from Washington [took] orders for uniforms [to be worn] to the exclusion of all other outer garments. Setting-up exercises [took place] outdoors every morning at 7:05 and at 7:25 the companies [were] formed [and would] fall in and march to the dining room for breakfast. [There was] formation for every meal, two hours of

drill every afternoon, and strict military discipline under the commandant, Captain McCarthy, disabled West Pointer.

The author attended EHS, 1915–17. We shall meet him again.
His Mr. Wilson, Mr. Cox and Mr. Seymour were, presumably,
RPW or "Twit" Whittle or Littleton Wickham (EHS 1911–15,
taught 1917–18 and again after the war), Hartwell Cocke (EHS
1909–15, taught 1917–18 and again after the war) and Alexander
Rives Seamon (EHS 1903–07, taught 1909–16, killed in action in
the Argonne, 1918).

Some 460 EHS alumni and boys served in World War I and
twenty-two of them died. Five were killed in the new machines
called aeroplanes, one (Quentin Roosevelt) in combat and four in
accidents. Of the others, six were killed in action and two died of
wounds, three died of disease, one of mustard gas, and five of
undetermined causes. (Of all U.S. casualties, some 53,000 were
killed in action or died of wounds as compared to some 63,000
who died of what the military men call "other causes", mainly
disease. Advances in medicine accounted for the dramatic decrease
in the relative proportion of disease-caused deaths since 1865.)
    That war dealt a mortal blow to the hopes of the idealists who
had thought it could never be. It killed more than ten million
fighting men in Europe and caused the deaths of perhaps forty
million civilians by starvation and pestilence. But it did not dev-
astate this country as "our" War had done.
    The School, despite drills and run-away enlistments and, soon,
reports of deaths, went on. Indeed, one of our Old Boys killed in
that war achieved a sort of immortality. The handsome face of
Lieutenant Richard H. Fawcett (1909–11), who died in an airplane
accident in Illinois July 8, 1918, "was selected out of two thousand
photographs as that of an ideal soldier." [ABK].

After the war the School quickly returned to normal. Here are
some memories of Joe Harrison (1921–25):

In 1921, coming out of the canebrakes and swamps of lower Georgia and South Carolina, it's kind of difficult to remember the various
happenings and people of E.H.S some sixty-five years later. However,
the atmosphere of the high school was so different from the docks of
Savannah, that there had to be an improvement in one's character if
one were allowed to stay.

Books and Stationery
Christmas Half.
Philbrick

1918

Oct.	2	Oral & Written Eng. I		52
		Ancient Hist		1 50
		Physics		1 20
		Smith's Latin		1 00
		Pencils⁹, Scratch¹⁰		20
	16	Telephone Call		10
	31	Hist. Note Book		25
Nov.	1	Dic. Book¹⁰, Oil²⁵, Note paper³⁰		65
		Ruler¹⁰, Gum Koz³⁰		40
		Arithmetic		60
	13	Scratch¹⁰		10
	15	Eye shade²⁵, Ex. Book¹⁵		40
	20	2 Pencil²⁰		20
	21	1 Tablet²⁰, Pencils⁵		25
	25	Tablet¹⁰, Dic. Book¹⁰		20
Dec.	10	Exam paper¹²		12
	12	Inf. Drill Reg.		40
		Drawing in Art.		65
1919				
Jan.	8	Charge for Drawing Instrument		40
		Sketch Book		30
	17	Ex. Bk¹⁵, Scratch¹⁰, Note paper³⁰, Oil²⁵		80
				10 24

A rat's expenses, 71 years ago.

LIEUT. RICHARD H. FAWCETT.
(Harris & Ewing photo.)

ALEXANDRIAN KILLED IN FLYING ACCIDENT

Lieut. R. H. Fawcett Falls at Scott Field, Belleville, Ill., Mother Is Informed.

ALEXANDRIA, Va., July 9.—Lieut. Richard Hartshorne Fawcett was killed at 6:30 o'clock last night in an aeroplane accident near Belleville, Ill. He was twenty-five years old, and lived at 517 Prince street, Alexandria. He was educated in the public schools of Alexandria, and afterward completed his education at the Episcopal High School of Virginia. After leaving school he became an electrician and was employed in that capacity in the House of Representatives. Later he took up this work

I had learned to play football and other sports in one of Savannah's downtown squares. It was a rough and tumble area ruled by the Savannah Irish. Being a member of one of the smaller teams on the little field at the High School, I remember one day I was on the bottom of a rather large pileup. I did not think that they were getting off of me fast enough, so I began using some of the Irish dock language—until I looked up and saw a well-shined Frank Brothers shoe on top of the ball which was in my arms. I looked up a little further into the cold gray eyes of one Archibald Robinson Hoxton, Headmaster. Nothing was said between us but I stopped cussing and using vile language from then on.

You could not be in Mr. Hoxton's presence without realizing that he was a real gentleman, to be compared with Robert E. Lee. He was a great help to me during the four years I was at the school.

Early in the Fall of 1924 word was sent around about 12:30 PM that the school was to meet in the Chapel at 12:45. After students and masters were assembled, Mr. Hoxton said "Gentlemen, the school has an emergency. The waiters have struck and the school cannot afford to pay them what they want. Therefore, I am forced to ask some of you to volunteer as waiters. You will be on every other week and the pay will be $5 per week. Now I know that your parents did not send you here to wait on tables, but as I said before, this is an emergency and we need help. Will anyone volunteer?" Whereupon the whole school stood up. Mr. Hoxton was shocked and very pleased, the $5 had done the job. So he said "I will just have to pick names at random." Which he did. The system still works 65 years later. It's considered quite an honor to be a waiter.

J. Harrison

The next year at Finals I was waiting on Mr. Hoxton's table at supper, carrying about twelve pieces of cherry pie covered with powdered sugar on one of those big trays. Never an easy job. Just as I was placing Mr. Hoxton's piece of pie in front of him it slipped off the plate and landed on his pants, spreading powdered sugar all over him. Well, Mr. Hoxton was not as embarrassed as I; he just looked up at me and said "Joe, do you want to get out of this school tomorrow?" I thought he was going to keep me there all summer but we wiped the sugar off, had a good laugh, and nothing more was said.

The house of a Seminary professor, Dr. Nelson, caught fire and some of us went to help. Chuck Carpenter and Harry Flippin pulled a really valuable piece of furniture out of the burning house—the kitchen stove!

There were many boys who were musical. One Sunday afternoon a bunch of us got together in Lower Blackford and decided to have a parade. What we lacked in finesse we sure put out in noise. As we were proceeding between Stewart Gym and Alumni Dorm there came Mr. Hoxton between the Infirmary and Blackford Hall. Nothing to do but run and I mean in a hurry into First Alumni, dump the trombone (thanks to Clarence Holland) and down the hall to Liggett Hall. The others got caught, but no penalties.

Mondays were tough days. Holidays, but if you were poor, no money to go to Washington, the days seemed endless. Some of us would hike to Cameron Run, about two miles from the school. It was where the Southern Railway and the Richmond, Fredericksburg and Potomac Railroad came together just outside the Alexandria station. The boys were sometimes allowed to throw the switches, a great thrill. Also, when the fast trains from New Orleans to New York came through, it was possible to see someone you knew. Homesick as we were, that was a great thrill too.

In those days, when you left home in January you didn't get back until June. Six months is a long time when you're homesick.

I think my greatest thrill of all during my four years at the school was to kick a field goal on November 23, 1924, at Orange. It beat Woodberry, 10 to 6.

Joe Harrison wasn't alone in taking his loneliness down to the railroad tracks. Remember, fellow older Old Boys, the magic of the trains, the pre-Diesel trains, that primordial magic in that lonely place, the rush and roar and the wail of the train whistle in the night, so primordial that no human joy or grief could withstand it?

"It is the place where you come up through Virginia on the great trains in the night-time, and rumble slowly across the wide Potomac and see the morning's sunlight on the nation's dome"— Thomas Wolfe, of course. He was there, in that time, rushing north from his native North Carolina, boiling with the wild juices which would, a few years later, burst forth, batter and delight us with *Look Homeward, Angel* and *Of Time and the River*:

"The train . . . leaps . . . springs . . . smashes on . . . demon's fury . . . terrific drive of eight-locked pistoned wheels . . . savage furnace-flare . . . hiss of steam. . . ." Remember?

It's a long rough road from Lynchburg to Danville. . . .

Then, that dying wail (for most of us our introduction to the Doppler effect), and "The old earth of Virginia . . . dreaming in the moon's white light . . . secret, immense and lonely earth. . . ."

"She'll be comin' round the mountain. . . ." Alexandria, 1927. And those boys stand on her waiting to be identified. Can you help?

As a matter of fact, for almost twenty years Thomas Wolfe often rushed past us in those magical trains, concocting that magical prose: ". . . a stone, a leaf, an unfound door . . . O lost and by the wind grieved ghost, come back again. . . ." Where now, racing along in what coal-burning heaven, are Casey Jones and the Old 97?

No. Lonely Joe Harrison was not alone.

At times when I wanted a little while to myself, I used to go down the hill and visit with the railroad switchman in the tower at Cameron Run, a wonderful vantage point from which to give a longing look at the homeward-bound overnight train from Washington. [J.T. "Skin" Lane, 1922–26.]

Brother Lane didn't spend all of his free hours with the switchman, though:

The Virginia Theological Seminary played a big part in our lives. We attended Sunday morning services there, and a group of their senior students would take turns conducting our Evensong services in our little chapel. There were some wonderful men in that group: Brooke Stabler, George Zabriskie, "Chuck" Carpenter, who was also my wrestling coach.

In 1923, after a happy (paper) union of eighty-four years, the Seminary and the School came to an amicable parting of the (paper) ways. The Protestant Episcopal High School, our official name, was set up as a non-profit corporation with its own Board of Trustees, to get no money from the Church. The separation was only on paper and students like Joe Harrison and Skin Lane hardly knew that anything had happened. Skin again:

Speaking of Evensong, the school used to have a lovely custom. On Sunday evenings, the married members of the faculty and their wives held open house. The boys were invited, but not required, to call at the house of their choice for refreshments and conversation. I found it delightful and visited all of them at one time or another, but I think Mrs. Carter's fudge was a shade better than the others.

There was one morning when "Flick" charged into the dining hall for breakfast with that rapid athletic stride of his, and took his seat at the table, to reveal to all that he had buttoned his collar but forgotten his tie. His embarrassed discovery of his oversight made for a hilariously cheerful morning for all of us.

OBLIGATION OF MONITORS

GENERAL CHARACTER

A few students whose character and deportment entitle them to special confidence are appointed each session as MONITORS. Certain minor duties incident to the conduct and discipline of the school are discharged by them and, in recognition thereof, they are allowed certain privileges denied to others. Monitors serve, in the order of their appointment, a week each, beginning at breakfas ton Mondays, seven being on full duty at a time.

Besides performing his peculiar functions, each Monitor is expected to exercise his personal influence at all times in behalf of good order and sound morals, and for failure to do so, as well as for violation of rules, is held to strict account.

IT IS REQUIRED OF EACH MONITOR:

1. To aid the master in charge of the bed rooms in maintaining good order in such manner as he may direct, never, except at his request, remaining up beyond eleven o'clock.

2. To report every boy found without leave in school room, bed room, or bed room passage not his own. This obligation extends to every Monitor who may see or know of the offender.

3. To read the lessons in turn in chapel, always in a white cravat.

4. To abstain from smoking in the school buildings and to report any boy who does so smoke.

5. To offer his resignation as soon in any month as he may have incurred twenty-five demerits.

6. To discountenance and, to the best of his ability, to prevent all bullying of boys by each other, especially improper teasing, beating and the like and, in particular, to prevent everything, whether individual or organized action, which discriminates unfavorably against *new boys.*

7. To abstain entirely from intoxicating drinks of every kind until twenty-four hours after the close of the session, or of his connection with the School if sooner terminated. "Connection with the School" can be terminated only by withdrawal by parent or guardian, by dismissal, by the close of the session, or by death: this obligation not to be affected by resignation or deposition.

8. To discountenance in every way gambling, and the use and possession upon the School premises of intoxicating drinks, reporting the same when necessary. Also, to take possession of and destroy immediately cards or dice whenever seen, reporting any boy who refuses to surrender them.

9. To see that no intoxicating drink is brought within the School buildings or grounds and whenever aware that such drink is there, to secure its immediate destruction.

10. To observe strictly the bounds as set by the School, never violating same without permission of the Principal.

IT IS REQUIRED OF EACH OF THE MONITORS ON DUTY:

1. To preserve order on the floor assigned them.

2. To distribute the mail, being careful never to leave matter in the satchel without instructions.

EPISCOPAL HIGH SCHOOL OF VIRGINIA.

". . . always in a white cravat." The twelve commandments, 1924.

He was mighty good at intercepting chocolate cake that my mother occasionally mailed to me. I would be called to his office, invited to take one slice and leave, wondering what privileged group was going to get the rest. One time a cake slipped through and then I faced the problem of where to keep it.

I found that my trunk in the cold damp cellar of Memorial Hall preserved it fairly well.

A favorite leisure-time activity was a trip to Bun's store for a coke or a package of cigarettes. To get there, one had to cross the athletic field and walk along a short path through the woods. The store contained a bench that bore the carved initials of many a High School student, including mine. I understand that the school obtained possession of that bench when Bun's store was closed, and now has it enshrined somewhere on campus.

The faculty was tops, but my favorites by a narrow margin were Dick Williams, who demanded discipline but was ultimately fair and had a great sense of humor, and Pat Callaway, through and through a good man.

The bench "that bore the carved initials of many a High School student" is now in the foyer of Centennial Hall. Among those initials is a brass plate bearing this inscription:

> *Presented to*
> *The Old Boys of EHS*
> *Past, Present and Future*
> *for the sake of*
> *'Auld Lang Syne'*
>
> *October* 14, 1950   An Old Boy
>   C. C. Carlin, Jr. '19

Charles Creighton Carlin, Jr., was the publisher of *The Alexandria Gazette*, "The Nation's Oldest Daily," as was his father before him. The bench was originally, according to local tradition, a pew in a rustic church located on Seminary Road not far from the Seminary. In those benighted days, again according to tradition, that church was called by the local Yahoos "Cologne Cathedral."

"Too old to cry and it hurt too much to laugh." Harry Blackiston (1923–28) found the Hill hard to climb:

In due course that awful moment arrived when our parents said goodby and my fellow rat Chalmers Nevius and I were left to fish for ourselves until suppertime. All the other boys seemed to be having the best time imaginable, laughing and joking and comparing their summer exploits and love affairs while Chalmers and I stared at our feet.

We noticed one other small boy about our age who looked even more miserable. He had on drab brown corduroy knickers, a coat to match, black knee-length stockings and high-button shoes. His homely looks matched his wardrobe. Instantly sensing a kindred lost soul, we quickly made friends. He was Smedley Darlington Butler, Jr., son of General Butler, one of the Marines' most famous and most controversial officers, said to be the only man ever to have won two Congressional Medals of Honor. His son promptly acquired the nickname of "Smelly."

Before long the dinner bell rang and the students fell in line waiting for the dining room doors to open. I squeezed in between two older boys. One of them said "If that kid could flap his ears, he'd fly." To borrow a phrase from Adlai Stevenson, I was too old to cry and it hurt too much to laugh.

The dining room accommodated the entire student body, about 180 boys. The atmosphere was spartan and the furniture the simplest. Each table had about fourteen places and was presided over by a master and, if married, his wife and any child old enough to attend meals. The white plaster walls were strung with photographs of the various teams of the past, many brown with age.

When the room was full, Mr. Hoxton gently tapped the little bell kept at his place. All stood in silence as he recited the grace which preceded every meal, "Oh Lord, make us thankful for these and all thy mercies, for Christ's sake. Amen."

Two hundred chairs scraped the floor in unison and the babel of conversation commenced. When Mr. Hoxton considered the meal over, he tapped his bell and all were free to leave, and not before.

J.T. Lane   H. Blackiston   A. Dudley

After supper the new boys assembled in study hall where various masters interviewed us to detemine how much math, history, language,
etc. we had had. As with most of the so-called Episcopal Church related schools, E.H.S. provided, at least theoretically, six forms. On
that somewhat casual basis we were initially assigned to what was
thought to be the appropriate form for each subject.

This guesswork did not always work. My fellow rat, Eugene Geismer, who for some reason was immediately nicknamed "Barney Google" after the then popular song and comic strip, was expansive about
his math background and was put in sixth form math. As the weeks
went by, he dropped to fifth math, then fourth, and by year end he
was in first math.

That charmingly casual, guesswork system of rats assigning
themselves to what they reckoned were "appropriate" forms went
on until the 1950's, when William Bee Ravenel devised placement
tests. Now the national Secondary School Admission Test (SSAT)
does it all.

Charley "C.V." Tompkins, who coached me in track, had more influence on me than anyone. I and others paid strict attention in his
class, as he was very accurate with chalk if he caught you dozing off.
In his chemistry class he would make up a conglomerate of all kinds
of metals, acids, etc., and the students were required to make tests to
determine all the various items. He really fixed me with my tests, then
he would come around to see what I had found, and chuckle over my
problems. I worked at his camp, "Yonanoka," for six years, where I
learned a lot of good from him. [Aldrich Dudley, Jr., 1924–30.]

Mr. Tomkins' summer camp for boys was in Linville, North
Carolina; it operated very successfully from 1924 to 1974; and it
was Yonahnoka ("Black Bear"). Aldie Dudley: better at running,
raffling candy, testing chemicals and learning good than at spelling.

The four and a half years that I spent at The High School were one
of the happiest periods of my life! I will never forget them, and I did
my share of walking off demerits. I had the greatest respect and admiration for Flick. When as a new monitor I had to practice reading the
first lesson for the evening chapel session standing up in front of him
in his office dressed in my blue suit and white tie my knees shook and
my hands trembled so much that I could barely read. He was so great
with me that when I got up in front of the school at chapel that evening I was so calm I felt like giving a sermon.

However, the person who had the most influence on me was Charlie

Tompkins. He coached football and track, which sports I liked, and he also taught chemistry, which I chose because of him. At the beginning of the year he told the class that we would probably not understand a word he was telling us in the first few sessions but if we kept thinking it would all suddenly clear up, and so it did, so much that I went on to study chemical engineering at Princeton! [Platt Okie, 1924–29.]

Jim Meem (1928–31) took delight in singing and swinging:

It seemed heavenly to be listening, long after "lights out" and on a radio held clandestinely under the bedcovers, to the music of Guy Lombardo!

Going before Mr. Henry Miller to try out for the choir must have been a terrible ordeal for him. Many of us applicants seemed to have only one aim in mind: to sing "Onward Christian Soldiers" just as loud as our lungs allowed. One of the reasons for such a "devoted" effort was that being chosen for the choir meant an extra trip to Washington. Later we found out that there were also extra bonuses, like being invited to sing in churches at The Plains and Middleburg, and the social amenities that went with it.

Swinging on ropes from the second floor in the old gym was a popular but not recommended pastime. One day I had just finished my swing and was getting ready to dismount when unbeknownst to me someone else was coming down from the second floor on another rope at full speed. Our heads, sideways, caught the full impact! The other student, whose name I do not recall, fell to the floor unconscious; I staggered dizzily to the infirmary to get treated for a bleeding ear.

A sad memory: When I arrived at EHS in 1928, Robert P. Quin of Houston, Texas, was beginning his second year. Yet in only those two years he established himself as one of the finest all-around athletes the High School ever had. He was also handsome, and a very friendly person. So imagine our shock and disbelief when we returned to school in September, 1930, to hear that Bob had died the previous July, from typhoid fever, I think, while travelling to Europe on a ship.

A joyful memory: Just before the end of my last term I learned that beside myself three other students—Edward P. Bailey, Charles W. Hancock and John B. Young—had chosen the Virginia Military Institute as the college they would attend. The selection of VMI by such a "crowd" of EHS students was truly unprecedented and naturally made me very happy.

And I could mention the excitement of becoming a monitor.

No one who was in the School with "Hot Shot" Quin (1927–29) will ever forget him. He did, apparently, die of typhoid fever, which

J.P. Okie   *Bob Quin*   *E.C. Moncure*

in those days was often fatal. Twenty years later he would not have died of that disease. Improved sanitation and antibiotics of the thirties and forties virtually wiped it out as a killer in this country. A room in the School's McAlister Hospital has been dedicated to his memory.

Four EHS boys in one year to VMI, that great old place which is coeval with us (chartered and opened as the first state military college in the country in 1839), was then and probably still is a record. For some insight into the griefs and joys of being one of the School's incarnate consciences, a monitor, see the section on Discipline.

As for that poor battered "other student" who fell to the floor unconscious after his head caught the full impact of Jim M.'s, it is to be hoped that the Infirmary, which was run by Dr. Hugh McGuire in those days, managed to restore him to full operational status within the hour. One wonders who he was.

A funny thing happened at Thanksgiving Day dinner. Ike Parrish was the waiter at Mr. Hoxton's table and was carrying a turkey on a big tray when the turkey slid off the tray to the floor. While the entire dining room roared with laughter and clapped their hands, Ike picked up the turkey by its drumstick and took it back to the kitchen. A moment later Ike reappeared with a turkey for Mr. Hoxton's table and everybody clapped again. It was the same turkey because there was no other one in the kitchen. [E. Conway Moncure, 1929–33.]

Ike Parrish's comment: "As I recall, Buddy Mizell was sitting at the end of Mr. Hoxton's table. He stuck his foot out and tripped me. I fell to the floor with the turkey sliding off the tray. I tried

*Roy Mason and Llewellyn
Thomas on Jim Meem,
1931—but whose is that
extra hand?*

to pick it up by the leg which came off, so I scooped it up in my arms, placed it on the tray and returned to the kitchen. There I was given the waiters' turkey for Mr. Hoxton's table."

And how does Buddy Mizell answer that tripping charge? Unfortunately we shall never know; he has joined the Majority.

Conway Moncure resumes:

Another funny thing happened that year. Rutledge Tufts was sitting on the end seat of the back row in Mr. Whittle's class and said or did something to provoke Mr. Whittle who told him to leave the room and return the next day. When Rut did not move, Mr. Whittle went to him and edged him off his bench to the floor, opened the door, and half-shoved, half-cajoled Rut to leave. The class roared.

My years at the High School are unforgettable and I look back on them with fond memories and nostalgia. My most unforgettable characters:

Mr. Hoxton ("Flick"), a great administrator, teacher and adviser, who ran a "tight ship." Mr. J. M. Daniel ("Dreamy"), a teacher who made a dull history course so very interesting. Mr. R. E. Latham ("Hawkeye"), a teacher who could spot a student's infraction from a mile distant. Mr. C.V. Tompkins, chemistry etc teacher who threw chalk at boys who gave dumb answers. Mr. Pat Callaway, God bless him!

Nat Barnwell (my classmate) as a rat being made to "flush like a toilet" and singing "Barnacle Bill the Sailor" in his native Charleston gullaw dialect. Robert "Czar" Train, great football player and leader. Ike Parrish, blithe spirit, good company, full of ideas. "Ma" Hearn, infirmary nurse who let students pretend sickness to spend night in infirmary to miss a test. "Saphead" Mason, Sultan of Egypt. Mrs. Clark, dietician in charge of kitchen, would give us waiters special food when we finished waiting. Wilmer, colored janitor at Alumni Hall, remembered and greeted me 25 years later. Will and Buster, head cook and assistant, baked delicious bread.

In the words of the old song, "Those were the days, my friend, we thought they'd never end." I like the words of Theodore Roosevelt, "If I could only be a boy again."

QUERY: Was boyhood "all in a rush with richness, juice and joy," as Gerard Manley Hopkins believed, or "Old, unhappy, far-off things, and battles long ago," as per Wordsworth—or did Longfellow say it best:

> *A boy's will is the wind's will,*
> *And the thoughts of youth are long, long thoughts. . . .*

And what about the Depression, which was out there when Conway Moncure left the Hill? Actually, the Great Depression of the thirties didn't hurt the School as much as it might have. Applications for enrollment dropped off somewhat, but prices of goods and services dropped off so much more that Proc Stuart actually saved some money.

What is the record for longevity at the High School, with or without graduating? My roommate, the late "Squinch" Goodwin, was there for six years, and I for five.

We both barely graduated. My last year I had only three periods in class, and five out! I had a lot of time on my hands, mostly sleeping and dreaming. I graduated about ten days after my class, while trying to pass the College Boards; I got a "gift" 75 on my third try at Fifth Form French and was handed my diploma by Rosalie, Mr. Hoxton's secretary, and was told, in effect, "Well done and get lost!" Needless to say, even my extra year at the High School was not wasted. *Fortiter et fideliter.* [E. Pinkney Wroth, 1935–40.]

Rosalie Nelson was Flick's secretary until about 1941, when she married Stewart Bell, Mayor of Winchester.

It seems that the record for EHS longevity is ten years, held by Walter Packard (1850–60) and two of Dr. Blackford's five sons: Ambler (1897–1907) and Staige (1907–1917). Two other sons went for nine years: Randolph (1900–09) and LM Jr. (1903–12). The fifth son, John, only went for eight years (1897–1905). OldFlick went for nine years (1886–95) and Young Flick for seven (1928–35). Others: Will Reade's son Frank (1905–14) and Arthur B. Kinsolving II (1906–14), the only long-timer who was not a teacher's son: his father was Lucien Kinsolving (1878–81), Bishop of Brazil. There are many more sevens.

Having done well, Pinkney Wroth did not get lost: he went on to the University and is now the Rector of St. Paul's Church in Washington.

Bill Hanson (1936–40) almost got a degree in UFOlogy:

On a Sunday evening in October several of us, following the tradition of visiting masters in their homes, went to Mr. & Mrs. Hoxton's. As I recall, David White had the office phone watch.

The Hoxtons and our group were conversing when the door that led to the office opened and David dashed in saying "The Martians have invaded the world and have landed in New Jersey!"

Mr. Hoxton leaped to the top of his couch and grabbed one of the crossed sabres beneath Robert E. Lee's portrait. "We had better get ready for them," he said.

Mrs. Hoxton turned on the radio and we all listened spellbound. The sound of gunfire and the frantic announcer describing the destruction of tanks, guns and infantry by "rays" from large dish-shaped machines on long legs had us terrified. Suddenly the announcer was cut

E.P. Wroth   *W.V. Hanson*   *J. Bryan III*

off. Then the White House came on the air imploring people to keep calm.

Some of us left to alert other students and other stayed glued to the radio.

As Paul Harvey would say, "Now you know the rest of the story."

It was October 30, 1938.

Old Flick's son Young Flick says that story is exactly true except it was a single sword not crossed sabres and it hung above not below a portrait of Llewellyn Hoxton not Robert E. Lee.

Some present-day historians believe that existing fears caused by international crises heightened the effect of that notorious radio broadcast of Orson Welles' *War of the Worlds*.

Italy was digesting her new "province" of Abyssinia; civil war was eviscerating Spain; Japan was continuing to overrun China.

Earlier that year German troops had occupied Austria and just one month before, September 30, 1938, Germany, Italy, England and France had signed the infamous Munich Agreement giving Hitler the Sudetenland and all of the important Czech military strongholds in return for what England's Neville Chamberlain called "peace in our time." Most Americans approved that policy of appeasement, but were very apprehensive.

Welles' Mercury Theater broadcast was extraordinarily realistic and an invasion from Mars didn't seem as wildly unlikely then as it does now. Space exploration has shown that the surface of the Red Planet is not nearly so friendly to life as it's portrayed in Edgar Rice Burroughs' Mars books, which were almost as popular in the twenties and thirties as were his Tarzans.

A year later, on October 14 and 15, we marked the hundredth anniversary of the founding of the School. (The story of how Centennial Hall was conceived and born may be found in the next chapter.) About two hundred and fifty Old Boys and friends of the School came for the occasion and there were some memorable speeches. Joseph Bryan, III told of what the place was like in his day, 1917–21:

The Seminary stood over here, Mr. Hoxton stood over there, and first bounce was out. I always thought of Mr. Hoxton as a sort of modern Medusa, one look from him and I would turn into stone.

When we dressed up we had on four-button, steam-heated suits, great big collars that stuck out like that, and bow ties no wider than that. We all parted our hair in the middle. When we weren't dressed

Above: OldFlick by his father's picture and sword, 1938. Right: Two Flicks, 1920.

Old Bar Blackford's five sons back for the Centennial, 1939. Left to right: Dr. John M., Rev. Ambler M., Rev. Randolph F., Dr. L. Minor, Dr. Staige D.

up we had on corduroy pants, and those were patched with adhesive plaster, whether they needed it or not, and everybody wrote their names on that. There was a group once that had shaved heads. My brother discovered the system of taking a felt hat and soaking it and working it down over a baseball bat. He could get that hat two feet tall.

Norborne Berkeley (1907–10) spoke of our sacred Three Words: "What has made the school, then, is the courage and devotion to duty of the soldier, the *fortiter*—thorough, faithful scholarship, the *fideliter*—the Christian spirit of the church, *feliciter*."

Our Poet-in-Residence Willoughby Reade presented a fine rolling Centennial Ode which paid tribute to our first hundred years— "A time full of dear memories,/ Of large endeavour in the cause of right"—and he called on us to "Fare forth anew, on great adventure bound/ Beyond the horizon's rim of things that are,/ Into a day of grander, nobler things to be."

The Reverend Arthur B. Kinsolving II (1906–14), nephew of our historian [ABK], said "If we are ever to establish on earth that kingdom of the Prince of Peace, then places like this must cradle the reborn citadel of peace. . . ." But even as he spoke our citadel of peace was disturbed by wars and rumors of wars in distant lands, and soon enough war came to us.

Once more the School gave generously to the Cause.

World War II took forty-three of us, our largest death toll since the War itself.

Charles J. Churchman (1945–47) came just after the war ended:

I remember arriving at EHS October 28, 1945, a rather lost, lonely, unhappy soul. An uncle, a close friend and fraternity brother of my father's at UVA, had determined, my father being deceased, that EHS was a good place for me to be. Since I was a country boy from a farm in Augusta County, Virginia, with a much greater passion for freedom to roam the countryside than to study Latin or math, I was inclined to want to be elsewhere.

The school had been underway for well over a month and I seemed to be a kind of loose entity rolling about without any real sense of purpose or connection. Being shy by nature, I didn't fancy living in the cubicle to which I was assigned on the second floor of Blackford Hall.

During my first night I noticed with some grief that boys were all around me, breathing far too loud, I thought, and even talking (after lights, no less). It just wasn't the peace and quiet of my big room on

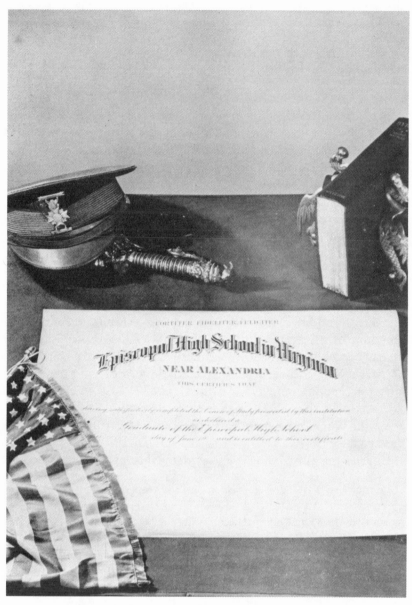

1942. The book is a collection of Byron's poems.

the farm. Consequently, not knowing anything at the time of the rat system, or even realizing I was one (I had missed the orientation), I called out and advised whoever it was making all the noise to be quiet and let me sleep. I later learned that the individual I had addressed in such an uncivilized and unthinkable manner was a monitor. Perhaps the shock of the action left him speechless, for he said nothing.

My first few weeks at the school were utter misery, for testing in Latin and math indicated that I was a hopeless incompetent in those disciplines, something that later tests have further substantiated. In any event I was required to repeat my second year algebra course, something I had already received credit for in my high school back home. I was, of course, failing second year Latin under Mr. Whittle, and so, for me, the clouds at that time hung oppressively low in the heavens.

With a torn cartilage in the knee I couldn't play any athletics (I was sort of off and on crutches) and the only activity I had to look forward to was study hall. It was at that time that Mr. Hoxton ("Flick," Sr., that is) came to my rescue.

This is an appropriate time to say something about teachers and headmasters, for I did and do have the highest regard for some of them. As for contact with my fellow students, I did have a few close friends but never saw the sense in all the competitive furor, zeal (madness, I would have called it, and probably still do) over athletics. Much of the time I just wanted to be by myself. So I spent many afternoons (since I couldn't engage in athletics) walking through Alexandria. In those days it was pine woods all the way from the school to the Masonic Temple.

"Flick" must have known I was at loose ends, a bit of a misfit really, for he called me in from study hall and set up regular tutoring sessions in math. Maybe it was about that time that I realized that if I hoped to ever leave the school, I would have to settle down and work.

N. Berkeley   *A.B. Kinsolving II*   *C.J. Churchman*

And the thought of being trapped there was appalling.

Certainly Mr. Hoxton inspired me in math, and my grades in math and geometry began to soar.

There was old Mr. Willoughby Reade, in his late eighties or nineties as I recall, anyway he was teaching his fiftieth and last year of English when I had him. A fine old Englishman, a real Victorian gentleman! He played tennis in his eighties with a green eye shade.

Actually I did appreciate the part EHS played in helping me to learn to study. It was there that an interest in English literature developed, as well as an interest in writing, mostly letters, to be sure, but even that is good practice; I became exchange editor of the little literary magazine, a position that was of most uncertain value. No one ever read my little entries, and for good reason, since I really had nothing to say, but it was fun to see my words in print.

Memories: by no means all bad ones: I did have some fun times, and it all seems so long ago. I think it was back then that I lost, like Thoreau, a hound, a bay horse, and a turtle dove, and-I've been seek-

Rifle team, 1943: Nathan Bundy, Billy Huger, David Walker, J.D. Baker, J.W. Bronaugh, H.H. Callaway, L.R. Craighill, F.A. Dusch, J.T. Fargason, J.A. Figg, W.H. Rogers, L.C. Shepherd, J.W. McCullough, H.H. Varner, S.G. Walsh, T.H. Willcox. The coach was Cooper Dawson, USNR. That team was ranked seventh nationally and first among the country's prep schools.

ing them ever since. It made me a bit strange then, and I suppose I'm a bit strange now, but I don't worry about that any more.

Then there was poor Mr. Rockwell, a likeable but terribly mistreated man. I loved to hear him smack his lips when he said "Chaucer."

Thoreau looked for his hound, horse and turtle dove in the woods by Walden Pond; CJC sought his in the groves of Academe.

After taking a B.A. in English from the University he got a commission in the Marine Corps, served in the Sixth Fleet in the Mediterranean during the Korean War, married, "taught here and there (three years in Taiwan), received an M.A. from UVA and a Ph.D. from the University of Tennessee. I am currently a professor of English at Bridgewater College in Virginia. During the 1986–87 school year my wife and I spent a year at the Dalian Institute of Foreign Languages in Dalian, People's Republic of China, directing a program for American students and teaching Chinese."

One little question, Professor: Are there *really* no flies in China?

Thoreauvian Churchman didn't say so, but his last year at the School was also Old Flick's last year as an extremely successful Principal. He retired in June, 1947, full of honors. Princeton and Harvard both made him Master of Arts, the University of the South made him Doctor of Letters (but he wouldn't let anybody call him Doctor), and the University elected him an honorary member of Phi Beta Kappa. Among his fellow preparatory school educators he was recognized as primus inter pares.

In his thirty-four years as Principal Old Flick took the institution which his predecessor had made great and made it greater.

"Of all the things I've shared with the High School, the best and most promising is my son, Hunter '81. I hope EHS will be for him as precious a resource as it has been for me." [Hunter H. McGuire, Jr., 1944–47.]

Old Flick continued Old Bar's tradition of getting and holding good masters who improved the quality of character-shaping as well as teaching. During his stewardship, in 1929, the School was able to increase its enrollment from around 170 to 200 by the building of a new dormitory, the new west wing of the main building (now used for classrooms).

He even pioneered in the gritty business of fund raising, absolutely essential but certainly a foreign field for him; and like a

Singers and slingers, 1944—don't they look alike?

Choir

Akeley, R. N.	Henderson, E. H.	Quaile, G. R.
Backer, W. M.	Hodges, W. L.	Randolph, R. L., Jr.
Berkeley, W. M., Jr.	Ingle, J. A., Jr.	Riddick, A. L., Jr.
Bucknell, J. A.C.	Kern, J. W., III	Rogers, F. W., Jr.
Burge, J. D., Jr.	Kilpatrick, H. C.	Rogers, R. J.
Cates, M. L., Jr.	Kinsolving, C. L.	Roper, J. L., III
Christian, F. P., III	LaRoche, E. P.	Salisbury, R. C.
Craighill, D. H., Jr.	Lemmon, F. T., Jr.	Sasscer, L. G., Jr.
Craighill, L. R., Jr.	Lloyd, R. B.	Vaill, F. S., Jr.
Craighill, R. M.	Massie, D. M.	Wannamaker, W. K.
Dana, T. F.	Miller, W. C., Jr.	Wardlaw, A. L., Jr.
Daniel, W. V.	Mobley, G. N.	Ware, J. W.
Englar, G. M.	Mobley, J. W., III	Washington, S. L.
Gant, C., Jr.	Morgan, H. J., Jr.	Waterman, A. B.
Goodwin, E. LeB.	Murph, D. S., Jr.	Welch, J. H.
Goodwin, T. R. L.	Page, R. B.	Wilson, E. E., Jr.
Greear, J. N., III	Page, W. L.	Choir Mother, Mrs.
Hagood, B. A.	Parker, L. W.	F. E. Carter
Hancock, E. H.	Phillips, W. C., Jr.	Organist, Mr. H. T.
Helfenstein, E. T., II	Pomfret, J. D.	Holladay

Waiters

Craighill, L. R., Jr.	Harris, J. M.	Sasscer, L. G.
Barrett, R. S., IV	Houstoun, W. G.	Semmes, D. H.
Berkeley, W. M. Jr.	Hyde, S. F.	Stites, J. W., Jr.
Bucknell, J. A. C.	Ingle, J. A.	Suthon, W. J.
Daniel, J. M., Jr.	Johnson, J. D. T.	Thompson, R. C.
Estill, R. W.	Kilpatrick, H. C.	Vaill, F. S., Jr.
Goodman, F.	King, F. D., Jr.	Wood, J. M.
	Prevatt, P. L.	

good and faithful servant toiling in the vineyards of the Lord, with no high pressuring he harvested nearly half-a-million dollars! Many of the present buildings are "his."

He ruled with such absolute, easy authority that . . . he was as firm and fair as . . . he was like . . . but similes fail. . . .

He was Flick.

He died October 14, 1951.

Bless that man, OldGod OldGod!

CHAPTER 6

Between the Wars
1919–1939

This entire chapter, so full of the sights and sounds and names and dates and measurements and colors and whigmaleeries of the middle twenty years of Old Flick's benevolent monarchy, was "dashed off" by Dick Daniel (1925–32), son of one of the oldest and staunchest of the famous "Old Guard" of masters, "Dreamy" Daniel.

"Dashed off"? Indeed! Elephants are supposed to have the best mammalian memories; they never forget. Well. The width, depth, precision and power of Dick Daniel's faculty of total recall, as evidenced in this incredible chronicle, would surely equal that of the champion rememberer among those wonderful pachyderms which, as "Dreamy" so eloquently told his ancient history classes, carried Hannibal the Carthaginian across the Alps in the year 218 B.C to attack Rome (unsuccessfully, but that wasn't the elephants' fault).

For such a brilliant illumination of a certain score of years of our temps perdu *as only the hardiest of Bede's sparrows could have flown through,* Tolle lege, tolle lege, *as Saint Augustine was so fond of saying: "Take up and read, take up and read!"*

EACH AFTERNOON a boy in khaki uniform with bugle in hand marched to the center of Hoxton circle, turned, faced west, raised the bugle to his lips and blew "assembly." He repeated the call facing north and again facing south. As the notes died away, khaki-clad boys came streaming from the dormitories carrying their rifles.

It was 1917, and the school had adopted military training. That training was continued through 1918–19.

Originally the rifles had been made of wood, but those were stored under Liggett Hall after they had been replaced with genuine U.S. Army Springfields. That cache of wooden guns under Liggett Hall became a wonderful source of supply for the small fry growing up on the Hill.

Sometime during the Fall of 1918 while the boys were drilling on Hoxton Field (the concrete steps behind Stewart Gym were very useful for this purpose) a column of black smoke curled up from the direction of Mudtown. It was a fire in Vic Donaldson's store. The boys broke ranks and streamed over the stile just east of Memorial Hall and across the cow pasture to the rescue. One of them grabbed me and I was carried piggy-back to the fire. It was too late to save anything except one glass show case full of candy. It was carried across King Street Road alongside the A.M.E. Church. The candy was liberated and thoroughly enjoyed by everyone including myself. Years later I learned from Felix Kloman that Mr. Hoxton insisted that the boys pay for the candy they ate.

R. Daniel

The school at this time had a faculty of a dozen members, five of whom were married. Mr. Hoxton lived in the main house (now called Hoxton House) with his wife, Sara Taylor, his daughter, Mary Earle, a teen-ager, and Archie, Jr., age two. It was not until later that his mother decreed that he should be called Flick.

The house south of Hoxton House was occupied by Mr. Shackelford, his wife Mabrey Page, and his three daughters, Evelyn, Flora Kinloch and Jane Byrd, ages ten, eight and four respectively. My father, John M. Daniel, lived in the north house on Hoxton Circle. The family included my mother Margaret Micou and three children, Jack, Margaret and myself; at the time of which I write we were aged eight, six and five respectively. Immediately to the north was Mr. Reade's home. His wife Mary Robertson and youngest daughter Mary Willoughby, a teen-ager, lived with him. The fifth married teacher was Mr. Carter who, with his wife Lucile Alvey and five-year-old son, Nick, occupied a two-room apartment at the east end of Lower Blackford. Three matrons, Miss Mary Jett, Mrs. Kennedy and Miss Roy were dietician, nurse and dormitory mother respectively. Mrs. Kennedy lived in the infirmary and the other two had rooms on the south side of the first floor of the main building between Hoxton House and the hall. The last staff member was the Proctor, Mr. George C. Stuart, who was responsible for the procurement of food, fuel and supplies and maintenance of buildings and grounds. He lived with his wife Anne (called Annie), a sister of Mr. Hoxton, in the house south of Liggett Hall.

Later Mr. Stuart became a justice of the peace and was forever after known as "the Judge." The unmarried teachers had rooms in the dormitories and the gymnasium, usually one to a floor except Second Alumni. That room was reserved for the Head Monitor and his roommate.

It should also be noted that at this time Mr. Hoxton's mother was living in Hoxton Memorial Cottage.

The success of any enterprise depends on the carrying out of the policies set by management. The High School has been particularly fortunate in its faithful cadre of servants. The dean of this corps was Uncle Jim Jackson, who had been born a slave and had served the school since 1866. He was too old to work but made himself useful by going around the grounds picking up loose paper with a walking stick with a spike at one end. The next in longevity was Joe Wanza who came aboard in 1890. He stoked the central heat furnaces under the main building behind Hoxton House. He banked the fires about 10 P.M. and retired to Mudtown for the night. At 6:30 A.M. he was on the job sending steam heat to the dorms and faculty homes. Hot water for showers was available only in the late afternoon. Joe made the rounds turning on the water and later turning it off. He was also a local musician of note, being much in demand for local entertainments and parties. But by 1918 he had "gotten religion" and given up the banjo. Another of his hobbies was building 12-room bird houses out of empty wooden butter chests.

Having voted for Harding in 1920, he was disillusioned by the G.O.P.'s refusal to live up to their promises and said he would never vote again. He knew every High School boy by name and many an Old Boy made it a point to look up Joe when returning to alma mater. His progeny was huge and many of them worked for EHS.

Next in importance was the head waiter, William Randall, a

Reflection in our now–non-existent lake, 1906

Aerial view, 1933

large mulatto whose duties included bell ringing and presiding over the other waiters. He rang the rising bell at 7:20 A.M. and all bells for meals plus the morning chapel bell at 8:40, after dinner classes at 1:50 and evening study hall at 7:20. Meals were always preceded by two bells five minutes apart: breakfast at 7:45 and 7:50, dinner at 1:00 and 1:05 and supper at 6:25 and 6:30. In the Spring term we had our own version of daylight saving time. Supper was at seven o'clock.

Then there was William Carpenter who ran the dairy. The herd consisted of twenty Holstein cows and a mean bull named Klondike who was a terror to all the children but we were not above teasing him. The cow pastures were the fields on either side of the main driveway and a lane just north of Memorial that led to an old barn situated on the present site of the Joseph Bryan library. There was a field just north of the lane where corn or cow peas were grown to fill the silo. After milking the milk was chilled in the barn and then brought to the basement under the kitchen where the refrigerators were located. It wasn't pasteurized.

During the day when dairy duties were light, Carpenter drove a one-horse light spring wagon to Alexandria to run errands and make sundry purchases. He also made daily stops at Burke & Herbert's bank to make deposits and cash checks. It wasn't until the mid-twenties that the wagon was abandoned in favor of a light truck, driven by John Thomas.

Heavy hauling was done by George Taylor with a team of mules, Jack and Kate. He was kept busy all the time hauling coal, ashes and ice. The services areas were located on the north side of the main building. The 300-lb. ice cakes were lowered to the refrigerators at the west end by block and tackle; coal was shoveled into the bunkers next to the furnace room. Ashes were lifted out by block and tackle into a dump cart.

Last but by no means least was Mr. Cleveland, the handyman, known as "Monkeywrench." He was a combination carpenter, plumber and electrician. He built the bleachers and board track from scratch. There was nothing the boys broke that he could not fix, except the wash basin in Alumni which had had its bottom blown out with a firecracker.

Food, Glorious Food!

Just as an army is said to march on its stomach, the morale of a boarding school is dependent on the quality of the food. The

High School has been most fortunate in this regard, particularly between the wars. One of the first topics discussed when boys from different schools met was food. Mr. Hoxton saw to it that the E.H.S. compared favorably. The dining room then as now was located on the first floor of the main building. Pictures of all the athletic teams lined the walls, the oldest beginning on the north side of the entrance door and progressing down through the years to the latest located south of the door.

Long tables seating six on a side, fourteen in all and oriented north and south, lined each side of the center aisle with its posts. Each table was presided over by a teacher. On the north side the first table's head was an unmarried teacher (later by Mr. and Mrs. Stuart), the second by my father, the third by Mr. Reade and the fourth by Mr. Williams. On the south side Mr. Whittle presided over the first, Mr. Hoxton the second, Mr. Shackelford the third and Mr. Carter the fourth. Later Messrs. Hoxton and Carter swapped tables so that the former would be more centrally located. The rest of the tables were presided over by the unmarried teachers.

The dietician, Miss Mary Landon Jett, presided over the kitchen with the help of Mr. Stuart. She had joined the staff in 1904 but her health failed in 1920 and she resigned. My one clear-cut recollection of her is of collecting mushrooms with her in the cow pastures. She taught me how to distinguish between the edible and poisonous varieties. Her brother, Robert Carter Jett, was elected first Bishop of Southwestern Virginia in 1920 and thus became a member of the Board of Trustees.

There followed a succession of short tenures. During the interim when no dietician was in charge, Mr. Stuart ran the kitchen. This was the era when the meal menus were repeated on a weekly basis. Breakfast consisted of hot or dry cereal followed by a main course and left over rolls. Milk, cream, sugar and butter were served.

Cereals were hot oatmeal, Cream of Wheat or Wheatena, cold corn flakes, bran or Shredded Wheat. Main courses were scrambled eggs with bacon, creamed chipped beef, fried apples with bacon, home fries, fish roe patties, sausage patties and a special pièce de resistance: salt roe herring from the Potomac. Most of the boys just ate the roe (if there was any) and did not touch the delicious sausage. Orange juice was an unaffordable luxury. Midday dinner consisted of meat, potatoes and gravy plus vegetables and sliced bread. No butter or milk was served.

Five days a week the meat was always a three-rib roast of beef, utility grade, which had to be carved by the master presiding over the table. The older teachers became quite proficient at making the meat go around for fourteen people. But the inexperienced ones had problems. Much later I asked my father how the school could afford a roast of beef every day. His reply was "It only cost five to ten cents a pound." Chicken on Sunday was an old custom, usually creamed chicken on rice but occasionally fried chicken cut in quarters. One Sunday a month the fare was usually a leg of lamb which also had to be carved, of course. For those who could not fill up on meat and potatoes there was always sliced bread and "treacle." This last was not corn or maple syrup but black-strap molasses.

"Boss" was served only three times a week. Sundays there was variety; but ice cream every Tuesday and pie every Thursday was the rule. Supper was also a big meal with a main course, hot fresh rolls with butter and milk. Here again the hot main courses followed a weekly rotation. Monday night was always Irish stew and Friday was steak night. In between there were such dishes as croquettes, liver and bacon and pork chops. Saturday and Sunday nights were disasters because the kitchen help was off. Cold sliced ham and tongue were standard with sticky buns or sliced bread.

The arrival of Mrs. Mabel Gardner Clark in 1924 changed everything. First of all she ran a tight ship, and this did not sit too well with the help. In the spring of 1925 the waiters, all but William and John Henry and William Randall, walked off the job just before dinner. Mr. Hoxton called a mass meeting in the chapel and asked for volunteers at a pay of 25 cents per meal. Enough boys responded and the school never went back to the old system. John Henry soon left to take a job as a chauffeur in Washington, but his brother Wilmer continued in the school's employ until his old age. William Randall continued until the late thirties when he was fired. He could not be broken of his habit of stealing.

The menus immediately became varied and non-repetitive. A universally approved change was boss every day—although prune whip and "fish eyes and glue" (tapioca) were less than sensational.

Gradually all the carving (except Thanksgiving turkeys) was relegated to the kitchen. Dixie cups of ice cream (and better refrigeration) came on the market and Mrs. Clark allowed the boys to buy them at odd hours.

Another improvement in the mid-twenties was the introduction of monogrammed dishes with EHS in block letters and decorated with the school colors to replace nondescript thick all-white china. At the same time silver-plated sugar bowls, cream pitchers and gravy boats monogrammed with EHS in flowing script replaced plain china and glass.

The introduction of pie à la mode or ice cream with fresh strawberries whenever the Board of Trustees were present met with universal acceptance. In fact it became common knowledge throughout the state that the High School had the best food of any boarding school.

Saturday Night Movies

David Wark Griffith's *Birth of a Nation* electrified the whole country in 1916 and made feature length movies popular and acceptable entertainment. For us at EHS the attractions of Washington increased markedly. Playing hooky and going to Washington on Saturday nights to see a movie were perceived to be a serious threat to the serenity of the Hill. So Father, who was an original do-it-yourselfer, conceived the idea of showing movies at the school. The school paid for the projector but my father was responsible for procurement of the machine and programs.

So in the summer of 1918 he visited C. Francis Jenkins, an inventor who worked in Washington and thought that Thomas Edison had stolen all his ideas. Jenkins is credited in *World Book Encyclopedia* and in a recent biography of Will Rogers with having projected the first commercial motion pictures in New York City in a theater in 1895. (Later he demonstrated a television system!) The projector that he invented incorporated several novel features which are no longer used.

The course of the film through the projector was at a right angle to the line from machine to screen. A prism was used to bend the light beam 90°. The film moved continuously past the light source and an outside rotating disc cut the beam three times in a revolution producing a stroboscopic effect. (A competing technology developed finger-like hooks to pull the film one frame at a time past the light source; this won out in the marketplace.) Another feature was an arrangement that permitted both supply and take-up reels to be located in the bottom of the machine, thus minimizing the chance of a fire. This was a real hazard in the days of nitrate film. The light source was a 600-watt bulb about two by six inches in size, operated on reduced voltage. The screen was the east wall of the chapel until the World War I memorial tablet was erected. Thereafter a screen had to be pulled down from the ceiling. Movies were shown on Saturday nights after the literary society meetings. Procurement of movies was a continual headache and rentals had to be reduced by early returns.

The average charge for a program of eight reels was about $20 and the admission price was 20 cents. So a hundred patrons was the break-even point. Having to deal with only one of many rental companies precluded getting a lot of the more popular movies but a number of great films were shown, the most famous being Charlie Chaplin in *The Kid* shown on March 18, 1922.

In the beginning my father had to go to Washington on Friday or Saturday to get a feature film, but later most of the films arrived by parcel post Saturday morning. However the return problem was never satisfactorily solved and he ended up taking the films personally to Washington Sunday afternoon.

Profits, if any, from the operation were for the benefit of the Missionary Society but they were extremely modest. Some were used to pay the fire insurance on the St. Agnes School building.

After the advent of the talkies in 1928, Saturday night movies went into decline. Later a 16mm sound projector was rented to show movies in Liggett Hall. Once in the late thirties I walked in at the close of a show and heard the U.S. Cavalry roundly booed as it rode to the rescue. The baddies were Confederates.

Infrastructure

Although electric lights had become common, it was not until 1910 that they came into the school, due to the high cost of wiring. Up until the mid-twenties there were only three telephones at the school. One was in Mr. Stuart's house, for his exclusive use. The second was the official school telephone (Alexandria 229) located in the office with an extension in Mr. Hoxton's bedroom. The third was a pay telephone located under the steps in the hall. When this phone rang during mealtime, someone near the door would answer it; then he would seek out the person wanted. As this person left to take his sweetheart's (probably) call, it was the custom for everybody to go "Sh-s-s-s!" By the time the boy reached the door, there would be complete silence.

Water supply in the early days depended on water collected off the roofs, and on numerous shallow wells, but by 1911 an artesian well was drilled in the woods east of school. An electric pump filled an adjacent storage tank. Another pump transferred it to an elevated storage tank located behind St. George's Hall at the Seminary, thus providing an adequate and dependable supply for both institutions. One of our faithful servants, Willis, was servicing the triplex piston pump one day when his sleeve got caught in the gears. He almost lost his arm but fortunately soneone was nearby who heard the screams and shut off the power. Willis recovered and went on to serve the school many more years.

By 1928 the Alexandria water company was planning expansion into Fairfax County and made a deal to take over the water system. In return for permission to hook new users to the system the Seminary and EHS were permitted to deduct these payments from what they owed. The result was that by the end of World War II the schools were receiving free water. The water company had long since connected the storage tank in the woods with a standpipe about one mile east. Also in 1928 a new cast iron line was run from the elevated water tank to the High School along the road in front of Liggett Hall to a point between Blackford Hall and the Stewart Gymnasium. Two fire plugs were installed.

During an athletic event at the Seminary, a student, Chuck Carpenter, spent the afternoon doing handstands on top of the elevated tank. (This was the same Carpenter who also coached the EHS wrestling teams of 1924–26 and who eventually became Bishop of Alabama.)

Sanitary waste was handled in the early years by cesspools located about where Pendleton Hall now stands; about 1928 it was hooked up to Alexandria's system. Paper trash was burned in the open north of Hoxton Field in front of the future Centennial Hall.

In the very early twenties there were no paved roads nearer than Stanton's store at the foot of Quaker Lane. King Street Road was paved to Janney's Lane, the western boundary of the City of Alexandria. Braddock Road was paved to Lloyd's Lane. Between these points mud reigned supreme, hence the name Mudtown.

At this time there were only five automobiles on the Hill: Reverend Paca Kennedy (school Chaplain and Seminary professor) had a 1914 Model T Ford, Mr. Stuart had a Dodge, Mr. Shackelford a 1916 Model T and Mr. Daniel had a 1915 Model T, all touring cars. Mr. Hoxton had the fifth car, a Dodge sedan that one had to enter in the rear. The only woman driver was my mother. She took us children once to a birthday party at the

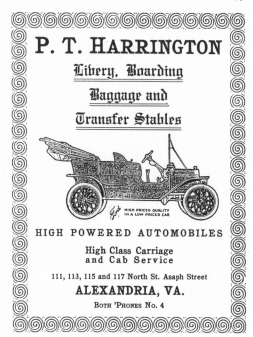

P. T. HARRINGTON
Livery, Boarding
Baggage and
Transfer Stables

HIGH POWERED AUTOMOBILES

High Class Carriage
and Cab Service

111, 113, 115 and 117 North St. Asaph Street

ALEXANDRIA, VA.

BOTH 'PHONES No. 4

Isn't she a beauty? 1911

Cooper Dawsons'. Hitting the wrong pedal she ran the car into a tree and my brother's head broke the windshield. He sustained a slight cut but there was no other damage. In 1920 a young teacher, Mr. Speidel, had a Saxon touring car and Mr. Carter got a Model T. By the mid-twenties Mr. Reade was driving a Dodge and Mr. Williams a Ford. After Mr. Carter got his Ford the first conversation between Mr. Carter and my father at the opening of school had to do with how much dirt road still remained between Richmond and Alexandria and how long the trip took. By the end of the decade nearly every teacher had a car and the school had built a garage to house them. My father had advanced to a Dodge, Mr. Stuart to a Buick and Mr. Hoxton to a Studebaker and then a Buick. Mr. Carter got the first Model A Ford, a big event, and Mr. Ailes gave Mr. Williams a new Model A in 1929. It sat between his house and Liggett Hall for a week at the opening of school because my father did not have time to teach him how to drive it. Dr. Kennedy traded his 1914 Model T in on a 1929 Model A.

Paving of the local highways and streets progressed all through the 1920's including the E.H.S. driveway in 1928, a gift from Mr. William Garrett Bibb (EHS 1879–82). Paving of King Street Road from Janney's Lane to Donaldson's store was delayed because both Fairfax and Arlington Counties were involved. The former did the two ends and the latter did the middle. Quaker Lane was paved around 1927. It later became the western boundary of Alexandria.

It is interesting to note that Mr. Bibb, who gave the driveway paving, also gave the wall in 1927 which marked the school boundaries with Quaker Lane and Braddock Road. In order to forestall future problems with the widening of Quaker Lane, the wall was set ten feet back of the property line but in the end this was not enough and the wall had to be replaced. The original wall cost about $5 per foot.

In the early years of this century there were as many as four ways to get to Washington. One could walk to Seminary Station (beyond Duke Street Road) and flag a train or one could walk to the foot of King Street and take the steamboat. But the most popular option was to walk two miles to Lloyd's station on the electric streetcar line which ended at 12th street and Pennsylvania Avenue. Commonwealth Avenue today follows the old right-of-way. Apparently Vic Donaldson got his start bussing students by taking them to and meeting cars at Lloyd's.

In the twenties there were two paved roads to Washington from Alexandria. From the Hill Braddock Road was followed to Russell Road. Here the choice was to either follow Russell Road to Arlington Heights then down through the U.S. Agricultural Station, between Hoover and Capital Airports (the latter had been built on a former burning dump) and on to the 14th Street Bridge. The other choice was to cross Russell Road and continue to Potomac Yards. A left turn was made here onto the Jefferson Davis Highway (U.S. #1) which went direct to the 14th Street Bridge. Short cut routes through what is now Shirlington and past the Army-Navy Country Club were mostly unpaved and very tortuous. The completion of Shirley Highway in the late 1940's finally opened up the shortest route.

Faculty Living Accommodations

When Mr. Blackford retired at the end of the 1912–13 session, he moved into his new home at Greenwood on Seminary Road, where my parents had been living since their marriage in 1908. The three of us had been born there. (This house, set on about sixteen acres, survived until 1956 when it was deliberately burned to clear a site for the synagogue now standing.) We moved into our own house on campus, newly built.

The Hoxtons, who had been married in 1903, occupied the main house with their daughter Mary Earle. It has now acquired the name "Hoxton House." Originally it consisted of two large downstairs rooms, a study and a parlor, and two large upstairs bedrooms. There was a large attic over the whole which provided a storage room and a large playroom for Flick. As part of main building remodelling of 1913 the space between the two structures was filled in with a new three-floor annex to match the old main building. This provided space for the matrons on the first floor, south side. The north side contained two rooms with a folding door partition that could make it into a single room. Originally this was used as a dining room when school was not in session. The football banquets were held in this room. The second floor contained the the enlarged chapel and the third floor contained four rooms, two of which were allotted to Mr. Reade and my father as classrooms. The third was the faculty lounge known as Social Hall. The fourth room with private bath was a part of Hoxton House. In the beginning this was the only bathroom for the family. In the early twenties a second bathroom was built in a corner of the south bedroom occupied by Mr. and Mrs. Hoxton. Young Flick was born here in 1916.

The one-room building to the north was the Wilmer Literary Society and the corresponding building to the south was the main school office. Originally there were one-story buildings north and south of Hoxton House.

The south unit had had a second story added probably around 1880 to provide accommodations for Mr. E. L. McClellan, a teacher and business adviser to Mr. Blackford, but it was now occupied by the Shackelford family. It had a living room, study, hall and pantry on the first floor with two bedrooms and a bath on the second floor. The space over the pantry was enclosed in the early twenties to provide a small room.

As part of the 1913 remodelling there was a plan to add a second story to the north unit, but it was unsound and had to be razed. A two-story duplicate of the Shackelford house was built for my family.

The old house to the northwest was occupied by Mr. and Mrs. Reade and their daughter, Mary Willoughby. My recollection of the living room is the number of stringed musical instruments scattered around, mandolins, guitars, ukuleles, etc. and also Ouija and backgammon boards. In addition there were a pantry and study on the first floor with bedrooms and a bath upstairs.

One of Mr. Reade's older daughters, Stella, had contracted tuberculosis. In accordance with the standard practice of the time a separate room with bath was built on to the west end of the house where she could be isolated. She divided her time between the High School and Saranac, New York. She died in 1929.

The only other staff dwelling on the grounds was the house next to Liggett Hall occupied by the Stuarts which had its own kitchen and furnace. All other faculty houses were on the central heating system.

In 1919 the school faced a housing shortage. The Carters' cramped quarters on Lower Blackford were made impossible by the arrival of little Bobby Carter. A double house was hastily constructed just north of the main building on the site of the old Fairfax Society. Each unit was almost an exact copy of the Daniel and Shackelford houses.

The next change in housing occurred on the death of Fanny Robinson Hoxton, Mr. Hoxton's mother, who was known to the small fry as Ga-Ga. Mr. Shackelford, having the largest family, moved into the cottage.

Soon, however, another housing crisis erupted. The impending marriage of Mr. Tompkins to Miss Margaret Bird and our own expanding family (my sister, Anne, was born in 1923) were the causes. It could be that the separation of the Board of Trustees into one for the Seminary and one for the High School facilitated the decision to build a new double house north of Liggett Hall. A new building costing $25,000 was finished in 1924; the new occupants, the Daniel and Williams families, moved in on the opening day of school. The paint was still wet.

Each unit had the usual living room, study, pantry and hall on the first floor. The second had three bedrooms and a bath but in addition there was a large room on the third floor. The school did not provide a second bath; so Mr. Williams and my father bought fixtures in Washington at a fire sale and had the attic space finished off and the fixtures installed for an additional personal cost of $200 each. The new homes were too far to be included in the central heating system, so a soft coal fired furnace and a bucket-a-day anthracite jack stove for summer hot water were provided. Mr. Williams and my father divided the furnace firing on a weekly basis. Our vacated houses were occupied by the matrons and the Tomkinses respectively.

In retrospect it appears that the masters' residences were as Spartan as the bunks in the dormitories were for the boys. Evidently the young men who had decided to make the training of youth their life's work were not going to let the lack of creature comforts stand in the way.

It must be noted though that in this period, when school was not in session, the families were all notably absent from the Hill. The Reades took off for Abingdon, Virginia, where they operated a summer camp for girls. Camp Glenrochie was one of the oldest in the country. The Shackelfords headed for their family homes, Cobham and Stony Point, in Albemarle County. The Carters spent their vacations in Richmond but in summer Mr. Carter was a counselor at Camp Greenbrier, Alderson, West Virginia.

He was later Director of the camp and died there in 1947.

Mr. Hoxton and my father had a unique arrangement during vacation periods. When one was off the premises the other was on. When Father was off, he always went to his mother's farm near Charles Town, West Virginia. He had been instrumental in planting a 60-acre apple orchard and building a comfortable brick house for our grandparents' declining years. There was nothing he enjoyed more than cultivating the orchard behind the wheel of a Fordson tractor. The division of vacation time with Mr. Hoxton followed this pattern: we took the week of Christmas off and the first half of spring vacation. In summer Mr. Hoxton always took the six weeks beginning in mid-July. His family usually visited a cousin at Fruit Hill near Shepherdstown, West Virginia, in July and spent all of August at Cape May, New Jersey.

The Williams family sometimes spent vacations with Mrs. Williams' family in Norfolk but more often set up housekeeping at home. Mr. and Mrs. Tompkins went to Linville on their honeymoon and the next year founded Camp Yonahnoka. Mr. Callaway and Mr. Williams were counsellors during the early years. Later Messrs. Latham, Fleming, Cardwell and Kaminer served on the staff.

This account would not be complete if I didn't mention the Tompkins nuptials which took place in Seminary Chapel in 1924 during Finals. It was an early evening wedding and the students were all invited. Naturally there was a conspiracy to impede their departure.

Mr. Moss in a Model T coupe was parked at the northeast door headed east. It was assumed that the car would have to turn around and head west to get out of the cul-de-sac. When the couple came down the aisle and entered the car, the church was evacuated at a rate that never before or since has been exceeded. The boys did not use the crowded aisles but jumped over pews in the mad rush. But Mr. Moss eluded them by driving out the little-used lane and entrance in front of Aspinwall Hall.

Other Capital Improvements

The circle in front of Hoxton House was once the top part of a figure eight. There was a lower, smaller circle so that one driving up to Hoxton's had to turn right (or left) before reaching the top of the hill. The south segment of the lower circle was rarely used. To continue to the school front or to Memorial Hall a U-turn was necessary. Most traffic proceeded toward Alumni and Blackford Halls. In the early twenties this was eliminated and the demerit track lengthened by moving the road in front of Memorial about thirty feet to the east.

Northwest of the kitchen was a nondescript group of frame buildings used to support the kitchen, dairy and maintenance operations. They consisted of servants' quarters, shops, garages and a barn. They were an eyesore and a fire hazard. The school mounted a concerted effort to get rid of them; but alternate facilities had to be provided. The first to go, about 1922, was the old barn.

A new barn with silo was built just west of the outdoor swimming pool next to Centennial Hall. Its construction was based on a new type of precast concrete blocks about a foot square and about four inches thick. This change cleared the site that was eventually occupied by the Joseph Bryan Library.

In 1925 it was decided to build a steam laundry in the woods in front of school. A deep well was drilled to supply water and a steam boiler with reciprocating engine to supply power through a ceiling-mounted pulley shaft and belts down to each piece of equipment. It was beautiful nineteenth century engineering. Later the belts and pulleys were scrapped and each piece of machinery equipped with its own motor.

Up until about 1925 the only book collections available to the students were those of the Literary Societies but these were mostly

Joseph Bryan (1856–61)

*Joseph Bryan's great-grandson,
John Stewart Bryan III*

Joseph Bryan Library in 1943

old and out-of-date books. The gift of a book collection formed the nucleus of a modern library. A librarian was needed and since Mr. Whittle had no coaching or other extra-curricular duties, he was appointed. Later Mrs. Virginia T. Bell, Mr. Tompkins' sister, held the position. The place to house the books was the west end of the little dining room. The east end had become social hall when a new teacher was added in 1919. In 1926 the school was electrified by the announcement that Mr. John Stewart Bryan had given $35,000 to build a library as a memorial to his father. The Williamsburg Restoration had begun so the building was modelled on that tradition.

The window capitals were carefully shaped and laid out on the ground by the brick masons before being laid up. The building included private quarters for Mr. Callaway and a room for the *Chronicle* and *Whispers*. Custom-made furniture as well as an automatic oil burner for heat were included in the gift. While this building was being constructed in 1927, the badly peeled white paint on the main building was removed by sand blasting . That same year the wall mentioned before was constructed.

Following the paving of Hoxton Circle and the main driveway in 1928 came the announcement of the gift of Dr. James C. Greenway (EHS 1890–95) of an athletic field as a memorial to his three brothers. It was to consist of two football fields, two baseball diamonds, a field house, parking space and a flag pole. The occasion was unique in two aspects. Congress had just made the Star Spangled Banner our national anthem and the boys actually learned two verses and sang it at the dedication. The occasion also featured what was probably the first raising of the Stars and Stripes since the Civil War, although the school had a large service flag for World War I (a star for each Old Boy who served and a gold star for each one who gave his life).

By the end of the twenties the kitchen had become almost impossibly cramped for space. All the refrigeration was in the basement which was very unhandy in spite of the dumb-waiter and in spite of the fact that an ammonia system of mechanical refrigeration had been installed in the early twenties.

Not only this but the science laboratories on the second floor had become inadequate.

So a decision was made in 1929 to scrap the two-story end of the main building and construct a three-floor ell-shaped wing. This was to include eighteen bunks and accommodations for a single master on the third floor. A criticism voiced at that time was: "Whoever heard of including student sleeping quarters, classrooms, laboratories and a kitchen all in one building?" The answer of course was that the school had no money for this much needed improvement. The $75,000 in bonds sold for the 1913 modeling were still out and there had been an endowment fund drive in 1926 which netted about 20 percent of its goal. By adding the 18 bunks the total school enrollment was increased about 10 percent and this plus the $100 per-boy increase in the annual fee enabled the improvement to be financed. As part of the program the rest of the frame buildings northwest of the main building were razed and replaced by a permanent brick structure with a garage for faculty cars on the first floor and servants' quarters on the second floor. All of this construction was accomplished in 1929. An unwelcome result of this was that the demerit track was now longer! This brick building served the school until the construction of Hummel learning center; the kitchen is still being used.

The stock market crash of 1929 did not adversely affect the school. In fact it thrived as never before. Tuition and board at this time was $850 and the school remained full.

Although the waiting list for admission was greatly reduced and management made many reductions in individual cases to enable boys to finish, there was no general reduction in charges. With the decline in the prices of food and fuel, a surplus began to build.

In 1934 the old infirmary was not that far out-of-date, but a new one was built, paid for out of school funds, and gratefully accepted. Ma Hearne, who had been in charge of the old one since 1920, retired when the new one, later named McAlister Hospital, for a non-alumnus, was built. Among other things it released space for other uses. Herr Whittle had been living in the upstairs apartment of the old Shackelford house. He now moved over to the infirmary upstairs which released his former quarters for Mr. Cardwell and his bride. The infirmary first floor became a social hall.

It should be noted that a room in the new hospital was dedicated to the memory of Bob Quin who attended the High School 1927–29 and died suddenly a year later. He was an outstanding leader, winning his letter in three sports and a monitorship his second year, an extremely rare accomplishment. His father was Bishop of Texas.

Early in the thirties the powers that be [*Aside to Memorician*

Daniel: shouldn't the "be" of those powers be "were"?] began planning a suitable event to celebrate the centennial in 1939. The most pressing need of the school then was more gymnasium space.

Stewart Memorial had been built before the size of the basketball court had been finally decided so that there are no sidelines. It had been designed to the specifications of A.J. Reach, a manufacturer of athletic equipment. The single court limited the number of teams that could practice. It had been the custom to excuse boys under fifteen from study-hall at 9:15. So a team of those boys had a half hour to practice every night during the winter.

So a decision was made to build a new gymnasium, to be known as Centennial Hall. A central building large enough for two courts side by side flanked by two wings was planned, one to be known as "The Cage" could be used for miscellaneous activities and the other to be an indoor swimming pool. The latter was never built. Incidentally it had long been rumored that the Packard-Laird Library at the Seminary was built in 1921 with money intended for an indoor swimming pool at the High School, causing the split of the Board of Trustees. There was no truth to this but it made a good story. Actually the school authorities did not favor a pool because of respiratory health problems.

Ground was broken for the new building in 1937; it was completed and in use well before the centennial date of October 15, 1939. The Old Boys Association met on October 14 in Liggett Hall and this was probably the last time that building with its potbellied stoves was used as an auditorium.

It should be noted that the date of October 15 coincided with the sesquicentennial of the adoption of the Book of Common Prayer.

Felix Kloman, rector of Old Christ Church in Philadelphia where the adoption took place, wanted Bishop Tucker to conduct a service of celebration there but instead the Presiding Bishop graced our celebration with his presence. The occasion was also notable for the presence of Dr. Blackford's five sons.

Mr. Carter used to keep the lower schoolroom during the day while also teaching two sections of ancient history and two sections of English history there. He also taught senior spelling and penmanship. He had the most beautiful flowing Spencerian handwriting. It was he who selected the eight four-syllable words (and

Centennial Hall

Blackford Hall, c. 1910

wrote them on the blackboard) that had to be used in writing columns (demerits).

Mr. Carter was given to making outrageous puns. "Dog in the ice-box" was "purp in de cooler" was "perpendicular." In 1929 we abjured Prohibition because the first two names on the school list of students were "Adams, Ailes" (Adam's ale: get it?—Joel B. Adams and Steve Ailes). The response to his quiet word-plays was deafening.

Mr. Carter's pet peeves were the fact that, according to him, the school worshipped the great gods of football and mathematics whereas he favored baseball and history.

In the evening study hall was from 7:20 to 9:45 and lights out in the dorms was 10:05. During examinations and just before there was a half hour of late study hall. A different teacher kept upper and lower study halls each night Monday through Friday. Those whose names began with a letter in the top half of the alphabet always sat in lower and the second half sat in upper. Lower was kept by Mr. Whittle on Mondays, my father on Tuesdays, etc. It was an article of faith that every new teacher would be severely tested as to his ability to keep a quiet study hall. Most passed easily but there was a notable exception. Mr. R. B. Campbell, who came in 1924 and was nicknamed "Boozy" (a nickname awarded him after he delivered a Philippic against drinking) kept upper study hall on Thursday nights. The amount of noise that came through the ceiling was amazing. A favorite teacher's device to find the cleverly hidden trouble maker's identity was to stick the whole student body involved five demerits. Then, invoking the honor system, the innocent could get theirs removed.

In this connection it is appropriate to recall the indignity heaped on Mr. Campbell by pieing (short-sheeting) his bed on Third Alumni. To the faculty this was not funny and the whole school was stuck 50 demerits to find the perpetrators. The two guilty boys lost their monitorships.

One of those boys later returned to the school as a teacher.

In each corner of the schoolroom was a large trash basket. On each nearby window was a pencil sharpener. By study-hall time the trash basket was generally quite full. On at least one occasion in my time an ingenious conspiracy took place. Someone put alarm clocks set to go off ten minutes apart in the bottoms of the trash baskets. The pencil sharpener shavings were dumped on top and the contents of an ink bottle added for good measure. The reader can imagine the rest of the scenario. It has been said that an EHS alumnus attending Massachusetts Institute of Technology perpetrated the same trick at a Boston Symphony concert.

The Big Game

Between the wars, that is between 1919 and 1939 inclusive, the High School beat Woodberry in football thirteen times and lost eight games, a creditable record full of memories. My first recollection of the rivalry is the bonfire which followed our victory in 1920. One of the matrons took me in tow and it was the first time I had stayed up through midnight. The next year we lost on Hoxton Field; but this was followed by three successive victories. The first was at Orange and was followed by a bonfire. This was the great undefeated team of George Morton, Hall Trapnell, Jimmy Bridges, Charlie Mackall, *et al.*

The typical procedure at the time was a telephone vigil in the office and when word of victory was received, the boys began building the bonfire. In those days "Monkeywrench" Cleveland built the bleachers which were exposed unpainted to the weather. After several years they would begin to rot so the two oldest were carried down to the front cow pasture and placed facing each other. Then the wooden food boxes that had accumulated behind the kitchen were placed on top with miscellaneous wood and paper. A collection would be taken up and my father would go to Alexandria and buy 30-ball Roman candles, enough for each boy to have at least one. Then came the wait for the team to make the rail trip from Orange to Alexandria. Vic Donaldson with his Reo Speedwagons would meet them and drive them out to school.

Mr. Hoxton would entrust his pistol to a teacher who would take up a position about a quarter mile down the road. When the Reo appeared, he would fire two shots and the fire would be lit. (One year Vic sabotaged the plan by driving out Duke Street instead of King Street.) The boys would then ring the bonfire and fire their Roman candles. After the fire died down everyone would adjourn to the porch of Hoxton House where the players and coaches would describe the game. This procedure was followed in 1920, 1922, 1924 and 1926. When we won on Hoxton Field in 1923 on a cold and windy day, there was no bonfire.

The next three years were lean but the pattern was broken in 1928. For the first time buses were chartered to drive the student body to Orange. The records of the two schools pointed to an almost certain Woodberry victory; but we were unprepared for the bonfire that our opponents had built just off the playing field before the game. No wonder Armistead Boothe lit it—between the halves! [Unhappy score: EHS-0, WFS-33.]

The next game was played in a snowstorm on Hoxton Field. The first thing our players did was dive in the mud before the game started. We played over our heads and held Woodberry and its big star, Bob Lassiter, later an all-American at Yale, to a single touchdown. [Heroic score: EHS-0, WFS-6.]

The year 1930 was a peak year for drama and excitement. Our team was undefeated and Woodberry had lost only one game. They had run up the score on one of our common opponents to intimidate us.

The game was to be played on Hanes Field, a gift of the Hanes Knitting Mill family; the field was to be dedicated before the game. The son of North Carolina's Governor, O. Max Gardner, played center for Woodberry; furthermore, a Woodberry alumnus, Lee Boatwright, was the fiancé of Sue Pollard, daughter of the Governor of Virginia. So both Governors and the entire student bodies of both schools were in attendance. [And did one Governor say to the other "It's a long time between drinks"?] As in 1928 a bonfire was built; but this time it was guarded by a man with a shotgun. It had been announced that the winning team's captain would light it after the game.

Woodberry had a quarterback, Walter Taylor, who had the reputation of being able to throw a football like a baseball. On the sixth play he connected with Ford for what turned out to be their lone touchdown. Charlie Hooff caught a short pass and ran 50 yards for our first touchdown. In the second quarter by hard slugging we managed to get a second touchdown and the score stood 12–7 in our favor. This was reported by phone to my father who was the only responsible person who had remained on the Hill. The second half was marked by many long unsuccessful Woodberry forward passes. The 12–7 score stood up and the game became one of our most dramatic victories. But that is not the end of the story. My father organized a bonfire and the boys arrived back at school before the team. This bonfire was built around the old horsedrawn omnibus that Mr. Mack used for years to haul High School boys.

There was no incentive or space to save the relic.

In 1931 for the first time ever a bonfire was built after our 9–0 win over Woodberry on our turf. How victories were celebrated after this I do not know but the string of five victories in a row beginning in 1935 must have exhausted the supply of combustible materials.

The Literary (?) Societies

The history of our literary societies need not be repeated here. Suffice it to say that by 1919 each one of the three had ample quarters, the Blackford Society occupied part of the first floor of its namesake building, the Fairfax Society the east end of First Memorial and the Wilmer Society occupied the little one-room building north of Hoxton House. It was later moved to the south one-room building. Membership in Wilmer was automatic for those boys under fifteen at the school opening but membership in the two senior societies was by invitation and blackballs were possible. By the early thirties Blackford had tended to become a club for boys from Baltimore and Georgia whereas boys from Richmond and Washington tended to be members of Fairfax. Each society member was required to sign a pledge which among other things prohibited entry on to the premises of another society. Meetings were usually held on Saturday nights before the movies and were supposed to feature reading, declamation and debating contests.

However, interest was flagging and the faculty had to coax the societies to run their contests to determine the Dual Contestants. It seemed like the biggest interest was getting in line after dinner to read the daily comics in the *Washington Post*. The societies subscribed to a number of magazines including *Life, Judge, Punch, Saturday Evening Post, Illustrated London News, Readers Digest, Literary Digest, Time*, etc.

The Fairfax vs Blackford rivalry was settled by the annual Athletic Day competition and the annual Dual Contest in the forensic arts. The former seemed to stir the most interest and came to be dominated by Fairfax which reigned supreme after 1918. In fact they were accused of padding their membership with all the promising athletes. Gold, silver and bronze medals were awarded the winners and it was customary for a member of the fair sex to hand out the awards in front of Stewart Gym at the conclusion of the games. Declining interest and the rapid development of track as an interscholastic sport prompted the demise of Athletic Day in 1923 after nearly fifty years of spirited intramural competition. (Athletic Day later became Field Day.) The annual Dual Contest continued to be held in Liggett Hall in the Spring during the twenties and thirties. Originally the contestants appeared in white tie and tails (borrowed of course) which were later downgraded to tuxedos. The joint celebration at Finals, also in Liggett Hall, was the culmination of the literary activities of the year and preceded the big dance on Final Monday.

Liggett Hall Entertainment

Dramatics were an off-and-on proposition during the 1920's and 1930's. Mr. Callaway was responsible for a revival of interest in 1924 with a spoofing of the teachers; "Faculty Follies" was an instant hit. The Tormentors Club was organized the following year and it put on one show a year for the next six years. Contrary to the custom of its predecessor, the "Liggett Hall Stock Company" which used local girls for the female parts, this club used boys to play both sexes. These productions were owing primarily to the talent and leadership of two Seminary students, Les Glenn (1925–27) and Bobo Baxter (1928–30). The former wrote original musical shows of which The Mad Mountaineer was the most memorable. The latter put on three plays: The Thirteenth Chair, The Man on the Box and Nothing But the Truth. The club was revived in 1933, again by Mr. Callaway, but interest was short lived.

The faculty always insisted that entertaiment must be provided for the boys whenever there was a free night. My father said more school property was damaged between the end of football season and the December examinations than at any other time during the school year. The night before Thanksgiving is a case in point. It was time to schedule one of Mr. Reade's inimitable readings, primarily from Dickens. These were given in Liggett Hall or the chapel. (Lectures were frequently given in both places. Through the 1920's the seating capacity of the Hall was adequate for most occasions; but once automobiles were in general use, more and more outside guests attended. In winter, heat was a problem. It was provided by pot bellied stoves located in alcoves along either side.)

An important entertainment in 1927 was a "musicale" presented by the combined glee clubs of the High School and Seminary. A featured artist was Mrs. Louise Homer Stires, the wife of a Seminary student. Her rendition of "The Italian Street Song" was certainly more memorable than Jeanette MacDonald's in the movie *Naughty Marietta*. Mrs. Stires was the daughter of Madame Louise Homer, one of the stars of the Golden Age of the Metropolitan who sang with Caruso. Mrs. Stires told the story of making an acoustical recording with her mother for Victor. Her own soprano voice was so thin in comparison with her mother's contraito that she had to stand a great deal closer to the horn when they sang the duet.

Avoca

In 1889 the Trustees ordered the construction of a residence on the site of the old High School garden for Dr. Carl E. Grammer, one of their new professors. This space is just east of the lower tennis courts. In 1898 my grandfather, Dr. Richard W. Micou, moved in with his family and occupied it until 1912. At this time the place was called (I don't know why) "Avoca." Dr. Cosby Bell then occupied the house until 1919 when the Rev. Dr. Thomas Kinloch Nelson, Seminary teacher and EHS chaplain, moved in. The Bells had no children and Dr. Nelson was unmarried. For one year, 1920–21, the house was occupied by Dr. Nelson's brother, Rev. R.B. Nelson, and his large family. His two older sons, Seddon and Bobby, aged about twelve and ten, attended the High School that year. I well remember an accident that occurred while they were there. The father in backing his Model T Ford out of the garage ran over his youngest son, Bruce, then aged about one-and-a-half years. The damage was only a broken leg!—which was repaired. The Nelson family moved to Winchester but all three sons returned to the High School later.

Dr. Tom Nelson resumed his occupancy of "Avoca" until the spring of 1926, when it was destroyed by fire. There had been in inkling of trouble during dinner the preceding Sunday. An alarm emptied the school dining room before boss was served. That time the fire was put out with hand-held soda extinguishers. However during school the following Wednesday (March 10) fire broke out again. This time it had gained too much headway to be put out by students and faculty; but the entire contents were saved. The Alexandria fire department pumped water through a hose laid to the skating pond but the house burned to the ground. The firemen pulled down the still-standing chimneys before leaving the site.

Since the Seminary and High School were now separate institutions, title to the vacant lot was now returned to EHS and the dividing line became a straight line from back of future Greenway Field all the way to Quaker Lane.

Real Estate

The original acreage of the school grounds was 80; it has grown to 130, owing to two gifts of William Winder Laird (EHS 1893–96). The first was in 1927 when the old Wise estate adjacent to the school on the northwest came on the market at approximately $1000 per acre. The size was thirty acres. My father opposed the deal on the premise that $30,000 at that time would have built several buildings; but he did not know real estate. The second gift came in the early thirties and added acreage farther west. At that time there was s public road between Seminary and Braddock Roads just behind Greenway Field, so the new Laird acres were separated from the rest of the campus. Since there were no homes fronting on this road, the school had it closed.

In the main hall there hung a map of the local area marked with a red line. This delineated "School bounds." Boys were permitted to roam this area without restriction.

The western limit was Bailey's Crossroads, the eastern was Janney's Lane and King Street Road. The southern boundary was Cameron Run and the northern was Glebe Road. A popular spot during the twenties was the railroad and Cameron Run because of the trains that took the boys home. The country's communication network at this time was the telegraph whose lines ran along railroad rights of way. Throwing rocks at the insulators was a fun thing to do until railroad detectives visited Mr. Hoxton. He threatened to put the tracks off bounds but in the end the culprits were forgiven.

In back of the school running for several miles were the remains of earthworks thrown up during the Civil War. In the twenties the line of forts could still be followed for a considerable distance.

No discussion of the times would be complete without mention of the "Boulevard" or "Bouly" as it was generally known. It was a gravel walk just south of and adjacent to Seminary Road beginning opposite the south entrance to the Seminary grounds and extending eastward in a straight line to Quaker Lane. At that time the intersection was about a hundred yards south of Janney's Lane.

From there it paralleled the west side of Quaker Lane to the top
of the steep hill about a hundred yards from Duke Street Road.
A beautiful view of the Potomac River and Hunting Creek could
be had at the south end. It was most popular as a place to take
girls.

(Before my time, EHS boys referred to their girlfriends as "cal-
ics" or "calicos.")

Just north of Leesburg Road (now occupied by Fairlington) was
a very large open field. In the early postwar years barnstorming
pilots kept a Jenny airplane there and took riders up for six minutes
at five dollars per head. The boys were not encouraged to patronize
but some did.

Recreation

Besides roaming the High School environs, the boys most enthusiastically patronized places where they could spend their
money. The opportunities were many and varied. Candy and
chewing gum were available at the "Mish," an arm of the Missionary Society. It had a room in Stewart Gymnasium basement
and representatives prowled the bleachers during athletic contests.
Their greatest coup was the introduction of Eskimo Pies during
the baseball seasons in the late twenties.

There were at least four nearby stores where goods of this nature
could be bought. First there were the Donaldson brothers, Victor
and Bernard, or Vic and Bun as they were more popularly known.
Vic operated the store in Mudtown (a brick building replaced the
one burned down in 1918) and Bun ran the one on Seminary Road
west of the School. The latter soon became the number one han-
gout.

There was also the store across Quaker Lane just south of the
school entrance. The owner, Mr. Mack, was the one-time horsedrawn omnibus driver. He died in 1918 and the store did not
long survive. Then there was Stanton's store on Duke Street Road
at the foot of Quaker Lane. This store was also the local voting
precinct.

The school prior to about 1930 did not provide any athletic
uniforms although it did provide equipment. Mr. Carter filled this
void by operating an athletic shop in the gym basement. He was
Mr. A.G. Spalding in person although other cheaper brands were
available. Afterwards the Athletic Association gradually began
supplying uniforms to the varsity teams.

Various boys would obtain concessions for supplying non-necessities such as school rings, other jewelry, memory books, writing paper, belt buckles, pennants etc, all emblazoned with the school seal or "E.H.S." or "Episcopal." At the end of the school year these concessions were sold to the highest bidder, but in 1932 the Athletic Association bought them all and used the profits to support the teams.

A small room between the chapel and lower school room was known as the "Book Closet." Every day after dinner it would be open for boys to buy stationery and books. Chits instead of cash were accepted. When Finals came, boys who were returning the next year could store belongings, including books, in marked boxes for future use; but most boys never bothered. School was out and that was that. Books were scattered everywhere and early returners could help themselves. The school decided these books should be collected and sold to the students at half price for the benefit of the Missionary Society.

But the student's biggest opportunity for splurging was the weekly trip to Washington. Vic Donaldson had a fleet of Reo Speedwagons which would seat about twenty to twenty-five boys on bench seats facing each other with roll down flaps for bad weather. They were used to haul teams to local contests. On Monday mornings after chapel the buses were lined up in front of Blackford and the infirmary. As soon as one was loaded it headed for Washington.

The objective of many boys, as I mentioned before, was to see as many movies as possible. All the major theaters opened their doors at 11 A.M. so it was no trouble to take in three films or sit through one for three showings. The charge before one o'clock was 25 cents. A favorite was the burlesque theater, Gayety, on 9th street between E and F streets, euphemistically known as the "9th St. Opera House." Vic's buses were parked on D street between 14th and 15th which was immediately behind Poli's theater. As soon as a bus was filled it pulled out and the last one left at six o'clock.

Boys could shop for almost anything they wanted on F street and frequently met in Peacock Alley in the Willard Hotel. But shopping for clothes was not necessary as all the big clothing stores frequently sent representatives out to school and displayed their wares in the northeast room on the first floor of Stewart Gym.

Those were the days, my friend,/ We thought they'd never end . . .
Red Duer, Jim Meem, Roy Mason, 1931.

. . . but they did. Rusty Anderson, Bo Mueller, Dean Smith, 1989.

Sunday

The rising bell was delayed to eight o'clock Sundays following the ten o'clock dorm bell on Saturday nights. Sunday was, above all, a day of rest. No manner of school work or organized athletics was required. Ample Sunday editions of the *Washington Post, Star* and *Times-Herald* were available. They were primarily bought for the funny papers ("Katzenjammer Kids," "Mutt & Jeff," "Happy Hooligan," "Hairbreadth Harry" etc) and the rest of the paper littered the campus.

Eleven o'clock service in the Seminary chapel was mandatory and we were all dressed to the nines. The boys occupied the north side of the nave and overflowed into the north and south galleries. The choir was composed of High School boys and attendance was carefully checked by a monitor sitting in the gallery. Mrs. Carter was choir mother which meant she was in charge of vestments. The collection was taken up by two monitors wearing detachable stiff collars. (Once when an Old Boy dropped a $50 bill in the plate, the monitor very nearly dropped it!) Communion was the First Sunday of the month and most boys, communicants or not, took the opportunity to leave just before the prayer for the Whole State of Christ's Church. Attendance at the four o'clock Bible Class was no longer compulsory, some time in the early 1920's, but boys were required to register their presence on the grounds by means of a check-off. So the bell continued to be rung and monitors were sent around with a school list to do the checking.

The day's devotions were concluded at a service of evening prayer at 8:30 in the school chapel at which two monitors in stiff collars and white cravats read the lessons. The canticles sung at the end of each lesson were the *Bonum est confiteri* and the *Nunc dimittis*. The chaplain preached a sermon one Sunday a month.

On the last Sunday before Christmas vacation Mr. Reade read, in his never-to-be-forgotten style, either the Bird or the Dickens Christmas Carol. Special hymns were sung at the first and last Sunday services of the session: "Lord, behold us with Thy blessing" and "Lord, dismiss us with Thy blessing." The latter was frequently sung to the tune "Sicilian Mariners."

During the remaining hour of the day boys were encouraged to make personal calls on the faculty in their homes or rooms.

Even study hall was never convened on Sunday. With the increasing ease of motor transportation, it became common to have a Saturday holiday when a major athletic contest was scheduled at another school. These were always followed by classes on Monday. In order to refresh memories of lessons studied the preceding Friday night, it was common to have a brief study hall after chapel on Monday morning. With this bit of history it would seem that the choice of a weekly holiday on Monday was eminently logical.

On the subject of religious services: for some unexplained reason Mr. Reade, who always played the foot-pumped organ in chapel, did not approve the Church hymnal of 1916.

The High School continued to use the edition of 1892, even though the Seminary had belatedly changed over. Invariably the first two and the last verses of hymns were sung. Mr. Reade had favorites, because we sang certain hymns repeatedly, especially militant ones. To this day when a familiar hymn is sung in church (which is not often), I find no need for a hymnal during the first two and last verses.

There were two reprehensible customs practiced in chapel in those days. The first was a practical joke: placing an open hymnal or prayer book upright under where the boy next to you was going to sit. The result was a damaged book and a surprised look. The second was writing game scores and miscellaneous comments on the blank pages at the beginning and end of these books. By reading these anonymous remarks the faculty could get some feedback.

Other Religious Observances

Mr. Hoxton always presided over daily chapel. On alternate days Mr. Reade read a lesson from the Bible after an opening hymn. Mr. Hoxton would lead the responsive reading of a psalm.

Every meal was prefaced by grace pronounced by Mr. Hoxton with the boys standing. Supper was always concluded (except on Sundays) with a Bible reading with the boys seated. Then we stood while the prayer "Lighten our darkness" was read. On one occasion Mr. Hoxton absent-mindedly recited grace again instead of the prayer. When the Principal was absent Mr. Reade did the honors and if both were elsewhere my father held forth.

This reminiscence would be incomplete without mention of Mr. Henry Justice Miller of the Seminary (1925–29). He was an accomplished organist who had never taken a lesson. He was also choir master during his three Seminary years; also one other year, when he taught English at EHS. Several times during the year

Hank would take over Sunday night chapel and conduct an all-hymn service which was very popular. To stiffen our morale during those lean football years, he wrote a fighting song: "Come on boys we've got to beat them," to the tune of "On Wisconsin."

On Wednesdays before the monthly communion service those boys planning to participate met with Mr. Nelson in the school chapel at the beginning of study-hall for a brief devotional service of preparation.

Friday night meetings before study-hall were conducted weekly by Seminary students. This was a regular feature of school life for many years. Usually three or four men were the leaders. Many were Old Boys, while others were men who were helping with the coaching of our athletic teams. Prominent among these was John E. Hines; he later became Presiding Bishop. All Seminary students were accorded the title Mr. because they were men and not boys. No first names were ever used. In fact the younger faculty members addressed the older ones by that title. No one addressed Mr. Hoxton as "Archie" except my father and Mr. Reade.

Public Events

There is no record of the school's reaction to the armistice in 1918; but the burial of the Unknown Soldier in Arlington on November 11, 1921, was granted as a holiday. Very few EHS boys saw both the parade on Pennsylvania Avenue and the ceremonies at the Amphitheater. The worst traffic jam ever to hit Washington clogged every route across the Potomac, and there were only two bridges. The 14th Street Bridge was plugged with four lanes of traffic, all headed south.

School was not in session on August 4, 1923, when Mr. Stuart appeared at breakfast in the main dining room with a newspaper announcing the death of President Harding. There were immediate expressions of regret although there were few supporters of Harding present.

A half holiday was announced for November 1, 1923, so that boys could attend the cornerstone laying at the George Washington Masonic Memorial on Shooter's Hill. President Coolidge did the honors.

A custom of long standing was honored on March 4, 1925, when a holiday was granted for the inauguration of Calvin Coolidge. It is reported that Dr. Blackford, in granting the holiday for the inaugural of Hayes in 1877, said he did not understand how anyone could witness the greatest thief in U.S. history taking the oath of office—in 1929 the day fell on a Monday, so I was cheated out of my only chance for a holiday in my seven years as a student. In 1937 the inauguration date was changed to January 20th.

On May 21, 1927, during the late innings of our baseball victory over Woodberry, the game was interrupted by newsboys rushing towards the bleachers from the outfield yelling "Extra, Extra!" The headlines screamed "Lindbergh Victor!" That was how we learned that *The Spirit of St. Louis* had landed safely in Paris.

Schoolroom decorum was interrupted in early December, 1927, by the drone of a very low-flying airplane. Pencils shot up for permission to look out the window. It was not until that evening that we learned that the plane was *The Spirit of St. Louis* which had just taken off from Bolling Field in Washington with a full load of gasoline and Lindbergh at the controls. He was struggling to gain altitude for his non-stop flight to Mexico City.

The U.S. Army airplane *Question Mark* flew over on March 15, 1929. This was the first plane to be refueled in the air; it set an endurance record. The technique was developed by planes flying out of Bolling Field.

The Hill Community

Besides the children at the High School there were others in the community. For the boys before we reached High School age, and for all the girls, education was a problem. The nearest public schools were at Bailey's Crossroads and Alexandria. Their reputation was poor. However there were three maiden Worthington sisters who lived at the foot of the Boulevard between Cooper Dawson's house and Richard Ely's house. (The former is well known in High School circles and the latter had been a prominent economist in Washington.) One of the sisters, Miss Maria, was the Seminary librarian. Another sister, Miss Virginia, ran a one-room school for children in her house. Her health failed in about 1920 and her place was taken by the third sister, Miss Mary. I began attending in the fall of 1920 along with my sister, Margaret. Other pupils were Nick Carter, Kin and Jane Byrd Shackelford from the High School, Charlie Hooff (who lived just across Quaker Lane), Virginia Cary Dawson (Cooper's sister), Ned Ely (who lived next door and was always late) and about half a dozen other neighborhood children. School was from 9 to 12:30 so we could get back to EHS in time for dinner.

Behind the house was an old Civil War powder magazine covered with dirt which stood about ten feet high. The sides were grown up with trees but the top was clear and level. Before school took in there was always a game of "chicken liver" on top. Anyone caught in the open by "it" in turn became "it."

After about three years, our parents decided that the education we were receiving was not adequate. So in 1923–24 Virginia Cary Dawson, Kin Shackelford, Margaret and I were tutored by Mrs. Joseph Waterman, the wife of a Seminary student, who lived in Miss Carrie Hooff's home on Quaker Lane. Charlie Hooff now lives in this house. Mrs. Waterman's son Joe was about two years old at this time. He later attended EHS. He gave his life in World War II.

While the boys usually entered the High School, the girls had no place to go; the need was so acute that parents on the Hill and in Alexandria got together and founded St. Agnes School in 1924. Boys were accepted until they were ready to attend EHS.

The arrival of babies born to faculty wives was not a subject for discussion. The pregnant ladies quietly stopped going to the school dining room and meals were carried out to them, as was the case when anyone was sick.

For eighteen years it seemed as if they operated on a three-year plan. Jack Daniel and Kin Shackelford were born in 1910, Nick Carter and I were born in 1913, Flick Hoxton in 1916, Bobby Carter in 1919, Dick Williams in 1922, Margaret Tomkins in 1925, John Daniel in 1928. Others born outside that cycle were Anne Daniel and Frank Williams in 1923 and Athlynn Williams in 1927.

Beginning with Captain Dick Williams' marriage to Miss Gertrude Bass in 1919 a number of weddings involving teachers or their offspring occurred prior to 1941. Mr. Daniel and Miss Marguerite Williams were married December 12, 1921. She was Mr. Williams' sister. Mr. Reade and his family were involved in the most marriages. There were about four over a five-year span. His daughter Evelyn married star EHS athlete Lee Trenholm '18. She went on the stage and began acting in films which raised a lot of eyebrows on the Hill. Frank Reade '14, who substituted during his father's sabbatical in 1922–23, was married during the Christmas holidays. Daughter Mary Willoughby married a teacher, Mr. William Andrew Copenhaver, in 1924. Mr. Reade himself was remarried during this period to Miss Nan Hutter Griffin.

The next wedding, that of Mr. Tompkins to Miss Margaret Bird during the 1924 Finals, has already been described.

On Tuesday, May 21, 1929, Miss Mary Earle Hoxton, daughter of the Principal, was married to William Whann Mackall '12 who had been head monitor.

Supper was at 5:15 so the boys could attend the 7 o'clock ceremony. At 9:20 study-hall was let out to give the couple a send-off. Someone rigged a stick through the steering wheel of Mr. Hoxton's car so that the horn would blow continuously and when the bride's father appeared with a plate of wedding cake, he was so thoroughly mobbed that the cake went flying.

The next wedding was that of Miss Evelyn Page Shackelford to James T. Murfee on October 4, 1930. Her sisters, Kin and Jane Byrd, were maids of honor and seven-year-old Frank Williams was ring bearer.

The marriage front was quiet until about 1934 when Mr. Cardwell and Miss Marion Calhoun, sister of Phinizy '29 and Lawson '32, tied the knot. This was followed later in the decade by the nuptials of Mr. Latham (the perennial bachelor) and Miss Ella Jesse. These last two marriages produced more children on the Hill. Young Charlie Tompkins was born about 1936.

This about covers the marriages and births in the faculty families up to 1941. Now I must sadly recall a few deaths. My mother was the first to go. She was caught in the flu epidemic of 1918 and died while school was temporarily closed, October 4–29. As a result my older brother, Jack, at the age of eight, began attending classes; my sister and I were sent to my grandmother's farm near Charles Town, West Virginia.

Jack continued in school and won the Liggett Gold Medal for excellence in general scholarship in 1920 at the age of nine. This award was open to all boys under fifteen at the opening of school. Three months later he caught diphtheria and died. Mrs. Mary Robertson Reade also died soon after my mother. She sat immediately behind me in the school dining room; she always wore a silver watch on a long chain, which fascinated me. She promised to give it to me if I would come and live with her. Their daughter Stella died of TB at Saranac Lake on February 12, 1929. The school was spared any more such occasions until Kin Shackelford developed a fatal brain tumor in about 1934. She had been serving as Mr. Hoxton's secretary and had won an affectionate place in the hearts of all who knew her.

Hallowe'en

Only once between the wars did the boys kick up their heels on "mischief night." They went on a rampage in 1920. Between supper and study-hall these pranks were accomplished: Mr. Carter's Ford was positioned alongside of Memorial. Mr. Shackelford's Ford likewise found itself next to Alumni. Mr. Speidel's Saxon automobile appeared on the gymnasium porch. Bobby Carter's baby carriage was suspended from the gymnasium roof, the children's velocipedes and toy wagons were put up the trees around Hoxton Circle and Mrs. Stuart's porch chairs disappeared under Liggett Hall. One wonders why the cars belonging to Messrs. Hoxton, Daniel and Stuart were not disturbed.

This type of mischief was quickly brought under control. Mr. Hoxton gave the boys from the end of breakfast until chapel to return all items to their proper places under a threat of a big demerit penalty.

Some years later a horn sounded in Mr. Fleming's study hall on Hallowe'en. This sparked a lot of tittering and a frown from Lukey. A few minutes later the horn sounded again with a louder response. Five demerits for the whole study hall was threatened if the disruption was repeated. No one to this day knows why Bobby Carter, under the open windows, did not blow his horn a third time.

U. S. Mail

Originally Theological Seminary was a separate and independent post office but Alexandria took it over and made it a branch station. It was located in the northeast first floor room in St. George's Hall under the postmastership of Miss Spofford. By 1925 a very small frame building had been built just behind St. George's for this purpose and Mrs. W.A. Cleveland was post mistress. Her husband, a cousin of "Monkeywrench," was in charge of the Seminary's buildings and grounds. They and their three children, Lucy, Billy and Anne, lived in a house adjacent to the Seminary barn on Seminary Road immediately south of St. George's.

There was at this time an official U.S. mailbox in the main hall

The mail, 1988. "If you are Mr. Jarvis Todd Baker, you may have already won One Million Dollars!"

at the High School where letters could be mailed. But this service was lost in the Coolidge economy drive of 1925. One of the servants had the daily job of pushing a hand cart to the post office to get the mail. This was sorted in the school office and faculty mail was put up in pigeon hole boxes under the steps in the main hall next to the pay telephone booth. Mail for the students was placed in a metal satchel-sized container which was taken to the dining room at the beginning of dinner. Monitors thereupon distributed it. This way, our correspondence was hardly private—feminine handwriting could be easily recognized and of course it was not always a mother writing to a son.

In the late 1930's, individual boxes with combination locks for each student were installed next to the office.

School Office

From Dr. Blackford's time until the late twenties, the south one-room building next to Hoxton House was the nerve center of the operation. I became quite familiar with it when school was not in session, because when Mr. Hoxton was not sitting at the desk, my father was. When I first knew the room, the outside entrance was on the west side and a window on the south. Because of prevailing westerly winds these two features were reversed. The school safe occupied the southeast corner. It was opened with a special key. Mr. Hoxton had one and my father the other which he carried in his wallet.

Next to the safe on the east wall was Mr. Hoxton's rolltop desk which was always locked when neither man was present. Mounted on a corner of the desk was the school telephone, Alexandria 229. The only extension was in Mr. Hoxton's bedroom. It was the kind that needed two hands to operate so it was mounted on an arm that could be swung 250° and extended about 30″. Next was the east window followed by the file cabinets. On the north side there were a door to Mr. Hoxton's study and shelves with glass doors. My father used to tell a story about the time Mrs. Blackford came in looking for something and not wishing to disturb her husband she began poking at some boxes on the top shelf. Soon a box came crashing down. At that the beloved Principal without looking up from his desk muttered: "Ah! My dear, may I suggest you get an axe."

Between the west door and the window was another desk for Mr. Stuart but, although it was piled high, he rarely sat at it. Along the south wall was a bookcase and another safe (combination type) that contained matters relating to the Board of Trustees and was rarely opened. In the center of the room was the typewriter desk and its trusty "Underwood No. 5." By 1930 the Wilmer Society was occupying the space and the office had been moved to the main building.

In the summer of 1922 Dr. Kinsolving in Baltimore was writing *The Story of a Southern School* and my father was constantly looking up facts for him.

One incident stands out in my memory. Late in August one summer a letter came to Mr. Hoxton from The University of the South offering him the honorary degree of Doctor of Literature. I was present when my father broke the news to him. Although he was not unmindful of the honor, he detested the thought of being addressed as Dr. Hoxton. If he could have, I believe he would have turned it down; but in the end he accepted it.

When school closed for the summer my father had two immediate jobs to do: first, close out the school books and, second, publish the school catalogue. One year (1929) I took on the responsibility of compiling the High List for the previous session. For some inexplicable reason I left off the name of James C. Meem and it had to be hand-written in each copy. I did not participate further in getting out the catalogue.

Although Mr. Stuart at one time had check signing privileges, only Mr. Hoxton had that privilege during this period. In order to allow bills to be paid in a timely fashion and provide money for daily operations during his absence, he would leave a number of checks signed in blank for my father to use.

Also during this period it was customary for Mr. Hoxton to have two boys from the school as secretaries or administrative assistants. They were more popularly known as flunkeys.

The Seminary

Just as the EHS was known as *the* High School and UVA was known as *the* University, Virginia Theological Seminary was referred to as *the* Seminary. Anyone who attended all three was said to have gone to *the* Trinity. The intimate connection between the High School and the Seminary has been amply documented.

From the beginning I attended the Seminary Sunday School. It met in prayer hall on the first floor of Aspinwall Hall with classes meeting in the various lecture rooms. The first superintendant that I remember was Richard H. Baker '16. Other teachers that I had were Big Tuie Kinsolving '14, Mr. C.V. Tompkins and Al Griffiths, who coached the cake team.

Athletic facilities for the Seminary were meager but there was a gymnasium just south of the central heating plant. I can recall going to a community Hallowe'en party in this building. By 1925 this building had been razed and Sparrow Hall had been constructed on the site. Prayer hall was moved to this building, but the Sunday School was moved to a frame building on Seminary Road that had been constructed as a mission chapel for black people. I continued to attend Sunday School through 1931 along with Nick Carter and a few others. Later the Sunday School was moved into Sparrow Hall. The only Seminary professor at this time with a child the same age as myself was Dr. Paca Kennedy, whose son was William Paca Kennedy.

The Packard-Laird Library was built in 1921. The old library, Wilmer Hall, was turned to new use as a refectory. Originally, Wilmer Hall had a circular staircase to reach the stacks; this structure was fascinating to the small fry.

There were six professors in 1919. Dr. Crawford, retired dean, still occupied "Wilderness" but was soon to be replaced by Dr. Bell. Dr. Wallis lived in "Oakwood" next to the chapel; he was succeeded by the Reverend Beverley D. Tucker. The last named served only three years and was replaced by his brother, Bishop Henry St. George Tucker. The Bishop was soon elected Bishop Coadjutor of Virginia and succeeded Bishop Brown in 1927. About this time a seventh professor was added to the faculty and a "Deanery" was built between "Oakwood" and "Melrose." The latter, across Seminary Road, had been the home of Dr. Berryman Green who was dean in the early twenties. Dr. Rollins occupied "Maywood" which was north of the main group of buildings.

The Seminary had a mandatory retirement age of sixty-seven or sixty-eight whereas the High School had none at this time. Under this rule Dr. Green retired as Dean and was succeeded by Dr. Rollins. He was later caught by the same rule and was replaced by Dr. Zabriskie. The latter had been a student in 1921–24 and was active in Friday night meetings at the High School before becoming a professor. Other professors who joined the faculty in the thirties were Dr. Brown-Sermon and Messrs. Stanley, Mollegen, Lowery and Ball.

The Honor System and Examinations

This system is probably the most written-about aspect of High School life, and Mr. Hoxton's talks certainly covered the subject. There has however been some discussion as to its origin. Did it come directly from the University, which instituted it in 1840?

Some years ago when a West Point cribbing scandal was in all the newspapers, I recall reading about their honor system and I was particularly impressed with its similarity with that at EHS. It is different in certain details from the UVA system, particularly as to emphasis on *not giving* aid. From this I have surmised that Colonel Hoxton [the Principal's father], who was a West Point graduate, brought it to the school when he joined Dr. Blackford's staff in 1870.

Blue books were not used for examinations in the 1920's and 1930's. Instead, special-legal sized ruled paper was issued. Each examination paper was bound with two brass fasteners at the top and included the question sheet. This discouraged the building of exam libraries. The last page reverse bore the signed pledge, date, subject, and the teacher's initials at the bottom. In order to pass a course, it was necessary to obtain a passing average on the Christmas, spring and final examinations. The passing grade was

75 out of 100 and daily class grades did not count. A common explanation for this was: "Would you want the surgeon in the middle of an operation to have to stop and refer to the textbook?"

One of my little jobs to help my father when I was old enough to count was to put fourteen brass fasteners in little envelopes for handing out with the special exam paper. History exams usually required fifteen pages and my father always spent upwards of the next three days reading some sixty papers. Four hours with a ten-minute recess at 11 o'clock were allotted on each exam day and no paper could be handed in until three hours had elapsed.

Spelling and Sacred Studies exams were on Mondays. The former took but a few minutes and more than eight words out of 100 missed constituted a failing grade. An average of four words missed during the year exempted a boy from senior spelling classes the following year. Sacred Studies exams lasted an hour. Since many a boy rushed through his math exam on the last Saturday to catch the train home, the two minor exams were shifted to the last day.

A major simplification of the commencement exercises took place around 1923. Prior to this, each boy received a certificate for each course taken, printed in black if he had failed one of the three exams, in gold if otherwise, and these facts were read out by Mr. Hoxton. The simplification was combining all examination grades on a single document which was then passed out to individuals in groups by all the teachers who were seated on the Liggett Hall platform.

Miscellaneous

There is a little known skeleton in my father's closet. He and Mr. Whittle made and drank home brew in our pantry in the fall of 1920. I should know because I helped to cap the bottles. None was made after my father's remarriage.

It is interesting to note that when Congress in 1933 passed a law legalizing 3.2 percent beer on the grounds that it was non-intoxicating, the school would have none of it. As far as the monitor's pledge was concerned the limit remained one-half of one percent.

A not so funny game was played by the boys on each other around 1930. It consisted of grabbing at each other's flies and saying "Three o'clock in Petersburg." Then the victim with em-

Monitors, 1924. Head Monitor: Woodard, E.L. Senior Monitors: Bridges, J.R., Holland, N.L., Page, J.G., Thomas, G.C. Monitors: Boogher, D.A., Boothe, A.L., Burwell, A.S.C., Ferguson, W.McL., Garnett, T.S., Greene, J.B.T., Hall, D.D., Hammond, L.M., Hemingway, W.R., Holbrook, W.G., Leigh, S.L., Mabley, J., Moncure, T.J., Morrison, F.M., Moss, H.H., Philbrick, H.C., Pinkerton, A.W., Randall, C.C., Randolph, M.E., Taliaferro, B.W., Taylor, J.M., Jr., Taylor, W.H., IV, Tyler, A., Jr., Tyler, J.P., Jr., Willett, J.A., Jr., Williams, A.A., Wilmer, C.B., Jr., Wood, W.H., Jr.

barrassment had to rebutton his fly. This was especially common on Sunday mornings when the boys gathered outside the Seminary chapel and ladies were present. Fortunately zipper flies render this game impossible to revive.

Radio came to the High School with a rush in 1923. There had been experimentation in the physics laboratory and Mr. Shackelford, who taught senior physics then, said that he had heard voice broadcasts as early as 1918. The big naval wireless station with its three towers, one taller than the Washington Monument, which was located south of Fort Myer, was easy to pick up; but there was little of interest broadcast except time signals at noon and 10:00 P.M.

Some of the boys had crystal sets in the dorms, probably as

Monitors, 1925. Head Monitor: Burwell, W.S.C. Senior Monitors: Marston, H.L., Moss, H.H., Randolph, M.E., Taylor, G.R., Tyler, J.P., Jr., Wood, W.H. Monitors: Albertson, R.B., Binford, C.T., Bryan, D.T., Buck, H.L., Buxton, R.V., Clay, W.L., Jr., Conley, E.T., Jr., Daniel, G., Jr., Every, E.H., Jr., Faulconer, P.H., Flippin, H.F., Gamble, E.L., Garnett, T.S., Jr., Hammond, L.M., Harris, F.M., Harrison, J.H., Hubbard, R.B., Mackall, L., Jr., Maulsby, D.L., Metz, J.D., Moncure, W.A., Moore, W.P., Jr., Morris, J.C., Jr., Sebrell, J.N., Strider, I.H., Swift, E.W., Jr., Taylor, W.H., Thomas, J.W., Tyler, J.P., Williams, F.C.

early as 1922. My father reported having heard one that used a bed spring for an antenna. The Hoxtons were the first on the faculty to get a crystal set. It was set up in their north bedroom and I used to be invited over at six o'clock to listen with Flick to a bedtime story using earphones. Shortly thereafter my father bought an identical set. It cost $8.50 and came complete with antenna wire, insulators, lead-in and ground wires plus the set and a pair of earphones. The set had a coil for station selection and a cat whisker to find a sensitive spot on the galena crystal. There were several Washington stations but the only one still on the air is WRC.

During the Dempsey vs Tunney fight in 1927 Jimmy Strider listened in over Mr. Hoxton's radio in the north bedroom and using a megaphone, rebroadcast it to the student-body assembled outside.

On January 25, 1928, a scarlet fever epidemic broke out. There were about ten cases in all. Dr. Dyer of the U.S. Public Health Service came out from Washington and administered the Dick Test for immunity to everybody lined up in the chapel. About two thirds of the school proved to be susceptible and the school was quarantined. Then Dr. Dyer began giving a series of five experimental serum shots six days apart after which everyone was re-tested. I do not believe the experimental vaccine was judged to be a great success. Because of the quarantine a Monday holiday was cancelled and a day added to spring vacation.

About 1931 there was a mystery man who came out and volunteered his services as an athletic trainer. He went by the name of Mr. Ball; but nobody knew whence he came. It was rumored that he was an FBI agent and carried a gun in his little black satchel. He must have been checked out by Mr. Hoxton and Mr. Tompkins, but no one ever knew for sure. Anyhow his work was much appreciated for about two years, and led to the hiring of a full-time trainer later, in the person of Al Seaman.

Graduation and World War II

It became quite evident during the Second World War that our conditions for graduation were out of synch with the rest of the country. In general, work at the sixth form level was equivalent to college work. Graduation requirements were completion of the sixth form in four major subjects and the fifth form in another. For financial or other reasons, many qualified boys were unable to return to graduate; but admission to college could easily be obtained with completion of the fifth form. As a result, the four-year curriculum was gradually adopted.

Demerits and "Voluntary"

As is still the case today, causing a disturbance in school or dorm and being late for meals, chapel or study-hall usually cost the guilty a demerit or two. If more than four or less than eleven demerits were incurred in one week, they could be worked off Monday morning by walking around the school buildings four times per demerit (equivalent to a mile).

If more than ten were incurred, the culprit was required to write them off at eight columns per demerit. Mr. Callaway was the disciplinarian in charge. There were no alternatives to these two methods until later in the 1930's. If the time required exceeded that available on Monday, the writing of demerits was continued in "Voluntary." This was a period from 5 to 6:30 during which the schoolroom was open for voluntary study, writing misspelled words twenty-five times and working off any other impositions. If anyone desired to leave the schoolroom during the day for any reason including going to the bathroom he could go "out on four" for ten minutes by raising four fingers. This meant he voluntarily agreed to write four columns in voluntary.

Just for the record: here is how the columns were written. Mr. Carter wrote eight words of four syllables on the blackboard. A special tablet of foolscap was required. This paper containing forty ruled lines was wide enough for four columns. Each column had to be set apart with vertical lines and numbered from one to forty. The blank spaces had to be filled in with the eight words in succession, five times for each column. Many a boy's handwriting was ruined by this procedure!

Summer School

At the close of each session there were a number of boys planning to go to northern colleges. This meant college board examinations, so key faculty members, heads of the various departments, would organize a summer school for two or three weeks after Finals. Boys who had completed some college equivalent work could take "advanced standing" examinations for UVA credit.

As an interesting sideline because normal school rules did not apply, it was not unusual for a summer school student to buy a well-used automobile in Washington for around $25. The big attraction was that a license and title could be gotten for $3.

Smoking

At best the school took a dim view of smoking. However, on attaining the age of seventeen and with written permission from home, a boy could indulge the habit. Violators were punished to the tune of 15 demerits for the first offense and 30 for the second. At this point a pledge to refrain was exacted and a violation meant instant dismissal. However, permission to smoke was hedged with numerous restrictions. Smoking in buildings was prohibited except in Egypt, the room in the basement of Stewart Gym. Also smoking on the afternoon of an athletic contest was strictly banned. Benches on the south side of Alumni and the gym were the most popular locales. On rainy days boys were tempted to indulge in the basement of the dorms.

There is a story that Mr. Hoxton sent a boy one afternoon to the basement of Memorial to tell the boys to stop smoking; he was about to make a tour of inspection.

Each boy was expected to make his own bed each morning. One clean sheet was issued each week. After chapel Mr. Tompkins and Mr. Hoxton made the daily inspection which included the trunk storage areas in the basements, so they were well aware of what went on on rainy afternoons. Locker inspections also took place periodically.

No discussion of smoking at the High School would be complete without mentioning where the faculty stood on the subject. The senior three teachers, Messrs. Hoxton, Reade and Daniel, were non-smokers. Mr. Shackelford smoked a pipe. (His zipper-closed tobacco pouch was the first zipper I ever saw, around 1924.) But Messrs. Carter, Williams, Whittle, Callaway and Tompkins were cigarette fiends.

Opening of School

In earlier days some older boys considered it appropriate to appear at opening supper somewhat under the influence—hence the monitor's pledge contained a provision outlawing alcoholic consumption twenty-four hours before school opening and after closing. School always took in at 6:30 supper, in September, January, March and April. Dormitory space was always assigned in advance but all other permanent seating was assigned later. Study hall commenced at 7:20 under the direction of Mr. Carter.

After chapel on the first day the literary societies were reorganized. Then the boys lined up to purchase stationery at the book closet. This was followed by a fifty-word spelling test for all except those exempt. To be exempt permanently one had to have missed no more than twelve words (increased from six in 1929) on the three hundred-word senior spelling exams of the previous year. This was followed by the writing of a short composition by all new boys to determine their level of English competence.

Prior to 1930 there was always a call for football candidates that first afternoon. But thereafter the candidates (by invitation) assembled about ten days prior to opening day for early practice.

The second day of school was a trial run with shortened periods through a preliminary schedule of classes. On the third day school began to function on a "full head of steam" (to use Mr. Hoxton's expression).

During the first two weeks each new boy met with Mr. Hoxton during study hall to review his course load, and the old boys met with my father to do the same. This was the extent of guidance counselling as practiced in those days.

Monitors, 1933. Head Monitor: Brookings, W.DuB. Senior Monitors: Fishburne, J.R., Moncure, E.C., Swift, H.W., Tufts, J.R. Monitors: Adams, A.P., Jr., Ballinger, P.F., Barnwell, N.L., Bird, R.M., Brawley, B., Brown, D.T., Bryan, J., III, Burke, J.W., Jr., Burwell, G.A., Byrd, C.M., Campbell, W.C., Cay, J.E., Jr., Davis, H.S., Gooch, W.R., Gordon, C.M., Gordon, W.T., Handlan, J.M., Hanson, K.M., Hoxton, A.R., Jr., Kopper, S.K.C., Lankford, R.E., Lee, L., Jr., MacRae, G.D., Mason, D.K., Mason, J.S., Meyers, J.H., Meyers, T.E., Jr., Nightingale, C.D., Rankin, E.S., Sands, C.S., Schley, R.L., Jr., Sherley, S., Tucker, W.M., Warren, F.C., Watson, F.L., Jr., Wetherill, W.C., Jr., White, R.J., Jr., Williams, F.D., Worthington, G.Y., III.

Training in the forensic arts was an integral part of the EHS curriculum. The literary societies were a prime instrument, supplemented by reading and declamation performances before upper study-hall during vacant morning periods under the tutelage of Mr. Reade. What boy does not remember the "hand supine," "hand prone," "hand clenched" and "finger index" gestures? In addition to being a fine speaker Mr. Reade was an accomplished tennis player and ice skater. One day as he was cutting his name in the ice on the skating pond by the front drive some one remarked "Watch him put M.El. (for Master of Elocution) after it."

High academic standards were maintained by the awarding of non-competitive prizes named for three Bishops of the Diocese of Virginia: Meade (1841–62), Johns (1862–76), Whittle (1876–1902).

"Eminent excellence" was defined as an average of at least 85 on the three exams in each course and an average of 90 on the daily work: to win the Meade Prize one had to attain eminent excellence in five major studies including Latin *and* Greek. Needless to say, not too many students qualified, but during the period 1920–33 fifteen Meade prizes were awarded—three of them to one boy, Bobby Nelson! He won in 1926, '27 and '28.

The Johns Prize required eminent excellence in Latin *or* Greek and four other major subjects, and the Whittle Prize required that excellence in any four major subjects. Those prizes have always fallen as the gentle rain from heaven. In one typical year, 1932, there were thirteen Johns and eleven Whittle Prizes awarded.

All subjects were classed as "major" except spelling and Sacred Studies. The spelling classes were held in the study-halls during vacant periods, and missed words had to be written 25 times in Voluntary. Classes in Sacred Studies were held weekly during an extra period before dinner. To allow proper preparation, a major subject such as Latin, math, English, French or history—in rotation—was omitted on the day of the class, usually Thursday. All boys aged 13 or under took Sacred Studies II, taught by Mr. Hoxton. The textbook was Charles Foster's *Story of the Bible*, a very readable condensation. (Today that book would be roundly condemned as anti-Semitic.) The Principal tolerated no flippancy in his class. He once ordered me to write four columns because I referred to Ruth as a "gal," but he later relented.

In addition to Sacred Studies Mr. Hoxton taught Second Math (algebra), Third Math (algebra and plane geometry) and Fourth

Math (trigonometry and solid geometry). I took all three of those classes under him.

My father also taught a section of Third Math. Once a student, Dean Hearne, who was taking that class for the third time got all of the answers to the exam questions right, but his calculations made no sense: he just knew the answers to every problem in the book. He never did get the hang of algebra.

New awards were added to the list during this period.

In 1925 Henry C. Blackiston established awards to two boys who were "outstanding leaders in the school," usually a cruise to a Caribbean island. (His son Harry, a student at the time, was one of the first winners.) In 1928 the C.C. Baldwin Sportsmanship Trophy was instituted, the winner to be determined by secret ballot of the students. Another award was the Graham F. Blandy Memorial Prize (the income from a $5000 New York Central Railroad bond) for a boy in need of financial help, the name of the recipient not to be announced.

During the early years between the wars there were four major sports: football, baseball, basketball and track. (Tennis was added in the thirties.)

The epitome of athletic achievement was to win an "E" in each of the four, and in the twenties there were at least five boys who managed that: George Morton (1921–22 and 1922–23), Jimmy Bridges (1923–24), Harry Flippin (1924–25 and 1925–26), Ben Boogher (1926–27) and Herbie Bryant (1927–28). When Mr. Hoxton gave Herbie the Rinehart Trophy for best athlete in 1928 he predicted that there would never be a four-letter athlete again— besides the difficulty of practicing for two sports simultaneously there were increasingly knotty problems of scheduling. (Once there was a track meet in Washington and a baseball game at the School on the same day. Harry Flippin won both hurdle races at the meet, changed clothes in my father's car, and hit the diamond running.)

[Editor's note: actually, after Dick Daniel's time Old Flick's prediction proved incorrect: Edward Stephens Martin (1957–61) won four letters. "Ned" Martin was also an outstanding student. He is now a physician in Charlotte and has a son at the School.]

Mr. Hoxton's Day

In addition to teaching three math classes and inspecting the dormitories every morning, Mr. Hoxton was in his office and available to any boy who wanted to see him between supper and study-hall each school night except Monday. That was the night set for the weekly faculty meeting in Social Hall. In between he performed administrative duties and answered his mail. There was no professional clerical help. In the early years two boys were detailed as secretaries, popularly known as *flunkeys*. Today they would be called *gofers*. They typed letters as Mr. Hoxton dictated, sent out scholastic reports, answered the telephones, summoned boys to the office, etc. Later he employed Kin Shackelford. After her death he did use a professional.

Faculty Social Life

Society on the Hill was very much an ingrown affair. With no facilities in the homes for preparing or serving meals, about the only amenity available was the serving of tea (or coffee). Of course during Prohibition, cocktail parties were out. The teachers got together after midday dinner frequently for coffee in their various homes. The Hoxtons served coffee every Sunday; Old Boys were invited if any were around. In the period after World War I there were in the vicinity probably less than a dozen families, outside of the two faculties, that would have been considered part of the "social scene." The automobile and neighborhood development changed all that.

At the beginning of each session formal calls were exchanged between the two faculties, complete with visiting cards to be left if the family called on was not at home. The Seminary families did not eat in the refectory but had their meals at home. Their homes had kitchens and dining rooms. Each family employed a cook and a maid as well. Some of the EHS families had maids too, and all employed nurses for their small children. The going rate for a child nurse was $3 per week. No one did their own laundry. It was all sent to Mudtown.

Teachers were employed under annual contracts which provided accommodations and meals. The latter applied only when school was in session. Compensation for new teachers was around $125 per month for nine months.

In all the years of my growing up on the Hill and attending the High School I never heard or saw a member of the faculty lose his temper or make an unkind remark about a colleague. I am sure there were some tense moments but each man respected the talents and strengths of his fellow teachers.

It is on this note that I conclude my reminiscence of the High School Between the Wars.

PS: Being a teacher's son on campus is not what it is cracked up to be. One misses out on dorm life and any conspiracies for mischief, etc.

(Editor's note: There. Is not that wide and deep and precise reconstruction of our Hill between the wars a nearly miraculous evocation of *le temps perdu*, or *déjà vu*, or *quelque-chose*?)

CHAPTER 7

Modern Times
1947–1989

In a little less than half a century this country's population in-creased to about 250 million (about 60 million rural, 190 million urban). Our center of population, moving southwestward, crossed the Mississippi from Illinois into Missouri.

The total population of the world grew to about five billion people. (It was about one billion in 1839, passed two billion in the 1920's, three billion in the 1960's and four billion in the 1970's.)

After nearly 200 years of counting people, in 1984 the Census Bureau counted robots. In that year some seventy-five U.S. com-panies manufactured some 5,500 robots, valued at more than 300 million dollars, mostly for automobile makers.

In 1947 Marshall Plan aid began rebuilding war-shattered econ-omies abroad, Bell Laboratories scientists invented the transistor, and Jackie Robinson became the first black to play on a major league baseball team (Brooklyn Dodgers).

In 1948 Gandhi was assassinated, the Jewish state of Israel was born and the Berlin airlift began (it ended in September, 1949).

In 1949 Mao Tse-tung proclaimed the Communist People's Re-public of China; the apartheid program was established in South

Africa; the Western allies organized NATO; George Orwell published Nineteen Eighty-four.

In the next year former State Department officer Alger Hiss was convicted of perjury; Wisconsin Senator Joe McCarthy started his anti-Red campaign; the Korean War began; cartoonist Charles Schulz created Peanuts.

In 1951 President Truman fired General Douglas MacArthur from his Far Eastern command. James Joyce published From Here to Eternity. *CBS telecast the first commercial color TV program.*

In 1953 Iosif Vissarionovich Dzhugashvili, AKA Joseph Stalin, died and Edmund Hillary of New Zealand and Tenzing Norgay of Nepal became the first men to climb to the top of the world's highest mountain, Everest (29,028 feet). In 1954 the Englishman Roger Bannister ran the first under-four-minute mile (3' 59.4"). In 1955 the American Federation of Labor (AFL) and the Congress of Industrial Organizations (CIO) merged and the U.S. Air Force Academy opened. In 1956 Elvis Presley sang his way to fame with "Heartbreak Hotel."

On October 4, 1957, the Age of Space began when Russia launched the first earth-orbiting artificial satellite, Sputnik.

The next year the United States launched its first artificial satellite, Explorer, *and sent a nuclear submarine under the ice cap at the North Pole.*

In 1959 Alaska and Hawaii became the 49th and 50th states. In 1960 a U.S. high-altitude U-2 reconnaissance plane piloted by Francis Gary Powers was shot down over Russia, and at age forty-three John Kennedy became the youngest man ever elected President.

The next year outgoing President Eisenhower warned against "the military-industrial complex" and incoming President Kennedy took full responsibility for our botched invasion of Cuba at the Bay of Pigs. The year after that he outbluffed Nikita Khrushchev and the Russians took their missiles out of Cuba.

In that same year (1962) Joseph Heller published Catch-22, *and James Meredith, a black applicant, was denied admission to the University of Mississippi; in 1963 there were race riots in Alabama, 200,000 "Freedom Marchers" came to Washington, and Martin Luther King delivered his "I have a dream" speech.*

On November 22, 1963, Kennedy was killed in Dallas. He was our fourth President to be assassinated (the others were Lincoln, Garfield and McKinley).

In 1964 U.S. ships and planes skirmished against North Vietnamese forces in the Gulf of Tonkin and the Senate empowered President Lyndon Johnson to escalate military action against that country. The Beatles became the world's most popular rock group.

At 5:15 PM November 9, 1965, an electrical relay switch in Ontario failed; parts of two Canadian provinces and all of our northeastern states were blacked out; thirty million people were without electricity for hours; nine months later there was a noticeable increase in the birth rate.

In 1967 Dr. Christiaan Barnard performed the first human heart transplant operation, in Cape Town, South Africa, and Israel fought Syria, Jordan and Egypt in the "Six-Day War."

In 1968 Martin Luther King and Robert F. Kennedy were assassinated.

On July 21, 1969, astronauts Neil Armstrong and Edwin Aldrin became the first human beings to walk on the moon. (Armstrong's exact words, as often misquoted as that famous Post Office motto which most people think begins "Not rain nor cold nor gloom of night . . . ", were "It's one small step for a man, one giant leap for mankind." The New York Post Office motto is, actually, "Neither snow, nor rain, nor heat, nor gloom of night stays these couriers from the swift completion of their appointed rounds." It is a paraphrase of a statement Herodotus made about the Persians, some 2400 years ago.)

As the decade of the 1960's ended there were student riots at schools across the country, and in 1970 National Guardsmen fired on a thousand Viet Nam war protesters at Kent State University in Ohio; four students were killed.

In 1971 a primitive people, the Tasaday, were found in the Philippines. They use Stone Age tools and have no words for "hate" or "war."

In 1972 police arrested five men for breaking into Democratic National Headquarters in Washington, and the Watergate scandal began. In 1974 streaking became a fad, and there was a gasoline shortage. In 1976 the unmanned space vehicles Viking I and II landed on Mars. In 1977 "punk rock" music became popular and President Carter pardoned ten thousand Viet Nam draft evaders.

Also in 1977 the National Women's Conference in Houston ratified and symbolized the change in the minds of women.

In 1978 this country established diplomatic relations with Red China; in Iran there were riots against the rule of the Shah; the movie Star Wars *set a world-wide attendance record, grossing more than two hundred million dollars.*

In 1979 the Shah left Iran; the Ayatollah Khomeini took power and proclaimed an Islamic Republic, dedicated to the destruction of "The Great American Satan;" on November 4 Iranians stormed the U.S. Embassy in Teheran and captured some ninety people including about sixty-five Americans. The Shah died of cancer the next year. Israel and Egypt signed a peace treaty; there was an accident at the nuclear reactor in Three-Mile Island, Pennsylvania; Russia invaded Afghanistan.

In 1980 we boycotted the summer Olympics, held in Russia, in protest against that invasion. Iraq started a war with Iran. The long-dormant volcano Mt. St. Helens in southwest Washington erupted. Jean Harris, headmistress of the Madeira School, shot and killed her lover, the diet doctor Herman Tarnower.

In a national poll two thousand U.S. eighth graders voted for "Heroes of Young America" and these were the winners: 1. Burt Reynolds, actor; 2. Steve Martin, comedian; 3. Eric Heiden, skater; 4. Eric Estrada, actor; 5. Alan Alda, actor; 6. Kristy McNichol, actress; 7. "Sugar Ray" Leonard, boxer; 8. Scott Baio, actor; 9. John Belushi, actor; 10. Kurt Thomas, gymnast.

In 1981 fifty-two American hostages set free by the Iranians got home twenty minutes after the inauguration of President Reagan. Terrorists were active around the world.

A group of extremists killed Egyptian leader Anwar Sadat; a deranged young man, John W. Hinckley, Jr., shot but did not kill President Reagan; a fanatic wounded Pope John Paul II.

In 1982 Argentine forces invaded the Falkland Islands and were defeated by defending British troops.

In 1983 The National Commission on Excellence in Education denounced our educational system for producing a "rising tide of mediocrity [which] threatens our very future;" indiscipline was thought to be the main problem. A 12,000-pound bomb killed 241 U.S. Marines and others in Beirut; Marines and Rangers and a small force from six Caribbean nations invaded Grenada.

In 1984 two trusted Sikhs of her personal bodyguard murdered India's Indira Gandhi.

In 1985 Mikhail Gorbachev came to power in Russia. Actor Rock Hudson died of AIDS. There were demonstrations against South Africa's policy of apartheid.

In November, 1985, Arab gunmen seized an Egyptian plane

bound from Athens to Cairo and the hijacking resulted in the deaths of sixty of the ninety-eight persons aboard.

January 28, 1986, the space shuttle Challenger *exploded just after take-off; all seven crew members died.*

Also in 1986 long-time dictator Ferdinand Marcos lost the Philippine Presidential election to Corazon Aquino and the search for his pilfered billions began. Robert Penn Warren became this country's first Poet Laureate. Responding to a terrorist bombing in Germany, U.S. planes flew from England to bomb targets in Libya. The core of a Russian nuclear reactor in Chernobyl, sixty miles north of Kiev, melted down.

In June, 1986, health authorities reported about ten thousand deaths from AIDS in this country, and predicted a ten-fold increase in such deaths by 1991. In July there was a four-day celebration of the hundredth birthday of the Statue of Liberty.

In 1987 a Senate Committee questioned Oliver North, John Poindexter and others concerning possibly illegal sales of arms to Iran and contributions of money and weapons to Contra forces fighting the Sandinista government in Nicaragua.

In 1988 for the fifth time in the last six elections the country, despite having more registered Democrats than Republicans, voted a Republican, George Bush, into the White House.

AFTER MR. HOXTON retired in 1947 the Trustees once more, as they had in 1913, found a new Principal on the spot.

Richard Pardee Williams, the "Cap'n Dick" and RPW who has already appeared ubiquitously throughout these chronicles, was the son of an Episcopal minister. Born in Richmond February 6, 1886, he attended the School from 1901 to 1904 and was Editor-in-Chief of *The Monthly Chronicle* and a member of the *Whispers* Board. He won the Johns and Meade prizes and the Historical Essay and English Composition and Fairfax Literary Society Debater's medals.

After graduation here he went to the University and took a B.A. in 1907 and an M.A. in 1908. He was a member of the Raven Society and Phi Beta Kappa and was on the Advisory Board of the General Athletic Association.

He came back to the Hill in 1908 as *caput/kephale* of the Latin and Greek departments and fulfilled that double-headed function with outstanding panache for the next fifty years—with two breaks:

From 1917 to 1919 he served overseas as captain of infantry in the Army's 80th Division and was in combat at St. Mihiel and Meuse-Argonne ("not wounded, just frightened"), and from 1947 to 1951 he was a third, so to speak, head. He was the Principal of this School.

Actually, while he was Principal he also kept one of his other two heads. Although he gave his Latin classes to Richard P. Thomsen (of whom we will hear a great deal more a little bit later) he continued to run the Greek department.

Cap'n Dick was famous for his wry wit, which was wont to manifest itself in any one of his three languages, and like King Cole (before he got old) he was a merry old soul. *The E.H.S. News* for Spring, 1948, had this to say of him as man, teacher and Principal:

Well-equipped for the broader aspects of his new duties by temperament, judgment and experience, Mr. Williams has the additional quality of a keen sense of humor, and a picturesqueness of speech that is its own copyright against imitation. The dining room, for instance, is a good place to be in, but it's a better room still when you can hear the joyous and contagious laughter of Mr. Williams above the noise—and you can!

And who is there who does not revel in the meaningful, laconic telegram that Mr. Williams sent from Woodberry way back yonder when we beat 'em in what the experts of the day predicted would be a close game? Asked to telegraph back to the School as soon as the game was over, giving all details, he wired back "E.H.S. 46, W.F.S. 0. Supply your own details!"

(The "way back yonder" of that game was 1916, and those experts probably shouldn't have predicted that the outcome would be close. Our team had won five of its six pre-WFS games, in four of them holding the enemy scoreless.)

Mr. Williams' years as Principal were tranquil.

The second World War was over and the Korean War had not divided the country; problems of drugs, sexual permissiveness and student unrest were unheard of; the Hill was, as it had been in Old Bar's closing years, in an Indian Summer.

As Cap'n Dick's *amicus* Pliny the Roman said, *Quanto innocentiore. . . .* —"Oh what a blessed, secure and harmless life was that." (Pliny was talking about first century AD farm life, actually, but *mutatis mutandis*—"If the shoe fits, wear it." Cap'n Dick was a great one for making classical shoes fit fresh feet: *e.g.,* any talk

Richard Pardee Williams, Jr., Principal, 1947–51.

of a party might elicit from him the poem beginning "Old Horace was an owl, sir,/ And when he began to prowl, Sir,/ He surely made Rome howl, sir . . . " He liked that poem much better than the more familiar "Latin is a language as dead as dead can be,/ It killed the ancient Romans and now it's killing me.")

Our Romanophile's reign was serene— and brief.

In 1951 he reached the age of mandatory retirement, 65. That June he abdicated.

Sic transit gloria? No no. He only gave up the job of Principal. He continued to teach Greek, resumed teaching Latin, and stayed in harness until he retired from all scholarly work in 1958. His last years were spent writing his history of the School.

R.P. Williams

Mr. Williams died January 4, 1966, in Alexandria.

Let it be noted that when our *kephale* retired he took classical Greek with him. That language disappeared from the EHS curriculum for almost three decades after the 1957–58 session. (And *kephale*, for the benefit of those poor unfortunates who never took Greek under him, means the same thing in that language that *caput* does in Latin: "head.") Recently Greek has been restored to the curriculum, much to the gratification of Old Boys who like the present writer were forced by Cap'n Dick to take it when they couldn't pass Latin—and came to enjoy it mightily.

Mr. Williams' memorial tablet in Pendleton Hall reads:

INTER SILVAS ACADEMI QUAERERE VERUM

which might be rendered "Seeking Truth within the grove of Academe."

After Cap'n Dick retired as Principal in 1951 the Trustees again had a relatively easy time finding a successor.

Richard Porter Thomsen became our first Headmaster. Before his time the official title of the School's leader had been Principal.

He was born in Baltimore December 8, 1912, and attended the School from 1926 to 1930, winning the Whittle and Laird prizes. He went on to Yale, where he was captain of the boxing team and a member of the Zeta Psi fraternity. Upon graduation in 1934 he was commissioned an ensign in the Naval Reserve.

Brooks Photography

Richard Porter Thomsen, Headmaster, 1951–67.

Then for five years he was "in business," which he describes as good experience but not very fulfilling. In Greek there are two words for "work:" *ergos,* which means productive enterprise, and *doulia,* drudgery. Business for him was *doulia.* Working just to make money wasn't enough. "The life unexamined," as Aristotle said, "is not worth living."

Home came the pilgrim, home to the Hill.

He taught Latin and history (ancient and English) here from 1939 to 1941, and then, in June, 1941, the Navy called him.

He served until November, 1945, on two troop transports— the *Chateau Thierry* and the *General J. R. Brooke*—in the Pacific, the north and south Atlantic, the Mediterranean, the Red Sea ("the only serious earthly competitor of Hell: sea temperature 92°, air temperature with a high wind 91°, humidity always 95 percent to 100 percent") and the Indian Ocean. ("I covered about 500,000 miles on those two ships, much of it on the *Chateau Thierry* in convoy at 7 to 10 knots.") He rose in rank from Ensign to Commander.

That *Chateau Thierry* (usually pronounced Chatter Theory by her crew) was a typical World War II grabbed-in-a-hurry transport, a cantankerous, mischievous, brave old bucket-of-bolts. Built at Hog Island in World War I she grew old in peacetime Army transport runs, died of honorable old age in 1938, and was snatched from the claws of scrap dealers in 1941. Her "uncompromisingly straight lines" made her look the same coming or going; a "slight topheaviness" made her roll almost all the way over in a heavy beam sea; "another unloveable peculiarity was the tendency of her steering gear to get stuck at crucial moments, such as when approaching the mined entrance to a harbor."

But she was a survivor, with a well-earned reputation for doing "the mostest with the leastest."

During Ensign-to-Commander Thomsen's tour aboard her she sailed through bitter cold and flaming heat, past submarines and flying fish and an albatross, and was hostess to a baboon (*not* her Captain—he was more irascible). And she took her crew, a "motley assortment" of inexperienced men, to four World War II firsts:

1. They established the first U.S base north of the Arctic Circle ("Bluie West," Greenland, September, 1941);

2. They carried the first American Expeditionary Force to the United Kingdom after war was declared (Belfast Lough, Northern Ireland, January, 1942);

3. They brought the first German prisoners of war to this country (soldiers of Rommel's once-formidable Afrika Corps, from Oran, Algeria, Spring, 1943);

4. They took part in the first major invasion of Axis territory (Sicily, July, 1943).

For a ship which had served faithfully, been declared moribund and consigned to honorable oblivion and then resurrected, the old Chatter Theory performed erratically, alarmingly, courageously.

Dick Thomsen wrote a little memoir of his war, "Innocents Aboard," which should be required reading for anybody who thinks that *Mister Roberts* and *The Caine Mutiny* said it all.

Our goodly, much-enduring Odysseus returned to the School in 1946 and resumed his teaching of Latin. When ex-Captain Dick Williams became Principal, ex-Commander Dick Thomsen was made head of the Latin department; when he (RPT) succeeded him (RPW) as head of the School he (RPW) took back command of that department. Clear? (Catullus might have gotten caught in such heady confusion. Cicero: *Numquam!*)

The power-passing from Captain Dick to Commander Dick, one Latinist to another, was as smooth as a *fluvialis unda*, a flowing wave.

In the Fall, 1951 issue of *The E.H.S. News* the new Headmaster wrote: "As I am fortunate enough to be the heir of a continuing program of change and progress which stems from Mr. Hoxton's and Mr. Williams' regimes, my first message [is to express] my pleasure at the eminently healthy state of our School."

Shades of the first four Principals, who strove so valiantly to save that same School from famine, debt, war and chaos! The bruised spirits of Rectors Pendleton, Dalrymple, McGuire and Gardner must have marveled that the battered place could ever have become "eminently healthy."

Gaudeamus igitur.

Of course, there were a few *muscae in unguento*, such as the Korean War abroad and McCarthyism at home, but on the Hill life rolled along tranquilly and rewardingly and—yes, Virginia—*feliciter*. (And yes, Virginia, *muscae* are flies and *unguento* is what they fly into.)

Mr. Ravenel and Mr. Karlson were the most impressive (and best) of the teachers in the fifties. Both were effective with opposite meth-

Captain Dick and Commander Dick.

Charles Vawter Tompkins, 1938.

Patrick Henry Callaway.

ods: down-home approach vs. intimidation respectively. [Pearce Connerat, 1954–57.]

However, as the quiet 1950's gave way to the troubled sixties
that ancient Ur-figure The Lord of Misrule seemed suddenly let
loose in the land. People, places, events and "happenings" were
blurred together in disorder. Flower Children and Hippies, sex,
drugs and loud music, Jack Kerouac *On The Road*, Woodstock,
Timothy O'Leary ("Turn on, tune in, drop out"), Black Panthers,
student riots, Haight-Ashbury and Watts, the Democratic Con-
vention in Chicago, Charles Manson, and underneath it all, Viet
Nam—"Hey Hey LBJ how many kids did you kill today?"

It has been said that in those decades the Western world went
through a convulsion of values and customs comparable in mag-
nitude to the blossoming of Athens, the fall of Rome, the explosion
of the Renaissance and the coming of the industrial age.

Maybe.

And maybe it was just the pendulum swinging too far. Now we
have ultra-conservative Yuppies.

In any case, our School weathered the storm as it had weathered
others. We were buffeted, twisted and turned, but our house was
builded on rock and stood fast. Only years later did we realize
that the very ground beneath us had moved.

I was a very happy camper. I actually thought that it was normal to
be locked up with 250 other boys for months at a time! In retrospect I
would wish that I had reached for more challenge and exploration. I
somehow settled in and was not stretched nor did I have the presence
of mind to stretch myself.

R.P. Thomsen   *P.C. Connerat*   *Cotten Alston*

For example, I remember shooting baskets in Centennial during the Kennedy Presidential inauguration after refusing an invitation to go watch it close up. My present theory is that those school years represent the very last time that we kids can be forced to consider things, forced to do things that ultimately accrue to our benefit, both in and out of the classroom. So I wish that I had read more, travelled more, and just generally pushed a little harder at the boundaries.

Of the Old Guard Mr. Callaway was the king by any measurement, but Mr. Tompkins was very special. Through his summer camp and at EHS he was a tremendous influence. [Cotten Alston, 1959–63.]

Lots of us found Mr. Tompkins special:

Peering over his bifocals, my senior adviser looked me straight in the eye. Although Mr. Tompkins had been a great teacher and athletic coach, this September, 1965, was the beginning of his last year of a fifty-year teaching career. "Mr. T." didn't even attempt any longer to hit misbehavers with well-aimed pieces of chalk, his trademark in the realm of classroom discipline. As he peered at me over his glasses I had good reason to be nervous. He knew perfectly well that I'd flunked two subjects the Spring before and that it was only because I'd just passed my two "re-exams" that I was even a member of the senior class. I said "Mr. Tompkins, my problem is that I just don't know how to study."

His hand holding a pen was shaking, but there was nothing feeble in the steely twinkle I saw in his eye. "Your problem isn't that you don't know how to study," he said, setting me up for the tough love he was about to deliver. "You're just afraid to do the dirty work!" Each of those last eight words hit me right between the eyes like so many pieces of his proverbial chalk. I remember nothing else about the remainder of our conversation, but I had heard the words I needed to turn my academic career around. Those words "cut more keenly than any two-edged sword . . . sift[ing] the purposes of the heart," as *The Book of Hebrews* tells us.

Throughout my senior year after that I made the High List, and day after day, sitting in Upper Study Hall, I can remember trying those impossible math problems one more time because, come hell or high water, I was going to "do the dirty work." [John B. Pinder III, 1962–66.

Brother Pinder now does whatever kind of work must be done in the vineyards of the Lord: he is a minister.

Having a clear complexion was extremely important to all EHS boys in the mid-sixties and no toilet kit was complete without a green

J.B. Pinder   *D. Orrick*

plastic bottle of Phisohex and a tube or two of Clearasil. To him seen eating a bar of candy one would say "Eat it now wear it tomorrow!"

The room over the Bryan Library was an ideal place to study. The quiet was welcome and the stacks of old National Geographic magazines piled high provided a pleasant diversion.

Mr. Johnsson the organist in church was an older man whose musical talents were stronger than his heart. One Sunday he had a heart attack as he struck the first note of the recessional hymn, "God the Omnipotent." His friend the choir president, Mr. Blakesley, reached into Mr. J's pocket, took out the nitroglycerin and popped it into his mouth, and the hymn went on to that magnificent conclusion: "Give to us peace in our time, O Lord." Nobody knew that anything had happened; it just seemed that that first note was a bit long. [DeCourcy Orrick III, 1965–69.]

DeCourcy Orrick's time at the School overlapped another changing of the guard. His four years were divided equally between the Principalities of Dick Thomsen and his successor.

Upon leaving office in 1967 Mr. Thomsen had this to say:

As strange as it may seem, I can think of no events taking place during my headmastership to which I attribute unusual significance or importance. I was, of course, proud of the school —its traditions, its faculty, its students—and I derive considerable satisfaction from having had a role in its history.

As one who is by nature much more of a conservator than an innovator, however, I am unable to "point with pride" at any landmark achievements. As to major sorrows, my follies and failures were too numerous to recount and much too painful to recall. I just wish that I had had the wisdom and clarity of vision during those years that hind-sight has since provided me.

As the Pennsylvania Dutch expression goes, it's a case of "too soon old, too late smart."

Pennsylvania Shmennsylvania. Our Richard, like Poor Richard, hides his light under a bushel.

Let the record show that during his sixteen years as Head the School got a handsome new chapel/auditorium (Pendleton Hall, completed in 1952), a new pipe organ (from Norborne Berkeley, EHS 1907–10), a big and comfortable new dormitory, and the better part of a new sports center. Flippin Field House, named for Harry Flippin, one of our greatest omni-athletes (letters in football, baseball, basketball and track, 1924–25 and 1925–26), was begun in 1967 and completed in 1968.

The endowment fund was increased from about one million dollars to almost four million. And, best of all, academic standards rose sharply.

Contrary to the practice of many school heads these days, he involved himself deeply both in admission processing and in college counselling, the school entry and exit points, and "I learned much about each. For instance, a senior decided, on his own, to try for Bowdoin College in Maine. I knew Bowdoin to be a fine place, but an unusual choice, since most of those wanting a Northern college, sometimes as many as a fifth of all of our seniors, aimed for Princeton or Yale or, less frequently, Harvard or Williams. Why was he choosing Bowdoin? His answer was most sensible: 'I want to go North for a while; I want a small liberal arts college for men, likely to have the best faculty and facilities, therefore the one with the largest endowment per student, and that's Bowdoin.' He did go there and it presumably did have its share of those best things."

Commander Dick found the School "eminently healthy" and left it more so. And he labored in fields of education far from the Hill. He was a charter member and headmaster of the National Association of Independent Schools, founded in 1962, and that Association's first representative in Washington. Washington and Lee made him an Honorary Doctor, and so did the Seminary.

Nowadays he keeps an avuncular eye on the Hill from nearby

Alexandria and is, if he the top-shining one will pardon the expression, our *éminence grise*.

Our ninth Head was the son of the sixth.

Archibald Robinson Hoxton, Jr. was born on the Hill, in, of course, Hoxton House, April 20, 1916. His first memory is of hearing the crack of baseball bats on Hoxton Field, "probably Mr. Callaway pitching for batting practice." (He was senior to Mr. Callaway on the Hill because he arrived by stork five months before PHC came by shank's mare. Sixty-five years later he spent his last night at EHS in the same room in which he was born, whereas PHC is still around, waiting for his new chapel.)

He was a student at the School from 1928 to 1935 (only seven years, as compared to his father's nine), and was Head Monitor, Valedictorian and captain of both the football and track teams. For three years he was Virginia prep school 440-yard champion and he held the school record in that event from 1933 until Oran Rowe (1970–74) broke it in 1974. He was awarded the C.C. Baldwin Medal for sportsmanship in both his junior and senior years, the first boy in the history of the School to win that medal twice (the only other has been his contemporary, Bill Rinehart, EHS 1933–37).

A.R. Hoxton, Jr.

Inevitably, he inherited his father's nickname.

He went to Yale, where he made three Y's in football, was a member of DKE, the Torch Honor Society and (shhhh) Skull and Bones, was Deacon of the University Church, and other things.

He then taught math and helped coach at The Hotchkiss School for two years.

From October, 1941 to October 1945 he was attached to the Research and Development Division of the Navy's Bureau of Ordnance and did "some unwitting leg work for the Manhattan Project" (which Project was of course the development of the atom bomb). He received a Commendation from the Secretary of the Navy.

Like our other Naval Person he came back to the Hill after the war, and taught math and coached for five years, managing to get a Master's degree from George Washington University in that time.

Young Flick, Headmaster, 1967–81.

In 1950 he was named headmaster of the Fairfield Country Day School in Connecticut and in 1953 he became HM of the Green Vale School in Glen Head, Long Island.

When he followed Dick Thomsen as EHS Headmaster in 1967 he had already had one more year of on-the-job training than his predecessor had tallied.

In Young Flick's first year as Headmaster the School was shaken by three especially disturbing sudden deaths.

On the night of April 4, 1968, I witnessed from the bank which stretches from Pendleton Hall to the Headmaster's house an extremely poignant moment in the history of the United States. That spot offers a most spectacular view of the city of Washington. From that vista, that night, a boy watched his nation's capital burn. Dr. Martin Luther King had been shot, the city was in flames, and with tears in my eyes I stared in disbelief as flames spread across the horizon. All I could think about was Sherman's burning of Atlanta. The South had all but perished in that conflagration, and I wondered if our union could survive this one. [DeCourcy Orrick, 1965–69.]

The next month, Sunday, May 12, that same boy experienced a more personal, more painful, grief.

When I came late in the dining room for supper I noticed that it was deathly quiet. There was not a sound except the clinking of ice as rats filled the water glasses and an occasional "Please pass the butter." Something was gravely amiss but I didn't know what it was and I was afraid to ask. Then the senior boy presiding at my table, who had the reputation of being aloof, dispassionate and completely unemotional, sensed my distress. Tears welled up in his eyes and he whispered "Mr. Ravenel died this morning."

William Bee Ravenel III was one of the most-respected, best-loved masters who ever graced our Hill.

Born in Charleston, he attended Davidson College and took a B.A. in 1935. He then went to Duke University and took a Master's degree, did more graduate work there and at George Washington University, and came to the School in that same year, 1936.

During World War II he was a Colonel in the Third Army's Sixth Armored Division, serving part of the time as a member of General George Patton's staff, and he was awarded a Silver Star and a Bronze Star with two Oak Leaf Clusters.

He returned to EHS, became head of the English Department,

"Neither snow, nor rain. . . ."
William Bee Ravenel, 1968.

and Assistant Principal. He wrote an immensely successful and readable *English Reference Book*. Samples: "Off the grass, not off of the grass; angry with, not at, a person." He was also, at one time or another, Director of Admissions, first adviser of the E club, and, for nine years, head of the very successful summer school program at Corolla Academy in Reading, England. He coached varsity baseball, basketball and JV football teams. He counselled, comforted, was there.

He died of a heart attack.

Twenty-four days later—June 5—Robert Kennedy, campaigning for the office which his brother John might still have held if he had lived, was shot.

Three such shocking sudden deaths in three months—and there were others, before and after: at the School (three other faculty and staff heart attacks in 1968–69); in civil rights confrontations, protest marches, student riots, Viet Nam.

It was a troubled, out-of-joint, time. Pain and change were blowing in the wind.

On the Hill the effects were muted. The lessons of the great storms were marked, learned and inwardly digested, and life went on. It has a way of doing that. As Pliny the Roman generalized, "This only point among the rest remaineth sure and certain, namely that nothing is certain." As Thomsen the Alexandrian particularized,

Since I had retired as Headmaster by that time, I could enjoy the luxury of being of two minds on the subject: as a traditionalist, I bemoaned the fact that the students no longer were exposed to the rigorously religious regime which had governed me and my contemporaries; as a pragmatist, I agreed that the changes were probably inevitable.

There is no question but that some students were "turned off" by what they considered excessive exposure to religion. On the other hand, it is my belief that most of these strays tend to return to the fold.

In addition, the rather intensive exposure to Biblical literature and church history that used to be characteristic of church-related boarding schools had the effect of creating what I would describe as religious literates, that is, persons who are reasonably comfortable when using or confronted by references to Adam's rib, Job's suffering, Judas Iscariot, or the miraculous events handled so deftly by Sportin' Life in *Porgy and Bess*.

If, as I strongly believe, one of the most important aims of education is to transmit an understanding of our cultural heritage, the concept of intensive exposure to our Judeo-Christian religious experience needs no further justification.

Bravo for you and the School, Commander Dick!

R. Burns

There is at the University the champion of champions of that position. In his best-selling 1987 book *Cultural Literacy: What Every American Needs to Know*, Professor (of English) E. D. Hirsch, Jr., stoutly maintains that "Only by piling up specific, communally shared information can children learn to participate in complex cooperative activities."

Asked to comment on the Thomsen view that "one of the most important aims of education is to transmit an understanding of our cultural heritage," Dr. Hirsch said, *con brio*, "Solomonic!"

No man is an island.

In 1965 our Board of Trustees voted unanimously to admit "any and all qualified applicants," and in 1968 two blacks, Reginald

Burns and Samuel Paschall, Jr., came to the School. "The next year Regi lived on my hall; three years later he was Head Monitor." [DeCourcy Orrick, 1965–69.] Now, about 20 blacks attend the School every year.

How do they like it?

In 1969 I was born to my proud parents, Jim and Nila Snowden. At this point in my new life I was unaware of the many changes occurring around me. One significant change that had occurred the previous year was one made at Episcopal, one which would later directly affect my life. In 1968 Episcopal High School enrolled the School's first black students. This change by EHS was very insignificant in my young life in South Bend, Indiana. However, sixteen years later, that same decision made in 1968 allowed me and several blacks before me to enroll into a "Rat" class.

I left a pretty good private boys' Catholic school to attend EHS, and I have never regretted my decision. I recall that on my first day at EHS I knew only two people, a classmate from Catholic school and an upperclassman from Hickory, North Carolina. After the New Boy Tea, I soon realized that there were very few black students at EHS. This was a surprise to me, since I came from and was used to an almost equally populated school of both blacks and whites. As I developed friendships with both blacks and whites, with very little attention to my race and that of others, it seemed that time flew by. Weeks turned into months, months into years, and before I realized, it was my senior year at EHS.

D. Snowden

My last semester was almost over. I found myself shackled with the responsibilities of being a Senior Monitor, Chairman of the Honor Committee and track captain, responsibilities I gladly accepted and enjoyed. These were responsibilities that fewer than twenty years ago blacks were not allowed to have at the High School or in most areas of society.

Looking back at my years at EHS I have captured something that is not only priceless but also blind to race or color: true friendships. My three years at EHS were filled with laughter, hard work, and, at times, frustration. I feel that there is no difference in my experiences at EHS from those of someone who is white or Japanese for that matter.

I am just as proud as the next EHS alum to say that I am an Old Boy! [Dane Snowden, 1984–87.]

In the 21 years since 1968 three blacks have been named Chairman of the Honor Committee, the School's highest elective position: Tony Chase '73, Dane Snowden and Vince Hodge '89. . . blowing in the wind. . . .

And the evening and the morning were the second day.

Other problems did not admit of such a happy solution. Young Flick thought back to an earlier, perhaps even harder, time, thought "This too shall pass," and managed to roll with it:

Dr. Dalrymple must have had his hands full dealing with a number of boys, not all, spoiled by free and easy plantation living, life styles not in keeping with his puritanical standards of behavior. In a different way the headmasters of the sixties, seventies and eighties have faced the same situation of meeting the influence of the counter culture of those years: blatant rebellion at the college level, drugs, sexual permissiveness, etc, etc. Of course, all those things filtered down to our age level in the sixties and seventies.

In my years, 1967–81, I had to dismiss boys for marijuana and alcohol; one year fifty-three were disciplined for alcohol, mostly off campus. The Reverend Charles Lester Kinsolving, EHS 1940–45, sometime-cleric-sometime-reporter, sensationalized that happening in a *San Francisco Chronicle* column headlined "Whiskey Rebellion at Episcopal."

On the rebellious yet humorous and salutary side were the two brothers who refused to stand up in Church, one of whom whispered to me the following year that he was teaching Sunday School at Pennsylvania. There was the football tailback who streaked through the dining room one evening and apologized for it publicly the next evening. I did nothing at the time although there was no mistaking the stride of the lad who had scored a touchdown on the kickoff against Woodberry the previous Fall.

Of course, youth rebellion was felt in our enrollment, yet the school was always full even though it accepted a few boys in the summers in two of those years. Many boys did not wish to give up the unstructured life of home and day school.

As at most schools, our College Board scores slipped and only began to recover in the late seventies and eighties. The Ivy League became especially picky, and one of our Trustees, also a trustee at Princeton, commented that young Ivy League directors of admission thought they could reform American society by whom they admitted to their freshman classes. However, both enrollment and scores began to pick up.

There were many problems in my time, problems that might have driven Dr. Dalrymple up the wall. But I wonder if he was as fortunate as I who had a supportive Board of Trustees, an excellent and strong faculty on whom I could lean for help in almost any area, and student leaders who, on the whole, were also actively supportive. Great boys all fourteen years.

Among the problems of that time was one bigger and darker than all of the others. *Apocalypse Now*. "Of course," Young Flick adds, "the rebellion against the Viet Nam War reached us. I permitted the Chaplain and a group of boys to hold a short protest vigil in the middle of the front circle. This was tough to take when Old Boys were being captured and dying, and my own son was flying a helicopter for his country in Viet Nam."

Five EHS men died in Viet Nam. And one suffered, as a prisoner of war: a captive of people who had no respect for international law, no mercy, he was starved, beaten, mentally tormented and physically tortured, almost beyond the limits of human endurance, for five-and-a-half years.

John S. McCain III (EHS 1951–54) is an Annapolis graduate and son and grandson of admirals.

On October 26, 1967, he was piloting his A-4 fighter-bomber over Viet Nam when disaster struck. As reported in an interview published in *U.S News & World Report* May 14, 1973, just two months after he came home, McCain's story is one of the most extraordinary and horrifying accounts recorded concerning that horrible war.

I was on my 23d mission, flying right over the heart of Hanoi when a Russian missile the size of a telephone pole came up and blew the right wing off my Skyhawk dive bomber.

I pulled the ejection handle, and was knocked unconscious by the force of the ejection. I didn't realize it at the moment, but I had broken my right leg around the knee, my right arm in three places, and my left arm. I landed by parachute in a lake. Some North Vietnamese swam out and pulled me to the side. People gathered, and they were all hollering and screaming and cursing and spitting and kicking at me. My right foot was resting next to my left knee, just in a 90° position. I said "My God— my leg!" That seemed to enrage them. One of them slammed a rifle butt down on my shoulder, and smashed it pretty badly. Another stuck a bayonet in my foot.

Pretty soon, they took me to Hanoi's main prison. For the next three or four days I lapsed from consciousness to unconsciousness. I was taken out to interrogation [and] hit with all sorts of war-criminal charges. They beat me around a little bit. . . . when they hit me it would knock me unconscious. They kept saying "You will not receive any medical treatment until you talk."

J.S. McCain

Then there came to the prisoner's cell an officer nicknamed "The Bug," "a psychotic torturer, one of the worst fiends that we had to deal with," and a "completely incompetent" doctor nicknamed "Zorba" who took his pulse and said "It's too late." But because he was the son of an admiral he was taken to the hospital, where the "treatment almost killed me."

Filth and dirt and water on the floor and a sixteen-year-old guard "right out of the rice fields" who would "slap me and hit me. He had a lot of fun that way." Manipulation of his arm, broken in three places, for an hour-and-a-half "without benefit of Novocaine. . . . I passed out a number of times." More interrogation, by "The Cat" and "Chihuahua," and more refusal to give any information other than name, rank, serial number. More beatings. Three or four spoonfuls of weak, gristly soup twice a day. "I was down to about 100 pounds from my normal weight of 155." The others "didn't expect me to live."

Solitary confinement: "The most important thing for survival is communication, even if it's only a wave or a wink or a tap on the wall, one tap for A, two for B and so on. It's vital to keep your mind occupied. Some guys were interested in mathematics, others would build [in imagination] a whole house. I spent days on end going back over history books. I thought a lot about the meaning of life. It was easy to lapse into fantasies. I memorized the names of all 335 of the men who were then prisoners of war in North Vietnam. I can still remember them."

(One of them was Ernie Brace, a civilian pilot who had been shot down over Laos and kept for three-and-a-half years in a bamboo cage in the jungle with his feet in stocks and an iron collar around his neck with a rope tied to it. He nearly lost the use of his legs but tried to escape three times. After the third try he was buried in the ground up to his neck. Others were Dick Stratton—"They peeled his thumbnails back and burned him with cigarettes"—and Mike Christian—"pounded hell out of him, busted one of his eardrums and busted his ribs.")

More interrogation, by "The Cat" and "The Rabbit." An offer

to be sent home, because that would show the other prisoners that the son of an admiral got special favors. "But I knew that the Code of Conduct says 'You will not accept parole or amnesty [or] special favors." He refused. "The Cat" broke his pen, kicked his chair over, and said "They taught you too well."

Dysentery. "Very severe treatment." Interrogations by "The Soft-Soap Fairy" and "Slopehead," who asked "Why are you so disrespectful of guards?" "I answered, 'Because the guards treat me like an animal.' When I said that, the guards, about ten of them, really laid into me. They bounced me from pillar to post, kicking and laughing and scratching. After a few hours of that ropes were put on me and I sat that night bound with ropes. For the next four days I was beaten every two or three hours. My left arm was broken again and my ribs were cracked.

"They wanted a statement saying I was sorry for the crimes I had committed against North Vietnamese people and that I was grateful for the treatment I had received from them. This was the paradox—so many guys were so mistreated to get them to say they were grateful. But this is the Communist way.

"I held out."

But finally "I reached the lowest point of my five-and-a-half years in North Vietnam. I was at the point of suicide. Every man has his breaking point. I had reached mine."

He wrote a "confession."

"Then the 'gooks' made a very serious mistake. They let me go back and rest for a couple of weeks." The next time "I was able to resist. . . . they couldn't 'bust' me again."

Anti-war groups and "peaceniks" like David Dellinger, Tom Hayden, the Berrigan brothers and James Johnson came. "I refused to see any of them. The propaganda value would have been too great, with my dad as commander in the Pacific."

Beatings, dysentery, boils. Torture for getting caught communicating: "Forced to stand up continuously for a couple of days. . . . [When] I sat down this little guard who was a particularly hateful man came in and jumped up and down on my knee. I had to go back on a crutch for the next year and a half." Torture for refusing to "cooperate:" "Forced to sit on a stool for three days and nights." Torture for nothing: "I had a turnkey who used to just bash me around for drill."

Exercise helped. "It makes you tired and you can sleep, and when you're asleep you're not there."

Hating helped. "If you are going to make it, you get tougher as time goes by. You get to hate them so bad that it gives you strength."

Prayer helped. "It wasn't a question of asking for superhuman strength or for God to strike the North Vietnamese dead. It was asking for moral and physical courage, for guidance and wisdom. I asked for comfort when I was in pain, and sometimes I received relief."

And "Finally came the day I'll never forget—the eighteenth of December, 1972. The whole place exploded when the Christmas bombing ordered by President Nixon began.

"I admire President Nixon's courage. There may be criticisms of him in certain areas, Watergate, for example. But he had to take the most unpopular decisions that I could imagine: the mining, the blockade, the bombing"—and those actions "ended the war."

After his return John McCain's health recovered. "I think I'm in better physical shape than I was when I got shot down."

And he was not spiritually damaged by those years of humiliation, sickness and pain. "Now I don't hate them any more, not those particular guys. I hate and detest their leaders.

"I think America today is a better country than the one I left. We have been through a sort of purging process, a re-evaluation. I had a lot of time to think over there, and came to the conclusion that one of the most important things in a man's life, along with his family, is to make some contribution to his country."

The contribution John McCain chose to make was to go into politics. He ran for public office in Arizona, served two terms as U.S. Representative, and in 1986 was elected to the Senate, succeeding Barry Goldwater.

After reading that U.S. News & World Report story Dick Thomsen, who had been Headmaster when John McCain was a student, wrote to him. He replied: "I often thought of the High School. I am convinced that the standards of behavior and conduct that were imparted to me at the High School were directly responsible for my ability to resist the Communists' attempts at subverting my honor."

Many of our Old Boys have died for their country. None has been brought closer to that death and survived—with honor bright.

DeCourcy Orrick (1965–69) again:

One disadvantage of the boarding school environment was that some boys assumed personalities which bore no resemblance to their true characters. One boy had a reputation for being callous and totally indifferent to those around him; he was the most sarcastic and cynical fellow on the Holy Hill. We called him "Bitter Bill." Over a decade after we left school we met again, and I could find no trace of the old "Bitter Bill." He confessed that the image he had projected was a total lie. He had felt that he needed to cloak himself in bitterness and sarcasm in order to protect himself from his peers, like me, who scared him to death!

Most boys who went to EHS grew up fast, though. The school offered a perfect opportunity to enjoy freedoms and independence unknown by those living their high school years at home.

My first-year contemporaries at the University literally cried as their family cars pulled away. Thanks to Episcopal, family partings were easy for me, and I was off to the Corner for a 3.2 beer before they could dry their eyes.

Taken altogether, the education EHS provided was first-rate. It was there that I learned how to study, how to organize a research paper, how to use the English language. But the most important lesson I learned was how to get along with others.

To this day when I feel happy about accomplishing something of value the tune and words of the hymn "On Our Way Rejoicing" come to mind. We sang that as a final hymn to signify that exams were over, and it was time to go home.

The first hymn we would sing at the beginning of a semester was *Ora Labora*, "Come Labor On." That wasn't as much fun to sing.

Ryvers Wright was at the School toward the end of the troubled times, 1972–76, but his most vivid memories are not of drugs, rebellions or any other counter-culture brouhahas:

In my junior year I took Shakespeare under the late George Dunlop. Mr. Dunlop often left academic discussions to talk about life, something that was fine with the boys in the class.

In the middle of a discussion about *Romeo and Juliet* Mr. Dunlop imparted to us in the class wisdom that I have found myself quoting many times over the years. He said: "If you have to ask yourself if you love someone, you don't, and if you have to ask yourself if you're ready to get married, you're not."

I have a memory from winter soccer (coached by Heslett Murray) of the weather being so cold and wet that our muddy, chopped-up soccer field was frozen solid, with thousands of mud ridges caused by footprints and water (now frozen to ice) covering the surface area. In order to make the field playable, the soccer team had to go onto the field a half-hour before game time and stamp all over the field, thus breaking the ice and levelling the frozen-mud footprints.

When playing on such a field, or on a snowy day, we put plastic bags on our feet between layers of socks to try to keep our feet dry and warm. The bags invariably failed, and we remained cold (the orange slices and tea at halftime also failed—it was too cold) until after the game and we returned to the dorm and had a hot cup of tea made in illegal coffeepots.

> "For this relief, much thanks; 'tis bitter cold,
> and I am sick at heart."
>
> —Hamlet.

Are you sick at heart, Ryvers Wright?

NO! I am happily married, and, à la Mr. Dunlop, my decision to get married wasn't really a decision at all. There I was, counting poles in my father's lumberyard, and suddenly something inside of me clicked and I knew that I should marry Pam. I had not been thinking about her, or about marriage. I called her, picked her up at the airport, proposed over dinner in Oldtown Alexandria, and we were married in July, 1982, and have lived happily thereafter.

As for that wise counselor George Dunlop (student 1945–47, master 1967–81, died October 10, 1981), Lance Koonce (1980–84) has elegized his "deeper sparks, tougher seeds"—gone up in smoke with "The Marlboro Man"—in an extraordinary poem written for a Duke literary magazine and reprinted in the Fall 1988 Old Boy magazine. It is, alas, too long for inclusion here.

During Young Flick's time some eight faculty chairs were established by generous friends of the School, and there was an increase in School enrollment to 280 boys.

As a builder he rivalled the Egyptian Pharaohs. He presided over the construction of two new dormitories (and the re-modelling of two others); an academic building which houses science laboratories, library and audio-visual facilities; a wrestling gymnasium (the old dirt-floor cage converted); a football stadium; an outdoor swimming pool. He changed first the main floor of Stewart Gym and then the Lower Study Hall into an Art Studio, complete with

R. Wright   L. Koonce   L.S. Ainslee

on-campus teacher. He converted a room in Blackford Hall into a small chapel.

The athletic program was expanded to four sports per season and the Summer Camp was started. So was the May Program which enables seniors to contribute their services and gain experience working in hospitals, on Capitol Hill and elsewhere.

The School had not had a full-time Chaplain for years; in 1968 he lured Jack Smith down from Exeter and the two changed both religious course work and worship. No longer were non-specialist teachers required to teach theology. That was (and is) done by the Chaplain and his assistant.

He introduced the custom of declaring a "Headmaster's holiday" about twice a year, usually after two six-day weeks came together and everybody was out of sorts.

He even managed to improve faculty housing—vastly. Now our masters can cook whole meals in their own kitchens!!

Taken altogether, Young Flick reckons that his stewardship was "a time for experiment—some good, some bad."

Time has already shown that there was much good, little bad.

His most important contribution remains as invisible as it is potent. It has been said that the greatness of a school's head is measured not by what he changes, but what he preserves. In troubled years of violence, disorder and savage attacks on ancient values Young Flick provided a fine balance between old and new, and resolutely kept our School on course. His father and his grandfather, who worked so hard to help set that course, would have been as proud of him as are his son and grandson, Old Boys who have followed it.

Our tenth Head, like his four immediate predecessors, attended and taught at the School before he was named to lead it. Lee Sanford Ainslie, Jr., was born in Huntington, West Virginia, June 24, 1937. His father's people came originally from Scotland, (which is why his name ends in -*ie* instead of -*ey*, as it would have if they had come from England.)

One of his great-grandfathers was also head of a school. After graduating from Washington College (later Washington and Lee), Joseph S. Raymond served during the War under Stonewall Jackson, was wounded twice and captured twice, but survived. Then for thirty-eight years he was President of the Jefferson Military College in Washington, Mississippi.

Sandy came to EHS in 1952 and graduated in 1956, having been Chairman of the Honor Committee, captain of the basketball team, co-captain of the track team and a player on the JV football team, president of the E Club, Senior Monitor, member of the Hop Committee, church usher, and winner of the J. C. Herbert Bryant Scholarship Medal. With Fred Wright he concocted most of the captions for the 1956 *Whispers*. One of those captions, which he did *not* write, reads as follows:

" ... His physical stature [he stands 6'6" and weighs 215 pounds] is unimportant by comparison with his standing in the opinion of the school. . . . Sandy is one from whom his classmates expect to hear a good deal in the future."

And hear of him they did, and do.

He went to the University of North Carolina on a Morehead Scholarship and was signally honored by being elected to a small social club so secret that its very name may not be spoken outside the walls of its crypt in Gimghoul Castle.

He graduated from UNC in 1961 and came back to the Hill. Here he taught English and Latin and coached basketball, track and tennis.

In 1974 he was named headmaster of the Virginia Episcopal School in Lynchburg. He learned that in order for the school to maintain its accreditation by the Southern Association of Schools and Colleges, the headmaster must have a master's degree in education with a specialization in administration, which meant that for the first two years while he was mastering Headmastery by day, by night he was taking courses at Lynchburg College.

In 1981 he came to the Hill for the third time, as the boss. In the eight years since then he has significantly changed the School's operation and direction.

Lee Sanford Ainslie, Jr., Headmaster, 1981–

Guided by a two-year study made by the chairmen of the various academic departments, he has completely revised the curriculum. Courses in math and foreign languages have been strengthened and computer work expanded. (Our library is one of the few secondary school libraries in the country to be completely computerized.) For the first time in the School's life we have a music teacher, and the requirements for graduation have been broadened to include introductory courses in music and art.

The Nation's Capital, long the School's playground, has become our workground as well: every student must work there for a whole semester in his sophomore year. That work can be anything from the obvious, such as politics, through the not-so-obvious, such as demographics or social work, all the way to the not-at-all obvious like the formal study of architecture.

Throughout all of their school years all of the boys use Washington as an academic and cultural resource. The Kennedy Center reports that it sells more tickets to the Episcopal High School than to any other institution except the Naval Academy.

For the faculty, there are now formal sabbaticals. (Mark Teeter used his to teach English in a Moscow public school; Riley Deeble and Al Phillips went to Scotland.)

For everybody, these are good and hopeful times.

Says Headmaster Ainslie:

In my comments at the Sesquicentennial celebration in October of 1988 I used as the theme of my talk the fact that Episcopal High School must continue to change in order to continue to remain the same. As I have thought about this observation, I have been reminded of the number of changes which have occurred in so many different areas since I was first introduced to the School in the early fifties.

Perhaps the most obvious changes which have occurred on our campus can be found in the physical facilities. Between 1950 and 1980, the following facilities were built: Pendleton Chapel/Auditorium, the new McGuire Dormitory, Hummel Dormitory, Berkeley Dormitory, the Hummel Library and Learning Center, Flippin Field House, the Hummel Bowl, the swimming pool, nine new dormitory apartments and ten new faculty houses. The building program has not stopped.

During the past decade, the School has added Penick Hall for admissions and development, a new Chapel [in progress], a greatly remodeled and expanded dining room, a new baseball field, a remodeled, rubberized-surface running track, three new dormitory apartments and five new faculty homes.

Walking away from politics? Left to right: Paul Thur de Koos, Kevin Williams, Dr. Ted Faunce, Peter Warfield, Rob Wyatt, David Wafle, Ben Tarbutton, Jeff Woodall. All of the boys were seniors this year.

THIS TREE COMMEMORATES A SCHOOL BOY FRIENDSHIP THAT LASTED A LIFETIME BLANCHARD RANDALL '37 JOHN S. MORTON '38

"THIS TREE" is a sturdy young oak planted by Jack Morton in memory of his friend Blanchard Randall near Hummel dorm last year.

The changes at EHS have not been limited, however, to physical fa-cilities. The curriculum has been revised and expanded dramatically. The School now offers five levels of English, six levels of mathematics, five levels of courses in six foreign languages, numerous general and specific courses in history, and several courses in theology, art, music and com-puter science.

Since 1950 EHS has seen its athletic offerings expand dramatically as well. There were five varsity sports in 1950, and there are now twelve: football, soccer, cross-country, basketball, wrestling, indoor track, squash, tennis, spring track, lacrosse, baseball and golf.

The student body has also grown, and its composition has changed. The enrollment now numbers 280, and incorporates students of many backgrounds, including blacks, other minorities, and foreign students. In 1959 there were 252 students. Thirty years later and on the anniversary of the School's Sesquicentennial, there are 287 students, representing twenty-four states and five foreign countries.

Even some of the School's oldest customs and traditions have been altered. All dormitory rooms now have doors; the floors are carpeted, and Rats no longer run relay. The majority of students spend study hall

Ground was broken for the Callaway Chapel at Homecoming a year ago. Now almost finished, that magnificent house of worship is, spiritually as well as physically, halfway between us and the Seminary.

working in their rooms and not in upper or lower study hall. A majority of the meals are now buffet rather than family-style service.

The character of the School during its proud 150-year history has never been defined by the number of students or the number of courses required for graduation or the number of sports offered. The true character of Episcopal High School has been defined by its philosophy, and that philosophy of developing the whole man remains unchanged. The School continues to see as its primary goal the nurturing of the individual boy, providing him an opportunity to grow spiritually, academically, athletically and socially.

In my opinion, the real essence of the Episcopal High School experience is found in two fields.

First, nearly every student who has ever attended Episcopal has been impressed by the School's high standards in all areas, be they academic, social, or moral. One common experience remembered by nearly all Episcopal High School students over all the generations of the School's existence is the expectation that they all strive to achieve at a level which is beyond the norm. It is a student's effort to reach demanding and challenging standards which results in the growth that is common to EHS boys.

A second significant area for which Episcopal has stood and will continue to stand in the future is the inculcation of a strong value system. Perhaps nothing so typifies this priority as the School's highly respected honor system. A good example of the high regard in which this system is held—and at the same time a testimony to its continued well-being—is the following excerpt from the Chapel talk of the Soviet teacher, Natalya Vikotorovna Nugaeva, who accompanied ten Soviet students to EHS as part of the reciprocal US/USSR High School Academic Partnership program last winter:

"The Episcopal High School honor system, with its four-point code, appeals to me greatly. . . . During our stay here, I have seen how both the teachers and the students live by this code in everything that they do. And I have seen that there is a great trust, respect and mutual understanding here between teachers and students. But what I especially admire is that your honor code is not just a series of abstract principles, but part of a larger *system* of honor. As I understand it, those who violate a point of honor are not just punished but are helped by the Honor Committee to understand what they have done and how their behavior affects both the community and themselves. I am also very impressed that it is the students themselves who watch after the system. I think that the Honor System has done much to create the sense of close community which we feel here at Episcopal High School."

Two other attributes of the School's character which while not as important as the aforementioned nevertheless have played a large part

"The Russians are coming!" And they came: February, 1989.

in the experience of the boys who have come here are the sense of camaraderie, the bonding of friendships, and the enthusiastic school spirit. Another common attribute of each boy's experience here, regardless of generation, has been good humor. The pranks played upon the faculty by the student body of the twenties are in many cases identical to—or at least identical in spirit to—those played upon the faculty today. The students today laugh about the same circumstances as the students of yesterday. In short, a spirit of humor transcends the generations at EHS.

Finally, one other element which has never changed at Episcopal is the faculty's concern for its students. Episcopal High School has always been a caring community, one which is genuinely concerned about the total development of each individual boy. The faculty members of the past and the faculty of the present have served as both parents and teachers for the boys enrolled at the High School.

I shall conclude this chapter as I have concluded almost every alumni talk which I have ever made. While Episcopal High School can be justifiably proud of what it has accomplished in the past in the way of increased and improved facilities, a sound financial structure and generous endowment, strong academic and athletic programs and rich traditions, the greatest strength and the true basis of the School's success is not found in these areas, but rather in its people: its students and masters. All else can be changed, and in many cases must be changed, to reflect the needs of the times. What can never be allowed to change is the spirit, good humor, integrity and devotion of the masters and boys of Episcopal High School. It is this relationship which has been and will continue to be the greatest asset of the School.

Here endeth the first sesquicentennial.

II
HIGHLIGHTS

SESQUICENTENNIAL

1839   1989

Activities

Talents unused do not atrophy; they fester.

—Pascal.

In 1839 there wasn't much organized activity to keep the boys busy outside of the classrooms, and ten years later their undirected energies were obviously causing disciplinary problems; Isaac Watts was of course right when he said "For Satan finds some mischief still/ For idle hands to do." In the 1849 catalog Mr. Dalrymple declared that the School was not intended to be a *"House of Correction* for boys who are unmanageable," and served notice that " 'bad boys' who are habitually idle or insubordinate will be removed by the School authorities."

But it was not until Mr. Blackford took office that the problem was addressed directly. He appealed to the Trustees for "a play-room, in a separate building"—an embryo gymnasium—and he started competitions in track and saw to it that the boys played football, baseball, tennis and lacrosse.

That remarkably prescient man also fathered our Literary Societies, with their forensic competitions, and he encouraged the formation of a choir and the Missionary Society (both in the 1870's) and student-edited publications like *The Monthly Chronicle* and *Whispers*, and whatever other groups might usefully siphon off youthful energies.

Since Mr. Blackford's time, and especially since the late 1940's and early 1950's when all of this country's schools were invigorated by eager GI Bill veterans of World War II, our out-of-classroom activities have multiplied bewilderingly.

There are all of the enterprises listed in the section on Curriculum, plus group work in the arts, music, drama, dance, publications, counselling, camping, whatnot.

Alexandria

Even by Virginia standards Alexandria is an old town.

Much of the present city was included in a 6,000-acre plot granted by Sir William Berkeley, Governor of the colony of Virginia, to one Robert Howsing, an English ship captain, in 1669;

the grant was authorized by King Charles II as a reward for the Captain's having brought 120 settlers from England to live in the New World. The tract overlapped a 700-acre patent which had been issued to a certain Dame Margaret Brent in 1654. The Howsing grant lay along the Potomac River from Hunting Creek north to Little Falls.

Less than a month after he had been given the land Howsing sold it for 6,000 pounds of tobacco, along with the casks in which the tobacco was packed, to John Alexander. Alexander was not through paying, however. He then had to settle with Dame Margaret's heirs for the 700 acres they owned. The original purchase cost him one pound of tobacco per acre; the second cost him 15 pounds per acre. It must have been painful for a Scotsman like Alexander.

In 1732 a group of Scottish merchants, seeking a suitable port for shipping tobacco, built a warehouse at the foot of what is now Orinoco Street in Alexandria, and around it there grew up a small development called Belhaven, after a titled Scottish hero. In 1749 a charter was issued by the Virginia General Assembly granting permission for sixty acres to be used for the establishment of a town, and the land was duly surveyed into lots (George Washington, then seventeen years old, was one of the surveyors) to be auctioned off. Over some protests, the name was changed from Belhaven to Alexandria, in recognition of the Alexander family connection, and in 1779 the town was incorporated.

Alexandria became a port of entry for foreign ships and a major center for export of flour and hemp. Brigs and schooners and ships of the line crowded its harbor; substantial brick houses graced its streets, and "hammer and trowel were at work everywhere," in the words of a French visitor, the Duc de la Rochefoucauld Liancourt. In 1796 he reckoned that "Alexandria is beyond all comparison the handsomest town in Virginia—indeed is among the finest in the United States." (Much colorful Alexandriana may be found in the little booklet *Know Your City* published by the City of Alexandria in 1987.)

In 1754 George Washington drilled militia troops in Market Square and in 1755 led them with General Edward Braddock's expedition in the disastrous attempt to capture Fort Duquesne (Pittsburgh) from the French. Braddock Road, which borders the northern boundary of the High School, is a reminder of that venture.

During the Revolution the town served as a supply and hospital center.

In 1789, the town (with an adjoining segment of Fairfax County) was ceded by the State of Virginia to the Federal Government to become part of the newly-created ten-mile-square District of Columbia. Alexandria had then a population of about three thousand people.

On August 27, 1814, three days after the burning of Washington in the War of 1812, British troops from ships anchored off Alexandria forced the citizens to give up huge supplies of flour, tobacco, cotton and wine, along with ships to transport these commodities. The town itself was spared.

When our School was founded the town had about eight thousand inhabitants, the District about three times that many.

Alexandria remained under Federal control until it was given back to the State in 1847. In 1852 it was declared a city and granted a new charter.

On May 24, 1861, Union forces occupied the city and made it a logistical supply center. Then it became the site of several forts designed to be part of the defenses of Washington. (Fort Ward Park now contains one of these forts, restored.) From 1863 to 1865 Alexandria was the capital of the Restored Government of Virginia, representing the seven Virginia counties which remained under Federal control throughout the War. Those counties were Accomack, Alexandria (now Arlington County), Fairfax, Loudoun, Norfolk, Northampton and Prince William.

In 1952 Alexandria annexed a portion of Fairfax County which included the Episcopal High School.

We are now part of a colorful, proud, peculiarly beautiful town, almost fifty years older than its country's capital.

NB: People who like to know just where they are, geographically, will be pleased to learn that according to the U.S. Coast Guard the Holy Hill's earthly coordinates are latitude 38° 49′ 18″ North, longitude 77° 05′ 56″ West. That means that if a tunnel were drilled from us straight through the center of the planet it would come out on the other side in the Indian Ocean southwest of Australia, near the Diamantina Deep; so far, our student with the longest commute would seem to have been Charles English Henderson III (1934–38), whose address is listed as Bullo River Station, Private Mail Bag 26, GPO Darwin, Australia.

Animals

He liveth best who loveth best
All things both great and small. . . .

—The Ancient Mariner.

Prisoners, it has been said, spend their "spare" time praying, cursing, and writing letters. They also—the lucky ones—befriend whatever wild life they can find sharing their quarters. People whose liberty has been only partially curtailed tend to bypass the first three of those occupations and focus on the fourth. Who knows how many birds, fish, turtles and other companionate fauna have lived on our Hill in secret? Insects, too.

Another thing was training squirrels. We used to get ink bottles and clean them up and smuggle in milk and feed the squirrels with an eye dropper. Then a squirrel would get loose in church. That happened quite often. I sat in front of Mr. Hoxton and I was the squirrel chaser. [Joseph Bryan, III, 1917–21.]

W.A.R. Goodwin

Egypt has become a luxurious smoking lounge. I believe, however, they did make one mistake down there. They put in a nature den. Then that was turned into a menagerie. They had all types of animals, owls and squirrels and dogs and hawks, everything in the world, and it was all right as long as they fed them, but occasionally we would get a little careless, and when they got hungry they started eating each other. Finally the survival of the fittest ended in a nothing to nothing tie. [William A.R. Goodwin, Jr., 1934–40.]

(Bill Goodwin was Head Monitor in 1940. He was killed in action in Sicily three years later. For how "luxurious" our "smoking lounge" ever has been, see the section on Egypt below.)

Pets have probably always been taboo for students at Episcopal, but this rule only challenged them to rise to new heights of deception. On Second Berkeley we had three goldfish in a small tank with a filter and pump all cleverly concealed behind a false bookcase. One fish was named Priscilla after Mrs. William F. Buckley, Jr.—I can't remember the names of the others. Success became boring and we sold our fish to Little Louis. He was carrying them in a big cardboard box across to First Dal when Mr. Ravenel's two playful retrievers jumped all over him. He talked politely to Mr. Ravenel while the dogs kept jumping and the water kept sloshing until the conversation came to an end, and then he walked on as if nothing had happened, which, actually, it hadn't. Sturdy lad; worthy companion for Priscilla. [DeCourcy Orrick, 1965–69.]

Study hall after dinner was a quiet but often boring activity, depending on the various degrees of supervision of individual teachers. On this particular evening, one of the students had brought along and released halfway through the study period a fly, to whose leg he had meticulously attached a piece of long thread. With this impediment the poor fly flew ever so slowly over the rows of students, many of whom added to the general commotion by bobbing and weaving as if it were an enemy plane passing overhead. The ruckus lasted until the fly could no longer move, much to the relief of the bewildered supervisor. [Jim Meem, 1928–31.]

There are a lot of things I remember about EHS and its personalities. One of the greatest nights was when someone turned a bat loose in Mr. Rodwell's study hall. The bat flew up and down the rows of desks while everyone screamed in mock terror and Mr. Rodwell's face got redder and redder. "Banjo Eyes" Hughes aimed his books at the bat and brought the fluorescent lights down on his head. The great finale was when young Flick Hoxton opened the door and demanded to know what was going on! At this point the bat flew directly toward young Flick, who dispatched it with one blow as only Superman could have done. It was awesome! [A. Eugene Geer, Jr., 1944–47.]

A.E. Geer

Young Flick says that that bat-batting took place in the Fall of 1945, and inspired some artist to draw a bat next to his demerit clip. Then, "while keeping 'my' study hall the next Spring, I overcame another bat with a ruler and earned a second bat silhouette. The headmaster who slew dragons in his young teaching days!"

Awards

Psalm 23 verse 5 might have been written for the number of awards now given at the School. The cup of honors runneth over.

The School's highest honor in Mr. McGuire's time was the Rector's gold medal for general merit.

Then Mr. Blackford established the Randolph Fairfax Medal "For Character, Conduct and Scholarship."

Since then Old Boys, families, friends and the School itself have given prizes of all sorts, from books through statuettes to gold medals, for achievements of all sorts, from scholarship through conduct to athletic prowess.

Even a partial list would be too unwieldy for this chronicle. The curious may consult the current Catalogue.

The Bell

The measured tolling of the school bell, a unique sound, civilized, calm, invincible, and final.
—John Knowles, *A Separate Peace.*

Our first bell was taken from a steamboat that travelled between Norfolk and Washington in the 1830's. It rang lustily for the opening of the first session, October 15, 1839, and four years later, October 4, 1843, it rang even more loudly, to sound the alarm: the Principal's house was on fire! The Sun and Friendship Engine Company came from Alexandria; fortunately the wind was blowing hard from the northwest, and the main building was spared.

The bell tolled faithfully for twenty years and then went silent, when the Yankees came.

After the War it roused sleepy boys again and marked the daylight hours for them with what Poe called "tintinnabulation." (It might, conceivably, have been his inspiration for the poem "The Bells." He visited the School in 1847 and that poem was written two years later.)

But then troubles began. The bell, so symbolic of Discipline and Duty, so vulnerable, was a natural target for mischievous young

Oh for Poe and his poem about bells! Ours summons just about everybody to just about everything.

gentlemen, and one bitterly cold night in the 1870's it was turned upside down and filled with water. The water froze and the poor old thing was probably cracked. Later it was unhinged and fell (or was pushed) from the roof, several times, and it was definitely cracked, and so was its voice. Subsequent equally irreverent man- (or boy-)handlings made it hoarser.

In 1911 it was replaced by the present bell, which was freshly minted just for us.

The sabotage continues. There's the inversion-immersion method, the ever-popular muffling of the clapper, and the "be-treacleing" of the bell rope. Merciful Time has obliterated the identities of most members of what must have been a small army of bell bashers, tippers, clapper-clouters, tricklers and suchlike— ask not for whom the bell tolled, it tolled—or went silent—for these.

There is a legend that Mrs. Blackford once found a student's book at the scene of a recent bell-boggling and quietly returned it to him, thus preserving his demerit-free anonymity. But not all toll-tamperers have been so lucky. It is of record that Edward D. Tayloe (1895–1900), did, "with one other fellow-student, at some ungodly hour invert the bell and fill it with water, which froze solid overnight." That is a rare instance of this classic crime wherein the perpetrator's identity is known.

In 1966 on Second McGuire there lived a senior who now holds a doctorate in chemistry but whose finest hour undoubtedly was the time he placed two sweat socks over the clanger of the bell. The whole school was late for breakfast. It was rumored that this same fearless lad placed the "whoopie" cushion under the Headmaster's red velvet kneeling pad in chapel. [DeCourcy Orrick, 1965–69.]

Bun

Vic owned and operated two seedy country stores. One was located in a brick building at the corner of Braddock Road and King Street at the foot of the hill in a small settlement appropriately named Mud Town. His other store was in the opposite direction past the football field through the woods beyond the pigpen and about a quarter-mile down a dirt country road. It was a one-room, dilapidated, unpainted frame structure reminiscent of the houses along the main street of an old cowboy movie. Vic's brother Bun ran this store. Bun was no Lord Chesterfield, but generally quite pleasant and well liked by the boys.

The honor system, which permeated every facet of school life, also prevailed at Bun's store. When a boy was ready to leave, he added up in his own mind his purchases and announced his total bill which Bun accepted and recorded in his account book. It was rare that Bun had to remind a boy of a forgotten item. The line of credit, however, was quite limited. After the account book showed several dollars due, Bun, having at least some of the instincts of his brother, was quick to remind his debtor that payment was in order. If this failed, Bun wrote his parents. [Harry Blackiston, 1923–28.]

One great experience was the winning of a large box of candy at Bun Donaldson's store, when I punched the right name on a card of chance. I took it back to school and had my own raffle. I did better as I raffled off each of the three trays of candy separately. [Aldrich Dudley, Jr., 1924–30.]

Oh, those relaxing strolls in the afternoon to Donaldson's store for a coke or a piece of candy! [Jim Meem, 1928–32.]

I remember going over to Bun Donaldson's store during the old days, just before the crash. ("How are you, Bun?" "Pretty good, pretty good.") All I could afford was chocolate milk or that awful stuff that I think was called Mavis. [Stuart Taylor, 1928–31.]

S. Taylor

Stuart Taylor weathered the crash by newspapering, first in Philadelphia and then in California, where he was editor-publisher of the Santa Barbara *News Press* from 1964 to 1985. What about recent charges that the U.S. press is arrogant and invasive? "I've been fed up with the press-bashing, and the dumbkopfs who are almost ready to yell for censorship. But I think the press, specifically television, brought on some of it with over-zealous investigative reporting with some characters acting more like prosecutors than reporters."

None of those characters worked for the SB *News Press*.

And Bun's invariable greeting was not exactly what is reported above. Precisely what he did say will be readily remembered by every one of the thousand or so boys who trudged across the field

---

V. C. DONALDSON

DEALER IN

General Merchandise and
Fine Groceries

COAL AND WOOD :: :: HAY AND MILL FEED OF ALL KINDS

BELL 'PHONE

THEOLOGICAL SEMINARY, VIRGINIA

1919

Bun's store, about 1925.

and through the woods to his snug little one-room chocolate-milk-Mavis-and-candy emporium in those years when it represented freedom of a sort, when it seemed almost a part of Beyond, the great waiting world where money could buy unimaginable pleasures.

So will each of those boys vividly remember the first time he ever came to that store and Bun, having greeted him on that little porch, led him into the dark inside, reverently pointed to a curious dried object hanging on the wall, and declared solemnly that it was a very special Something that had once belonged to George Washington.

What exactly were they: Bun's greeting, and the special Something?

For those who don't remember, let them, like Bun, and his store, and those remote, slightly sticky, innocent days, rest in peace.

Characters

O brave old world, that had such people in't!
—The Tempest (modified).

The boy who got the most astounding grades during my years at the School, and did it with comparatively slight effort, was Littleton M.

Wickham. He was brilliant in both math and languages, a rare combination, and carried off practically every scholarship medal and prize in
the place. He was scornful of athletics. A dedicated snob, as he himself was the first to admit, he was descended from Charleston, South
Carolina, aristocracy and John Wickham, the famous defense attorney
in the Aaron Burr trial of 1807.

L.M. Wickham

After graduating in law at the University of
Virginia, "Lit" Wickham taught for a few
years at Episcopal High and then began practicing law in Richmond. He would spend
hours rummaging through dictionaries and
other reference books in search of precisely
the right word or phrase for a legal brief,
when such exactitude was by no means that
important. Given a jury case by his firm, he
invariably lost it because of his top-lofty attitude toward the jurors. An intellectual, he
made no bones about it and wanted everybody to know it. A unique achievement was
his reading all the known works of Homer,
Virgil, Dante and Rabelais in the original. He
scorned American authors and paid no attention to their writings.

Littleton Wickham was *sui generis*. I don't suppose there has been
anybody like him, before or since. He didn't care tuppence what anybody thought of him. Wickham was against nearly all the changes
that had taken place since the Civil War. He didn't go quite so far as
a gentleman with the incredible name of Mountjoy Cloud, who visited
the University of Virginia from time to time. Cloud, a native Missis-
sippian, said he wished he had been born in 1835 and been killed in
Pickett's charge at Gettysburg. [V Dabney, 1914–17.]

The School seems to have survived Lit, but what if Mount had
come here too?

Every class, I am sure, has its "character," and ours was no exception. We had a boy who lived on Second Memorial who loved to lie in
his bed and spit at the ceiling; then he would hastily pull the sheet
over his head in the event his projectile fell short. His ceiling was
mute testimony to the fact that he was pretty good at his trade. [J.T.
"Skin" Lane, 1922–26.]

Colleges

Getting into a good college wasn't such a big deal until fairly recently. This is how our own Cooper Dawson did it, precisely sixty-one years ago:

S.C. Dawson

W. Shiers

In the Spring of each year Mr. Hoxton would announce in chapel that any boys going to the University of Virginia for next year should check their names on the list under his clip that day. I didn't hear the announcement as day students were not required to attend chapel. Nobody asked me if I was going to college although it was my seventh year at EHS.

So I got a roommate and a room and gaily went to Charlottesville with my good friend Bruce Gunnell to enter the University in September, 1928. On registration day I paid my fees, a total of $105, and walked up to the table to register with the D's. The gentleman at the table did not have my name on his list and refused to register S. Cooper Dawson, Jr. He sent me to the Dean.

I walked into the Dean's office with two pieces of paper stating that I had gotten advanced standing in Latin and in math at the University and asked to be admitted. The Dean looked at me and said "I guess I had better call up Archie Hoxton," which he did by the use of central and a little delay. When he got Mr. Hoxton on the phone he said "Archie, I have a young fellow here who says his name is S. Cooper Dawson, Jr., and he wants to come to the University. Shall I let him in?" Evidently Mr. Hoxton said "Yes, please take him off my hands, I have had him for seven years," and the Dean gave me a note for the man at the D table and I was in.

It was all so simple.

Nineteen years later? Bill Shiers (1945–47):

Having recently endured with two children the coldly calculating process of modern college applications (PSAT's, SAT's, essays, letters of recommendation and the like) I marvel at how truly simple life was back in 1947—if only you had the right people on your side.

I had attended a small-town public high school for two years and somehow managed to survive the academic rigors of EHS for another two. Possessing good grades and enough credits for college entrance, but not the right quantity nor mix to qualify for an Episcopal diploma, I sought a recommendation from Mr. Hoxton, certain that he had the single-handed CLOUT to get me admitted to Washington and Lee.

I'll never forget the interview, with Flick's laser stare knifing through the event. I argued that, as a prospective journalism student, it would be costly and unnecessary to return to Alexandria for another year just to shore up my credentials in math and science. He countered from an entirely unexpected direction. "Son," he inquired, "who makes the decisions in your home, you or your Father?" I blurted, "Sir, in matters that pertain to me I am usually given a say." I was sure he would think this answer impertinent and summarily close the interview. But he was impassive.

We reviewed my plight in more detail, then at length he said, "You must understand that until you are a graduate of the High School, it would not be proper or fair to others for me to give you an official recommendation for college." I knew for certain that I had lost the contest until, after a long pause, he volunteered, "However, I can write Dean Gilliam a personal letter saying that, if admitted, I think you will do well." Such a letter, in that era, was currency of value far greater than any transcript I could ever produce. And, not incidentally, the episode taught me a lot about the quality of mercy.

As a seventeen-year-old, I thought of my situation in 1947 as unique and entirely special, but often over the years I have wondered how many hundreds of times Old Flick had been begged in similar fashion to put his credibility on the line for a parade of youngsters with modest prospects. Boy, did he have CLOUT!

And was Old Flick's confidence in his non-graduate justified? Says Bill Shiers, "My first year at W&L went swimmingly. EHS had prepared me too well. My second year was miserable. I had gotten out of the habit of studying. After that I settled down, got my B.A. and Certificate in Journalism, and would have gone to law school but the Korean War came along and besides I was broke. Still am. Flick never said I'd get rich."

In the past four years two or more EHS graduates have applied to and been accepted by these thirty-five colleges and universities:

Boston University, Brown, Bucknell, Cornell, Dartmouth, Davidson, Denison, Duke, Emory, English Speaking Union, Florida, Georgetown, Georgia, Hampden-Sydney, James Madison, Middlebury, Morehouse, North Carolina, North Carolina State, Pennsylvania, Princeton, Rhodes, Richmond, Roanoke, Rollins, St. Andrew's (Scotland), University of the South, Southern Methodist University, Tulane, Virginia, Virginia Polytechnic Institute, Wake Forest, Washington and Lee, William and Mary, Yale.

Cubicles

I am pent up where there is not room enough to
swing a cat.
—Smollett, Humphry Clinker.

Except for a small number of select old boys who had conventional bedrooms and a roommate, all others slept in cubicles consisting of a chair, a locker and a bed with a green curtain in place of a door. Rugs were not permitted. Students were not allowed to enter any cubicle other than their own. Everything else in the drab, box-like, old-fashioned three-story dormitory was equally simple. One or two monitors bunked on each floor and were responsible for keeping order, seeing that lights were out on time, etc. I could see the Washington Monument from my cubicle window. At night I looked longingly at it and agreed with others that where I was could be more accurately described as as a "Hell Hole" rather than a "Holy Hill." [Harry Blackiston, 1923–28.]

Studying after "lights out" presented a challenge to enterprising students in the 1960's. One year I was fortunate enough to have a bed the head of which abutted a wooden wardrobe that had a loose panel which easily slid aside. This enabled me to stick my head inside the locker and with a flashlight read in comparative safety the likes of *Anthony Adverse, War and Peace, Gone With The Wind* and other titles recommended for extra credit by William Bee Ravenel. [DeCourcy Orrick, 1965–69.]

For another way of achieving cubicular study after "Lights Out," read Mud Churchman's stirring account of how he memorized the whole of Caesar's *Gallic Wars*, filed in the section on Latin.

Needless to say, those old green-curtained unlighted cubicles

"In dorm," 1914. *Behind those curtains were rows of cubicles like the one shown.*

"In dorm," 1979. *Billy Hughes and Gordon Lowman in their far-from-Spartan pad.*

have themselves gone with Decy Orrick's wind. Today's young EHS gentlemen abide in large, comfortable, brilliantly lit, lavishly (an old cubiclean would say) furnished, hyperimaginatively bedizened and loud-with-music rooms.

Curriculum

Instruction which enlightens the understanding not separated from the moral education which amends the heart.
—de Tocqueville, *Democracy in America*.

When the School was founded the Trustees intended that it should prepare its boys so well that they could enter the Seminary directly, without going through a college, and so a curriculum almost equivalent to that of a college was laid out.

Old records show that in the first sessions the boys studied Latin, Greek, English, mathematics and "natural philosophy," which included physics, chemistry, astronomy and mechanics. Of course, as Dr. Pendleton said, "Religious instruction is imparted more or less fully and systematically by all the teachers; this is expected to be a matter of chief interest to them all."

Ever since then a notably high level of scholarship has been maintained here. It is not uncommon that a graduate of this School finds his first year or so of college so repetitive that if he doesn't take thought for the morrow he forgets how to study.

The greatest change in our curriculum has been in the shift in emphasis, common in all Western institutions of learning, from the arts to the sciences—from the medieval Trivium, of grammar, rhetoric and logic, to the Quadrivium, of arithmetic, geometry, music and astronomy—and the corresponding lessening of the importance attached to religious instruction.

At the present time, an EHS student may take courses in English, Russian, French, German, Spanish, creative writing, art, music, photography, environmental science, math, computer sciences (the whole Holy Hill hums with high-tech/"user-friendly" artful intelligences), biology, chemistry, physics, history, anthropology, government, economics, public affairs, international relations and war as well as aviation, ethics, theology, evolution, "Problems of Existence" and Latin and Greek. (Greek, abandoned in 1957, has been reinstated.)

$$\frac{1}{p} = 2a \cos\left(\theta + \frac{\pi}{6}\right)$$

$$\frac{1}{2ap} = \cos\theta \cos 30 - \sin\theta \sin 30$$

$$\frac{1}{2ap} = \frac{\cos\theta \sqrt{3}}{2} - \frac{\sin\theta}{2}$$

$$\frac{1}{a} = p\cos\theta\sqrt{3} - p\sin\theta$$

$$\frac{1}{a} = \sqrt{3}x - y = \frac{1}{a}$$

$$\frac{\sqrt{3}x - y}{\sqrt{3}+1} = \frac{1}{2a} = ?$$

Ewing Lawson (1896–98): math: November 12, 1896.

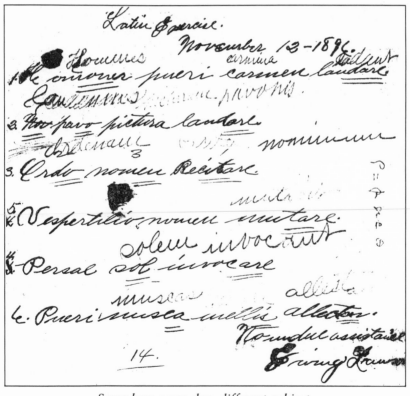

Same boy, same day, different subject.

In addition to these in-house nourishments the School offers arranged work in Washington (the May Program) and access to innumerable cultural happenings in the Capital.

There are summer foreign language programs in Spain, France, Germany and the Soviet Union, and the School participates in the programs of School-Year Abroad and the English-Speaking Union.

'Twas not always such a smorgasbord.

Former Headmaster Dick Thomsen reports thus about curricularity and allied matters of the past:

Exam questions recorded by Littleton Wickham as an EHS student, 1911–15, were quite formidable. Sample arithmetic question: "Divide 219.60 in the proportion of 36.41 and 45." When Wickham came aboard as a teacher in 1917 his contract called for him to teach "the two highest forms of French, both classes of Spanish, Latin I, II, III and possibly IV."

For this he was offered $660, "with room, light, heat, and attendance." The salary was reduced by $16 per month for board and $4 per month for laundry. (A letter to him from Mr. Hoxton later on contained the good news that the charge for board would be eliminated beginning in the session 1920–21.) Wickham's salary was raised to $1150 for 1918–19, and was $1300 by 1920–21. (My beginning salary, for the 1939–40 session, was $1200, and this was raised to $1400 for 1940–41.) Wickham's stationery accounts as a teacher indicated that he bought some of the books (used by himself) for his classes and that the most pervasive charge was for blotters at five cents a package. (No clue as to number in a package.)

Of what value are directed studies?

Said the philosopher/doctor Sir Thomas Browne, with typical seventeenth-century eloquence: *The wisedome of God receives small honour from those vulgar heads that do rudely stare about and with a grosse rusticity admire His workes; those highly magnifie Him whose judicious enquiry into His acts, and deliberate research of His creatures, return the duty of a devout and learned admiration.*

Said that other philosopher/doctor, Hippocrates, with typical classic Greek brevity: *Many admire, few know.*

Through its wide and deep curriculum this School aims for the best of both of those essentials: to generate knowledge of, and magnify admiration for, all of His acts and creatures.

Customs

Be not the first by whom the new are tried,
Nor yet the last to lay the old aside.
—Pope, Essay on Criticism.

Headmaster Dick Thomsen collected for Principal Dick Williams' history, *The High School,* such an intriguing treasury of facts, near-facts and fancies about old EHS customs and folklore that with his permission it is re-included almost in its entirety, with a few minor changes, here.

Bosses

One of the oldest customs of the School is the practice of referring to desserts as "bosses." The fact that bosses have constituted down through the years the only legal tender recognized by the School for betting purposes has kept this gustatory outlet for the gambling instinct in the public eye. The loyal booster for some college or professional team, or other cause, is frequently called upon to put up "a week's boss" (or two, which has been established in recent years as the maximum one can commit and still be within the School's anti-gambling regulations) in support of his vocal claims of superiority for his team, or his foul-shooting prowess, or something—or else to shut up.

The expression itself is seemingly lost in the mists of antiquity, and no alumnus has yet been uncovered who can speak with real authority on the origin of the term. The Reverend Churchill J. Gibson (EHS 1902–05) advises that desserts were a rare, once-a-week occasion in his time and that the day on which they were served was therefore the top day of the week, or "boss day." Dr. A. Colclough Dick (EHS 1919–23) states that in logging camp tradition the day when the boss visited the camp was generally marked by an extra good meal, complete with dessert, and that he believes the School somehow fell heir to this boss-equals-dessert association.

Mondays

Less elusive is the reason for the High School's practice of having Monday as the weekly holiday (or classless day) instead of Saturday. The following letter from Dr. Blackford to Mr. W. D. Cabell, Esq., headmaster of Norwood School, Norwood, Virginia (where the former was assistant headmaster before coming to EHS) is self-explanatory:

September 28, 1870

My dear Sir:

A change in the established custom of schools in Virginia which I have (by the example of the preparatory department of the University of the South) been led to introduce strikes me as so admirable that I venture to recommend it to you. It is to have Monday, not Saturday, the rest day. This removes all temptation to boys to study on Sunday, and all necessity to keep their lessons in mind during the long interval from Saturday night until Monday morning. It leaves Sunday freer and less cumbered with secular thoughts or anxieties, and seems to me in every way an improvement. My boys like it well.

The School today may be less concerned about tempting the boys to study on the Sabbath, but the Monday holidays have continued with the enthusiastic endorsement of faculty and students alike. Saturdays and Sundays are thereby unencumbered by study halls, and Washington on Mondays is a far less crowded place in which to shop, dine, visit movies, museums, galleries, etc, than it is on Saturdays.

[Editor's note: In recent years the need to coordinate our activities with those of other schools has caused EHS to make Saturday instead of Monday the holiday almost every week. Pity.]

Colors

Just as well documented is the origin of our present school colors. The following letter written in 1951 to Mr. Christopher C. Baldwin, Jr. (EHS 1912-17), then alumni secretary, tells the story:

Dear Chris:

In accordance with your request for my recollection as to the adoption by the Episcopal High School of its present colors, my recollection thereof, though vague in some respects, is as follows:

When I entered as a student in the fall of 1888, the school colors were black and blue. There was considerable dissatisfaction among the students as to said colors [apparently the School's athletic opponents were wont to talk of beating EHS "black and blue"], so a committee was appointed to determine the advisability of changing the colors and if advisable to make recommendation as to other colors. This was during the session of either 1888 or 1889-1890. I do not remember the names of [all] the five members of the committee, but Dick Thomas, Lewis Machen and I were members of said committee.

We obtained samples of a large number of colors from merchants, and, after many conferences decided that Maroon and Black were the most satisfactory; not only because they were well matched, but because they were characteristic of the dignity and high standing, both collegiate and otherwise, of this school.

Before making a definite selection, we obtained information from a number of universities, colleges and high schools as to their colors, and, to the best of my recollection, none of them adopted the Maroon and Black.

The colors were then adopted. They have waved for nearly sixty years. May they ever wave.

Although nearly sixty years have elapsed since I left the High School, I still glory in the recollections of the days spent there by me, and of the faculty and students who made life worth living.

> With best wishes, I am,
>> Sincerely yours,
>> William W. Old, Jr.

Whispers

The first EHS yearbook was published for the session of 1891–92, but for the next ten years its appearance was sporadic and uncertain. A more stable tradition was established by the appearance in 1903 of *Whispers*, as our present annual is called, which has regularly and faithfully recorded the passing years since its inception. The name "Whispers" has a gossipy connotation, and there *have* been issues in which were printed revelations quite unsuitable for a manly, straightforward group of young gentlemen. The name, however, does not derive from such inclinations or episodes, but from far more romantic sources.

We are fortunate in having a report from the Reverend Oscar deWolf Randolph (EHS 1899–1903), the first editor-in-chief of *Whispers,* to the effect that: "In our day at E.H.S., 'having the whisper' was an expression on the Hill which connoted about the same thing as being crazy about a girl." The inimitable Churchill Gibson gives an expanded account of the eponymy, and his version is quite obviously based on solid first-hand experience. He writes as follows:

When we went "fussing" at the dawn of the century, i.e. scouting the "Kalic," which is short for "calico"—to you moderns, calling on the girls—we hunted in packs. On a Saturday or Sunday night a girl's "parlor" would be crowded with E.H.S boys.

When the time grew nigh when our presence was requested back at school, all left at once—but perchance some lucky devil dawdled and had just one last word ere he left at the end of the line. That one was said to "have the whisper" and was set up above his fellows.

The "whisper" was a great prize—and so came the name *Whispers* to be applied to the annual.

In short, when you had "the whispers," you had the last word. It would be hard to imagine a more appropriate name for a school yearbook; too bad the word has lost its earlier connotation.

Egypt

Egypt is an old and unofficial school organization, a rather exotic club which draws its members from those students who are addicted to the smoking habit and who, having reached the ripe age of seventeen and having obtained written permission from their parents, are allowed to smoke in a specially prescribed area on campus. The origin of the name, stemming from some scatological association with pyramids of a bygone day, is a closely guarded secret. Leadership reposes in a Pharaoh or a Sultan, with other ceremonial duties assumed by a High Priest, a Scribe and other impressive functionaries. Various indoor areas have proved to be quite inadequate for housing this spirited group, and the members now pursue their activities—smoking cigarettes, singing songs, spinning yarns and assassinating characters—under the open skies, rejoicing in the fresh, bracing air of Northern Virginia.

Waiters

The High School's "elite corps" of waiters, two teams which serve on alternate weeks throughout the session, constitutes a system that appears to be unique among schools. The high prestige and morale of these teams are such that the selection of waiters is a highly competitive process, and, although there is some remuneration (circa 35 cents a meal), financial need is not a factor, and successful candidates are as likely as not to be well-heeled.

Few realize that the system began as a strike-breaking action in the mid-1920's when the hired waiters walked out. Mr. Joseph

H. Harrison (EHS 1921–25) has told how Mr. Hoxton assembled the school and announced the crisis just ten minutes before lunch, and how the entire student body arose in response to his apologetic call for volunteers to serve at the handsome pay of five dollars a week.

Trickle

And then there is the tradition of having syrup regularly on the table at meals and designating it as "treacle" (pronounced "trickle" in EHS lore). There was a time when "treacle" was served with all meals, but conventional jams and jellies have replaced it at breakfast, it was deemed unwanted at lunch, and only at supper does it now make a daily appearance, in conjunction with the hot rolls which are equally traditional. We have no less an authority than Mr. Robert L. Whittle (EHS 1903–06, Faculty 1910–1965) for the claim that the nomenclature, if not the custom itself, derives from Dickens' *Nicholas Nickleby*. In that novel (published in 1839) the brutish wife of the ogreish schoolmaster of "Dotheboys Hall" forces gobs of a "delicious compound" of "brimstone and treacle" into the mouths of the underfed pupils "partly because if they hadn't something or other in the way of medicine they'd be always ailing and giving trouble, and partly because it spoils their appetites and comes cheaper than breakfast and dinner."

[Editor's note: speaking somewhat defensively off-the-record, Dick Thomsen says of EHS's trickle, "I *loved* it—and especially on chief baker Buster's rolls!"]

White Ties

Another old tradition was the practice of having two monitors, wearing white four-in-hand ties, read the Bible lessons at the regular Sunday evening chapel services. Each monitor was expected to perform this duty at least once during the session, and possibly twice. No one seems to know just when or how the custom began, but it is probable that Dr. Blackford introduced it after observing it at some English public school during one of his frequent summer trips abroad. We can surmise further that the ties were intended to help solemnify the occasion and to help sanctify the readers, at least temporarily.

The practice was discontinued in the early 1950's, not because white ties were increasingly difficult to obtain (although this was the case), but because the situation changed. For one thing, the Sunday evening chapel service has been replaced, except on occasion, by a diversified program of lectures, cultural events, educational movies, etc. For another, the students—both monitors and non-monitors—have been taking increasing responsibility for the conduct of chapel services, and they now read the daily lessons both in morning chapel and in the dining room after supper. The wearing of white ties seemed somewhat incongruous under these circumstances. The tradition is gone, at least for the time being, but we believe that the broadened base of chapel participation and experience constitutes a net gain for the School.

Eggs, Hams, and Sausages

From the mid-1850s there are stories of how the appearance in downtown Alexandria of EHS students, fresh in their uniforms (prescribed until 1861) and equally fresh, no doubt, in their attitudes, was enough to set the town boys to howling "eggs, hams, and sausages" (a title derived from the School's initials). This town-and-gown tension was marked by frequent battles between our uniformed predecessors and a particularly savage group of townies known as the "Blood Tubs," according to reminiscences left us by Alexander Hunter (EHS 1855–61).

Demerits

We have left undone those things which we ought to have done, and we have done those things which we ought not to have done, and there is no health in us.

Lost in the merciful mists of time are the origins of the School's present system whereby spiritual health can be restored to young committers of sins of omission and commission by the working off of demerits. Perhaps Dr. Blackford substituted that method of restoration for the thrashings favored by his predecessors.

For decades demerits were discharged by walking around "the bull ring," the road which still circles the central School buildings, four laps (one mile) per demerit, or by writing them off, as here described by Mr. Callaway: "Eight four-syllable words are to be written in order. The words are chosen by the master in charge of demerits. Sometimes a short word such as 'epitome' or 'epilepsy'

Chris Wollak of the class of 1984 writing off demerits.

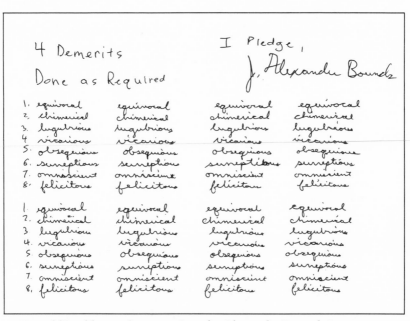

One-fifth of four columns written by Alexander Bounds (1986–89).

will take the place of a word of ten or more letters such as 'conflagration' or 'incompatible.' I remember once a boy tried to write off demerits using two pens at the same time! The words were fairly legible but it was not the right way, as no word should be written twice in the same group."

During or soon after World War I a third method was devised: demerits could be discharged by work done for the School (but not for personal service).

At first an ordinary citizen had to work off demerits if he got four or more in one week; a monitor needed six or more. Now it is five or more for everybody.

PHC: "Once a teacher requested that a boy be allowed to 'study off' demerits at the rate of one per half-hour. The nearest thing to acceptance of this novel proposal was permission for the boy to read an assigned paperback book while walking off demerits in the usual way. He walked, read, and tore out each page of the book as he finished it—and after a few pages decided that what he gained in reading was not worth what he lost in walking speed."

One Monday in my first year I "hooked" to Washington without permission with Ike Parrish and Hugh Cathcart and of course was seen and reported by Mr. Carter and "The Hawk" Latham. The penalty was 60 demerits or 240 times around the school buildings on the circular driveway. Each demerit was one mile. [E. Conway Moncure, 1929–33.]

"One boy had ten demerits. He put 40 pebbles in his pocket when he began to walk them off. After each lap he threw away a pebble. When he had thrown away the last one, he reported ten demerits walked. In figuring the time per mile he saw that his time for *walking* was much better than the school record for *running* a mile. Then he discovered that he had a hole in his pocket!"—PHC.

A somewhat dubious distinction: in four years at EHS I never had to work off a demerit! The complicated system of awarding demerits and working them off could best be described as byzantine. The rules were microscopically detailed and demerits could be awarded for anything from an improperly folded newspaper at the breakfast table to an unauthorized absence from school. To quote from the Sixth Edition of the Handbook for Students (September, 1966): "For every demerit incurred during a week (if as many as four) a boy is required on the following weekly holiday, immediately after chapel (or the study period if he is required to attend it) to copy in the prescribed order in the schoolroom twenty sets of eight words of not less than four syllables each, selected by the dean of students. If a boy has not more than ten demerits, he may work them off by walking, four laps for each demerit around the drive which circles the main building, Blackford Hall, McGuire Hall, etc."

I was cautious in my conduct but not really a goody two shoes. Dozens of times I received less than four demerits and twice I was "stuck" over ten. But thanks to the carefully prescribed rules governing how demerits could be awarded ("Reports of demerits must be posted by the masters before the end of supper of the following day") I eluded punishment.

I remember well skipping junior football practice my rat year to go to the soda fountain in the Bradlee Shopping Center. For that transgression Mr. Shelor awarded me thirty demerits. Luckily, he failed to post them in time as required by the Handbook, so I got off scot-free.

When I left EHS I thought that my performance had gone unnoticed, but not so. Mr. Callaway later told me that ever since 1969 he had cited my demeritless record to exhort good conduct from each new class. [DeCourcy Orrick, 1965–69.]

According to Allen Phillips, who has for a quarter of a century sat in judgment and execution on matters disciplinary, the actual champion dealer-with-demerits was and still is Matt Quarles. In three years, 1971–74, he reaped *not one* of the pesky things!

And what was his formula for success?

I wish I could write an entertaining satirical account of my experience on the Hill, but my "formula for success" was simple.

M. *Quarles*   W.F.K. *French*   C. *Gaines*

My formula for successfully graduating from Episcopal without receiving a single demerit stemmed from my realization that the rules imposed by Episcopal were established for our general welfare—and if nothing else adherence to them made life easier. Whether I agreed or not, I did appreciate the need for them and the authority from which they sprang.

After a point in time I had maintained so clean a record that it became self-perpetuating, as much a matter of pride and seeing how long I could maintain it as it was following the rules.

My saying that I was always the mischievous instigator or a step ahead of the faculty would prove better reading but the truth is that being the youngest of three boys I was up against some kid-wise parents. By the time I reached the hollow halls of the High School I had already been through fifteen years of boot camp. Episcopal was a piece of cake.

PS: My older brother was expelled during his senior year—I'm sure that this came into play as well—a compulsive desire by a sibling brother to redeem the family name and move ahead in a friendly rivalry.

William Fuller K. French of Midland, Texas, and the class of 1983, thought of infame and exdemeritation:

If one was fortunate enough to be caught drinking alcohol and not be dismissed from school, the 100 demerits automatically initiated him into the infamous "Century Club." At Episcopal there is, unfortunately, no way to accrue merits to counteract one's demerits.

Actually, says Mr. Callaway, there is now such a way: "Recently a 'merit system,' which applies only to seniors, has been instituted. A boy gets two merits per week if he does not get 'workable' demerits that week. Those merits may be used to cancel demerits. The maximum number of such merits that a boy can have at any one time is ten."

John E. Cay, Jr. (1930–33) earned his membership in the Century Club thanks to "Nourishing Nora":

My last year was 1933. In the Spring of that year I had been accepted at the University of North Carolina and my good buddy Joseph Benjamin Chestnut Denmark, also a Savannahian, had been accepted at Princeton.

As all Old Boys will recall, Spring in Alexandria is beautiful and a young man's fancy turns to a subject not necessarily involving academics or athletics. Joe and I had read in the Washington paper that the Gaiety Theatre, known to the students as the 9th Street Opera House, was featuring "Nourishing Nora Ford" as the headline performer. In spite of the fact that we were only two weeks from the end of our last year, the appeal of this actress was too much for us and we decided to "hook to town."

On a Friday evening, after lights, we succesfully made our way off campus, bummed a ride into Washington, and thoroughly enjoyed the midnight show. We did not sit in the front row, as we thought that would be too conspicuous, so with an abundance of precaution we sat in the third row. We returned to the High School without incident and were very proud of how clever we had been. What we didn't know was that Mr. Robert Latham, our math professor, was also a devotee of "Nourishing Nora" and had attended the same performance.

The next morning after chapel we were told to come to Mr. Hoxton's office. He questioned us about our activities the evening before. The honor system being what it is, we of course told him the truth. Mr. Hoxton told us what we already knew, that "hooking to town" was a shipping offense. He also told us that inasmuch as we were within two weeks of leaving the High School and had been accepted in colleges he would not invoke the usual penalty. Instead he would give us each 100 demerits which we would be required to walk off prior to our leaving. Also we were told that we must write our parents advising them of what we had done and what the penalty was. He further said that the letter to our parents would be a personal matter between us and them, but that he would like to see their replies.

My father was a widower and fortunately was the type who would understand his son's unwise and untimely behavior. I advised Dad of the facts and explained to him that I would have to walk off 100 demerits prior to coming home. Dad, not being much of a letter writer, sent me a telegram which simply said SORRY FOR YOUR PROBLEM STOP START WALKING HOME.

It will be hard to believe, but Joe and I finished the 100 demerits on graduation day. No one had ever walked 100 demerits before.

Mr. Hoxton came out near the end, saw us walking and called us up to his porch. Joe and I, of course, thought he was going to remove the rest of the demerits. He asked us how we were getting along. We stated that we were making it, whereupon he stated that he would remove *one* lap because he had interrupted us.

When we were completing the 99th demerit, we decided to walk one extra lap so that we could truthfully say that we had walked 100 demerits; I get tired just thinking about it.

PS: I am not sure that the vision of "Nourishing Nora" was worth the effort nor am I sure that the punishment fit the crime. But to become a legend at the High School makes it all worth while.

PPS: When my son was born I entered him at birth at the High School. Mr. Hoxton was still the headmaster. He wrote my wife a letter acknowledging the fact that my son was entered and he suggested to her that she start walking the young man around the crib, pointing out that if he was anything like his father he would need the experience. [John Cay is among the 1933 monitors pictured in Chapter 6.]

The record for most demerits awarded at any one time was probably set in 1976. Because of scheduling requirements there had been two six-day weeks in a row, and suddenly the word "Boycott" turned about three-quarters of the students into a mob; the mob conglobulated, was assured by Clarence Gaines that "They can't stick us all," and boycotted some classes. Result: "They" did "stick us all"—a total of 5,900 demerits.

Clarence Gaines (1973–76) is the son of the famous "Bighouse" Gaines of Winston-Salem State University, who with 790 victories and counting is the second winningest amateur basketball coach of all time. (The first: Adolph Rupp of Kentucky, with 875.)

Discipline

*A bird that can sing and won't sing must be
made to sing.*

—Mr. McGuire.

"The discipline of the School is based on the principle that the divine law requires obedience to parents, and makes it the bounden duty of parents to enforce that obedience; that the teacher stands in the parent's place, and that, while requiring submission, he must not neglect to inspire, if he may, such sentiments of honour and moral responsibility as will lead the pupil to govern himself."— Mr. Blackford.

Throughout the nineteenth century this school, like most other American and English schools, maintained strict discipline by liberal application of various forms of corporal punishment, with, it would seem, generally beneficial results. Hear one of the victims, looking back:

There has been a great deal said of the barbarism of whipping at school, and the superior and effective influence of moral suasion, but I am fully persuaded that the fact that personal chastisement awaits an idle and rebellious small boy, who will not respond to the milder methods of discipline, is an indispensable agent in preserving and insuring good order in a large school composed of all sorts of boys.

I recollect when I had just reached my twelfth year that the Rector appeared one day in the study and called me out into the passage, and told me that it was time for me to begin to study Greek. I mildly remonstrated that I did not wish to study Greek. The Rector's conclusive answer was, "Boy, if I slap your head off, I will teach you to study Greek." [Joseph Bryan, 1856–61.]

The Rector's conclusive answer also proved to be a wise one:

In after years I often thanked him for settling the question. I am sure that nothing but positive treatment would have overcome my great and unreasonable prejudice against the most beautiful and perfect of classical languages.

Indeed, with us corporal punishment—softened considerably—continued until fairly recently. Harry Blackiston (1923–28):

During the summer of 1927 I had received word from Mr. Hoxton that I had been appointed one of the school's seven senior monitors. After several years as part of that amorphous group known as the "common herd," I could now look forward to the elevated status of one of the undisputed "big dogs." Senior monitors had no specific privileges beyond those of other monitors. They were, however, subject to the supervision of the faculty, the final judges of matters involving the honor system and in general the conduct of the students. Breach of the honor system, such as cheating on an exam, called for instant expulsion. On a matter of such seriousness, it fell to Mr. Hoxton to make the final decision. Senior monitors met one night each week in the Head Monitor's room during the last half-hour of study hall. If it was decided that a particular boy needed to be disciplined, one of the senior monitors would quietly enter the study hall and whisper to the master sitting on the raised platform presiding over the study hall that we wanted to talk to a particular boy. The master would nod, the senior monitor would go to the boy's desk and tell him to come along. The nights of the senior monitors' meetings were anxious times for every boy in study hall. Everyone froze until the unwelcome visitor stopped at another boy's desk.

Once selected, the victim then had the terrifying experience of appearing before the quasi-judicial student panel, hearing his shortcomings spelled out and receiving such admonition or other punishment as the circumstances required. Senior monitors had the authority to administer corporal punishment, subject to specific faculty approval. This happened once during my tenure. It was expected of every boy that he demonstrate the "proper attitude" and "school spirit" at all appropriate times, especially at football games, and other sporting events, by, among other things, cheering continuously until his throat was dry. Jimmy, a first year boy about fourteen years old, seemed to fall short of the expected guidelines. It was agreed that nothing short of a few whacks with the paddle would drive the point home. I was selected to get the necessary faculty approval. I called on Mr. John M. Daniel. He agreed.

J. Mizell

The boy was terrified. His sins, mostly of omission, were recited to him and he was told to bend over. The Judges of the Star Chamber administered the authorized number of blows in the manner of a slave master in an ancient Roman galley.

Jimmy was in tears. I don't think the pain was significant, humiliation being the cause of the tears. This was the only experience I ever had with handing out or receiving corporal punishment. I was not entirely happy with it at the time and feel uncomfortable now when I think of it. It was a clear violation of the constitutional guarantee of freedom from "cruel and unusual punishment."

Jack Mizell (1926–30) was a Senior Monitor two years later, had the same job to do, and remembers it very differently:

R.D. Tucker

George Coles was the Head Monitor and he told me to administer the "whack." Why he chose me, I don't know, except I was a left-handed hitter on the baseball team. On the first swat the paddle split and that was the end of it. I don't think it fazed the boy mentally or physically. My view of this was that it was not very humiliating or painful to the average guy, but was similar to what boys' club members and fraternities routinely do. I just don't remember this Senior Monitor procedure being such a big deal.

Both Harry Blackiston and Jack Mizell have practiced law and their opinions *re* the possible unconstitutionality of the Senior

Monitor swatting also vary markedly. Says JM, "I think that in a case where there is no injury a court would not interest itself in the disciplinary measures employed by a boarding school. I believe that nowadays even some public schools allow some physical punishment as an aid to maintaining discipline. After all, a boarding school is legally *in loco parentis,* 'in the place of a parent,' and so has the duty as well as the right to maintain discipline."

All forms of corporal punishment were abolished at the High School in the 1940's.

However, there has long been a rumor that in the Head Monitor's room on Second Alumni there hung on the wall a paddle with three holes in it "so it swings faster and hits harder" and that rumor persisted certainly into the 1950's and probably beyond. Good rumors are hardier than old soldiers; they not only rarely if ever die, they just swing faster and hit harder.

When my friend Joe Harrison and I entered the High School in 1921 the School had a Board of Monitors presided over by the Head Monitor, all of them selected, I believe, by Mr. Hoxton. There was no such thing at that time as a "Senior Monitor." Later, I believe in 1923–24, the practice of selecting from the Monitors three individuals to serve as Senior Monitors was established.

Joe and I ultimately became monitors. Each monitor had the rather frightening duty of reading the Bible lesson at Sunday night chapel, the lesson being assigned by Flick, who listened intently and stood ready to catch the Monitor if he passed out from fright or was unable to speak. I remember very vividly the tongue-twister Joe had to read: "Here beginneth the fifth chapter of the Epistle of Paul the Apostle to the Ephesians." [Bill Clay, 1921–25. Clay is among the 1925 monitors pictured in Chapter 6.]

> *Let joy be unconfined!*
> —*Childe Harold's Pilgrimage.*

Believe it or not, my own son is in the seventh grade now! I'm sure that the experience of raising him has helped to give me a better perspective on my experiences at EHS, and to realize that the rigid structure which I rebelled against was the very feature I would be grateful for later in life. I'm surprised to say that, even now! [Richard D. Tucker III, 1970–74.]

Grateful father Tucker was indeed a spirited rebel against the School's "rigid structure," and holds what may be a unique distinction: at his graduation exercises he turned a somersault as he walked away from the Headmaster with his diploma.

Egypt

... fog & filthy air ...

—Macbeth.

Smoking must have been a problem on the Hill *ab initio*, from the beginning. "Old Bar" Blackford himself seems to have struggled against it in vain.

In the 1889–90 School catalog it was stated categorically that "All use of tobacco is disapproved, and the smoking of cigarettes is positively prohibited," and the December, 1890, *Monthly Chronicle* quoted this stern ultimatum by "a well-known physician of Baltimore" (Dr. Robert Taylor Wilson of the EHS class of 1879):

"It is impossible for the boy who *smokes* to be perfectly healthy; and, if his physical growth is not stunted by the early use of tobacco, he is mentally less keen and receptive, less refined and manly, and, in the majority of instances, shows evidence of im-

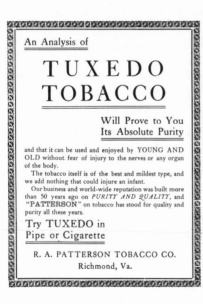

An Analysis of

TUXEDO TOBACCO

Will Prove to You Its Absolute Purity

and that it can be used and enjoyed by YOUNG AND OLD without fear of injury to the nerves or any organ of the body.

The tobacco itself is of the best and mildest type, and we add nothing that could injure an infant.

Our business and world-wide reputation was built more than 50 years ago on *PURITY AND QUALITY*, and "PATTERSON" on tobacco has stood for quality and purity all these years.

Try TUXEDO in Pipe or Cigarette

R. A. PATTERSON TOBACCO CO.
Richmond, Va.

paired health in the lack of power, feeble digestion, weak eyes, pallor of face and general inability to meet and resist disease of any kind."

There were other such cautionary pronouncements (the impassioned fulminations of "Wileyboley" Reade against nicotine were as eloquent as Cicero's castigations of Catiline) and in the 1910 *Whispers* there appeared that very defensive ad.

The Patterson Tobacco Co. could have saved its money, however, because then, as now, young lungs needed no encouragement to defy adult wisdom and fill themselves with smoke. And so they did, in a most unlikely place. Some time after the coming of the Stewart Gymnasium in 1913 a dingy back room in the basement of that temple of health was officially/unofficially ceded to smokers. Foul with fog & filthy air, it was called Egypt. (Why Egypt? The name seems to have stemmed from ancient outhouse days and certainly antedated the arrival of the Stewart gym. See Dick Thomsen's speculations about it in his section on Customs.)

Any EHS boy over seventeen years of age who had written parental consent and wasn't in athletic training could smoke (if not breathe) in Egypt.

In the Jazz Age 1920's smoking on the Hill was not only permissible, it was admirable, and not just for boys. The full-page full-color dedicatory picture opposite adorned the 1921 *Whispers.*

As time went by Egypt steadfastly kept its name but occasionally changed its location.

Smoking in the basement of Memorial Hall, and making it "legal" by sticking one's head out of the building, through a small casement window, seemed much healthier than inhaling that concentrated, nicotined air of the most popular place called "Egypt." [Jim Meem, 1928–31.]

Egypt in my day occupied a couple of grey wooden benches on a cement slab located between the windows of the dining room and Blackford Hall. There, exposed to wind and rain, small groups of boys would huddle to puff away. The number of Egyptians was never great because most boys were in training most of the time. [DeCourcy Orrick, 1965–69.]

In 1949 the American Cancer Society first publicly warned that cigarette smoking could cause cancer, and gradually it became

*Egypt, 1946. "Peace! At Any Price" Sultan—Finley Shepherd;
Prime Minister—Boss Barrett; Sheik—George Wash. Connors;
Bouncer—Paw Cromwell; Shoveleers—Big Ace Parker, Zerk Zer-
kle, Bison Kaminer, Bones Haydock; P.B.I.—Pida Morgan, Delsey
Willcox, Clem Welch, Birdie Quaile, Dick Paynter; Fanwavers:
Prunehead Stoney, Gus Daniel, Phil Phillips, Russian Reid; Mar-
tyrs—Yankee Akeley, Stew Cassilly, Bunny Broyles, Cheese Hol-
land, Monk Clark.*

clear that tobacco is worse for lungs than four columns are for
handwriting.

"Gyp" was an anachronism. It infuriated me that I was forced to
breathe the air that careless smokers were polluting—silly habit, especially after all of the documentation published about smoking causing
cancer. Some things are hard to explain. [William Fuller K. French,
1979–83.]

For several years "legal" boy smokers could huddle together
like poachers in what Dick Thomsen called "the fresh, bracing air
of Northern Virginia," but now smoking is not allowed anywhere
on the School grounds. Where there is unofficial smoke there is

official ire: 15 demerits for first offense, 30 for second plus probable appearance before faculty and in some rehabilitation program like "Smoke-Enders."

Egypt?

One with Nineveh and Tyre.

Faculty

A teacher affects eternity; he can never tell where his influence stops.
—Henry Adams, *The Education. . . .*

The School has always been blessed with excellent teachers. Appreciations of various ones of them are scattered throughout this book, and here are a few more:

Then there was the math class with Grigsby Cave Shackelford ("It's so easy, boys") and the occasions when his false teeth would fly out ("Those blamed teeth!"). [Stuart Taylor, 1928–31.]

Mr. Shackelford's deep-voiced, soothing "It's so easy, boys" actually did make math seem easy, and exciting.

"The New Old Guard." Joe Shelor, appointed 1962; Riley Deeble, 1951; Ben Johns, 1958 (retired 1989); Allen Phillips, 1951 (between 1953 and 1955 he had to teach elsewhere because no married quarters were available here); Ernest Helfenstein, 1957. Between them they have taught here a total of 159 years.

Faculty.

Session of 1894–'95.

Principal.

Launcelot M. Blackford, M. A.

Masters.

Frank S. Hall, M. D.   Buckner M. Randolph, Jr.

James W. Kern.   Willoughby Reade.

Winslow H. Randolph.   Lewis H. Machen.

Faculty, Then and Now

Episcopal High School Faculty 1984–85.

Lee Sanford Ainslie, Jr. (Headmaster), John Minot Walker, Jr., David Randall Dougherty, Patrick Henry Callaway, William Riley Deeble, III, Allen Carleton Phillips, Ernest Helfenstein, III, Benjamin Irving Johns, Joseph Badger Shelor, Richard Fenner Yarborough, Nelson Bell McDaniel, John James Lisanick, Edward Adams Rice, John Michael Miller, Steve Six, Lucien Miner Geer, John William Wires, James Robert MacDonald, Evan James Male, Jr., James DuBois Farrar, Jr., Tony Lynn Shaver, Richard Myers Stubbs, Lewis Edward Cobbs, Ernest Fraser Richards Hubbard, John Michael Carroll, Jr., Grant Charles Kornberg, Rodney Kroehl Brown, Benjamin Blaine Swan, Carroll Bennett Robinson, Jr., Richard Kendall Allen, Jeffrey Alexander Streed, Mark Hale Teeter, John Stanley Blanton, Jr., Ray Marvin Keck, III, William Evans Hannum, Victoria N. Salmon, Katherine Early Roper, Susan F. Miller, Blair Dabney Buck, Brent Mason Myers, Theodore Swift Faunce, Charles Henry Skipper, Jeffrey Yates McSwain, Thomas L. Clement, Barbara Garside, Gregory J. Shaia, Nathaniel H. Acker, William M. Boothe, J.E.G. Craig, Jr., John Kellogg Haines, Virginia N. Settle, R.N.

I really enjoyed my brief stint at the High School. Grigsby Cave Shackelford was the greatest teacher that I ever encountered in my whole life, but there were other good ones. [William Fitzhugh Rust, Jr., 1930–32.]

Benjamin E. Harnley was an exceptionally good teacher of French: didactic but theatrical. He made it fun by having us sing songs like "Auprès as de ma blonde" and acting scenes from Molière and Racine. Thanks to his noble efforts at least one of my classmates scored a perfect 800 on the French Advanced Placement exam and countless others were encouraged to pursue French in college. [DeCourcy Orrick, 1965–69.]

EHS was the best thing that ever happened to me. They taught me how to study and although I went to school for a long time thereafter it was always easier. We had a great time—but then times were simpler. [Russell Boyd, 1948–51.]

Peggy Tompkins says her father, CVT, had an easy-to-remember way of demonstrating what an isosceles triangle standing on its apex looks like:
"He would hold a boy's feet with his head in a wastebasket."

The number of students per teacher is an important ratio.
In those famous "good old days" when life was uncomplicated and tranquil and there weren't so many ideas and things to be done, avoided, marked, learned, inwardly digested or otherwise dealt with flying around, the concept of the teacher as character model as well as instructor, inherited from Elizabethan times, still prevailed, and a good old teacher had time to be personally and professionally close to a large number of boys.
For most of our years the number of boys per teacher was 15 or more, and as recently as 1950 we had 242 boys and only 20 faculty members. Now, however, for 285 boys we have 54 faculty members.
So much to learn, so little time to think of what it all means.

> *I shot a curse into the air,*
> *It fell to earth ... THERE???!!!*
>
> —Longfellow (modified).

"Mrs. Carter told her crowd how impossible it was to keep Bobby from chewing gum and Mrs. Hoxton was lamenting Flick's frequent use of the word 'damn.' 'I don't know where he gets such horrible language,' she would say, 'for I never let him go in the office during faculty meetings.' "—*Whispers*, 1925.

Food

Parents who prefer their sons should not lose time by
headache and indigestion will not send them boxes of eatables.
—EHS Catalogue, 1889–90.

For us growing boys, the desserts provided by Mrs. Mabel Clark to crown her fine meals were simply "out of this world." A dessert was commonly called a "boss"—why, I have no idea—and it was the monetary unit for most bets. After all the other students had eaten, Mrs. Clark would allow her waiters to have two bosses! To me that was a greater reward than the $10 a month we were paid. [Jim Meem, 1928–31.]

Just as a cold wind reminds me of the brisk walk from Berkeley Hall to the main building, so weak maple syrup reminds me of that staple of the EHS dining room, treacle. Having successfully made the transition from the Old World to the New, treacle was an integral part of life at the School. Delightful as it was, however, treacle could not stand alone. It required warm rolls and butter. "When liver and cabbage were the fare, we all thanked God that trickle was there." Treacle and bread could provide main course or dessert, and the combination was universally admired. [DeCourcy Orrick, 1965–69.]

The overwhelming favorite was creamed chipped beef, although everybody knew that salt-peter was the main ingredient. [William Fuller K. French, 1980–83.]

Bill Clay (1921–25) had to wait until Thanksgiving for his favorite:

The man in charge of ordering the food and determining the menu for every meal was known as "Proc." He gave us terrible meals, probably not his fault alone but also due to the tight budget. The diet we were subjected to often resulted in a protest march around the demerit road—the protesters would sing

Proc, Proc, Proc, the boys are marching!
Give them food or they will die!
What the Hell do you think we are,
We come from home so far,
Just to be fed like pigs in the sty!

These protests never accomplished anything.

A vivid memory of the dining room revolves around the head waiter, William, who reigned supreme there. He was very dependable and his many duties included ringing the old bell in the tower of the main building by pulling the rope that hung down just outside the door to the dining room to signal the time for each meal, also the time to get up, the ten-minute warning, study hall, chapel, lights out, etc etc.

I will never forget the so-called "rolls" served at supper time. They were very deceiving, very tempting-looking on the outside but nothing but solid, clammy dough for their "innards." As a result we only ate the outsides and dumped the rest into a plate.

It seemed as though we had turnip tops, or so-called "greens," at lunch every day, along with mashed potatoes and meat that was so tough that students would bring all sorts of knives and razors to try to cut it. Many of us would make a three-tier sandwich that we would fill with the heavy treacle, or molasses, that was always available. That always played havoc with our ability to compete in time trials for track or in fact to do anything satisfactorily other than just sit still until we could get over the effect.

Every rat had to take his turn pouring milk and water and in the spring the ice tea that was stored in a large white pitcher on each table. I remember that a famous tumbler (origin unknown) would appear from time to time; it had a hole in the bottom, impossible to see until the water or milk would start streaming out. Chaos!

We had many rules including one that prohibited receipt by mail of a package containing any food or candy. If such contraband arrived and was detected the boy to whom the package was addressed would find his name posted on the bulletin board just outside the entrance to the dining room followed by the frightening words "See Mr. Hoxton." This happened to me in my rat year! I went to see Mr. Hoxton in his office. He greeted me with a big smile and handed me a heavy, heavy package addressed to me and bearing the label "Contents - Collars." Flick said "Bill old Bill, those 'collars' must be made of iron. Please open the package and let's take a look. If they are what I think they are I will let you eat one and the rest will be sent to the Old Folks Home." When I managed, with shaking fingers, to open it, there inside was a huge box of delicious chocolate fudge candy. Flick actually

let me have not one but two pieces, which I had trouble swallowing
due to my upset condition. I am sure the rest of the fudge was enjoyed
by the Old Folks.

The one real feast we had at the High School was our Thanksgiving
dinner. On that occasion the school outdid itself and we had huge
turkeys with all the trimmings.

A short-lived underground publication called *The EHS Mudslinger* in its May, 1979 issue featured the "School Menu" for a
supposedly typical day:

BREAKFAST: stale bread, fried fat strips, battery acid, oatmush, cream of
grits soup, skum milk. LUNCH: deathball sandwiches. DINNER: choice of
mystery meat, baked elephant scabs or biology cat stew, strange yellow
pudding, essence of Viet Nam tea, coffee grounds.

Fruits (One)

By their fruits ye shall know them.
—Matthew 7:20.

This place has been a dear and good home-away-from-home
for most of us—but what about its professional performance?
How well has it educated us?

Of course, it is difficult today to measure accurately the worth
of a school by weighing the successfulness of the after-school careers of its alumni, because there is now no general agreement
about what "success" is. We are quick to admit that we don't
know what a properly educated man should do because we don't
know what a proper education is; we question each other's basic
values; desperately we search for "meaning," "fulfillment" and
such-like esoteric things which, supposedly, bring "the good life."
Desperately and fruitlessly—like Milton's hungry sheep, we look
up and are not fed.

*What is Truth?, said jesting Pilate, and would not stay for an
answer.*

The trouble is, there is no other way—at all—to measure a
school's performance. And yesterday's way may not be accurate
today, but it is not bad, and perhaps some day we will return to
its traditional values.

So here, with that *caveat*, are some of the brightest jewels in
our crown.

Churchmen

In our 150 years about 150 of our Old Boys have entered the ministry, many of them going directly from the School into the Seminary, and of that number these seventeen have become Bishops:

Richard H. Baker (1913–16). North Carolina
George L. Cadigan (1928–29). Missouri
Herbert A. Donovan, Jr. (1944–49). Arkansas
Robert W. Estill (1941–44). North Carolina
Robert A. Gibson (1860–61). Virginia
Frederick D. Goodwin (1905–08). Virginia
Edward T. Helfenstein (1880–83). Maryland
James A. Ingle (1882–84). China
John L. Jackson (1899–1902). Louisiana
Arthur B. Kinsolving II (1906–14). Arizona
Lucien L. Kinsolving (1878–81). Brazil
John B. Newton (1854–56). Virginia
George W. Peterkin (1856–58). West Virginia
Ernest M. Stires (1881–85). Long Island
Albert R. Stuart (1920–24). Georgia
Francis M. Whittle (1839–41). Virginia
James R. Winchester (1866–69). Arkansas

Some others have been elected to the office but declined it.

E. Felix Kloman (1917–19) was Dean of the Seminary from 1952 to 1956. Cornelius Walker (1840–42) was a Professor there from 1867 to 1894. Kinloch Nelson (1854–58) taught there from 1876 to 1894, as did his son Thomas Kinloch Nelson (1890–96), from 1919 to 1940.

The Rev. D. Francis Sprigg (1842–43) was for many years editor of *The Southern Churchman*.

Presidents of Colleges

John Stewart Bryan (1886–89). College of William and Mary, Va.
James M. Garnett (1853–57). St. John's College, Md.
Dabney S. Lancaster (1906–08). Longwood State Teachers College, Va. (and Virginia State Superintendent of Education)
Donald M. Lay, Jr. (1931–35). Acting President, Rhode Island School of Design, R.I. (and Headmaster, Palm Beach Day School, Fla.)

Robert Edmund Lee (1936–37). Georgia State College for Women, Ga.

William S. A. Pott (1903–09). Elmira College, N.Y.

Frank R. Reade (1905–14). Georgia State College for Women, Ga.

Robert E. L. Strider II (1934–35). Colby College, Me.

Headmasters of Other Schools

Lee Sanford Ainslie, Jr. (1952–56). Virginia Episcopal School, Va.

Francis E. Carter, Jr. (1925–32). Summit School, North Carolina, and Montgomery Bell Academy, Tenn.

Rev. W. Page Dame (1893–96). Christchurch School, Va.

David R. Dougherty (1960–64). North Cross School, Va.

Archibald R. Hoxton, Jr. (1928–35). Fairfield Country Day School, Conn., and Green Vale School, N.Y.

John P. McGuire, Jr. (1852–54). (Founder) McGuire's University School, Va.

William S. Peebles IV (1969–73). Powhatan School, Va.

Rev. Oscar deW. Randolph (1898–1903). Virginia Episcopal School, Va.

Winslow H. Randolph (1886–89). Emerson Institute, D.C.

Rev. W. Brooke Stabler (1918–21). Avon Old Farms School, Conn., Cranbrook School, Mich., and Tower Hill School, Del.

Rev. Roger A. Walke, Jr. (1928–32). Porter Military Academy, S.C., and Virginia Episcopal School, Va.

John I. Yellott (1923–27). Phoenix Country Day School, Ariz.

Scholars

Ten of our Old Boys have gone to Oxford as Rhodes Scholars:

Benjamin May Baker, Jr. (1919—Balliol—he ran against the real *Chariots of Fire* hero)

Staige Davis Blackford, Jr. (1948—Queen's)

Armistead Lloyd Boothe (1924—Brasenose)

Edwin Parker Conquest, Jr. (1949—New)

Samuel Clark Oliver Holt (1953—Christ Church)

Caleb Kimball King (1977—Christ Church)

Arthur Lee Kinsolving (1917—Christ Church)

Augustus Blagden Kinsolving (1956—Christ Church)

Addison White, Jr. (1903—Christ Church. He must have been one of the first Rhodes Scholars; Cecil Rhodes died in 1902 and the scholarships were established by his will)

Philip Tyler Zabriskie (1941—Balliol)

Statesmen

Philip Henry Alston, Jr. (1926–29). Ambassador to Australia

Robert K. Woods Bliss (1887–89). Ambassador to Argentina

Langhorne Bond (1951–55). Director, Federal Aviation Authority

W. Gaston Caperton III (1955–59). Governor of West Virginia

Phillips L. Goldsborough (1873–79). Governor of, and Senator from, Maryland

Richard E. Lankford (1928–33). Congressman from Maryland

John S. McCain III (1951–54). Senator from Arizona

Robert Walton Moore (1872–77). Congressman from Virginia and Counselor of the State Department

George S. Vest, Jr. (1931–37). Director General of the Foreign Service, press spokesman for Henry Kissinger, other high State Department jobs

Richard S. Whaley (1890–93). Congressman from South Carolina

Joseph E. Willard (1879–82). Ambassador to Spain

Way Chin Williams Yen (1895–97). Minister of Foreign Affairs, Republic of China (1920); Premier of China (1924); Chinese Minister to U.S. (1931); Chief Chinese Delegate to League of Nations (1932)

In addition to those Statesmen we have had four Secretaries of War or Army:

Newton D. Baker (1887–89). Secretary of War, 1916–21

Kenneth C. Royall (1909–11). Secretary of War (the last) in 1947 and Secretary of the Army (the first—he was given that new title when James Forrestal became the first Secretary of Defense), 1947–49

Stephen C. Ailes (1926–29). Secretary of the Army, 1964–1965

Howard H. Callaway (1939–44). Secretary of the Army, 1973–1975

Arma Virosque Canimus

Does it seem strange that our small peaceable kingdom should have hatched four civilian directors of military might?

Steve Ailes says: "It is amazing that four alumni of the school have served as Secretaries of War/Army, but it is nothing more than coincidence of course." Bo Callaway agrees: "I have no idea why EHS has produced so many secretaries of war and army. I really believe it's just a coincidence."

Left: Newton D. Baker as cartooned during WWI. He was accused of egotism but proved to be a good and faithful SecWar. Right: Which of these formally attired gentlemen became his country's first SecArmy? They are the unidentified Dual Contestants of 1911: Launcelot M. Blackford, Jr., Harrison M. Robertson, Donald M. Faulkner, George C. Wallace, Jr., Walker J. Suthon, Jr., Robert K. Massie, Jr., Kenneth C. Royall.

Steve Ailes   *Bo Callaway*

Our two most militarily knowledgeable OB's also agree about the prospects for World War III:

SA: "I would be very surprised to see nations of any size decide to try to solve their problems by military means. Everybody has to stay relatively strong, militarily, to prevent war, but I suspect the level of strength thought to be needed will decline over time. Let's hope so anyway."

BC: "I don't think we are very close to World War III, because WWIII would be such a disaster for both the USSR and the USA. I believe strongly, however, that we may prevent WWIII through preparedness and strength and that a good defense against incoming missiles (SDI) will go a very long way in deterring war."

As for what the School did for them:

SA: "It never ceases to amaze me how a short tour at EHS, in my case three years, seems to have a major impact on one's life. I suppose everyone looks back on the period fourteen to seventeen as one in which the world changed a great deal, but I think of Captain Dick Williams, Mr. Shackelford and Mr. Hoxton quite often and still feel somehow that I am a representative of the school and want to live up to their ideals."

BC: "What Episcopal did was to prepare me, not only academically but mentally, for the two colleges that I attended [Georgia Tech and West Point] and prepared me for all the challenges in life after college."

Four of our Old Boys so high-ranked in the Army! Perhaps a friend of the Wheat family, James Barbour, was prescient rather than just careless when he wrote in 1861 that Roberdeau "was educated at the Military [sic] High School under Rev'd now Col. W. N. Pendleton."

Arts and Humanities

Of course, the School has had its share of very successful artists, writers, musicians, architects, doctors, lawyers, scientists, financiers and other creative folk.

For instance, "superstar pediatrician" Dr. T. Berry Brazelton (1934–36) is, according to child care experts, "arguably this generation's top baby doc."

Richard Henry Horner Bales (1927–32) was for forty-two years the Director of Music for the National Gallery and Conductor of the National Gallery Orchestra. He is now Conductor Emeritus of that Orchestra. Ernest Stires (1939–43) is a popular composer

ELEGY FOR A MASTER

In Memory of Robert Edward Latham (1903–86)
A Master at the Episcopal High School (1924–69)

by RICHARD BALES, EHS '32

For String Orchestra or Septet   Fairfax County, Va., August 15, 1986

Robert Edward Latham.   *Richard H.H. Bales.*

whose latest work, "Sonata in C Major," has been called "a serious, substantial piece of music that incorporates many elements of jazz."

A.S. Jones

Our eminent writers have been legion. Among them: Pulitzer Prize winners Virginius Dabney (1914–17) and Alex Jones (1960–64), Launcelot Minor Blackford, Jr. (1903–12), Joseph Bryan, III (1917–21) and his son C.D.B. Bryan (1949–52), Pete Martin (1946–47), Bill Shreve (1925–28), Charles Wertenbaker (1915–19).

Theodore Wong (1892–94) was Head of the Chinese Educational Mission in U.S. and John Denley Walker (1937–40), one of the most decorated Navy fliers of World War II, was Executive Director of the English Speaking Union in the United States.

John Payne (1926–27) is an actor who started on radio and went through movies like *Dodsworth, Sentimental Journey, Miracle on 34th Street* and *Captain China* to TV (*The Restless Gun*).

Fruits (Two)

... and by their other fruits ye shall know
them also....

What would a school be without pranks—capers—escapades—
hacks—whatever you want to call them, those often-ingenious,
often-infuriating, seldom-harmful, sometimes-amusing bendings
and breakings of rules?

Answer: It most assuredly would not be this School.

Just as we have had our share of Eminences and Movers &
Shakers, so have we been blessed with our fair share of Others—
those without whose sayings and doings this gray world would
be even grayer, and the devil, who finds work for idle hands,
disgruntled.

There was once a fire in the Main Building and I tried to lead a
bucket brigade over the belfry roof. As I broke through the window,
there was the one and only Mr. Hoxton, with two of these machines
that put out fires. The story runs that he had left his class where he
was discoursing on the *Pons Asinorum,* and he left the *asini* far behind. He ordered me, in that perfect military voice, "Old Arthur, let
her fly." And I threw the bucket of water, every drop of which landed
on him. There are few Old Boys of this school who can boast of having poured a whole bucket of cold water on Mr. Hoxton and lived to
tell the tale. [Arthur B. Kinsolving II, 1906–14.]

Joseph Bryan, III (1917–21) remembers creative idlenesses:

Well, when we were loafing what did we do? We used to spend
hours copying the teachers' initials. Then we had a junior Edison with
us, Jimmie Biays. He rigged up a gang pen which would write four
columns of words at the same time. He spent more time making that
pen than it would have taken to write a hundred and fifty columns.
We used to spend a good deal of time writing letters to important
people and betting on whether we would get answers. My one
triumph was winning a week's boss by getting an autographed photograph from the President of France. The guy who wrote to the King of
England never got an answer.

Charley Wertenbaker was the first to discover the potentials of a
wastebasket, in the summer, when the teachers wore white suits. He

would go to study hall and put an alarm clock in the bottom of a wastebasket and put other wastebaskets on it and on them dump ink wells. The teacher would come and plunge his arm down to get the alarm clock—a mess!

Wertenbaker would go to sharpen a pencil in study hall and by some dexterity hit himself in the back of the head with a book. It was a beautiful thing. He would go down with a crash and that whole row of study hall was stuck with demerits—but not him. You would set a chair on the edge of a locker with one leg right on the corner and load that chair with tin cans and bottles and anything you could lay your hands on and then tie a string to it and tie a ball to the string and throw the ball over the roof of the dormitory. That night, safely on the far side, you would pull the string, which would break, so it was foolproof.

Jim Meem (1928–31) also remembers certain unholier-than-thou happenings on the Holy Hill:

Once a week evening chapel was held on the second floor of Main Building. It was a solemn event held in a large room with many marble plaques memorializing former Principals, teachers and students some of whom had died in the Civil War or more recent wars. Monitors, who were to read the lessons from the Scriptures, were required to wear white ties! All this solemnity would sometimes be broken during the singing of an old Episcopal hymn entitled "The Son of God Goes Forth to War." That hymn had a catchy refrain that included three deep notes: when it came to that line, several students in different parts of the chapel would go down in various stages of a half-knee bend, in unison and to the beat of the tempting music. There were usually scattered laughs among the students, but as far as I know, no one was ever caught in that irreverent act.

For his monthly quiz, Mr. Carter often liked to include a questionnaire of current events taken from the then-popular magazine The Literary Digest. The events covered were occasionally well known to the students: but for me, recently arrived from Brazil, some were a complete blank. One question was "Who won the World Series that year?" My answer was "Princeton." That blooper was bandied about the School for many a day!

Another event traced directly to my Brazilian background was a squib which appeared in The Monthly Chronicle. It pointed out that there were two students at EHS whose English others could not understand. One was from Brazil (guess who) and the other was from South Carolina (Hugh Cathcart, I think).

Cathcarts belong in South Carolina all right, but Meems in Brazil? Jim Meem explains:

My father was teaching at V.M.I. when he decided to become an Episcopal missionary. After finishing three years at our well-known Seminary in Alexandria, he opted to go to Brazil. He was probably influenced in this decision by the fact that his father had spent three years in that country just before the Civil War, helping to build the main railroad between Rio and Sao Paulo.

It was in the southern city of Rio Grande that father met my mother. Her grandfather had gone to Brazil when he was eighteen years old to enter the india rubber business in the Amazon region. Some years later he moved to Rio Grande. Subsequently he served two separate terms of six years each as the U.S. Consul in that port city.

Jim's name is indeed arresting—or something: in Chapter Six Dick Daniel tells how "for some inexplicable reason" he left it out of the 1929 catalog "and it had to be hand written in each copy." Where does it come from? Unknown, says Jim: "No one in the family has really discovered where the name MEEM originated. Could be a Dutch name. But I think this cartoon from *The New Yorker* comes closest to hitting it on the head, even though my wife says it doesn't *look* like her."

Joe Harrison (1921–25)—saved by the Honor System:

A boy from Richmond went home for the weekend but before he went he gave one of the colored help four alarm clocks to be placed in Lower Study Hall wastebaskets, one in each corner, set to go off at 8, 8:15, 8:30 and 9 p.m. All went according to plan. The first clock went off. Consternation and uproar! Finally everything quieted down—until the second one went off! More consternation and uproar! But then Mr. Copenhaver, who was keeping study hall (I think), was wise enough to check the wastebaskets, and the other two were found. When the culprit arrived back on Monday he noticed that the whole school was glum. He asked why. "Have you seen the bulletin board?" Posted was a notice: "School fined 100 demerits for causing or having anything to do with causing disturbance in the Lower Study Hall Friday night." Well, there was nothing else he could do but turn himself in, which he did. Thereby acquiring the 100 demerits to be worked off over numerous Mondays and volunteer study halls.

"Breaking the rules was so sweet."

Johnny Ball, Bill Shiers and I planned a big night escape. Breaking the rules was so sweet—that is, if you weren't caught. The idea was to

"Whom? Meem?"

(Drawing by Lorenz; ©1975 The New Yorker Magazine, Inc.)

escape without letting any of the monitors or the master at the end of the hall hear us. It took hours, I think, edging along on squeaking boards. We went into D.C. in the early hours of the morning (an unthinkably dangerous venture today). As I recall, some drunk kept trying to give us money and we kept putting it back in his pocket, so someone else could come along and get it all, I suppose. We really did nothing wicked, but we felt mighty brave and competent. [Charles J. "Mud" Churchman, 1945–47.]

Shiers' comment:

Indeed I do remember the occasion—but for forty years I have convinced myself that it was only a very bad dream. Now that Churchman has broken the faith, I demand a jury trial and defy the prosecution to produce credible eyewitnesses. Churchman recalls accurately the difficulties of escaping, but he omits details of our pre-dawn return and the agonies of a day of classes followed by an evening study hall without the benefit of any sleep whatsoever. We paid dearly for the alleged crime. He indeed is the victim of that selective memory so characteristic of the aging process. No court would ever accept such testimony.

I'm Forever Blowing Bubbles. . . .

By sort of cupping your tongue you could blow tiny little bubbles, and a secret sport was to sit in the Seminary church balcony during Sunday morning service and blow those little bubbles out over the people below. They were so small that I don't remember anybody ever looking up. [An Old Boy who even after a safe number of years would still just as soon remain anonymous.]

After forty years of building, buying and operating about 25 radio stations I have thrown in the towel. Loafing isn't so bad after all. I remember one of my early radio businesses: It was a cable radio system in the "new dorm." My illegal radio served my neighbors in adjoining alcoves if they supplied their own headphones and extension cords. My charge was 1 cent each per night which covered the cost of my batteries. Now and then my radio was discovered and confiscated until the end of the school year. My "business" continued and at the end of the year I recovered quite a few old radios. [William Fitzhugh Rust, Jr., 1930–32.]

This picture reflects an incident in the winter of 1963–64. Sandy Rowe had gone home for a weekend. Some of the boys decided to fill his room on 2d Dal with newspaper. (I believe that Dick Kopper and Kenny Davis were among the ringleaders.) It was Sunday, and the stream of boys carrying newspapers from the other dorms to Dalrymple was continuous.

When Sandy returned that evening he was surprised at how many of his friends had turned out to greet him. He was even more surprised, entering his room, to walk into a wall of paper.

All participants were required to turn to after Sunday program, to clear the room and cart the paper to the incinerator. Someone lost a shoe in the sea of newsprint; it was never recovered and is presumed to have perished in the flames.

The figure seated reading is H. Thomas Hall, AKA Joe Crow. The standing boy is Skip Styers. [Charles Sheild McCandlish, 1962–66.]

Says H. Thomas Hall III (1960–64), "Apparently I am the person who 'lost a shoe in the sea of newsprint' although frankly I don't remember it: there was a lot of monkey business." H. Thomas also doesn't remember how he became Joe Crow but that nickname stuck to him all through college.

C. McCandlish   H.T. Hall, III

Tom (AKA Joe Crow) Hall sitting in newspaper-packed room of Sandy Rowe reading—a book. 1964.

"Gardy-loo!" ("A warning cry," says any good dictionary, "uttered in old Edinburgh before throwing dish water into the street.")

The recipe of the redoubtable DeCourcy Orrick (1965–69) for beating the system:

Drinking was extremely popular with a relatively small group of boys. It was never done openly, and I never saw a student drink on campus. I was no saint. In blatant disregard of the rules my roommates and I and our dates drank a bottle of wine in Georgetown before the formal dance during the Finals weekend our senior year. I brushed my teeth well and gargled liberally with mouthwash before going through the receiving line in the Gym that night.

A boy tapped into the study hall bell system using a simple splice and a length of electrical wire. He could ring the schoolroom bell from the comfort and safety of his own desk, but he was cautious in using his power and would wait until just before the master's finger reached the button before he made his connection. The mysterious bell ringing went on for about a week, to the great consternation of faculty schoolroom keepers.

Ghosts

I can call spirits from the vasty deep.
Why, so can I, or so can any man, but will they come. . . ?
—I Henry IV.

One occasionally hears a pleasantly scary story that Hoxton House is haunted by the ghost of Dr. Blackford's mother, that fierce old lady who in life used to stand in the front hall and call out loudly "Launcelot, Launcelot!" (accent on the last syllable) while running her cane up and down the spokes on the stair railing, making a horrible din.

But Young Flick and his sister Mary Earle, who grew up in that house, say that never did they encounter that restless spirit.

YF believes that the ghost story was "dreamed up by Nelson Mc-Daniel to amuse the boys at the first summer camp."

Best-beloved Lanty's mother Mary. On his wedding day she gave him her "most precious possession. . . . this work of genius," Uncle Tom's Cabin.

Misfortunate.

A good ghost can go a long way toward cooling a house in summer.

However, in the old Stuart house, just south of Liggett Hall, things—"things"—are different.

"Proc" Stuart's wife was of course Mr. Hoxton's well-beloved sister "Miss Annie," a somewhat legendary character in her own right: it was said that early in the mornings her nightgowned barefooted figure might be seen walking through the dewy grass because she deemed this activity good for her complexion.

The Tompkins family moved into the Stuart house in 1944, just after Miss Annie had died. The first night little Peggy Tompkins was sleeping in Miss Annie's room and, she remembers vividly, "I heard the front door open, and steps coming up the stairs. Miss Annie? I had been fond of her so I wasn't badly scared."

Twice again it happened, once to Peggy, and once to a friend: the sound of the door opening, and steps.

"And we're not very fanciful people."

The Helfenstein family moved into the house when daughter Margot, now a young lady, was five years old. One night after they had been there about a week Miss Margot said, without much evidence of fright, that she saw "an old lady standing in the door looking at me." Less than two years later she reported, again unruffledly, that she had seen the same old lady standing in the same door again, again just looking.

Mr. Ernest Helfenstein is "not very fanciful" either. To be the Associate Headmaster of this School these days you had better be pragmatic. And he is a sound sleeper (which helps, too). He listened to his daughter's ghost stories with polite skepticism.

Until one night a few years later. Then as he was sleeping, "soundly as usual," he was aware of noises as of a door opening, and a coldness.

And he did not sleep so soundly the rest of that night.

Envoi: Dean Runk, a Trustee of the School, came to spend the night with the Helfensteins a while ago. They told him the story of the ghost. Said he, "I haven't seen Miss Annie in so long—leave the door open."

Miss Annie didn't come that night, but the Helfensteins want her to know that she will always be welcome.

Girls

*One cold morning Mr. Blackford came upon two
boys shivering at the school gate, their hands
and noses blue from the biting air. He said,
"What are you sniveling for, lads? This is no
school for girls." [ABK].*

Should the School take girls?

That question has often been asked, especially by Old Boys with daughters, by faculty members seeking bright(er) students, and by some—not many—boys. No official action, yea or nay, has ever been taken, but a committee is now studying the matter and is scheduled to report in 1990. The present student body seems opposed, and most Old Boys also say No with a capital NO.

The dances were great events. "Dates" were housed and chaperoned by teachers' wives. Every one had a list of dates recorded. Breakfast, lunch, "before lunch," "after lunch," etc. I remember quite well hiring an unknown Washington band for $35 for the Saturday night dance: Meyer Davis. [Ben Baker, 1916–19.]

Two of my best friends were Harry Flippin and Hunter Faulconer, both from Charlottesville, both excellent athletes, and both in trouble a great deal of the time. One Sunday afternoon they called on a local girl who was very popular. Flippin left first and had gotten about fifty yards away when Faulconer came steaming across the lawn shouting "Flip, I've spilled the beans!" It seems he was kissing the girl goodbye when her mother came out on the porch. [Joe Harrison, 1921–25.]

Cooper Dawson says that those two excellent athletes and lovers were also enterprising businessmen. "When Faulconer and Flippin owned the rights to the memory books in 1924–25 they pushed very hard to persuade every rat and indeed everybody to buy one of those books, because the profits, at $5 apiece (a tremendous price then), were considerable. The next Spring Mr. Hoxton told Harry Old Harry and Hunter Old Hunter to stop pressuring people, so they sold the rights to Jim Cathcart and Dick Chichester. The next Fall when those two found out about Mr. Hoxton's pronouncement Faulconer and Flippin were gone.

"In the Spring a young man's fancy," also in the Fall, Winter and Summer. 1904.

Captain Flippin and Trooper Faulconer.

Vice versa.

"Some thirty years later all four of those people plus a lot of others were in my Penn-Daw Hotel after a reunion, reminiscing about the good old days at EHS, and the facts of the matter came out. Flippin and Faulconer were slightly embarrassed and Cathcart and Chichester were ready for mayhem."

Jim Meem (1928–31) dared the unknown:

Inviting a girl to a dance at Episcopal, especially if she were from out of town and not from a local girl's school, was a daring but exciting affair. In my case, I had met my intended date only once, when through arrangements made through Robert B. Harrison, I had attended the Bachelors' Cotillion in Baltimore. So it was really a happy surprise when, several months later, I invited her and she accepted my invitation to come to a dance at the High School. In the days of students having no cars at their disposal, one had to rely on the good graces of the wife of one of the teachers who would agree to have the girl stay at their house. The rules for your date's staying out and coming in after the dance were few but very specific. The result of it all as I remember it was that we all had a very good time!

Decy Orrick (1965–69) fared not quite so well:

Never date a friend's sister! I made the mistake of asking the younger sister of a classmate from Georgia to the Finals dance; when that fresh young Georgia peach stepped from her daddy's car she was wearing an E-normous petticoat which made her white dress billow out like that of Scarlett arriving at Twelve Oaks for the Wilkes' party. As we danced (to the music of "Willie T and the Magnificents") I managed to tread on that garment so often and so heavily that by the end of the evening the floor was littered with little pieces. For days thereafter my friends ceremoniously presented me with sentimental mementoes.

In the fall of 1967 an historic meeting took place between the students of two exclusive secondary schools, the Foxcroft School and the Episcopal High School. The forum for this meeting was a dance at the girls' school—never before had the young ladies of Foxcroft been permitted to invite boys to a mixer. The ground rules were carefully set. The heights of the girls who would attend were recorded and sent to the EHS Hop Committee, which had the task of matching couples by stature.

We boys were somewhat apprehensive because we knew three things about Foxcroft girls: 1. They had to wear uniforms. 2. They had to sleep in open porches. 3. They drilled with toy guns. Most of us had seen the old movie *Tarzan and the Amazons.*

The dance was a huge success. The girls wore grey skirts and green jackets, they had no toy guns, they treated us kindly. The only stressful moment came just before the pairing off of the preselected blind dates. Then our tallest boy, Elmore Grant, 6′5″, was matched with their most diminutive lass, who stood way under 5 feet—everybody chuckled, and all went well.

There was not a single bathroom for visiting females anywhere in the High School grounds until the coming of Centennial Hall.

Honor

In action faithful, and in honor clear . . .
—Pope.

It is generally thought that our present Honor System is as old as the High School and that we got it directly from the University, but tain't necessarily so. It is not known precisely when we first adopted a formal code of honorable behavior with specified admonishments and punishments for violations thereof.

It is, however, known that the University, which had opened in 1825 with Thomas Jefferson as its first Rector, did not set up its code of honor until 1842, three years after we were born, and that it did so because of explosive tensions culminating in an action far more serious than cheating on an examination. As the University's present Honor Committee chairman, J. Brady Lum, tells the story, "It was not terribly uncommon in those days for students to ride up and down the Lawn on their horses taking 'pot shots' at a bell which hung on the north portico of the Rotunda. As rough and rowdy Virginia gentlemen, this was one way in which they could vent some anger and frustration. Professor John A. G. Davis lived in Pavilion X which is on the Lawn. He heard the activity outside and decided that it was time to put a stop to this practice. When he found George Semmes, a student, George was masked. Professor Davis removed the mask and George shot him." Shot and killed him.

The shock of a murder at the University gave rise to a new formulation of discipline that covered several areas of wrongdoing—trivial, of course, by comparison to capital crime but still important to an educational institution. The overall tension between faculty and students, which had its roots in classrooms, was decisively addressed, and Henry St. George Tucker, a popular professor of law, offered this resolution:

"Resolved that in all future examinations . . . each candidate shall attach to the written answers . . . a certificate of the following words: I, A.B., do hereby certify on my honor that I have derived no assistance during the time of this examination from any source whatever."

Acceptance of that relatively simple "certificate," quite similar to the first part of the present pledge, was regarded as a show of confidence in the students by the faculty, and thus began an Honor System which allowed the students to establish their own standards for classroom and community conduct, and procedures for dealing with violations. That System has served the University ever since, effectively because flexibly: at first it encompassed, *inter alia,* such esoteric activities as "cheating at cards, drinking on the day of a dance, gambling with first-year students, and insulting a lady"— today it (like ours) concentrates on the three worst secret crimes against self and society: lying, cheating and stealing.

There is, however, reason to doubt that we took our honor code directly from the University: at the crucial time relations between Us and Them seem to have been strained. At our Jubilee celebration (as reported in the July, 1889, *Monthly Chronicle*) Major John Page, a brother-in-law of Principal Pendleton and a master at the School for the first four sessions, "dwelt on Bp. Meade's distrust of colleges at that day, and spoke of the profound impression produced and the prejudice fostered against the University by the killing there in 1840 of Prof. J.A.G. Davis."

Of course, in the early years this School had its own standards of behavior for its boys, but those standards could vary widely from one Principal to the next, and admonishments (often minimal) and punishments (often maximal: beatings) tended to be arbitrarily administered.

It seems likely that the first codified Honor System was introduced to EHS by the fifth Principal, Launcelot Blackford, soon after he took office in 1870. He *may* have gotten it from the University, where he had been a student, or he *may* have gotten it from West Point, where his chief assistant, Colonel Llewellyn Hoxton, had studied—the Military Academy had had an Honor System since its founding in 1802.

Whatever its origins, our Honor System has become a vital part, perhaps the most important of all, of our School's life.

For a long time the System was enforced by the Principal, with advice, if called for, from senior faculty members. Violators of the code were usually expelled from the School. Then, beginning in the 1920's, the System was administered by a committee composed of the senior monitors and some teachers.

After World War II students were given control of that committee.

Now the Honor Committee consists of seven students, elected by the student body, and four masters. The chairman is a student. Violators are carefully, and privately, questioned and heard by the Committee, and—often enough—cautioned, comforted, and let off with a warning. If a boy is expelled it is done with surgical despatch. Transport is arranged, his parents are told, and he is gone before sunset.

Many of the violators who were pardoned, and some who were expelled, have later expressed gratitude for a lesson learned.

What is "Honor"? It can be very different things to different people. For us, it is three prohibitions and one command:

I will not lie.

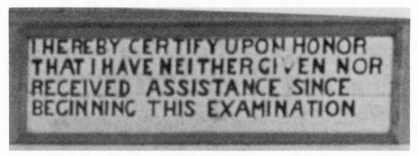

I HEREBY CERTIFY UPON HONOR THAT I HAVE NEITHER GIVEN NOR RECEIVED ASSISTANCE SINCE BEGINNING THIS EXAMINATION

"The Pledge."

I will not cheat.

I will not steal.

I will report any person who does so.

That command bothers every boy who comes to the School with the ancient inhibition against squealing or ratting on a friend.

It is necessary to explain, to make it truly clear, that in this kind of trouble what may seem to be betrayal of friendship is actually a gift of deeper friendship. "Am I my brother's keeper?" Cain cried. Each of us should reckon himself to be more than that. In matters of honor we should be our brother's loving, loyal friend, and do what may hurt ourselves to help him. At best we may save him from greater stain—at worst we may protect ourselves and others from further injury.

The Honor Committee keeps in mind, always, that EHS boys are indeed boys, not men, and that the School's duty is to prepare those boys for responsibility as well as achievement.

Says Allen Phillips, Dean of Students and permanent member of the Committee, "We must show the same patience and understanding in developing a boy morally that all of us show in developing him academically and athletically. Our job is to prepare rather than to get rid of."

And is the System working?

Numbers of boys reported (often by themselves) for violations are increasing, but not as fast as the ambient level of morality, especially as depicted and perhaps furthered in movies and on TV, is falling. If one sees our Holy Hill as a sort of Holland protected from the sea by a little boy with his finger in the dike, one may be sustained by the thought that Holland is still safe. So, so far, are we.

Says the Headmaster, "Locks, lie detectors, trained dogs to locate illicit drugs, breatholyzers—far fetched? I have heard of schools which use such tactics." Not us. Not yet.

Si monumentum requiris, circumspice—"If you seek his monument, look around you," Londoners who wanted to see the works of Christopher Wren, master architect, were told. If you want to see the monument of our Honor System, look at the School, at work and at play, yesterday, today, and—God willing—tomorrow.

As "Big Tuie" Kinsolving said at our Centennial:

We have and hold an institution whose ideals are summarized in loyal Christian integrity. No one can fail to treasure the implementation of the Honor System.

To quote an Old Boy, "Do your duty only where honor lights the path and there can be no real failure—whether you reach to grasp the golden key of success or whether disasters buffet you and beat you down. Like Rostand's famous hero Cyrano de Bergerac, whose hands so nobly sought the prize and so nobly failed, may you finally lift high the credentials of integrity this School has given you; and say, like him, with choking breath: My stainless crest of honor! My white plume!"

This appeal is no escape from the dismal dusk of threatening storm on every horizon and the flash lightning of nuclear testings. But we still see the kindly light of The Faith on which cornerstone this School was built. The testing is going to need this as we persist in following the Prince of Peace.

For in the Citadel of Peace hang the trophies of the world
Yet no barons don their mail and no pennons are unfurled
But there we daily robe the Golden Fleece, daily cup the Holy Grail.

The honor system has not changed and it never will change. [Bill Goodwin, 1934–40.]

In my second year when I was about 15 I shot a small percussion-type pistol off in study hall when Mr. Campbell ("Boozy") was keeping study hall. He stuck the entire school 25 demerits and of course I went to him and told him that I was the one that did it and he removed the 25 demerits from everybody else. What really impressed me about the High School was its Honor System. I have wished many times that this was more widespread through our society! [Harry Klinefelter, 1925–30.]

It was strenuous but quite rewarding, to make that final effort to finish walking off your demerits in time to catch the last bus to Washington. It was very impressive to me that there was no one but myself counting how many laps I had run off for each demerit. It was part of the great honor system of the High School! [Jim Meem, 1928–31.]

The Honour System in my opinion worked magnificently. Years later when I was in Europe I met a Swiss gentleman who had gone to EHS when his parents were living in Washington. When I asked him what he remembered most about the High School he replied quick as a flash, "How inspiringly a perfect sense of honour pervaded a large group of school boys." God bless old EHS. [Ben Baker, 1916–19.]

H.F. Klinefelter, Jr.

I know of one mother whose son, here for the first time, wrote her in surprise: "All the boys here tell the truth, even the little ones." [Norborne Berkeley, 1907–10.]

"In the Fall of 1952 the School was playing its opening football game with Gonzaga High School and the score was tied 7–7 in the fourth quarter. A loose ball rolled out of bounds, hotly pursued by Jay Corson, the Episcopal captain, and several Gonzaga players. The referee ruled that Jay had been the last person to touch the ball before it went out of bounds, entitling his team to possession thereof. Jay thereupon went up to the referee and stated that he had been unable to touch the ball in the scramble and that Gonzaga was therefore the rightful possessor.

"Alas, virtue had to be its only reward that day; Gonzaga scored again to win 13 to 7. But, as we were so often told in olden times, 'It isn't whether you win or lose. . . .' " [Dick Thomsen.]

There about 275 students at Episcopal, and invariably about one percent every year turned out to be thieves. Thievery absolutely turned my stomach. [William Fuller K. French, 1980–83.]

The Honor System was put through much scrutiny during my four years, but it worked surprisingly well. [Lance Mangham, 1983–87.]

Peggy Tompkins says that her father, the redoubtable "Mr. T," used to have an honor system of his own. He would let boys work alone in the chemistry lab if they didn't work on bombs. "So one day a boy landed on the ground at my father's feet, clearly having come from above, where the lab was. Nothing of him seemed broken, so my father looked at him and said 'You seem to be all right,' and that was the end of it. Turned out the boy had been sitting in the lab window studying and had fallen asleep—and out."

The purpose of the EHS Honor System is not to prohibit dishonorable behavior but to inhibit it. [Dylan Glenn, 1983–87.]

Headmaster Ainslie sums it up: "It is my belief, based upon talks with literally hundreds of Old Boys, that it is the Honor System—high and demanding standards coupled with honorable values —which has bonded us together as a community of brothers."

—which has, which does, and which, with good will, hard work and good luck, ever shall.

Howard

The name "Howard" has graced our Hill longer than even the Seminary has been here. It was the name of our tract and it may have been the name of the owner of our original building, now called "Hoxton House." And it seems that that house is older than the United States.

In his very informative book *Mine Eyes Have Seen the Glory* Launcelot Minor Blackford, Jr., said: "About the middle of the eighteenth century a wealthy Virginia planter selected for the site of his country home a hill three miles west of the newly founded town of Alexandria. There he erected a mansion he called Howard. It still stands. The thickness of the walls suggests that he feared Indian raids; the lofty ceilings of the two large rooms on the first floor with their beautifully carved woodwork also indicate that he built soon after 1750."

As told in the chronology, we were often called "Howard" at first, and for a considerable time thereafter, and Principal Blackford always thought that we should have been officially given that name.

Recently the name appeared here again, in a different context. In the early 1950's the Minnie Howard School, named for a de-

How Howard House became Hoxton House, in five stages.
1839: (artist's imagining).

1878.

1893.

1940: *Note balcony.*

Now.

ceased Alexandria public school principal who was no relation to the original tract owner, was built across Braddock Road from EHS. It was at first an elementary school, then it was a "middle" school, and now it is administrative HQ for the Alexandria public school system.

For us, the old name "Howard" will always be redolent of antebellum magnolia, like Tara or Twelve Oaks, or Arlington.

Latin

Amo, Amas, Amat?

I hated Latin. The only exam I ever failed during my five years at Episcopal was fifth form Latin when we were reading *The Aeneid*. Fortunately I passed the final exam. Immediately after learning of my final success, on a warm June night in 1928 several other boys who shared my feeling about Latin and I built a bonfire near the pigsty behind the baseball field and tossed into the flames, with shouts of damnation reminiscent of the Grand Inquisitor sending heretics to the stake, all our copies of one of the world's great classics, *The Aeneid* of Publius Vergilius Maro.

I have long felt there is something wrong with the way Latin is taught in most schools. Little attention is paid to the dramatic events being described and their historic setting. [Harry Blackiston, 1923–28.]

My Latin teacher, Mr. R. P. Williams, told me that I would have to stand on tiptoe and reach up to touch bottom in Latin. It appeared that I was very poorly prepared before going to EHS. [E. Conway Moncure, 1929–33.]

Then there was R. P. Williams ("Captain Dick"). I've never known a teacher who could look so ferocious—glaring at you over his glasses, and sounding so mean—but have such a kindly heart. After failing Mr. Whittle's Latin, I reached an agreement with Mr. Williams that a pass in third year Latin under him would erase my hopeless record in second year Latin. This was my second year and I was sharing a room with Bill Shiers on the ground floor of Blackford. To do well in Latin I figured I would have to memorize all of Caesar's *Gaelic Wars*. To accomplish this formidable task, I wired our tiny closet so I could continue my studies after "lights out." On several occasions I nearly suffocated, and constant replenishing of the oxygen by fanning the door was the standard procedure. I will never forget the thrill I felt when "Captain Dick" walked over to my table one evening in the dining hall to shake my hand and tell me I had received a high grade on my Latin exam. ["Mud" Churchman, 1945–47.]

Well now Mud, weren't those wars more French than Irish, Gallic than Gaelic?
And this is Shiers' comment:

Aha! Churchman poses as the devoted academician, ever ready to recite Caesar into the dark hours. Yes, I remember his nightly Latin recitations well, because they were always done aloud— interminably. For me, it was like traveling on safari and attempting to sleep by campfire in the presence of muffled native chanting in entirely unknown tongues. But I devised a strategy. I arranged to have our Philco table-model radio fitted with receptacles for World War II surplus earphones.
Then, instead of after-hours erudition, we enjoyed a little night music and, as I recall, became regular patrons of an early Arthur Godfrey radio talk show. It was not at all difficult to wean Charlie away from the Punic Wars. *Et tu*, Churchman!

Postscriptum: nobody (*nemo*) seems to know where our most illustrious of all Latinities, our *Fortiter, Fideliter, Feliciter*, came from.

Legends

Although it is often said that in 1755 the occupants of Howard House stood on their porch and watched Braddock and his Red Coats march by on their way to the disastrous battle of Fort Duquesne, Young Flick has found that story to be only a story.
BUT: "It is true that the northern boundary of the farm was the road taken by General Braddock on that ill-fated expedition against the French and Indians." [*Mine Eyes Have Seen the Glory.*]

A century ago there was an old willow tree just south of old Howard House which was said to have grown from a riding switch thrown away by the young George Washington when he came over from Mount Vernon one day to call on the young lady of the house. That story also is legendary.

BUT: Young Flick says it is true that on the black gum tree behind the present Headmaster's house certain small branches turn crimson in the Fall. What is not (necessarily) true is the story that from one of them was hung a Confederate spy. HOWEVER: "That tree is as beautiful as ever. As a child I caught tadpoles in the spring at its base."

Old Bar's mother had an ex-slave, Peggy, who grew up with the Blackford family and went with her to the School. She and Mrs. B. were installed in the north "office" by the Principal's house.

Mrs. B. used to demand audience with her son whenever she chose, and in her presence that masterful man was as meek as a lamb.

One day Mrs. B. announced that she wanted faithful Peggy to be buried at her feet. Peggy objected: "I don't want to be buried at nobody's feets." There the matter rested. Mrs. B. died in 1896 and was buried in Lynchburg. Mam' Peggy succeeded to the matriarchal position of her mistress in a way probably incomprehensible to any one but a Virginian.

It is doubtful if she ever left her room after Mrs. B's death. Old Bar and his sons and all honored visitors had to pay respects to her there as a monarch. She died in 1911 and was buried in Old Bar's lot in Ivy Hill Cemetery, Alexandria. Then, ". . . When he died three years later, it so happened that Launcelot's body was laid at the feet of Mam' Peggy."

Legend? That's what son LMB Jr. wrote in *Mine Eyes Have Seen the Glory*.

"Call me Bob."

One of the best-loved legendary characters of the War was the invincible indomitable inimitable etc. etc. "John R. Curd of Buckingham County." At our Centennial ceremony, October 14, 1939, Norborne Berkeley (1907–10) favored his hearers with this morsel of vintage Curdiana:

"It was in one of the last battles of the war," said John R. Curd. "I had just killed a great number of Yankees, more than I could count, and had captured from them large quantities of guns and ammunition. I continued slaying as fast as I could shoot my muskets and I used several of these weapons because they became so hot I had to change them every minute or two. I was thus engaged when who should ride up behind me but General Robert E. Lee. He said 'John R. Curd of Buckingham County, cease firing. I'm sick of this bloodshed and carnage.' I said 'General, leave me alone for a minute or two and I'll kill 'em all.' Looking me squarely in the eye, General Lee replied 'John R. Curd of Buckingham County, don't call me General, call me Bob.' "

While the foregoing may arouse the skepticism of some, the following, reported by Young Flick, is Gospel Truth:

"When Henry St. George Tucker was Presiding Bishop of the Episcopal Church, his secretary received a call from the White House. The King and Queen of England were to visit Franklin Roosevelt, and the President wanted Bishop Tucker to come to Hyde Park to conduct a service for those gathered there for the weekend. The Bishop sent word back, 'I am sorry that I cannot come. There is a Board of Trustees meeting at the Episcopal High School.'

"I understand that he *went* to Hyde Park."

Q: Is it true that Mr. Callaway once pitched both games of a double-header, the first game with his left hand, the second with his right?

A: We-e-e-e-ll . . . but he did pitch with the semi-legendary Eppa Rixey at UVA.

Malaprops

Ut Sit Mens (not quite) Sana.

Malaprops abound in every school, of course. Just as in Boston all young Hallowells believe that the Lord's Prayer begins with "Hallowell be Thy name" so in Charleston most little Ravenels probably believe it is "Ravenel be Thy name," and everywhere "Surely goodness and mercy shall follow me all the days of my life" becomes "Surely good Mrs. Murphy," and "Gladly the Cross I'd bear" has been construed by the classic "Gladly the cross-eyed bear." Unfortunately most of these little gems are preserved only in family lore, but here are a few that have enlivened our Hill:

"A volcano is a mountain with a hole in it that is called the creator." [George B. Lee, 1883–88].

EXAMINATION ECHOES, from *The Monthly Chronicle*, July, 1889:

Q: Give the two plurals of DIE and GENIUS.

A: DEAD and DIES. The singular means just for any one to die; the second means when a person dies, and is used for the future.

GENIUS and GENUS. The first means more than one; the second means that the time is to come before he will be a genus.

Q: How are SHALL and WILL distinguished?

A: WILL is used in many ways, as "A man makes a WILL."

Q: What are the principal forms of composition?

A: UNITY, HARMONY AND BRIEFNESS.

Clarence W. Robinson Jr. (1917–20): "Do you want to buy a memory book?"

Lorimer McLaren (1919–22): "I don't know. Who is it in memory of?"

Lorraine Pitman (1919–20), seeing the laundry list: "Do we have to wear that much every week?"

PHC contributes these jewels from long-ago jewelers:

Assessing Shakespeare's *Julius Caesar*, "Mark Antony was the biggest trader in the entire Mediterranean area." (For "trader" read "traitor"?)

"A polygon is a quadrilateral triangle with five sides."

"After studying for the bar one becomes the best bar tender in town."

"QED means Quite Easily Done."

"ETC means Everything That Comes (later)."

Miracles

Reports *quondam* Headmaster Thomsen, "One evening there was a blackout in the dining room caused by a thunderstorm and I was reading the old prayer 'Lighten our darkness, we beseech Thee, O Lord, and by Thy great mercy defend us from all dangers and perils of the night," and lo and behold the lights came on!"

Miscellanea

"A fourteen-year-old first-year boy at the Sunday service in the Seminary chapel sat in the pew right in front of the preacher. After the service a teacher asked him what he thought of the sermon. He replied 'I guess the sermon was all right but the preacher kept spitting on me.' "—PHC.

Some Virginians "revere the past, regret the present and fear the future." [V Dabney, 1914–17.]

"Remember the time in 1925 when Hollis Hand, just named a monitor, was up on Third Alumni with a hand gun and shot himself in the—where else?—hand? And put two bullet holes through the wall of his bunk, scaring the daylights out of the double-bunk folks next door? Hollis didn't lose his monitorship but there was a lot of commotion concerning this event." [Cooper Dawson, 1921–28.]

[Editor's note: not only did Hollis Hand not lose his monitorship, he went on to become, two years later, Head Monitor.]

Lester Kinsolving (1940–45) is an inexhaustible fountain (geyser? volcanic eruption?) of EHS reminiscences, his own and others'. He remembers his father, Big Tuie, telling this version of the memorable story of what could have been a confrontation between the High School and the White House.

Big Tuie was in the School in 1909 with Quentin Roosevelt, whose father was then President. Young Quentin was "as wild as mountain scenery," so wild that he was stuck so many demerits

| B.H. Hand | C.L. Kinsolving | A.L. Kinsolving |

that it was decided that he needed five whacks. The School asked the White House for permission. Said TR "Beat him good! Bully!!"

He—Les Kinsolving—remembers that whenever a certain boy's mother came out to the School the whole Hill went on red alert, because she was "fearfully and wonderfully made."

He remembers breaking every rule in the book from keeping his bicycle in the furnace room to sleeping under his bed (at least that is what Mr. Latham, making a spot check, thought—actually he was in town—"O'Donnell's Sea Grill at 4 AM." So when "The Hawk" stuck him ten demerits he said, to himself, "Ha! Ninety less than I deserve!").

"I was so bad that the senior monitors beat me twenty-eight times with a chair leg."

He remembers much merriment and much excellent teaching, especially by Messrs. Dreamy Daniel and Wileyboly Reade.

And the School remembers him. For many years he used to give a radio broadcast on the morning of the Woodberry game. Those broadcasts were often more exciting than the games.

His eloquent father called Robert E. Lee "the uncrowned king of the Anglo-Saxon race." Les, who has made himself an embattled minister as well as a much-read, much-abused, first-rate muckraking reporter, might be called "the self-crowned king of the rebel race."

Our School needs more Les.

Misspellings

Not long ago an Old Boy who shall be nameless lest his name be misspelled remarked to a recently retired Headmaster that there are two EHS names which are misspelled at least as often as they are spelled correctly. Said he, "One of our greatest athletes was Harry Flippin. That is the correct spelling: *Flippin*. But how often have you seen it spelled FLIPPEN? And one of our greatest math teachers was Mr. Shackelford. And how often he is spelled *Shackleford*!

"Do you know," asked the OB, "of any other EHS name so commonly misspelled?"

The retired HM nodded his head and pointed. To himself.

"Thomsen," he said, "as in Thomson, Thompson, Thomason, Tomsen. . . ."

So, it will be remembered, did Mr. C. V. Tompkins lamentably often become Mr. Tomkins or Thompkins or even Thompkhins.

Official School records have not infrequently stripped the middle name of Thomas Rutherfoord Moncure (1927–30) to Rutherford.

Tayloe is one of the proudest names in the South, but in the unSouthern word processers: Taylor.

We have had, at last count, thirty-nine *Lees* and only two *Leas*— Anthony A.(1947–50) and John Willis (1893–94)—so it is understandable that those lonely *a*'s have become sociable *e*'s. How could our one Daniels—Ernest Marvin, Jr. (1934–37)—keep his *s* in the presence of sixteen students named Daniel?

Dulany to Dulaney or the other way around is probably inevitable.

And so it goes.

Fortiter, Fideliter, Filasiter.

Mysteries

"Where is the stone window sill that was used to sharpen knives in the old main building kitchen, taken down in 1988 when the new addition was started?" [Cooper Dawson, 1921–28.]

Who was the enterprising gardener (now gardener-emeritus) of the 1960's who, after having been expelled from the School for growing marijuana in a window box, was voted *in absentia* "Greenest Thumb"?

Who was our first casualty? *The Monthly Chronicle* of July, 1889, notes that in 1840 the infant School's "first death had occurred near the beginning of the session" and records without identification, amplification or comment that the victim was "an interesting youth from Petersburg."

Our first casualty of non-war violence seems to have been Theodore Wong (1892–94)—but who killed him? ABK says that he was the son of our first native Chinese priest and "was an earnest Christian, a brilliant thinker, a fine speaker and a charming gentleman." In 1919, soon after the close of the war, he "had charge of all the Chinese indemnity students who were pursuing courses in this country and was assassinated in Washington. It is supposed that the motive was robbery." Supposed by who? (Whom is necessary only for Jim Meem: see section on Fruits 2.) RPW, writing forty-two years after ABK, names no suspects and indeed doesn't even mention the murder.

"HELLO, CENTRAL . . ."

The 1889–90 Catalogue announces proudly that "The School is connected with Alexandria by telephone."

WHAT WAS OUR TELEPHONE NUMBER?

In Chapter Six Dick Daniel says that in the mid-twenties the School's number was 229. But what about thirty years before?

Of all the numbers ours could have been, a hundred years ago, there is one which it very probably was not: the dread number of *The Book of Revelation*:

Let him that hath understanding count the number of the beast: for it is the number of a man; and his number is Six hundred threescore and six.

Whose understanding? What beast? What man??

That number—666—has puzzled numerologists, Biblicists, historians and everybody else ever since John dreamed it on Patmos two millennia ago. It is the best-known, most-feared number in the Western world.

Imagine saying to a devout Victorian telephone operator "Hello, Central, give me that Episcopal number, 666."

In the twenties and thirties our boys used to greet each other with this whatchamacallit: Q—"Why is a mouse when it spins?" A— "The higher the flier the fewer."

What mouse? How spin? Higher and fewer than what?

Was there really, as Bill French and everybody else always thought, salt-peter in all the food??

Names

You would think that an old Southern school like this would be topheavy with old Southern names like Washington, Lee, Randolph, Fairfax, Taliaferro (pronounced of course Tolliver), Rhett, Ravenel, Huger (U-G), and so forth, wouldn't you?

Not so.

We have had, down through the years, our share of those redolent names: as of last count, eleven Washingtons; thirty-nine Lees; thirty-eight Masons; twenty-eight Randolphs; four Fairfaxes; ten Taliaferros; thirteen Rhetts; five Ravenels; five Hugers; sixteen Blackfords; twenty-four Bryans, and so forth.

But our most numerous names have been those also most numerous in the rest of the country: Smith (82); Williams (62); Brown (51), Jones (45); Taylor (44). . . .

Nicknames

Nicknames, it seems, are the name of the prep school game.

EHS has been, is, and evermore, doubtless, will be singularly blessed in the richness and strangeness of the sea-changes which our boys have wrought on each others' names.

In that wonderful fourteenth century poem *Sir Gawain and the Green Knight* the narrator tells us that on his way to The Green Chapel the hero met so many marvels that "a tenth would be too tedious to tell." Well, to tell here a hundredth of the nicknames that have adorned and merrified the Hill would be not too tedious—not at all—they are as funny as they are, almost always, apt. There just isn't space. Nor would there be if this book were ten times as long.

Here are a few that Dick "Tommy" Thomsen remembers from the forties and fifties:

Douglas Stevenson "Sea Food" Bradley, Ashby Robertson "Elmer" Carver, James Ely "Proboscis" Bradfield, Edward Watts "Crash" Gamble III, Jaquelin Marshall "Buzzard" Harrison, John Gibson "Blackout" Semmes.

And here, generously provided by DeCourcy "Augie Doggie" Orrick, are some more, from the fifties and sixties:

Mole, Piglet, Bobo, Ook, Hondo, Squeaks, Droopy, Crazy Legs, Hose Nose, Hound Dog, Red Dog, Chipmunk, Iron Pig, Wild Duck, Whooping Crane, Shadrach, Tweedledum and Tweedledee, Carrot Top, the Goobe, the Beggar, Gloomy, Froggy, the Monk, Leemo, Little Czar, Little Storm, Round, Natty Bumppo, Big Red, Daily Duck, Joe Bod, Y'ahtch, Woody, Chunk, Buckshot, Patman, Gentle Ben.

Of course, Headmasters and masters are not exempt. A few:

R. P. Thomsen—Tommy; R. E. Latham—Uncle Bob or The Hawk (several Old Boys, perhaps influenced by the TV series *Mash*, have mistakenly called him "Hawkeye"); C. V. Tompkins—Mr. T.; A. C. Phillips—Big Al; W. R. Deeble—Double O; B. E.

Harnley—Hi-Ho; P. H. Callaway—Pops; W. M. Boothe—The General; A. C. E. Pleasance—Ace; M. J. DeSarno—Spike; S. S. Walden—Sleepy Sid; L. E. Hollinger—The Colonel; D. S. Walker, Jr.—Doak; R. F. Yarborough, Jr.—Big Daddy; H. Burn—Hubba Hubba Harry; G. E. King—Sky King.

Some sixty years ago there was here a teacher of English and French, Mr. Robert Bailey Campbell, who was nicknamed "Boozy." Why? Because in that most boozy of times, the wild twenties, all through Washington and Lee he never drank. (Cooper Dawson says he left us to become a minister.)

Nobody has been exempt. Dick Thomsen's wife Betsy was, because of her snow-white hair and aristocratic features, George.

Cap'n Dick, Dreamy Daniel, Wileyboley Reade, Herr Whittle, Old Bar, Old Dal and all the others were there. (Why was Dreamy Dreamy? In the 1926 *Whispers* it is written: "Dreamy—an adjective usually applied to a man skilled in the art of uncovering mysteries and interpreting strange handwritings. Has its origin in *Daniel VII:*1, "Daniel had a dream and visions of his head . . .")

Nicknames, like their more portentous cousins, myths, usually have some logical point of origin. So, like myths, they usually have a ring of authenticity. But, unlike myths, they almost always make us laugh.

To expand upon that little boy's statement of 1840, *Homo natus est titillari nominibus peregrinis*—"Man is born to be tickled, by outlandish names."

Two nicknames are especially memorable hereabouts.

Archibald Robinson Hoxton was Flick and his son is Young Flick. Arthur Barksdale Kinsolving II (EHS 1906–14) was Big Tuie and his cousin Arthur Lee Kinsolving (1913–17) was Little Tui.

The provenance of Flick has been established. Tui(e) came about thus: When Lucien Lee Kinsolving (EHS 1878–81) was Missionary Bishop of Southern Brazil the Brazilians localized the name of his little son Arthur into the more Portuguese-ical Arturo, and thence on to Tuie. He was Tuied all through eight years of this School (1906–14) except that when his cousin Arthur Lee came along (1913–17) he became Big Tuie and his cousin Little Tuie. (Little T later dropped the *e*.)

Like our Flicks, our Tui(e)s had distinguished careers.

Big Tuie became the first Bishop of the Diocese of Arizona and Little Tui served for many years as the rector of St. James Church in New York City.

*The Rt. Rev. Arthur B.
Kinsolving, "Big Tuie"
(1906–14).*

Big T was a magnificent preacher and story-teller, famed far
and wide for his seamless weaving together of hilarious tales and
eloquent perorations. As Dick Thomsen once observed, "His mag-
netic personality was very much in evidence during his visits to
the School and, like a modern Pied Piper, he would be followed
about the campus by an admiring and spell-bound group of students and teachers."

One of those visits was just fifty years ago, when he came to
give our Centennial Address. Part of that unforgettable address is
inscribed on a memorial plaque placed in the chapel:

> *Old Boys of an old school: we cannot fail this place which
> has helped us so many times. This is the Hill which
> cradled our youth, and to this Hill as boys and men we
> shall forever lift our eyes for help.*

Tuie Kinsolving wasn't all magnificence, though. As befits a
nickname like that, there was much more to him (dare one say
Tuiem?). In School he won prizes as a reader and declaimer, was
named Head Monitor and voted best athlete and most popular
boy, and he shared with Johnny Dunlop (1910–14) what must
still be a *sui generis*, one-of-a-kind, football fabulosity.

As the story has come down through the decades, it was in the second half of the immortal Woodberry game of 1913. Our undefeated team, comfortably ahead, whomped up a play the very thought of which can, even at this great remove of time, make one slightly queasy.

Big Tuie, an end, was cross-eyed and Johnny Dunlop, a back, was also cross-eyed, unusualnesses which didn't escape the attention of the enemy since players didn't wear face-guards in those days. So Big Tuie dropped back and passed to Johnny (the rules were different then). Whoooeeeeee . . .

The attackers couldn't tell which way the passer was going to throw the ball and defenders couldn't tell which way the receiver was going to run.

Voilà!

On this Hill which cradled his youth the boy Tuie lifted his eyes and that, in the expression which came along a little later, was all she wrote. You can still hear echoes of the bleachers laughing and hollering YAY JOHNNEEE YAAAAY TUIEEEEEE!!!

We won that game 62–0, the most voluminous drubbing we have ever administered unto the Orangemen.

Nicknames, nicknames. . . .

Would that there were more space here for more of them.

All hail, Boche Spinoza, Pinky Connor, Weepy Williams, Rat Brawley, Black Rhett, Evo Frost, Bits Sherrill, Buffalo Cary, Cottontail Randolph, Tarbaby Baker, Farmer Burn, Brutey Stocker, Honest Ned Parrish, Rabbi Holt, Greaseball Nulsen, Gloomy Herbert, Sunny King (and Insect, No-Key and Gator King), Bone-rack Castleman, Animal Skoggard, Stump Philbrick, Skin Lane, Joe Crow Hall, Rusty Gates, Possumtrot Pott, Coo Coo Cooke, 9-Toes Davis, Czar Train, Wilmington Flash Woodbury, Tigger Alexander, Red Man Crosland, Bumpsy Woodruff, Sugar Mackall, Poet Lanier, Speed Sexton, Son Trask, Mr. Mom Smith, Barney Google Geismer, Smelly Butler, Hot Shot Quin, Boota DeButts, Dreamy and Wileyboley and Herr and Nick and Flick and Old Bar, Lava Bryan, Saphead Mason. . . .

I loved football and found a place at quarterback on one of the teams. I often complained to the coach that he always put the best players on the other team. One day he did me the favor of putting my classmate, Albert M. Rhett of the old Charleston family, at halfback on my team. He had been given the nickname of "Mole-eye" because his eyes appeared half-closed. Mole-eye could run like a startled deer and that day our squad was unbeatable. [Harry Blackiston, 1923–28.]

When I was at EHS I bore the nickname "Mud," an appellation awarded me by a friend because I had once said that if such and such weren't so my name was mud. I remember that I had another name in Mr. Shackelford's solid geometry class. The poor man was not well that year. I would have sympathy now, for it was his last year of teaching and his memory was playing tricks. The students gave me some strange name and he took it for my real one. [Charles Churchman, 1945–47.]

All hail, "some strange name" on top of Mud!
All hail, THE High School!!
All hail, Eggs, Hams and Sausages!!!

Nobility

No matter how loudly democratic, every school should have some quiet connection with Nobility, some King or Baron or Sir or Lady or Something roosting discreetly up some studential family tree.

Fortunately, our School boasts three such scions (at least—if you are an unknown other, please notify the Transcendent Alumni Office).

Randolph Fairfax (1857–59) could trace his American lineage back through a welter of First Families of Virginia to that First of all First New World Ladies, the Indian Princess Pocahontas (c1595–1617); his English entitlement went back to a certain Sir Thomas of Denton who was raised to the peerage as Lord Fairfax, Baron of Cameron, in 1627.

The official blue-bloodedness of Harry Blackiston (1923–28) is three hundred years older. He is a descendant of Richard III, King of England from 1312 to 1377, and of the English noble families of Mortimer and Percy; a many-greats grandfather was the Sir Henry Percy (1364–1403) who became Shakespeare's incandescent Hotspur.

Ernest Helfenstein III (1945–50), our present Associate Headmaster, is the undisputed Doyen of our aristogenes, however. His patricianity goes back more than a thousand years. The Grafs von Helfenstein were nobles in the Court and prelates in the Church

Fairfax.

Percy.

Castle Helfenstein, as it may have looked a thousand years ago.

"Noble is as noble does" or *"It's all in the mind"* or something:
instant knightification. 1929.

in Swabia (modern Germany) from the ninth century on; one was a son of Maximilian I, Holy Roman Emperor from 1493 to 1519.

About the year 1100 they built a castle atop a mountain northwest of the city of Ulm but during the Peasants' Revolts of 1513 the castle was stormed and the Graf of the time was killed. (His little son was tossed into the air and caught on a pitchfork.) The first Helfensteins came to this country during the Revolution and were all ministers until Ernest's father broke the succession; he was the first Helfenstein not to be a minister or priest since about the year 800. He and five noble kinsmen, including Ernest, all went to EHS.

In modern German "helfen" means "help," a perfect name for men of the cloth. "Stein" means "stone."

A German Graf equals an English Earl.

Numbers

At 14–18 years of age four years at EHS represents about 22% of one's life up to that point! A fairly hefty chunk of time! And there we all were inside those walls for a good 250 days with 250 boys, tight times; and if it all worked out then they were amazing and close times. They were for me. [Cotten Alston, 1959–63.]

You haven't seen speed until you've seen any practised old boy taking his morning shower. Using somebody else's soap and shampoo, it takes him at the most one minute, thirty-five seconds. (Then he rushes to his closet to apply the necessities of adolescence—deodorant, mouthwash and Clearasil.) [William Fuller K. French, 1980–83.]

Others

We are not alone.
—Isaac Asimov, *Is Anybody Out There?*

The Reverend Milo Mahan, one of our three first teachers, brought something besides a profound knowledge of the classics to the fledgling school.

He had taught at the Flushing Institute on Long Island under the Reverend William Augustus Muhlenberg, an Episcopal minister, and there he had encountered the concept, brand new to this country, that a school could be a home as well as a lecture hall for boys.

This concept, which seems quite normal to us now, was a departure from the prevalent academies (*i.e.* secondary schools) of the period which had succeeded the earlier Latin grammar schools and which were called boarding schools because they were patronized by students from a distance in addition to those who lived in the area. The so-called boarders, however, lived as a rule with reputable families in the community rather than in dormitories on campus, and were subject to school authority only for class and chapel attendance.

Inspired by the precepts and examples provided by the Swiss education reformers Pestalozzi and Fellenberg, the Round Hill School was founded on the new model at Northampton, Massachusetts, in 1823, and this in turn provided the pattern for Dr. Muhlenberg's school at Flushing. Round Hill and Flushing were both under the auspices of the Episcopal Church.

Both of those schools became casualties of financial and administrative problems, possibly because they were ahead of their time, and perished a few years after they were founded, but fortunately the innovations they had begun were preserved by two other schools founded shortly after their demise.

The first of these was the Episcopal High School in Virginia, which means, of course, that we were then and are now the oldest boarding school for boys in the direct line and tradition of Round Hill and Flushing.

The next school to adopt the new format was the College and Secondary School of St. James (now St. James School), established near Hagerstown by the Episcopal Diocese of Maryland in 1842. Like the others, St. James was designed as "an educational institution that would function as a church family, a Christian home, in which the rector would act as father to the whole community."

That school inherited several of Dr. Muhlenberg's former colleagues and pupils.

The impact of the new movement was felt soon enough.

The first two principals and six other faculty members of St. Paul's School in Concord, New Hampshire, founded in 1856, had been students and/or teachers at St. James.

Subsequently many other eminently successful Episcopal boarding schools benefitted from the same legacy.

In the 1850's there was another boys' school near us. The Fairfax Institute, principaled by the Reverend George A. Smith, flourished for a time, and in the fullness of time, 1861 to be exact, when the Yankees came, vanished. It left a riotous memory. This is a tale that Cooper Dawson's father used to tell:

About 1853 our Principal, Dr. Dalrymple, was driving into town one morning in his carriage with his coachman and two-horse team and they approached a duck on the side of the Leesburg Pike, halfway to Alexandria. The duck tried to cross the road, was run over, and quack, quack, the poor duck fell dead. In his sermon that morning the good Principal used the death of the duck to illustrate some point in his sermon. The sermons in those days ran at least a full hour and the service at least two hours. The Fairfax boys sat on one side of the aisle and the EHS boys on the other and all of them were generally pretty tired when the service was over.

Going out of the church the Fairfax boys were shouting "Quack, Quack, Quack!" The EHS boys took offense and a pitched battle occurred there in the church yard. EHS outnumbered Fairfax, and—legend has it—our boys seized a Fairfax boy and shoved his head so far down into a pipe that it took two sturdy teachers to pull it out. That boy was none other than Fitzhugh Lee, nephew of Robert E. Lee.

Good thing Himself wasn't around that morning, although he might not have recognized his nephew. There were lots of Lees in Virginia then, and another Fitzhugh Lee had gone to EHS just five years before. Nephew Fitzhugh, once he got his head out of that pipe, went on to become a Confederate General, then Governor of Virginia, and finally a United States General in the Spanish American War.

He was one of two Confederate Generals who later put on the old blue uniform and reached an equal rank in the armies of the North. (The other was Fighting Joe Wheeler.)

The Fitzhugh Lee who went to the School in 1848–49 had a father, Cassius, who was in a quiet way one of the most remarkable men of that remarkable family. While his cousin Robert became a Confederate General and his cousin Smith Lee, Robert's brother, became a Confederate Admiral, Cassius decided that his duty lay at home. He lived at the house called "Menokin," just across Braddock Road from the north entrance of the School, and was treasurer of the Seminary as well as a member of its Board of Trustees. He remained a civilian, and did the best he could to protect the property of the Seminary and the High School.

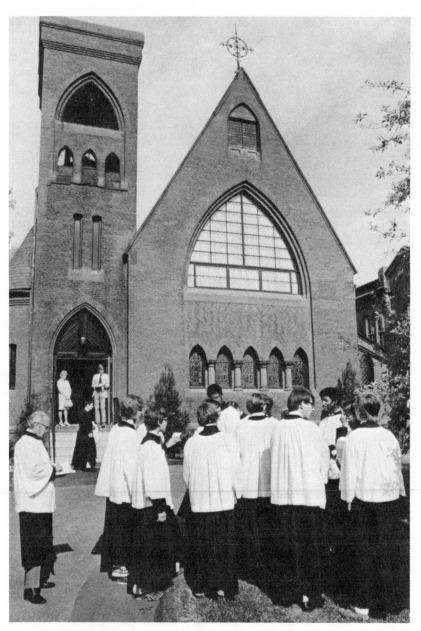

Did somebody say "Quack quack?"

He managed to save the Hill's buildings from being more damaged than they had been at the time they were used as hospitals by the Federals, and thanks to his efforts and those of the son-in-law of the Dean of the Seminary, Dr. Sparrow, the great grove of oak trees around the Seminary was spared. The trees of the School grounds were not so fortunate.

Cassius Lee lived for the rest of his life at "Menokin," and in 1870 his cousin Robert spent the night with him there on his last visit to Alexandria, a few months before his death.

On the morning after that night cousin Robert paid a visit to a neighbor, Samuel Cooper.

Samuel Cooper, West Point 1815, was appointed a full general of the CSA in May, 1861 and served throughout the War in Richmond. As "adjutant and inspector general" he outranked Robert E. Lee. Indeed, he was the highest ranking officer in the Southern Army. He was the great-grandfather of him who has been the source of all these stories, none other than EHS's Old Boy General, Samuel Cooper Dawson, Jr.

In 1878 the Fairfax Institute was reopened, as the Worthington School. That school lasted twenty-six years. The old Fairfax-Worthington building still stands, a private home behind the brick wall on Quaker Lane near Duke Street.

> *There is a tide in the affairs of men*
> *Which, taken at the flood, leads on to fortune.*
> *—Julius Caesar.*

General Samuel Cooper

There can also be a tide which is not so good. In 1901 Churchill Gibson found himself washed up on the Orange shores of the Woodberry Forest School. He played center on the football team in the first game of the long series against EHS, and WFS lost that game 54–0. The next year he came here, played center on our team, and the best we could do against his recentmost alma mater was eke out a scoreless tie.

Of course, not a few boys for not a few reasons have gone to more than one school. Billy Evans went to three: first VES, then WFS, then EHS (1929–31).

And of course many of our faculty members have taught elsewhere; both our present Headmaster and his immediate predecessor taught at and were HM's of other schools before they came here.

Plant

Build thee more stately mansions. . . .
—Oliver Wendell Holmes,
The Chambered Nautilus

Cooper Dawson (1921–28) was the School's business manager from 1969 to 1983, and with the help of his old friend David Bayliss he supervised an enormous amount of construction, thus:

Hummel Field and field house; cage, redone; Hummel Learning Center; Hummel dormitory; McGuire dormitory (for which old Memorial was torn down); Dalrymple dormitory (which is old Alumni redone); Penick House; seven faculty residences; west wing of main building redone; swimming pool.

Cooper says that he always tried to have things built "boy-proof." How do you boy-proof a building? "It's hard to do. Dreamy Daniel used to say 'Make them simple, solid, tough.' " If it wasn't boys proving that nothing on this malleable earth can be "proof," it was men.

There was the time in 1976 when the contractor mistook this pipe for that and dumped 5000 (five thousand) gallons of oil into our sewer. Interest in that event was promptly expressed by the Environmental Protection Agency, the City of Alexandria, the State of Virginia and the United States of America. For more than a week Flick's office smelled so bad that he couldn't stay in it.

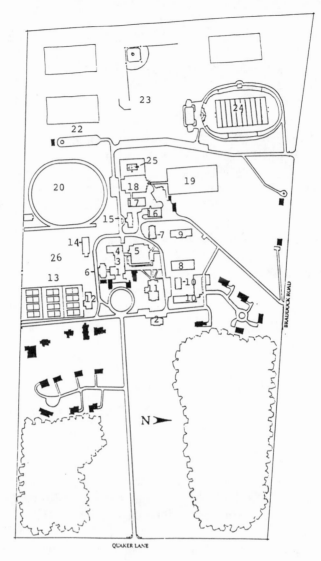

The Episcopal Campus

1. Hoxton House
   Main Building
2. Penick Hall
3. School Dining
   Room
4. Williams Wing
   Classrooms
5. Hummel
   Learning Center
6. Blackford Hall
7. Bryan Library
8. Pendleton Hall

9. Berkeley Dorm
10. Hummel Dorm
11. McGuire Dorm
12. Dalrymple Dorm
13. Tennis Courts
14. Stewart Gym
15. McAllister
    Infirmary
16. Maintenance
17. Wrestling Cage
18. Centennial Gym
19. Flippin Fieldhouse

20. Hoxton Field
21. Bryant Squash
    Courts
22. Greenway Fields
23. Bryant Fields
    Cooper Dawson
    Baseball Field
24. Hummel Bowl
25. Outdoor
    Swimming Pool
26. Callaway Chapel

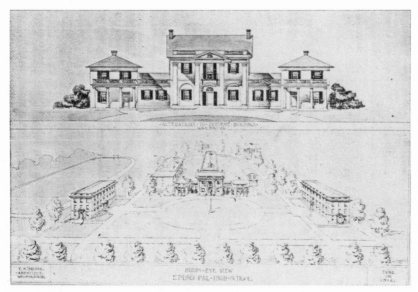

How we looked in an architect's dream, 1913.

In 1979 the front end loader of a contractor digging a trench for a new gas line broke the electric line in front of Blackford Hall. "The business manager," reports that business manager, "had warned about the electric line and he was so irate and raised so much sand that the Principal finally came out and suggested that he leave the scene." Our Cooper has never been exactly a "Milquetoast." It would have been educational to see him raising sand.

There was also the time, back in 1927, when Old Cooper's father and other shrewd businessmen thought that the School was unwise to pay $750 per acre for the thirty-three so-called Laird Acres to the west. "I wonder what they would think today when the assessed price of an acre of land in that area is probably $150,000."

In McGuire Hall, when the weather turned cold I used to be awakened early each morning by what I assumed was some upper classman beating on my steam pipes with a baseball bat. Rats were used to intimidation like that so I tried not to let the noise bother me. Only later did I learn that the banging was caused not by some malevolent Old Boy but by an antiquated heating system which was shooting hot steam into cold pipes.

Pendleton Hall

Tucked behind the Bryan Library was a brick building known informally as "Black McGuire." In it lived half-a-dozen old school workers who were all black and *very* good company for anybody lucky enough to be their friend. [DeCourcy Orrick, 1965–69.]

Poetry

Will Reade did all kinds of good things for us, one of which was public speaking, reading in chapel, sight reading to groups to achieve confidence, memorizing various bits and pieces. I remember memorizing bits of Shakespeare and believe it or not the entire *Ancient Mariner* of Coleridge. I can still do most of it. [Ben Baker, 1916–19.]

I'm so thankful Mr. Reade had us memorize lots of poetry. Teachers should require their students to do that while they are young. I can still utter, at most inauspicious times, lines such as Tennyson's "The Ptarmigan that whitens ere its hour woos its own end." Although I have never found the appropriate moment for such a pronouncement, I am happy to know that my brain does contain such gems. ["Mud" Churchman, 1945–47.]

Teaching by rote and by using memorization is no longer popular among modern educators, but I am particularly grateful to A.C. Phillips for not falling victim to popularity. That distinguished gentleman from Fredericksburg, Virginia (pronounced of course Firdicksburg) compelled me to memorize among other things the prelude to Chaucer's *Canterbury Tales* in Middle English. If I have recited those verses once in the past twenty years I have recited them a thousand times. I derive endless pleasure from being able to recall those phrases committed to memory in Mr. Phillips' English classes. I'm not well read and I've never been considered a scholar, but I've impressed a lot of folks by quoting from Shakespeare and the English romantic poets, and, of course, Chaucer.

I credit another gentleman, R. E. Latham, for my initial exposure to memorizing. In Ancient History Uncle Bob used to say "Dates are the pegs upon which to hang the facts of history," and he had us memorize the dates of reign of every English monarch from Ethelred the Unready to Elizabeth II. I studied harder for his final exam than I have ever studied since, and those pegs are with me still. [DeCourcy Orrick, 1965–69.]

Publications

*Any resemblance to persons living or dead is
entirely their own fault.
—The Monthly Chronicle, November, 1939.*

This School sang—sort of—before it could rightly fly.

In February, 1842, a secretive and solemn paper called *The Monthly Record* appeared. It was published by the faculty and meant to tell parents, in strictest confidence, how their boys were doing: grades were written opposite fictitious initials and each boy was represented by initials known only to his parents and him. Considering that there were 110 boys and postage was expensive it was a sensible method. Presumably to make the paper more interesting, articles like "Christian Education," "The Student's Death Bed," "Filial Disobedience," "The Rod" and "Infinity" were featured, but despite such enticements the *Record* did not survive after its first year.

In 1847 a sort of rudimentary catalog containing the course of study, terms, regulations and the names of the Rector (Mr. Dalrymple) and the Trustees was issued.

Ten years later the first journal written by the boys was produced. It was called the *Howard Miscellany* and contained contributions from older students, but it wasn't printed. The editors read it to the assembled School on Friday afternoons. Then the younger boys, whose contributions were being ignored, put together their own paper, the *Weekly Venus*. That effort was heroic. Every article in it was handwritten by the editor-in-chief. Its motto was *Omnia Labor Vincit* but *Omnia* was too much and it perished after only a few issues. The *Miscellany* lasted a year.

In November, 1888, our most venerable still-existing publication, *The Chronicle*, was born. That journal, originally named *The Monthly Chronicle*, served as literary magazine, editorial voice and purveyor of miscellany.

In its first issue the editors promised "to report faithfully all trials of strength or skill among the boys," and their description of one such trial—football—may be found in this book's section on Sports. In the second issue we learn that London's St. Pancras railroad station "is 700 feet long, and it includes 9,000 tons of iron, 80,000 cubic feet of stone and sixty millions of brick." In 1915 it spoke out against what it called overemphasis on examinations. In November, 1919, it named the Old Boys who had served, and those who had died, in World War I. In 1925 it criticized the School's leave policy and demerit system. For a hundred-and-one years the sturdy old *Chronicle* has entertained and informed the boys of this School and alerted the masters to their concerns. May its ink-stained shadow never grow less!

In 1890 there appeared a sassy little journal called *The Lightning Bug*. Its masthead listed as editors "Ironsides, Major, Queer Boy, Pilgrim, Shepherd, Deadeye, Boulevarde, 1492, Plant, Confessor," and its statement of intent was: "We give all our jokes in good nature. If we hurt your feelings, we don't mean it, if we bore you it is your fault."

It mentioned two apparent contemporaries, *The June Bug* and *The Cockroach*, which have vanished without a trace. A third contemporary, *High School Topics*, sported the motto *FAS EST AB HOSTE DOCERI* ("It is right to be taught by an enemy"), the enemy being the *Bug*, but it wasn't taught well enough and it too failed.

The Lightning Bug flew brightly about and published the first *EHS Annual* before it expired in 1893.

In 1903 *Whispers*, called by ABK "a more stately and imposing

The Monthly Chronicle.

EPISCOPAL HIGH SCHOOL, Near ALEXANDRIA, VA.

VOL. I. ———NOVEMBER, 1888.——— No. I.

COUNSELS FOR YOUNG MEN.

[From a private letter of a father to his son at school.]

It is said that happy men profit by the experience of others; wise men, by their own experience; and fools, by the experience of none. The best way is to min-found in every stratum of society and in every walk of life, and, wherever found, make their impress deep, and broad in the community around them. Cromwell and Luther, St. Paul and Mahomet, Dr. Guthrie and George Muller, Bismark and Andrew Jackson, in different degrees and different spheres are illustrations of this power. It is, however, found in every circle of society and in every grade, and the man who has it

FIAT LUX!! Page one of issue of The Chronicle. *Of the eight movers and shakers praised in those "Counsels" two are now known but to God: Thomas Guthrie was a Scottish clergyman/ philanthropist whose book* Plea for Ragged Schools *was published in 1847 and the German Georg Müller (1850–1934) pioneered in psychophysical studies.*

➤THE LIGHTNING BUG.◄

——ISSUED BY——

Ironsides, Major, Queer Boy, Pilgrim, Shepherd, Deadeye, Boulevarde, 1492, Plant, Confessor.

Vol. I. No 3. { EPISCOPAL HIGH SCHOOL OF VA., FEB. 7, 1891. { Price 50 cts. a Year.

This is the dullest time of the whole year. What with the mean weather and the examinations, the former of which blows your hat off, gets your feet wet and gives you a cold; the latter of which makes you work, won't let you loaf, makes you mad, sick and tired—it is about as little gay now as it ever gets. What then? Why, THE BUG, of course. That's what we are here for, and the darker the night the brighter the BUG, and we try to be modest about it, too, but just can't

THE BUG wishes to acknowledge right here the kindness of the Seminites in subscribing so liberally. We shall endeavor to give them fame in our columns often.

There is a sweet dudeling named B--c, Whose eyes have such a sweet l--c.
Do you notice the style of his elegant smile? His tongue runs on just like a br--c.

It is rumored in polite circles that the following conversation took place in town: M-ll-r—Shall I come and talk to you while you are having your tooth pulled? She— No, I never take gas. Marry, snick-up and and go to!

Mr. W-ll--ms says Indian Fritz, or Man-not-afraid-of a Cuban, put such a Hayes over B-rtl-tt's eye that he was unable to see. "Hath the fellow any wit that hath told us this?"

We were sorry to see that our esteemed contemporary, The June Bug, like all such insects this time of the year, died without a flutter a few minutes after its appearance. The Cockroach is still here, but it's too funny to live.

Mr. Gr--r's bevelled mirror on his desk is a work of art. We can well understand the pleasure he must take in looking at himself in any glass.

Because the old Roman's name was Brutus, is that any reason for A-dd-s-n's saying he was very brutal? We trow not.

It is passing strange that H-ld should be scared to death when he sings a solo in chapel. He's not the one to be scared then.

Vol. 1 No. 3. With such editors, how could that Bug *not enlighten? And note requiems for "esteemed contemporary"* June Bug *and too-funny* Cockroach: *might copies of those fellows still be somewhere in our crowded archives?*

DOWN THROUGH THE YEARS WITH
THE MONTHLY CHRONICLE

January, 1890. OUR DEPARTED CHIEFTAIN (Jefferson Davis died December 6, 1889)

January, 1893. THE INAUGURATION (of Grover Cleveland): ". . . think of the moral grandeur of the time in which we live. Turn back to the days when the transfer of power . . . was only accomplished with bloodshed."

March, 1900. TRANSVAAL VS ENGLAND: ". . . fight it all out by yourself."

February, 1919. THE SPIRIT OF FRANCE (magnificent!)

June–July, 1922. THE EFFECT OF PROHIBITION: "The majority of clear-thinking Americans are its loyal supporters. . . ."

June–July, 1941. LABOR CONDITIONS AND UNIONS IN THE U.S.: "Industrial peace . . . depends on . . . common sense."

January, 1942. THANK YOU, JAPAN: ". . . your treacherous attacks . . . have accomplished more in one day than ten Roosevelts could have done in ten years."

May, 1963. CHRONICLE POLL (most popular subjects: math, English, history; sports: football, soccer, baseball)

February, 1966. RECORD SNOWFALL ISOLATES CAMPUS (two feet in six days)

March, 1966. WAR HAWKS SUPPORT VIET NAM ESCALATION IN EHS POLL

January, 1967. GUMBLY-WADS, BANANAS, SISTERS TANGLE IN TRIVIA CONTEST

December, 1967. IS THERE TOO MUCH EMPHASIS ON ATHLETICS? (yes and no)

February, 1969. SIDEBURN CRAZE HITS CAMPUS: FACULTY YIELDS

December, 1973. ENERGY CRISIS REACHES EPISCOPAL

October, 1974. RAT SYSTEM SEEN AS NECESSARY EVIL

WHISPERS

PUBLISHED BY THE STUDENTS OF
THE EPISCOPAL HIGH SCHOOL
OF VIRGINIA, NEAR ALEXANDRIA

FORTITER, FIDELITER, FELICITER

A sober beginning.

For Paris, the Holy Hill; for Notre Dame, our bell tower.

publication," succeeded the *Annual*; it has been going its stately and imposing way ever since. Also in 1903 *The Bug* revived and formed a partnership with *The Chronicle* which lasted for three years. Then it went dark for good. A pity, because it was a sharp as well as merry little thing.

Many journals and chronicles of varying merit have sprung up like mushrooms since our early days. Our Hill is as Loquacious as it is Holy. But most of those ephemera have like mushrooms quickly perished.

One of the hardiest and best survivors has been *The Daemon*, a literary magazine started in 1957 and still flourishing. The daemon of its title was presumably the twentieth century incarnation of the famous afflatus which ordered Socrates around; or was it something less stern, more whimsical, out of Kipling? That great story-teller advised other writers thus: "When your Daemon is in charge, do not try to think consciously. Drift, wait, and obey." E. A. Poe might would have written for *The Daemon*. So might H. Melville, N. Hawthorne and W. Whitman. Maybe even, under an assumed name, E. Dickinson. Principals Pendleton, Dalrymple, McGuire and Blackford might not have. Why not? *The Daemon* should address that question in an editorial.

Notes Dick Daniel,

Anonymous publications were the rage in the twenties in many colleges and schools and the High School was no exception. At Finals for several years "The Black Book" had appeared. It was intended to be a humorous compendium of gossip about prominent boys and the teachers. However about 1926 the bounds of propriety were overstepped. Among other things a veiled reference to Mrs. Tompkins' pregnancy appeared. That did it. The school assembled in the chapel and the two boys responsible had to stand up and apologize to the student body. All the copies, which had been sold at the Saturday night dance, were confiscated. (*De gustibus est disputandum—et corrigendum.*)

The Monthly Chronicle and *Whispers* reigned supreme between the wars. The aforementioned Black Book died suddenly. Eight issues of *The Chronicle* per year were published at an annual subscription rate of $2. Payment was not mandatory and only about half the students paid. Advertising carried the freight. Printing cost about $40 per issue of 40 pages. Competition for board membership was not particularly keen. To be considered one had to submit a short story. For editor-in-chief an editorial was required. In 1930 when I became editor-in-chief only one other editorial was submitted.

As mentioned earlier, by 1931–32 the Depression was extremely severe; but the school remained full and did not cut its consumption. Hence advertising for both *The Chronicle* and *Whispers* held up. In fact at an average charge of $50 per page about $800 and $1000 were raised for each respectively. Many of us thought *The Chronicle* should become a weekly, so in May of 1932 two weekly issues were published, financed by the advertising surplus, with the hope that the idea would catch on. It did not.

The *Whispers* board was appointed by the editor-in-chief who in turn had been elected by the preceding board. The Read-Taylor Company in Baltimore had been producing the annual since 1922 and had set a high standard for excellence.

However their costs were high and the 1932 contract had to be their last. The company did not survive the Depression. The economies that year were as follows: there was a base cost for a fixed number of copies and a schedule of fixed charges for zinc and half-tone cuts. Extra copies were $1.25 each. The estimated cost including extra copies was around $2000 for a 200-page annual. At a $5 price to the students, 200 copies sold meant $1000. This plus the $1000 from advertising covered the cost; there turned out to be a surplus. (The actual cost in 1932 was $1,616.57.)

Now that potent word-processers are everywhere and potential word-processer-processers almost as ubiquitous, may we hope that in the future our Hill will be even more blessed with journals, chronicles, broadsides, serious manifestoes and light-hearted ukases than it has been in the past?

Rat

Breathes there the rat with soul so tough
Who never to himself hath said "Enough!"
Who never in that lo-o-o-ong first year
Hath moaned and groaned "Why am I here?"

One of my experiences which I remember vividly was when I was a rat. A group of "mean" old boys sent me over to Flick Hoxton's house for the "keys to the pitcher's box." Flick turned me around and sent me back with the message that the "mean" boys had the responsibility for those keys and they should find them. [Aldrich Dudley, Jr., 1924–30.]

There was no hazing as such, the only officially sanctioned chores imposed on rats being closing dormitory windows in the cubicles early in the morning well before the rising bell, waking the other boys at their chosen hour and pouring milk and water at meals. Boys being boys, and some with the sadistic pleasure of picking on those least able to retaliate, a little relatively mild hazing was inevitable such as the game of "bug in the rug." Selected new boys were invited to join in. The victim and an old boy lay on the floor, their heads covered with a blanket so they couldn't see. The boys standing around were given a paddle and took a whack at the victim's rear end. He would guess who hit him. If correct that boy would have to substitute for the new boy who theoretically would then join in spanking the new victims under the rug. Unfortunately the victim's partner under the rug wielded the paddle. The victim either never guessed the true state of affairs or was too frightened to say what he knew. In either event he continued to suffer until the others had satisfied their lust for inflicting pain. In practice it was generally more humiliation than real pain. Another sport was dumping a boy out of his bed. [Harry Blackiston, 1923–28.]

My most vivid and terrifying memory was of that first Sunday night mass meeting, being paraded as a Rat with other Rats over to Stewart Gym for the indoctrination (merciless quizzing as to who were captains, monitors etc) by the Old Boys. September 1954 was the last year for that. The victims wore white handkerchiefs. [Pearce Connerat, 1954–57.]

Philosophizes DeCourcy Orrick (1965–69):

Boarding school is not for every young boy. Sometimes chronic homesickness can only be cured by running away. A rat living across from me left the dormitory late one evening in order to arrive at Alexandria's train station for an early morning train south. On his way over the then-brick wall he fell and broke his leg.

This unfortunate event did not deter him, however. In the morning the Headmaster found him, fractured femur and all, at the station with ticket in hand, patiently waiting for the Southern Crescent and home.

In 1965 there was no greater insult than to be exposed to an unexpected and shocking "moon" from someone you considered an inferior. My roommate Jason was the victim of such an assault one morning as he left our room for breakfast. Three scantily clad rats had arranged themselves on all fours in a human pyramid just outside the green canvas cloth which served as the door to our room. When Jason emerged the rats quickly dropped their shorts exposing Jason to three moons in the full phase. One moon would have been insulting enough. Three was overkill. Jason grabbed the nearest weapon, our broom, and bashed away, scattering rats and straw all over the hall.

Not all rats on the Holy Hill had two feet. Once a large recently deceased *rattus commonus* was discovered in the baggage room under McGuire Hall. We put it in a paper bag and stuck it under the business manager's demerit clip.

Being a rat at EHS was really not all that bad. You had to learn by heart the names of all the varsity captains, the football schedule, and all the cheers and songs, and, of course, hold doors for upper classmen and pour and stack at meals. Only once did I forget a captain's name and have to sing a song from on top of my wardrobe.

Super rats were sophomores or juniors, and they usually attracted more attention because of their size. Seniors and monitors always called rats by their surnames. There seemed a great social abyss and it never occurred to me that the high and mighty would deign to learn the Christian name of a miserable rat. Great was my surprise when the senior monitor who lived in the room next to mine for a whole year called me by my first name on the day of his graduation. On that day I learned that the fellow really had cared about me. That realization made me feel for the first time that I was a part of the Episcopal High School, and it would forever be a part of me.

As an Old Boy I participated to a limited degree in the hazing of deserving rats. The son of the Suffragan Bishop of Virginia did something disrespectful, I forget what it was, so we held him by the legs and slowly dunked his head in the toilet—until we saw a shiny gleam from a gold cross fixed on a sea of purple. It was the Bishop, come unexpectedly to see his son. As luck would have it, the Bishop was an Old Boy, so he understood.

Lance Mangham (1983–87):

My first day I was standing outside the dining room door when someone told me "You better go back and get your rat tag right now!" I ran as fast as possible and got back just in time to sit down right next to a teacher (of course I was told that that seat was for seniors only and to never sit in a senior seat again). After dinner I learned what a rat run was. Too bad I didn't know where the "center" was yet. By the end of that day I swore that I wouldn't last a week at this school.

Though other classes argue the statement, my class was the real last rat class. We were the last class that had to wake up the entire hall in the mornings and call every single bell during the day. In fact, we were also the last class that had to do rat runs to the Center.

I have never been more nervous than when I sat up in upper study hall that first quarter of freshman year watching the senior monitors walk through. Were they going to tap me on the shoulder? Please, Lord, don't let them pick me. Please!

That year was also the last year of weekly mass meetings during which anything could happen. Two meetings come to mind. The first one I ever went to they picked a boy out of the crowd, Dale Bender, to do the E-P-I-S-C-O-P-A-L cheer. Dale, unfortunately, didn't know how to spell Episcopal. He never lived that one down. The second meeting of the masses that I remember was in the winter when everyone was wearing their wool coats. Some of the old boys had the great idea of slitting pillows and letting the feathers go everywhere. It only took all night to get them out of my hair, face, and especially my coat.

The "rat tag" was a tag that every rat had (has?) to pick up on his first day. It had his name on it and he had to wear it wherever he went. Old Boys told him that when he went to the shower he should pin it to his skin. It could not be taken off until after the first football win. The "rat run" was (is?) running to get anything any OB wanted, usually something to eat and a Coke in the Blackford lounge but sometimes all the way to the "Center," Bradlee's shopping mall just outside the front gate.

Apprehensive Rat Mangham lasted four years, graduated first in his class, and is now majoring in electrical engineering at Duke.

Running what was known as "morning relay" was an important duty performed by rats. It involved waking up the Old Boys and other rats on your floor in time for them to get to breakfast before grace. Each Old Boy had to be waked in a different way: this one had to be shaken gently by the shoulder, that one vigorously by the legs, this one not touched at all; some slept through a good shaking and needed a second or third, others leaped up, some screamed "I'm awake get out!", others made do with a polite "Thanks," others were as silent as the tomb. Woe to the rat who didn't get every single one to breakfast on time! [DeCourcy Orrick, 1965–69.]

R.A. "Bone-rack" Castleman (1870–75) had a rattier time of it:

In the autumn of 1870 a small boy learned that the dream of his life was to be fulfilled. He was to go to the Episcopal High School. Dr. Blackford had just taken charge. Six or eight boys formed a "gang," as they called it, whose sole aim and pleasure seemed to be to make life miserable for the small boys. Tom Brown at Rugby presents but a faint picture of what we endured. At last one of our number could endure it no longer, and induced his father to let him leave. So thoroughly intimidated was he that not until at the station homeward bound would he name to the Principal any of our persecutors.

A positive assurance from the Principal to the members of the "gang" that, should any knowledge of further operations in their chosen line come to his ears, his carriage would be at the door for them in twenty minutes, assuaged considerably the horrors of our situation. At the beginning of the next session one of them tried something of the same sort. A sudden simultaneous assault of five or six kids laid him in the dust, humbled his pride, and marked the end of "fagging" at the E.H.S.

". . . . The end of 'fagging'. . . ."—really?

Walton Moore (1872–77) may have had the rattiest time of all:

I distinctly recall the hour when I, a very small boy who had been tied very fast to the apron string of a mother who had but one son to spoil, found myself in the midst of the new surroundings. It was an hour of pride and triumph and rose-colored dreams without even a vague suspicion of faltering or failure. This feeling of exultation lasted about sixty minutes. I went from the Principal's study to the baseball field. I fancied that my playing attracted the same sort of admiration as had been accorded me at home.

I imagined that all eyes were turned in my direction, when suddenly (at that moment I was diverted by a cross-examination on ancient geography not knowing that the big boy was guying me) a hot liner took me full in the diaphragm and curled me up on the ground. Then home sickness began; what better evidence of the intimate relationship between the mind and the body?

At that time in Mr. Blackford's head-ship the young boys entering the School were not treated with the consideration by the older ones that has become the unvarying rule since. In fact there was a marked tendency towards hazing and I, obviously pining for home, dispirited, with all my flags flying at half mast, so to speak, became a victim of boy's inhumanity to boy. I escaped a head foremost ducking in the lavatory tank by pleading chills. This was hardly admissible for the chills in question had left me years before. The excuse was not accurate and by this admission I now make the only atonement I can for the departure from the literal truth, still glad however that I was not ducked.

Then, summoned to the play room which was a forbidden precinct to the kids, I was given the alternative of singing or having my face blacked and submitting to other indignities. I sang "Rock of Ages" and my voice, unmusical at best and on that occasion full of tears, inflicted such punishment on the audience that I was not allowed to proceed beyond the first verse.

The fellow who put me through the ancient geography examination seemed to think that fate had consigned me to his unmerciful custody. He made me the most miserable of mortals. He was an expert in the art of delivering a quick and stinging cut with a damp towel on the person of a half-clad kid. He taught me to regard the bathing squad as a most uncivilized institution. He taught me what is meant by "running the gauntlet." No human being ever manufactured a harder snowball than he or sent it to its human destination with more unerring aim. I shall always believe that he was the one who placed a snow man of ample proportions in my bed one night, a performance resembling that which leads to the exclamation in Alcestis "Cold comfort, I ween!"

In a word this individual brought me, young as I was, to constant melancholy musing on the question "Is life worth living?"

I made a step away from my troubles when my application for membership in the Fairfax Society was offered. There was but one Society then and its membership somewhat restricted and I thought then and I know now that being admitted was one of the most fortunate things that could happen to me.

The old building is gone, but I can never forget it. Of it I often fondly think, for it was a house of refuge to me, the scene of my earliest friendships, the medium by which I caught the first glimpse of the professional and political domain in which my life has been spent.

Evidently that house of refuge and its friendships more than made up for the miseries inflicted on the poor rat by his "ancient geography" tormentor, because Walton Moore stayed in the School for five years and went on to become one of the most capable, versatile and distinguished diplomats ever to serve this country.

Ratdom does end, one finds. Usually before you realize it a whole school year has slipped away. And then . . .

Thucydides said of the Greek lads who fought and lost at Syracuse "Having done what men could, they suffered what men must." Rats who survived Rat Year might say "Having suffered what little boys must, they do what big boys can."

But that was in the past.

Nowadays rats are "new boys" and in addition to the faculty advisors who look after all students they have monitors especially assigned to be their "big brothers."

Rogues

On Monday, April 13, 1778, James Boswell tells us in his *Diary*, Dr. Johnson boasted that he could repeat a complete chapter of Horrebow's *Natural History of Iceland*, and proceeded to do so, saying, "Chapter LXXII. Concerning Snakes. There are no snakes to be met with throughout the whole island."

And so, it seems, it is with this School. In all of our 150 years there is no record of any notorious scapegraces, criminals, villains, blackguards or rogues to be met with. (The mysterious William Orton Williams, hanged as a spy in 1863, was spying for the right side.)

Is our Hill really that Holy?

Sports

Ut Sit. . . .

Before the War and immediately thereafter there were no organized sports at the High School—or, for that matter, anywhere else in this country. Boys ran around, threw sticks and balls, hit each other, wrestled, and played whatever unruly games suggested themselves. Remember Rector Pendleton playing "bandy"?

Formal sports at the School began in the 1870's. The energetic new Principal, Launcelot Blackford, valued exercise as a vital outlet for youthful high spirits, and he liked organization and competition. His very successful efforts to start track, baseball, football tennis and lacrosse have been recounted in Chapter Four. Under Flick Hoxton, that superb athlete, team sports flourished even more vigorously, as they have ever since.

If EHS should ever decide to have a second motto, it might be— since for us Exercise outranks Cleanliness which is supposed to be next to Godliness—*Pure, Robuste, Sancte* = "Cleanly, Strongly, Godlily." Today, the School offers a bewildering assortment of ways to keep one *in corpore sano*: football (3 teams);

Some of the sports trophies won by the School and her boys as of 1926. Today, our trophies overflow out of the Bryan Library into a room of their own in Centennial Hall.

cross country (3 teams); soccer (3 teams); tennis (Fall and Spring); basketball (3 teams); wrestling (2 teams); track (indoor and outdoor); squash; lacrosse (3 teams); baseball (2 teams); golf.

Perhaps one day somebody will revive Mr. Pendleton's bandy?

Meanwhile, here is what the very first issue of *The Monthly Chronicle* (November, 1888) had to say about that era's prince of pastimes:

Foot Ball is the most manly and exhilarating of all games. In order to be proficient in it, one needs to have a quick eye and quick muscles, good judgment, and plenty of pluck. We read of Foot Ball in the days of King Arthur, but the game as it was then played and as we see it now are totally different. All of its fine points have been developed, and it now takes no inconsiderable amount of skill and method to excel in it. In early times the ball was nothing more than an ox bladder blown up and tied at the neck. In the days of Tom Brown the bladder was still there but it had been covered with leather. The ball now used is composed of a bladder of India rubber enveloped in pig skin.

The game was formerly played by any number. It was then reduced to twenty on a side, then fifteen, and then eleven, which number is decidedly preferable, as more men are apt to impede the action of each other.

It is unnecessary to write a description of the game as many of our readers have seen more contests than the writer. If not, let them read the

That famous football team of 1901. "First" in upper right means first to play Woodberry.

account of the match in Tom Brown at Rugby. Their game was not as we play it, but a good idea of its general character may be formed from this description.

To have a good Foot Ball team it is first necessary to pick the men and in doing this considerable judgment must be exercised. The rushers should be the largest, strongest men in the eleven. The three heaviest are generally played as centre rush, and the other two on either side of him, the right and left guards. The most active men in the rush line should be played as end rushers; and the weakest, between the guards and the ends. Next comes the quarter back. If he is capable, he should be made captain, as he has more opportunity to use head work and has a better view of the field. He should be a small, or at least a very active man. It is indispensable that he should have a quick mind and a decided one, ever ready to take advantage ofthe slightest opportunity offered. The two half-backs should be the speediest men on the team, for they have most of the running to do. They should also be able to pass the ball well, and with judgment. The full-back must be able to run, kick and tackle well.

To have a winning team they should be well trained. up to all of the tricks, for nothing gains ground like a good trick well executed. Every man should follow closely the member of his side running with the ball and be ready to receive it should it be passed to him. Accurate passing of the ball is the key note to a team's success.

Dick Thomsen has this report of less formal exercises: "On Athletic Day (presumably the precursor or successor of Field Day) in 1914 events included 'throwing the ball' and a 'potato race,' along with other more normal track events. Prizes were: a baseball glove, a collar bag, a knife, a pen, watch chain, and studs."

My first year my brother Rutherfoord played in the Woodberry game which we lost 6–0. It was played in wet snow on a muddy field. We beat Woodberry my third year and were undefeated. Our coach secretly installed the "T Formation" instead of the old "single wing" and we sprang it on Woodberry 9–0. I got jaundice my last year and missed two weeks from school. That year we lost to Woodberry 13–0 at Woodberry. Their team outweighed us by twenty pounds per player. Eight of their team later played major college football. Henry Swift was our halfback and weighed 125–130 pounds. I saw him get up after tackling a big back—his knees were wobbling, his head was shaking, and he was not walking straight. I'll never forget his courage. [E. Conway Moncure, 1929–33.]

"Dialogue between player and coach after a Cake Team football game: 'The guy in front of me kept holding me.' 'Didn't the referee see it?' 'He must not have.' 'What did you do?' 'I said Nice going, Buddy.' 'What did he say?' 'I didn't say it loud enough for him to hear it.' "—PHC.

When EHS played the Lawrenceville School for the last time, as a rat I fashioned FORGET HELL! rebel banners from bed sheets laid out on the floor in the basement of Pendleton Hall. We made good use of those banners and the famous Rebel Yell in New Jersey October 9, 1965. EHS lost the game 40 to 15 through no fault of the malevolent-looking Confederates we painted on the sheets. [DeCourcy Orrick, 1965–69.]

> By the rivers of Babylon, there we sat down,
> yea, we wept. . . .
> —Psalm 137.

Football team of 1894–95.

P.R. Meade (Manager), B.M. Randolph, E.W. Robertson, J.A. Berger (Captain), F.P. Helm, D.B. Tennant, P.R. Meade, J.O. Steger, W.H. Randolph, R.M. Menefee, W.A. Clason, A.R. Hoxton, C. Himel, M. Griffin, E.T. Massey, B.C. Nalle, L.G. Hoxton.

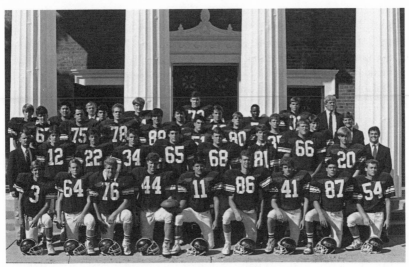

Football team, 1988.

Lance Mangham (1983–87) sat by those rivers:

L. Mangham

Arriving at school that first day was kind of like a nightmare. I had dreaded that day all summer. As my father drove me up the long front drive I was shaking. I hated changes and this change was going to be major. We pulled up in front of Hummel and me and my dad, both in coat and tie, hopped out to find out where I would be living. Thoughts of what my roommate would be like raced through my mind. "Yes, Laurance will be living in Berkeley and he has two roommates." Oh, great! The worst dorm and stuck with TWO roommates. Meeting new people was not my favorite thing to do. As the day progressed I met both of my roomies and they seemed okay.

I made a decision the second day of school that was probably the best that I have made in my life. I was unsure of what sport to go out for. I had played a little tennis and football but I knew that I wasn't very good at either. I had played soccer for two years but I dreaded every minute that I was on the field. After talking to a couple of Old Boys and seeing the signs that Mr. Male had posted I decided to try cross-country.

The first day of cross-country was almost as bad as the first day of school. Mr. Male seemed pretty nice but he made us run an entire mile! I thought I was going to die. By the end of four years everything had changed: running a mile was trivial. The question now was could I break five minutes. Mr. Male was the best coach I will ever have.

During my freshman and senior seasons our cross-country teams were ranked in the top ten schools (private and public) in the state, quite a feat figuring that we were up against schools ten times as big as us, but our team in my junior year was perhaps the best we ever had. Senior year was really special for me. I was finally running on the varsity team. Although against Woodberry I finished 13th out of 14 my time was 17:30 for three miles and I have never been so happy.

But my most vivid memory is disappointing. I was down to my last race ever: the Interstate Athletic Conference Championships senior year. Our team was in the top six in the state. This was it. I was running varsity in the Championships! As I stood at the starting line many thoughts raced through my mind; this was the last race I would run at EHS; I might finally get one of those nice IAC Championship sweatshirts. (We later learned that that was the last cross-country race Mr. Male would coach at the School.)

Seventeen minutes later I was down on the ground crying in disbelief. I refused to believe that we had lost. That race still haunts me.

Mens Felix in Corpore Incorporated

Among our super-athletes like Harry Flippin and the others there may have been some who had they been so inclined might have made professional sports teams, but none have tried. The closest we have come to such glory seems to be at one remove.

In 1915 Old Flick decided that the School needed a baseball coach, so he hired a most remarkable fellow.

Eppa Rixey was born May 3, 1891 in Culpeper, into an eminent old Virginia clan; one of his uncles was the surgeon in charge when McKinley was assassinated in 1901 and then was President Taft's surgeon general, and another uncle served in Congress during the early 1900's. Eppa didn't go to the High School but he did go to the University, and loved it. Trouble was, he was a terrific athlete, a six-foot-five natural at baseball, basketball, tennis and golf. He was such a powerful left-handed pitcher that, legend has it, "when Ep pitched for Virginia, the batters often fainted." The Philadelphia Phillies grabbed him right after he took his BA in chemistry, in 1912. (He managed to get an MA in Latin by working in the off-seasons, but was never able to drink deep of the Pierian Spring.)

In twenty-one years with the Phils and then the Cincinnati Reds he racked up 266 wins, a record for left-handers which stood until Warren Spahn of the Milwaukee Braves topped it in 1959. In 1963 Eppa Jeptha, as the sports writers liked to call him, became the tallest player ever to be immortalized in the Baseball Hall of Fame. And the most amazing thing, what certain writers call "the beauty part," was that he never lost his easy-going good humor. For a score of years in a milieu not notable for innocent enthusiasm he was a happy, playful, likeable elf. His only complaint: sleeping car berths were so short that he had to sleep in the aisles.

He came out to coach our worshipful diamond aspirants on October 26, 1915. He was as athletically awesome on the Hill as OldFlick himself, and not just because of his pitching prowess. Serving in tennis, another legend has it, he would toss the ball·"as high as Third Alumni," and then—woe to the boy, or the racket, or the net, that got in the way!

He also taught math.

Alas alas the Phils called him back in the Spring, and Mr. Carter was detailed to coach our 1916 team. The next Fall Mr. Callaway was given the coaching job, and the rest is history. Alas, because our Hill would have been if not holier at least hilariouser if happy Eppa Jeptha had stayed on.

Nine years after that brief but splendid era one of our Old Boys turned down a chance to reach the very peak of world amateur athletic distinction. As told in Chapter Five, when Ben Baker (1916–19) was a Rhodes Scholar at Oxford he ran against Cambridge's Harold Abrahams, hero of the movie *Chariots of Fire* and winner of the 100-meter dash in the 1924 Olympics. BB himself was invited to compete in those Games, but declined. Who won when he ran against Abrahams? "Can't remember. Oxford-Cambridge meets were casual, almost more social than competitive— lovely relationship."

Ben Baker was a track man for all seasons. He ran whatever sprint race needed to be run, and when he wasn't sprinting he was broadjumping. Once he was jumping and there, standing by the pit watching, was the King of England, George V. But as a photograph later showed, at the moment BB was at the top of his jump His Majesty was looking at his program. No matter: "He said to me later that he greatly admired the University of Virginia."

We did have one other brush with professional sports:

In the early 1970's the Washington Redskins football team needed an extra place to practice, and borrowed our Hummel Bowl. Afterwards they were so grateful that they donated two season tickets to the School. About five days before each Redskin home game the Headmaster would draw names out of a hat to see who the lucky ones would be. [William Fuller K. French, 1980–83.]

In general, Hoxtons have been to EHS almost as oxygen is to air: for more than two-thirds of the School's life (103 years, to be exact) at least one of them has been on the Hill in one capacity or another.

In particular, in EHS football they have set a record which any other family will have to work hard—for about a hundred years— to equal. Four (4) generations of them have played on about a dozen (12) varsity teams, the middle two generations on Hoxton Field.

Flick1 played in the backfield while he was a student here (1886–95) and then coached the first Episcopal football team to play Woodberry, in 1901 (we won, 54–0).

First Basketball team, 1913. Front Row: *R.G. Rhett, Jr., W.D.G. Boaz (Captain), W.A. Rinehart* Back Row: *O.M. Holmes, F.R. Rutledge, Mr. J.L. Hughes (Coach), A.G. Thurman, J.A. Ingle*

Ben Baker jumping in front of King George V (at right, with cane).

TITLE *St. Louis and Washington*

PLACE *Washington Ball Park*   DATE *May 15, 1920.*

NOTES *The stars were Courtney, Sisler, Gideon and Rice. Shannon got a three bagger. Went with "Jelly" Richardson*

Stump Philbrick and Jelly Richardson (1919–22) were able to go to this game because May 15, 1920, was a Saturday.

His son Flick2 (1928–35) played in the backfield, was captain in 1934, and was later an assistant coach.

His grandson Arch (1958–62) played in the backfield.

His greatgrandson Rob (1979–84) played guard and was one of the three captains in 1983.

Total points scored in eight Woodberry games in which Hoxtons played: EHS 106, WFS 90.

Cotten Alston was such a hero of the fabulous 1962 Woodberry football game (which we won 14–13) that "even today people remind me of it." At School he was one of the biggest of big dogs. "Football was the dominant sport then. Coach Sydnor Walden was very good, we had excellent teams and successes, the chemistry was almost mystical." What Homer said seemed overflowingly true: *There is no greater glory for a man so long as he lives than that which he achieves by his own hands and his feet.* BUT:

Now, looking back, I realize that football was It. The school offered no other worthy outlets or challenges, no other attractive opportunities, such as a good glee club, or arts program. Thus sports took on a larger-than-life sort of air that reinforced the existing atmosphere.

No, that 1962 game was not the highest point of my entire existence. Actually, I had played a terrible game, missed a lot of blocks,
so I was happy to have a little redemption. The real catch that day
was the first TD by Ed Carrington, who took it out of the defender's
hands. Then when the score was tied 13–13 the extra point snap was
low—"Gator" King pulled it out of the dirt and Mayo Gravatt
punched it through the uprights. Heroes all. That game was a lot of
fun, and it gave my roommate's father and my father a real thrill, but
it wasn't the apex of a lifetime.

Cotten Alston (whose roommate was Dick Yarborough) is now
happily "employed as a photographer, 'a solver of visual problems,
a visual confessor.' " The apex of his lifetime? "Yet,"—he hopes—
"to come!"

As for his retrospective dismay at the School's lack of other
worthy outlets or challenges in those days, let him marvel at the
profusion of such outlets today, as noted in the section on Curriculum. For the boys of the class of 1989–90 football is all right,
but this brave new world hath other creatures in it.

Herbie Bryant, who won the Rinehart Trophy for best athlete
in 1928, was not our greatest scholar. His mother was Mrs. Hoxton's sister, which didn't make his low marks less noticeable. According to his classmate Cooper Dawson, "Back in the Fall of
1923 we were both little skinny guys taking second math under

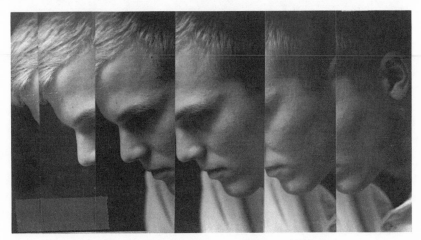

Cotten Alston as Cotten Alston sees him.

the strict supervision of Mr. A.R. Hoxton, Sr. and Herbert often came to class improperly prepared. On one of these occasions Mr. Hoxton looked at him and said 'Herbert old Herbert you are my nephew and sometimes I am not very proud of it.' He was much better prepared for the next couple of weeks."

About that same time Cooper old Cooper "broke the door in Wilmer Literary Society running from the clutches of Robert Cochran and had to report to Mr. Hoxton. He looked at me and said 'Cooper old Cooper I am sorry that you have broken the door and I will have to send your father a bill.' "

Such were a Principal's pressing problems, sixty-six years ago.

Marvin McCrary Giles, III (1957–61) did very well in athletics at the School, lettering in football, basketball and track. (He was also a monitor, headwaiter and member of the Honor Committee.) After school, however, he concentrated on another sport: golf. And in seven years he made himself a world-class player.

Vinny Giles plays to the seventh green on his way to an 8-and-7 victory over Mark James to win the British Amateur at Hoylake, June, 1975.

In 1962 he won the Virginia Amateur Championship (and in succeeding years won that title six more times, the last in 1987). He played in nine invitation-only Masters Tournaments, and in 1968 his 288 was the lowest amateur score in that Tournament. In 1972 he won the U.S. Amateur. The next year his 291 was the lowest amateur score in the U.S. Open. In 1975 he won the British Amateur.

Over the years he has represented the United States on four Walker Cup teams which played against teams from Great Britain, and on three teams representing this country against other teams from all over the world. He is noted for his putting and his short game.

Why didn't he play golf for EHS? Simple. "The School had no golf team." Now, of course, it has.

Aside from no-golf-team frustration, what are Vinny Giles' most vivid memories of his four High School years? "How much I hated it as a rat and loved it the last two years, and those hundred demerits." He got those demerits in the winter of his last year, for "hooking" (not the golf stroke) it down the road to Richmond and St. Catherine's School on a Monday leave.

Bill Clay (1921–25) might have fared better if he had gone out for golf, or tennis, or mumbledy-peg (a strange contest, popular in those long purple Washington Springs, of stabbing a knife blade into the ground between one's fingers, the faster the better, and the more dangerous):

> I decided to go out for track. I did not have any ability whatever and managed to suffer god-awful shin splints and the misery of running during the winter months on the wooden track that was laid on the little varsity football field. It seemed as though we had nothing but ice and snow all winter. We would slip and fall very often on a piece of unseen ice and go flying off into the snow bank that rimmed the track. The only thing that made the sport at all worthwhile was participation in the big college invitational meets in Washington and Baltimore. There we saw some world-famous runners, like Paavo Nurmi, the "Flying Finn," and Joie Ray, the great American miler. Nurmi had two unusual habits: he timed himself with a wrist watch while running and he never wore a jock strap. How he won race after race in that state of "undress" was a miracle to me.
>
> We wore long johns when we practiced and since we each had only

one pair on which was spilled a lot of the wintergreen liniment made by Coach Charlie Tompkins we were perpetually enveloped in a god-awful smell.

I also went out for football at which I was no better than at track. At first I weighed 114 pounds and played tackle on the Cake Team (our prize at the end of the season was a cake baked in the school kitchen). Then I worked my weary way up to the scrubs and got worked over every afternoon by the Varsity. My friend Joe Harrison did much better. He became a talented drop kicker and it was not unusual for him to hit one from the 50-yard line. The football in those days was much rounder than the skinny one used today, which is designed more for passing than for kicking.

Batter Up!

Last April 22 on Bryant Athletic Field the School took part in a ceremony as fitting as a faithful fielder's glove: the dedication of the Dawson Baseball Diamond.

Who Dawson? One guess only. . . .

Of our Cooper, third baseman non-pareil, the 1929 *Whispers* said that in the 1928 Woodberry game "His sharp fielding and one-hand pick-ups featured our defensive play." (Sad to say, despite that sharp defensive play our offensive play wasn't quite offensive enough. We lost the game 5–4.)

Transport

On Our Way Rejoicing . . .

Vic was an important part of our lives. First the store but then he owned a much banged T-model Ford bus. I drove it to take teams to nearby schools or to the railway station or to Washington for Monday holiday. I forget how many it could carry but it would be pretty full on Monday: fare 15 cents round trip. It barely made it on the level, did fine going down hill but not a prayer going up hill so that passengers had to get out and provide the power needed. [Ben Baker, 1916–19.]

A few years later the fare was a few cents more. Reports Bill Clay (1921–25):

Our carriage, 1894.

1910.

The Donaldsons operated several Reo Speedwagon trucks, each equipped with a canopy over the back and a hard bench running down each side of the truck that held about ten boys. It looked sort of like a covered wagon of the old days, minus the mule team. Bun was able to recognize a new boy almost immediately and would greet him with "Hi young fellah! Give me the check for your trunk and get into my bus. It will cost you $1.50 for your ride and 50 cents for your trunk."

I never learned how Bun and his brother Vic were able to obtain the

School carriage in front of Pendleton Hall, 1988. Waiting to be wafted warmly to Washington are (from left) Jamie McDaniel, Ross Reynolds, and Joel Dubenitz.

sole franchise for hauling students to and from the High School at the beginning and end of each school year, for the trips to Washington, and for carrying the athletic teams to various contests. Of one thing I am absolutely sure and that is that Flick would not have given them the franchise unless he had had complete confidence in their honesty and driving ability.

And his confidence was not misplaced, for Bun hauled us on all of our many trips, in all kinds of weather, without having but one accident that I heard about in my four years at the School, and that probably was not his fault.

It occurred on a return trip from Washington, on a cold and rainy night, when the Speedwagon skidded and almost turned over. No one was hurt, but I remember that Harry Flippin was sitting on the tail end of the truck and he fell out.

Another well-remembered trip with Bun was coming back from Washington after a track meet. A dense fog developed and it was almost impossible to see the road ahead. It finally became necessary for someone to run in front of the truck and help the driver find his way. We were all pooped out from the meet and I don't know how it came about that D. Tennant Bryan was selected by Coach Tompkins but selected he was, and he jogged much of the way back to school right in front of the old Reo, showing all of us the way.

D.T. Bryan

Tennant Bryan (1921–25) says "From 1924 to 1989 is a right long time and it is conceivable that a few details of daily happenings might be forgotten, but.... I would like to believe Billy Clay's account of my having led Bun's vehicle through the fog at night, but I have no recollection of any part of it and must say it sounds very unlike me to have displayed such stamina and/or heroism."

Will the Real Revere of that Midnight Run please stand up and take credit?

Transportation to Washington was provided by a truck owned by Vic Donaldson. Had Vic been alive when *A Christmas Carol* was written, Dickens would surely have used him for his model when he described Scrooge, for Vic was indeed "a squeezing, wrenching, grasping, scraping, clutching, covetous old sinner," and a low-grade, coarse, redneck to boot. A boy once said to Vic, "Vic, when you die they're going to paint a dollar bill on your tombstone." "Won't hurt my feelings none," was his reply.

The truck had wooden benches along the sides and a canvas cover for a top. The trip to and from the city in bad weather, with slippery, winding, narrow country roads, was horrendous, and only by the Grace of God was there never an accident. The dozen or so boys huddled together under the canvas top had no protection whatever, and any accident would probably have caused fatalities, or at least serious injuries. [Harry Blackiston, 1923–28.]

Vic Donaldson's truck had benches along the side of the body and canvas curtains which rolled down during cold weather and trapped the exhaust fumes. [Aldrich Dudley, Jr., 1924–30.]

The bus truly resembled a covered wagon, even to the part of the tarpaulin and some very hard benches. [Jim Meem, 1928–31.]

Train trips from home to school and back could also be memorable. Thus the same Bill Clay who profited by whoever it was's epic forerunner-run along the road:

Some of my most vivid memories of those long-ago days are the long trips to the High School on the Atlantic Coast Line railroad, leaving Savannah around 8 PM and arriving in Alexandria about eighteen hours later if the train was on time. The old Pullman cars were in charge of fine old colored porters who would make up the berths around 9 o'clock and hang the curtains for the uppers and lowers. The trains were very long and carried fourteen or more Pullmans and day coaches. The engines all burned coal and a tremendous quantity of coal cinders came into the windows in spite of screens.

I forget the number of the ACL train that carried us, Joe Harrison and me, north, but coming south we went on ACL #85. It was a wonderful train, since it was carrying us home. We spent Easter at School and got home only for about fourteen days at Christmas. What a thrill it was when the railroad representative called at the School during early evening to take the orders of students wanting reservations! He would set up his office in a little store-room just outside lower study hall and each of us would be summoned, one at a time. The tickets would be delivered about ten days later and we would lose ourselves in blissfully thinking about the coming trip home.

In our rat year Joe and I did our best to keep out of sight of any old boys riding the same train. Otherwise, we ran the risk of being forced to "propose" to any pretty, but completely strange, girl on the train. I had better luck than Joe. He had to get down on his knees to one extremely good-looking girl.

Joe Harrison didn't suffer. "The girl was indeed very pretty. Kneeling, I said 'Will you marry me?' She said 'No.' And that was that."

Vivant et Mulieres . . .

Most of you who are reading this will recognize the words above as part of the *Gaudeamus igitur,* which has been sung at academic exercises from time immemorial. They follow the *Vivant omnes virgines* line, translate alliteratively as "and long live the ladies," and are the male students' heartfelt toast and tribute to those adult females—described in the verse as "tender, lovable, *bonae* (which connotes all kinds of excellence), painstaking"—who have provided nurture, comfort and inspiration in their lives.

It is altogether meet, right and the bounden duty of these chronicles to salute the immensely important roles played by women throughout the history of the School, even if such a salute must because of lack of space be regrettably short and, thanks to the ineluctability of the Doctrine of Invincible Ignorance as applied to incautious compilers of exemplars, even more regrettably skewed. (That Doctrine, incidentally, also offers exoneration for those with proper credentials of ignorance.)

Down through the years the wives of headmasters and teachers have devoted much time and effort to bringing some home atmosphere into boarding school life. In his *Story of a Southern School* ABK describes Mrs. McGuire, wife of the School's third principal, as "the personification of all that was gentle, lovable and tender. . . . She was guide, counselor and comforter of all the homesick lads, and, when they were ill . . . nursed them with loving care."

As was Mrs. McGuire, so have been the wives of other principals and teachers of the past, especially Mrs. Blackford, Mrs. Llewellyn Hoxton and Mrs. Archibald Hoxton, all of whom have marble plaques testifying to their devotion to the School and its students; and Mrs. Williams, wife of the seventh principal. Betsy Thomsen and Ruth Hoxton, wives of the eighth and ninth headmasters, have both received the School's Distinguished Service Award for their many contributions, and future chronicles will doubtless recount how this kind of feminine service is continuing.

One custom of the past, now replaced by other activities, is worthy of note. Until the 1960's the married members of the faculty and their wives opened their homes to the boys on Sunday evenings and served cocoa, soft drinks, cookies and other delectables along with conversation and companionship. It was the female element, which sometimes included faculty daughters and their friends, that enhanced the pleasure of these evenings and helped put the visitors at ease. Old Boys of those days remember with gratitude the warmth and hospitality of those ladies who have already been named and also of Mesdames Reade, Daniel, Carter, Shackelford, Tompkins, Latham, Ravenel, Walke, McLaughlin, Walden, Bobbitt, Murray, Phillips, Seidule, Helfenstein, Johns, Ainslie, Shelor and others.

In addition to holding those Sunday soirees these ladies housed, entertained and chaperoned the girls who came for School dances, a form of hospitality which during Finals of the past extended over two days and nights! Along with these special services their presence on campus, whether in their homes or at their tables in the dining room, helped to provide a civilizing influence and some relief from the otherwise overwhelmingly masculine atmosphere.

Of the women who served the School in professional capacities several names stand out. The first of these is Miss Mary C. Leeper, a cousin of Dr. Blackford, who was the Matron from 1870 until her death in 1895. Suffice it to say that there is a marble plaque in her memory, and that ABK's book devotes seven pages to the eloquent tributes paid to her — far more lineage than was given to any other EHS notable, female or male.

Next on the list is Miss Mary Landon Jett, sister of the then Bishop of Southwestern Virginia who served as our Matron from 1904 to 1921. So beloved was she that in 1920 the students dedicated *Whispers* to her. Then there is Miss Annie Glascock, who was the Nurse from 1944 until her death in 1969 and for whom a well-deserved marble plaque was placed in Pendleton Hall. Miss Annie was amply constructed, somewhat along the lines of The Powerful Katinka of early comic strip fame, and her gentleness, warmth and understanding of boys made her an ideal person for her job. She sensed when there was a genuine need for a lad to be admitted to the infirmary for a little mothering, but the goldbricker seeking refuge from a test or the consequences of neglected homework was likely to receive short shrift.

Another name for this special pantheon is that of Mrs. Claude L. Hoover (now Mrs. R.S. Westervelt). She was the School Secretary from 1945 to 1962, riding herd on three headmasters (Hoxton, Williams and Thomsen). Mildred Hoover handled all the official correspondence and most of the telephone calls, maintained the files, and in general performed like the proverbial one-(wo)man band. When this remarkably able and energetic woman retired in 1962 she was immediately replaced by two persons, and in the more complex School of today her functions are being performed by an awesome number of secretaries, bookkeepers, computers and wordprocessors.

The list of those women who have served the School long and well in professional positions would not be complete without the name of Mrs. Virginia Tompkins Bell, who presided over the Joseph Bryan Library from 1940 until 1964 and whose unfailing patience and helpfulness were appreciated by the students of that period.

Up until the late 1970s classes were taught exclusively by men, but since then the professional role of women in the School has widened, and a number of them have served and are serving as regular members of the faculty.

Back to the volunteers. In 1949 there came into existence the Parents and Friends Association, an organization which has con-

Miss Jett. The boys of 1919–1920 *dedicated the eighteenth edition of* Whispers *to Miss Mary Landon Jett, "whose untiring devotion and sympathy have endeared her to all the E.H.S. boys with whom she has been associated."*

ferred many benefits upon the school and which, at least in its early years, was entirely female in its composition. The founding group was outstanding in terms of charm, talent and dedication, and these qualities have happily accompanied succeeding generations of the Association's leaders and supporters. They have provided valuable service in enhancing the aesthetic aspects of the campus, in promoting good relations for the School, and in raising funds for its continuing welfare.

The final all-male bastion at EHS was breached in 1983 when Suzanne F. (Mrs. William G., Jr.) Thomas, the mother of two alumni, was elected to the Board of Trustees. The breach was widened in 1984 with the election of Roberta Bryan (Mrs. Frederick S.) Bocock, the wife, mother, daughter, grand-daughter and great grand-daughter of Old Boys, and she was joined in 1985 by Douglass K. (Mrs. Hugh L.) Patterson, whose twin sons graduated in 1981.

The presence and influence of women in the life of the Episcopal High School has been benevolent, beneficial, and increasingly bountiful. To borrow another fragment from the *Gaudeamus igitur: Semper sint in flore.*

—(RPT *scripsit.*)

Washington

Tower'd cities please us then,
And the busy hum of men.
—Milton, *L'Allegro.*

On arrival in Washington, the first stop was the barber shop, shoeshine parlor and men's room in the basement. The sole purpose of a visit to Washington was to get some decent food and see as many movies as possible before the truck left for school about 5:30 PM. Three movies in three different theaters was considered par. A chocolate malted milk and toasted cheese sandwich at People's Drug Store was a good appetizer. It was on these holidays that I learned to love shrimp cocktails, the standard dish for our noon meal, usually at the Olmstead Grill. [Harry Blackiston, 1923–28.]

A student could go to Washington only once a month on Mondays. What seems almost incredible to me now is that he might see a movie in the morning, sometimes with an organ recital and vaudeville thrown in on the bill; eat a fine luncheon at the Olmstead Restaurant, starting off with a delicious shrimp cocktail; see a burlesque show at the Gayety Theater; and if his "cultural" leanings so prescribed, top it all off with another movie at the Earle, Palace or Fox Theater. All this and still have time to catch the last bus back to the High School and dinner! [Jim Meem, 1928–31.]

We parked a block or two off Penn. Avenue. Most went to the Washington Lunch: hot cakes and syrup 10 cents. Then to Peacock Alley of the Willard Hotel to watch the passing scene until Keith's Vaudeville Theater opened. Then into the Peanut Gallery for 10 cents and eventually back to the bus. [Ben Baker, 1916–19.]

We would get a lunch that seemed superb at Child's Restaurant, especially appetizing after the dreary meals at the School, and very often we would walk through Peacock Alley in the old Willard Hotel hoping to see some pretty girls go by. If we could find empty chairs we would sit and watch the parade and listen to the string quartet that always seemed to be playing beautiful tunes like "Tea for Two" or "Sonny Boy" or "Rose Marie" or "Indian Love Call" or even "Rhapsody in Blue." We also tried to listen to the music from Washington that came over the radio on a "crystal set" that got fairly good reception after lights out. We used ear phones, so we could listen far into the night, but it took quite a bit of skill to scratch the crystal with the "cat's whisker" in just the right way to tune in. For many consecutive nights we listened to the tragic story of Floyd Collins who was trapped by a fallen rock while exploring a new cave in Kentucky. It was impossible to free him and he died after an ordeal of several weeks. In those days "big" stories like that seemed to come only one at a time. [Bill Clay, 1921–25.]

Addenda

Fortiter, Fideliter, Tarditer.

When this book was being patched together many bits came late or, like the Prodigal Son, were lost and are found. Here are some of them.

From Bill Boothe (1938–43):

My strongest memory of EHS? The Old Guard, and Mr. Callaway. My second strongest memory is of a Sunday in December, 1941. We were sitting around outside the can listening to a Redskins-Eagles football game on a ten-dollar radio. (Each dorm was allowed one radio.) Suddenly the announcer broke in to say that the Japanese had attacked Pearl Harbor. We were angry that he had interrupted the game, and then to rub salt in the wound the Redskins lost.

My third strongest memory was also involved with the radio. It was October, 1938, and there was all that excitement about the invasion from Mars. Some students ran out onto the playing field and looked up expecting to see the green men.

And in 1940 or '41 the School put up some British sailors who came from Norfolk where their ship was being repaired. They made the war seem a little closer, but not much.

And I remember in the fifties all of the archives of this school were stored higgledy-piggledy in a small room off the hall in the main building, along with the Communion wine. Later they were moved to Pendleton Hall.

W.M. Boothe

Bill Boothe knows a great deal about the innerness of the School, and even more about its outerness. From 1951 to 1987 he was Alumni Secretary and Director of Public Relations and Endowment. He endeared himself to Old Boys with his self-styled "Victorian, Edwardian" low-pressure approach to matters of who gives what.

> *'T'were only a shote.'*
> —Kipling, *The Day's Work.*

In Chapter Four there is a little story about Quentin Roosevelt (1908–09). Here are two more stories about young Quentin, late but lively. The first is from Margery Hall Fawcett, whose brother, Percy Hall, was a rat with Roosevelt.

The two rats became friends, and one day Percy's father, who was rector of St. Timothy's Church in Catonsville, Maryland, came to see his son, "and one of the EHS masters asked him if he would see that Quentin got to the White House, where his father was living as President, for the weekend.

"When it was time to start, Quentin appeared with a pet pig one of the neighboring farmers had given him. The pig was just a piglet and Quentin had a dog's harness on it.

"In those days one walked from EHS down Braddock Road

and Lloyd's Lane about two miles to the Washington and Old Dominion trolley line where one boarded the car and rode to 12th and Pennsylvania Avenue in Washington. There they got off and walked up Pennsylvania Avenue to the White House. In those days the family had no secret service to guard them.

"They arrived safely, and Quentin was allowed to keep his pig!"

The other QR story comes from that elephant-memoried custodian of Hill lore, Dick Daniel (1925–32):

"It happened at my father and mother's wedding reception which was held in the Micou house just east of the tennis courts on December 15, 1908. Egged on by fellow students, Quentin was boosted in a window and was caught passing out wedding cake to the boys. My grandfather showed him to the door to the cellar stairs, pushed him in and closed the door."

(Wasn't it our own Edgar Allan Poe who said "the most beautiful word in the English language is *cellardoor*?")

Laurance "Lance" Mangham (1983–87):

If I had to vote on the best teacher in the school it would have to be Mr. Richard M. Stubbs. He is a wonderful math and computer teacher. The school owes him a great deal. He doesn't even get mad when I beat him at golf. (Golf tournaments were very big in the spring, inspiring putting contests in the halls and rooms of Hummel and Berkeley; pickup basketball games were favored during the winter.)

During my years at the School we started having a rotating schedule and Egypt was discontinued and seven students were kicked out after being caught with drugs (mushrooms). There were so many University of North Carolina fans that I turned into a Carolina hater within my first month.

Chapel was always the way that students greeted the day. Most came stumbling in at 7:55, five minutes late, only half awake. Singing verses out of the Hymnal and searching all through the Prayer Book were a little too much that early in the morning. It must have been hard for Reverend Brown, but he tried to add a little excitement. Everyone's favorite announcements were Mr. Craig's, which ended ". . . also today I will be giving out textbooks. When I say 'Who's next?' don't say 'Me!' "

Q: Who was the first person to win a race on the new track?

A: The day it opened, October, 1984, the cross-country team ran a mile on it, and Chad Anderson beat Billy Smith, who almost always won warm-up miles—an incredible upset!

Q: What was the score of our first official football game?

A: ¼–0. That is correct: one-fourth to zero. In 1881 EHS beat a place called Kendall by that score. I don't know how we got ¼ but that's what Coach Robinson, Mr. Hathaway, Paul Pelosi and I found when we dug back into the records. The computer wouldn't accept ¼; it insisted on 14, so the score 14–0 appears now in the books. Maybe some day some sports maven will account for that ¼;

My advice to future classes: enjoy your last month in school, your class will never be completely together again. During my first day I never thought graduation would arrive. When it did, I wished I could put it off. You will never have a chance to have as good friends as you have at EHS; I thank everyone who was a part of my time there; I hope Episcopal High School can last for another 150 years.

In 1839 the four most popular occupations throughout the South were (all figures approximate): "Farming"—250,000, "Commerce, Manufacturing, Mechanic Arts, Mining"—130,000, "Navigation"—12,000, "Law, Medicine and Divinity"—10,000.

In 1989 the four most popular occupations for about 3000 living Old Boys of the High School were, again approximately: "Law, Judiciary"—390; "Finance"—270; "Health Service"—160; "Manufacturing"—130. Only about sixty of those OB's were engaged in "Farming, Forestry," about forty in "Ministry (All)."

Three weeks before the Presidential election of 1960 a poll was taken of the 255 EHS students. Of the 230 who declared for one or the other of the two major candidates, 184 opted for Richard Nixon, 46 for John Kennedy—precisely four times more votes for Republican "Experience!" than for Democratic "Youth!"

NOTE: after the section on Misspellings had been completed, laying it down as law that the name of our best beloved math teacher was ShackELford, not repeat not ShackLEford, but before the text for this book was graven in stone, a chance trip through all of the copies of *Whispers* from 1903 to 1989 yielded along with a welter of nostalgia an astonishing fact:

In the forty-one *Whispers*es from 1907, when he joined our faculty, to 1947, when he retired, Grigsby Cave's last name is spelled ShackELford thirty-one times, ShackLEford ten times! And those ten times are not even all contiguous. He started off as LE and stayed that way for six years, 1907 to 1912. He then shifted to EL, but returned to LE for 1914 and 1915. He was EL again for the next three years, returned briefly to LE in 1919 and then

Shack, in the 1916 Whispers *which was dedicated to him. And that's how* he *spelled himself.*

was steadfastly EL for the rest of the way except for two one-year relapses to LE (1919, 1937).

In 1916 *Whispers* was dedicated to him as EL and in 1934 it was dedicated to his daughter Kin as EL but in 1937 there was a little confusion: that volume was dedicated to his wife Mabrey ShackELford whereas he was listed as ShackLEford. And in 1918 one finds confusion worse confounded: in the written list of faculty members he is ShackELford but under his picture that same name is spelled ShackLEford.

RPW's book has him EL throughout but in ABK he is EL in the text, LE in the index.

Oh well. He didn't seem to care how he was spelled, or elled. Maybe that soothing murmuration of his, "Isn't it easy, boys, isn't it easy," really meant that he more than agreed with Ralph Waldo Emerson, who held that "A foolish consistency is the hobgoblin of little minds."

Q E D

Homecoming Thoughts

by Todd Waters 1985–89

IT WAS HOMECOMING 1987. Episcopal was playing Wood-berry on a soggy field that had just recently been cleared of several inches of snow. The day, however, was bright and sunny and the stands of the Hummel Bowl were filled with members of the Episcopal community—faculty, alumni, friends of the school, and us students, inspired by a speech in chapel that morning by Mr. Dougherty and a mass meeting the night before.

We cheered ourselves hoarse, despite the sad fact that Episcopal trailed for most of the game. Losing that game hurt a lot, but we never lost our spirit, and cheered just as loudly during the last minute as during the first.

What sets this game apart from others in my memory, however, is an incident that took place during the second half. Episcopal was behind and we students were about the only people in the Bowl making any noise. Then the cheerleaders appealed to the alumni who were seated around us. "C'mon," yelled a raspy voice, "stand up—cheer!!" And those Old Boys did, just as if they were once again students at the school.

It would have been perfect if our team had rallied to beat the Tigers, but that was not to be. Never mind. The fact that those men stood up and cheered is very important to me. It made me think: what am I going to be like when I come back for my tenth, twentieth, or thirtieth reunion? What kind of mark will Episcopal have left on me? Will I stand without hesitation to cheer the Maroon?

The most marvelous quality about the alumni at that Homecoming game was their sense of belonging to the Episcopal community. That they were comfortable cheering along with the students was proof of this feeling that everyone has at the High School. Episcopal *is* a community, to which everyone belongs and for which everyone works.

The Headmaster guides the school, keeping it steady on course. The faculty members have many duties. They teach and try to excite in their charges the love of learning; they coach; they serve as dorm masters, advisers and members of action groups such as the Honor Committee; they do whatever else must be done. The students are also many-faceted. There are scholars, athletes, leaders, actors, poets, comedians, and various combinations of these. Seniors are role models for underclassmen, and monitors help New Boys get accustomed to life on the Hill. The New Boys also are important, for they represent the future of Episcopal, and it is up to them to carry on its traditions. Having a role to play at the school gives each student a vivid conception of his worth, enabling him to say "I am important. I am somebody." That feeling will never leave the student, even after he graduates, or after his fiftieth reunion. That feeling starts here.

Why is this sense of community so strong at Episcopal? It is probably because we are a small school, with only about 275 students and 40 teachers. Everyone knows almost everything about everyone else. You can hardly feel alone when 274 other students know your name, home town, personality, interests and achievements. Episcopal's smallness is a very good thing. It strengthens the bonds of community and makes the school the friendly, open, Southernly-hospitable place that it is.

Our small size also nurtures strong friendships. You can't help getting to know someone well when he is in your English class or plays on the same athletic team or sits at the same table or lives on the same dorm floor. These friendships are diverse and meaningful. Chances are that the alumni at that Homecoming game could not remember much about courses or sermons, but could and did remember friends and good (and bad) times shared. At Episcopal a boy comes to appreciate just how important friends are. They are the people with whom you share your successes, and in whom you seek consolation in your failures. They are the people who give you honest advice, and come to you for guidance. They are simply *there* when you need them, even after you have left school.

The final thing that I thought about at that game as I looked ahead to Homecoming in my own future was less tangible than the network of friends made here, but no less important. It was the school's sense of tradition. Being able to say "I went to the High School" has countless implications, such as "I was once a New Boy" or "I lived under the Honor Code" or "I learned to get along peaceably with a roommate" or simply "I survived four years of coats and ties, 7:45 A.M. chapels, and sit-down meals," but one element remains fundamental. Although externals have constantly changed, and always will, beneath all change there is an unwavering Episcopal tradition of taking New Boys and molding them into young men prepared to face the challenges of college and the responsibilities of life thereafter.

The Episcopal experience is amazing. It becomes a part of your character, and its values stay with you forever. You leave this School as a member of a special community, and you understand others, as well as yourself, better.

At my Homecoming, when I stand to cheer on the Maroon, these things will be in my mind.

Todd Waters

Lauds

BISHOP OF THE DIOCESE OF VIRGINIA:

The High School has its roots in the church, where intellect is disciplined by faith, and the value of the whole person is celebrated as the creation of a loving God. . . .

Peter James Lee

THE WHITE HOUSE, WASHINGTON:

Abraham Lincoln called education "the most important subject which we as a people can be engaged in." . . . . Throughout the years, your school has been engaged in this vital mission, enriching its students with knowledge and a love for learning. . . . God bless you.

George Bush

GOVERNOR, COMMONWEALTH OF VIRGINIA:

. . . very best wishes for continued success. . . .

Gerald L. Baliles

PRESIDENT, NATIONAL ASSOCIATION OF INDEPENDENT SCHOOLS:

The Episcopal High School has been important to NAIS from our founding 27 years ago. . . .

John J. Esty, Jr.

HEADMASTER, WOODBERRY FOREST SCHOOL:

. . . Woodberry's greetings. . . .

Emmett Wright, Jr.

Epilogue

To whom can I speak today?
Brothers are evil
And the friends of today unloveable.

To whom can I speak today?
Gentleness has perished
And the violent man has come down on everyone.

To whom can I speak today?
The wrong which roams the earth,
There is no end to it.

It is 1989. There are some five billion human beings on the planet, nearly 250 million in this country, and about three billion of them are living in poverty.

Explosion of population, rape of Nature, pollution and other man-made blights threaten to destroy civilization. The old Four Horsemen—War, Plague, Famine and Death—loom again out of our past, and are led by a fifth, more terrible: The Bomb.

There have been troubled times before. The little cry above was uttered by some despairing Egyptian four thousand years ago.

When this School was in its tender infancy Henry Lyte felt impelled to write that despairing lament,

> *Abide with me: fast falls the eventide;*
> *The darkness deepens; Lord, with me abide.*
> *Change and decay in all around I see,*
> *Help of the helpless, O abide with me.*

When the School was a struggling adolescent Matthew Arnold, son of the stern headmaster of Rugby whose fanatic discipline was aped by most early principals of American boys' schools, saw the Western world as desolation, "a darkling plain . . . where ignorant armies clash by night."

A few years ago Federal Communications Commissioner Newton Minow called this country's television fare, and by extension our whole intellectual domain, "a vast wasteland."

Today, through the troubled air sound Coleridge's ancestral voices prophesying war, and worse: Armageddon—oblivion.

Decay, ignorance, waste, these three; but the greatest of these is ignorance.

To survive, we must educate ourselves.

"Educate" is a deep and wide word. Derived from the Latin educere, *it means "to lead out."*

It is the function of schools, like this one, along with families and churches and other benefactors to lead people out of ignorance and its constant trouble-making companion, fear, into knowledge, and, God willing, more.

Wisdom is the principal thing; therefore get thee wisdom: and with all thy getting get understanding, *the Good Book tells us.*

The High School has always nourished understanding and caring as well as knowing.

The time has come. The peril and the promise are at hand. The School stands ready.

As the traditional School song goes, "God bless old EHS."

May we now and for another century and a half run our good race, fight our good fight, "and gladly teach."

May the Lord bless and keep us, may He make His face to shine upon us, and give us, and the whole troubled world, wisdom, understanding, compassion, and peace.

Bibliography

These books have to do with the High School and its boys; they are Required Reading:

Alvey, Edward, Jr., *Days of My Youth*: Fredericksburg, 1987.

Beymer, William Gilmore, *On Hazardous Service*: New York, 1912.

Blackford, Charles M., *Letters from Lee's Army*: New York, 1874.

Blackford, Launcelot Minor, Jr., *Mine Eyes Have Seen the Glory*: Cambridge, 1954.

Blackford, W. W., *War Years with Jeb Stuart*: New York, 1945.

Blackiston, Henry C., *Those Happy Years*: Princeton, 1986.

Bryan, C. D. B., *P. S. Wilkinson*: New York, 1965.

Dabney, Virginius, *Across the Years*: New York, 1978.

Diary of a Southern Refugee, During the War, by A Lady of Virginia (Judith McGuire): New York, 1868.

Dufour, Charles L., *Gentle Tiger*: Baton Rouge, 1957.

Goodwin, William A. R., *History of the Theological Seminary in Virginia. . . .*: Rochester, 1923.

Jones, Terry L., *Lee's Tigers. . . .* : Baton Rouge, 1987.

Kinsolving, Arthur Barksdale, *The Story of a Southern School*: Baltimore, 1922.

Lee, Susan Pendleton, *Memoirs of William Nelson Pendleton:* Philadelphia, 1893.

Wertenbaker, Charles, *Before They Were Men*: Alumni Edition, 1973.

Williams, Richard Pardee, Jr., *The High School*: Boston, 1964.

These books have to do with other schools, other boys (with the same problems), and other things of EHS interest; they are Recommended Reading:

Anson, Robert Sam, *Best Intentions*: New York, 1987.

Auchincloss, Louis, *The Rector of Justin*: Boston, 1964.
Bloom, Allan, *The Closing of the American Mind*: New York, 1987.
Botkin, B. A., *A Civil War Treasury*: New York, 1960.
Cookson & Persell, *Preparing for Power*: New York, 1985.
Davis, Burke, *The Civil War*: New York, 1960.
Dickens, Charles, *Nicholas Nickleby*: London, 1839.
Hirsch, E. D. Jr., *Cultural Literacy*: Boston, 1987.
Hughes, Thomas, *Tom Brown's School Days*: New York, 1883.
Johnson, Owen, *The Tennessee Shad*: New York, 1911.
The Juhl Letters to the Charleston Courier: Athens, Georgia, 1974.
Kipling, Rudyard, *Stalky & Co.*: New York, 1900.
Knowles, John, *Separate Peace*: New York, 1959.
Ravitch & Finn, *What Do Our 17-Year-Olds Know?*: New York, 1987.
Salinger, J. D., *Catcher in the Rye*: Boston, 1951.
Taylor, Richard, *Destruction and Reconstruction*: New York, 1877.
Tidwell, Hall & Gaddy, *Come Retribution*: Jackson, Miss., 1988.
Wolfe, Thomas, *Look Homeward, Angel*: New York, 1929.
———, *Of Time and the River*: New York, 1935
Wyatt-Brown, Bertram, *Honor and Violence in the Old South*: New York, 1986.

Index

"A bird that can sing . . . ", 21, 256
Abolition, 4, 64f
Acker, Nathaniel H., 265
Across the Years, xvii
Activities, 227
Adams, A.P., Jr., 181
Adams, Joel B., 154
Aeschylus, 27, 53
AIDS, 189f
Ailes, Eugene E., 143
Ailes, Stephen C., 152, 272f
Ainslie, L. Sanford, Jr., 215–223, 265, 271,
  291, 293
Ainslie, Sharon, 351
Akeley, R.N., 130, 262
Alaska, 53, 62, 187
Albertson, R.B., 177
Alcohol, 4, 180, 208, 282
Alexander, Tigger, 308
Alexandria, 227ff + *passim*
Allen, Richard K., 265
Alston, Cotten, 198f, 312, 342f
Alston, Philip H., Jr., 272
Alvey, Edward, Jr., xvii, 84ff, 98
Anderson, Chad, 357
Anderson, Rusty, 163
Angell, Norman, 105
Animals, 5, 230f
Antibiotics, 93, 119

Apartheid, 186, 189
Appomattox, 32, 48, 67f, 71
Aristotle, 195
Arlington Cemetery, 54, 166
Arlington House, 5, 7, 54, 59, 296
Armistead, J.C., 82
Arnold, Matthew, 80
Arnold, Thomas, 80
Athletic Association, 161
Atzerodt, George, 50
Automobile, 5, 90, 142f, 159, 170, 179,
  346–350
Avoca, 159
Awards, 182, 232

Backer, W.M., 130
Bailey, Edward P., 118
Bailey's Crossroads, 160, 167
Baird, John P., 40–44
Baker, Ben, 103ff, 271, 285, 292, 320,
  340f, 346, 355
Baker, J.D., 128
Baker, Jarvis T., 171
Baker, Newton D., 91, 98, 272f
Baker, Richard H., 173, 270
Baker, Tarbaby, 308
Baldwin, Christopher C., Jr., 183, 202,
  246f
Bales, Richard H.H., 274ff

Baliles, Gerald, 364
Ball, Johnny, 279f
Ballinger, P.F., 181
Balloon, 27, 29f
Bandy, 13f, 333f
Barbour, James, 274
Barnwell, Nat, 121, 181
Barrett, Boss, 262
Barrett, R.S., IV, 131
Barton, David, 38
Bartow, Henry B., 77
Baxter, Bobo, 158
Bayliss, David, 317
Beall, John Y., 52
Beall, William, 52
Before They Were Men, vii, 107
Bell, Cosby, 159
Bell, Stewart, 121
Bell, the, 137, 232ff
Bell, Virginia T., 150, 352
Bender, Dale, 330
Berger, J.A., 337
Berkeley, Norborne, 124, 201, 292, 298f
Berkeley, W.M., Jr., 130f
Beymer, William G., 40–46
Biays, Jimmy, 277
Bibb, William G., 143f
Binford, C.T., 177
Bird, R.M., 181
"Black Book", 326
Blackford, Ambler, 84, 122, 124
Blackford, Charles, 89
Blackford, John, 122, 124
Blackford, Launcelot M., 38, 64–89, 122,
    144f, 152, 166, 171f, 174, 227, 232,
    246, 249f, 256, 260, 264, 289, 293, 298,
    326, 330f, 333, 351
Blackford, Mrs. L.M., 78, 172, 233, 351
Blackford, Launcelot M., Jr., 66, 122, 124,
    273, 276, 293, 297f
Blackford Literary Society, 73, 75, 107, 157
Blackford, Mary (L.M.'s mother), 64ff,
    283f, 298
Blackford, Randolph, 122, 124
Blackford, Staige D., 122, 124
Blackford, Staige D., Jr., 271
Blackford, William (L.M.'s brother), 8, 66,
    88
Blackiston, Henry C., 183
Blackiston, Henry C., Jr., xvii, 115, 234,
    240, 257ff, 296, 308f, 328, 349, 354
Blacks, 207ff
Blandy, Graham F., 183

Blanton, John S., Jr., 265
Bliss, Robert K.W., 272
"Boarding schools", 313
Boatwright, Lee, 156
Boaz, W.D.G., 341
Bobbitt, Emily, 351
Bocock, Roberta B., 354
Bond, Langhorne, 272
Boogher, Ben, 183
Boogher, D.A., 176
Book of Common Prayer, 3, 152
Booth, John Wilkes, 48–52
Boothe, Armistead L., 156, 176, 271
Boothe, William M., 265, 306, 355f
"Boss", 100, 104, 139, 245, 267
"Boulevard", 160
Bounds, Alexander, 251
Boyd, Russell, 51, 266
Braddock, Edward, 297
Bradfield, James E., 305
Bradley, Douglas S., 305
Brawley, B., 181
Brawley, Rat, 308
Brazelton, T. Berry, 33, 274
Bridges, Jimmy, 155, 176, 183
Brittingham, Jacob, 57
Bronaugh, J.W., 128
Brookings, W.DuB., 181
Brown, D.T., 181
Brown, F.S.R., 82
Brown, John, 4, 23
Brown, Rodney K., 265
Brown, Willing, 105ff
Browne, V.H., 82
Broyles, Bunny, 262
Bryan, C.D.B., xvii, 276
Bryan, John Randolph, 29
Bryan, John Stewart (1889), 270
Bryan, John Stewart III (1956), xixf, 149
Bryan, Jonathan III, 181
Bryan, Joseph (1861), xix, 23, 149, 256f
Bryan, Joseph III (1921), 122ff, 230, 276f
Bryan, Tennant, 348f
Bryant, Herbie, 183, 343f
Buck, Blair D., 265
Buck, H.L., 177
Buck, W.H., 82
Buckingham, Mrs. B.H., 96
Buckle, Cuthbert C., 104
Bucknell, J.A.C., 130f
Bundy, Nathan, 128
Bunn, Robert, 51
Burge, J.D., Jr., 130

Burke, J.W., Jr., 181
Burn, Farmer, 308
Burns, Regi, 206f
Burroughs, Edgar Rice, 90, 123
Burwell, A.S.C., 176f
Burwell, G.A., 181
Butler, Smelly, 116, 308
Buxton, R.V., 177
Byrd, C.M., 181
Byrd, E. Wickham, 73

Cabell, W.D., 246
Cadigan, George L., 270
Calhoun, Lawson, 169
Calhoun, Marion, 169
Calhoun, Phinizy, 169
"Calicos", 161, 248
Callaway, Howard H., 128, 177, 272f
Callaway, Patrick Henry (PHC), 96, 115,
    121, 147, 150, 158, 178, 180, 198, 202,
    250, 253f, 265, 299, 306, 340, 355
Cameron Run, 111ff, 160
Campbell, Robert B., 154, 291, 306
Campbell, W.C., 181
Caperton, W. Gaston III, 272
Cardwell, Bickerton, 147, 151, 169
Carlin, Charles C., Jr., 115
Carpenter, Chuck, 111, 113, 128, 142
Carpenter, William, 137
Carrington, Dick, 103
Carrington, Ed, 343
Carroll, John M., Jr., 265
Carter, Bobby, 146, 168, 170, 266
Carter, Francis E., xvii, xx, 84ff, 96ff, 134,
    138, 143, 146f, 152, 154, 161, 170,
    179f, 252, 278, 335, 340
Carter, Francis E., Jr., 271
Carter, Jimmy, 188
Carter, Lucile, xvii, 84ff, 98, 113, 130, 134,
    164, 266f, 351
Carter, Nick, 135, 167f, 173
Carter, Samuel P., 46
Carver, Ashby R., 305
Cary, Buffalo, 308
Cary, Jefferson, 37
Cassilly, Stew, 262
Castleman, Bone-rack, 308, 330
Cates, M.L., Jr., 130
Cathcart, Hugh, 252, 278f
Cathcart, Jim, 286
Cay, John E., Jr.,181, 254ff
Centennial, 123ff, 291, 298f, 307

Centennial Hall, 115, 123, 142, 148, 152,
    198, 287
Characters, 235ff
Chase, Tony, 208
Chateau Thierry, 195f
Chaucer, 36, 128
Chichester, Dick, 286
Christian, F.P., III, 130
Christian, Mike, 211
Chronicle (see *Monthly Chronicle*)
Churchman, Charles J., 125–131, 240,
    279f, 296f, 309, 320
Civil rights, 187
Clark, G.L., 335
Clark, Mabel G., 121, 139, 267
Clark, Monk, 262
Clason, W.A., 337
Clay, Bill, 177, 259, 267f, 345f, 346–350,
    355
Clement, Thomas L., 265
Cleopatra, 102
Cleveland, Anne, 170
Cleveland, Billy, 170
Cleveland, Grover, 102
Cleveland, Lucy, 170
Cleveland, "Monkeywrench", 137, 155
Cloud, Mountjoy, 237
Cobb, Ty, 100
Cobbs, Lewis E., 265
Cochran, Robert, 344
Cocke, Hartwell, 108
Cocke, W.R., 335
Cockroach, 322
Coleman, Leighton, 77
Coles, George, 258
Collins, Floyd, 355
"Cologne Cathedral", 115
Colors, 246f
Conley, E.T., Jr., 177
Connerat, Pearce, 198f, 328
Connor, Pinky, 308
Connors, George Wash., 262
Conquest, Edwin P., Jr., 271
Conrad, Tucker, 25f
Cooke, Coo Coo, 308
Coolidge, Calvin, 166, 171
Cooper, Samuel, 316
Copenhaver, William A., 169, 279
Corson, Jay, 292
Craig, J.E.G., Jr., 265, 357
Craighill, D.H., Jr., 130
Craighill, L.R., Jr., 128, 130f
Craighill, R.M., 130

Crawford, Angus M., 264
Crawford, C.B., 335
Cromwell, Paw, 262
Crosland, Red Man, 308
Cubicles, 71, 80, 99, 221, 240f
Curd, John R., 298f
Curriculum, 220, 242ff + passim
Customs, 245–250

Dabney, V, xvii, 98–103, 105, 237, 276,
    301
Daemon, 326
Dalrymple, Edwin A., 16–20, 77, 196,
    208f, 227, 306, 314, 321
Dame, G.W., 82
Dame, R.N., 82
Dame, W.P., 82, 271
Dana, T.F., 130
Daniel, Anne, 146, 168
Daniel, G., Jr., 177, 262
Daniel, J.M., Jr., 131, 335
Daniel, Jack, 134, 168f
Daniel, John M., xvi, xx, 83, 96f, 105, 120,
    133f, 142, 168, 170, 180, 258, 264, 302,
    306, 317, 357
Daniel, Margaret M., 104, 134, 167ff, 351,
    357
Daniel, Richard M., xvi, 51f, 133–185,
    279, 304, 326, 357
Daniel, W.V., 130
Daniels, Ernest M., Jr., 303
Davis, Burke, 29
Davis, H.S., 181
Davis, Jefferson, 8, 10, 48f, 71
Davis, John A.G., 288f
Davis, John S., 103
Davis, Kenny, 281
Davis, 9–Toes, 308
Dawson, Cooper, 128, 143, 167, 238f,
    285f, 301, 303, 306, 314, 316f, 344, 346
Dawson, Virginia C., 167f
Days of My Youth, xvii
DeButts, Boota, 103, 308
Deeble, Riley, 218, 263, 265, 305
Dellinger, David, 211
Demerits, 148, 154, 170, 178f, 250–256,
    291f, 345
Denmark, Joe, 254f
Depression, 92, 121, 326f
DeSarno, M.J., 306
Diary of a Southern Refugee, xvii, 23
Dick, A. Colclough, 245
Discipline, 119, 256–260

Disease, 27f, 31, 91, 108, 178
Donaldson, Bun, 100, 115, 161, 234ff,
    347ff
Donaldson, Vic, 100, 134, 143, 155, 161f,
    234ff, 347ff
Donovan, Herbert A., Jr., 270
Dortch, G.H., 82
Dougherty, David R., 265, 271, 361
Doyle, Arthur Conan, 62, 80
Dual Contest, 157f, 273
Dubenitz, Joel, 348
Dudley, Aldie, 116f, 234, 327, 349
Duer, Red, 163
Dufour, Charles, 32–36
Dunlop, George, 213f
Dunlop, Johnny, 307f
Dusch, F.A., 128

Earhart, M., 82
Echols, William H., Jr., 68f
Edward VIII, 92
"Eggs, Hams and Sausages", 22f, 250, 309
Egypt, 121, 179f, 230, 248, 260–263, 357
EHS Annual, 102, 326
EHS Mudslinger, 269
E.H.S. News, 191
Ely, Ned, 167
Ely, Richard, 167
Endowment, 11, 95, 131, 201
England, 3ff, 21, 61f, 64, 75, 79f, 87, 196,
    299
Englar, G.M., 130
Englehardt, C.F., 82
Enrollment, 11, 15f, 59, 70, 121, 131, 221
Epilogue, 365f
The Episcopal High School, xvf + [RPW]
Estill, Robert W., 131, 270
Esty, John J., Jr., 364
Evans, Billy, 317
Every, E.H., Jr., 177
Examinations, 174f

Faculty, 263
Fairfax, Bryan, 37
Fairfax Literary Society, 38, 73, 75, 107,
    157, 190, 332
Fairfax, Orlando, 37f
Fairfax, Randolph, 37ff, 73, 80, 309
Fargason, J.T., 128
Farrar, James D., Jr., 265
Faulconer, Hunter, 177, 285f
Faulkner, Charles J., Jr., 264
Faulkner, Donald M., 273

Faunce, Theodore S., 219, 265
Fawcett, Margery Hall, 356f
Fawcett, Richard H., 108
Ferguson, Homer L., 104
Ferguson, W.McL., 176
"FFV's", 37, 39, 309
Field Day, 105, 107, 158, 336
Figg, J.A., 128
Fishburne, J.R., 181
Fleet, R., 82
Fleming, Julius ("Juhl"), 54f
Fleming, Warner L., 147, 170
"Flick", whence the nickname, 93
"Flick"—see Hoxton, A.R. & Son
Flippin, Harry, 111, 177, 183, 285f, 302,
  339, 348
Flunkeys, 173
Flushing Institute, 312f
Fontaine, Berkeley M., 264
Food, 11, 86, 99f, 116, 121, 137–140, 221,
  267ff
Four columns, 178f, 277 + Demerits
Freeman, Miss I.C., 96
French, William F.K., 253f, 262, 267, 292,
  312, 340
Frost, Evo, 308
Fruits (One), 269–276
Fruits (Two), 277–283

Gaines, Clarence, 253, 256
Gamble, E.L., 177
Gamble, Edward W. III, 305
Gant, C., Jr., 130
Gardner, William F., 56–60, 64, 196
"Gardy-loo", 282
Garfield, James A., 42ff, 187
Garibaldi, 34
Garnett, James M., 21f, 38, 64
Garnett, T.S., Jr., 176f
Garside, Barbara, 265
Gates, Rusty, 308
Gaudeamus igitur, xx, 196, 350, 354
Gayety Theatre, 100, 162, 254f, 355
Geer, A. Eugene, 231
Geer, Lucien M., 265
Geismer, Eugene, 117, 308
General J.R. Brooke, 195f
Gentle Tiger, 32
Gettysburg, 27, 32, 83, 88, 237
Ghosts, 283ff
Gibson, Churchill J., 245, 247f, 317
Gibson, Robert A., 270
Giles, Marvin McC. III, 344f

Girls, 8, 285ff, 350
Glascock, Annie, 352
Glenn, Dylan, 293
Glenn, Les, 158
Goldsborough, Phillips L., 272
Gooch, W.R., 181
Goodman, F., 131
Goodwin, E.LeB., 130
Goodwin, Frederick D., 270
Goodwin, Squinch, 121
Goodwin, Thomas R., 98, 130
Goodwin, William A.R., 230, 291
Gordon, C.M., 181
Gordon, W.T., 181
Grammer, Carl E., 159
Granger, Gordon, 41
Grant, Elmore, 287
Gravatt, Mayo, 343
Greear, J.N., III,
Greek, 15, 190–196, 257
Green, Berryman, 174
Greene, J.B.T., 176
Greenway, Addison, 107
Greenway Fields, 107, 160
Greenway, Gilbert, 107
Greenway, James C., 107, 150
Greenway, John, 107
Greenway, William, 107
Griffin, M., 337
Griffiths, Al, 173
Gunnell, Bruce, 238
Guthrie, Thomas, 323

Hagood, B.A., 130
Haines, John K., 265
Hall, D.D., 176
Hall, Frank S., 264
Hall, H. Thomas, 281f, 308
Hall, Percy, 356f
Hall, Sellman, 103
Hammond, L.M., 176f
Hancock, Charles W., 118
Hancock, E.H., 130
Hand, Hollis, 301
Handlan, J.M., 181
Hannum, William E., 265
Hanson, Bill, 122
Hanson, K.M., 181
Harding, Warren G., 91, 135, 166
Harnley, B.E., 266, 306
Harris, F.M., 177
Harris, J.M., 131
Harrison, Jaquelin M., 305

Harrison, Joe, 108–113, 177, 248f, 259, 279, 285, 346, 350
Harrison, Robert B., 286
Hathaway, David L., 358
Haydock, Bones, 262
Hayes, J., 82
Hearn, Ma, 121, 151
Hearne, Dean, 183
Helfenstein, Edward T., 270
Helfenstein, Edward T. II, 130
Helfenstein, Ernest III, 263, 265, 284f, 309–312
Helfenstein, Mrs. Ernest, 351
Helfenstein, Margot, 284
Helm, F.P., 337
Hemingway, W.R., 176
Henderson, Charles E. III, 229
Henderson, E.H., 130
Henry, John, 139
Henry, Wilmer, 139
Herbert, Gloomy, 308
High School Topics, 322
High List, 199
Himel, C., 337
Hines, John E., 166
Hodge, Vince, 208
Hodges, W.L., 130
Hoge, G.P., 335
Holbrook, W.G., 176
Holladay, H.T., 130
Holland, Cheese, 262
Holland, Clarence, 111
Holland, N.L., 176
Hollinger, L.E., 306
Holmes, O.M., 341
Holt, Rabbi, 308
Holt, Samuel C.O., 271
Homer, Louise, 159
Honor, 68f, 74, 154, 174f, 221f, 255, 279, 287–293
Honor and Violence in the Old South, 22
Hooff, Carrie, 168
Hooff, Charlie, 156, 167f
"Hooking", 255
Hoover, Mildred, 352
Houstoun, W.G., 131
Howard, 7, 32, 47, 67, 293–296
Howard House, 7, 23, 294, 297
Howard Miscellany, 321
Hoxton, A. R. (Flick), 85, 87, 90–185, 190, 196, 230, 238f, 244, 249, 255ff, 259, 266, 268, 274, 277, 286, 306, 327, 333, 340ff, 344, 352

Hoxton, Mrs. A.R., 100, 12, 145, 184
Hoxton, A.R., Jr., (Young Flick), 100, 145, 168, 202–216, 271, 306, 340ff
Hoxton, Arch, 342
Hoxton, Fanny R., 135, 146
Hoxton Field, 96, 134, 142, 155f, 202
Hoxton House, 7, 134f, 145, 148, 155, 157, 171, 202, 283, 293, 295
Hoxton, L.G., 337
Hoxton, Llewellyn, 69f, 87, 123f, 174, 289
Hoxton, Mrs. Llewellyn, 351
Hoxton, Mary Earle, 134, 145, 169, 284
Hoxton, Rob, 342
Hoxton, Ruth, 351
Hoxton, Sarah T., 100, 134, 351
Hubard, R.B. 177
Hubbard, E. Fraser R., 265
Huger, Billy, 128
Hughes, Banjo Eyes, 231
Hughes, Billy, 241
Hughes, J.L., 341
Hughes, Thomas, 4
Hunter, Alexander, 250
Hunter, E.P., 335
Hyde, S. F., 131

Influenza, 91, 104, 169
Ingle, James A., 270, 341
Ingle, James A, Jr., 130f
"Innocents Aboard", 196
Iverson, Alfred, 31

Jackson, John L., 270
Jackson, Stonewall, 216
Jackson, Uncle Jim, 135
Jefferson, Thomas, 37, 288
Jenkins, C. Francis, 140
Jett, Mary L., 105, 135, 138, 352f
Jett, Robert C., 138, 352
Johns, Ben, 263, 265
Johns, Betty, 351
Johnson, Andrew, 50, 53
Johnson, J.D.T., 131
Johnson, James, 211
Johnson, O.H., 82
Johnson, Worthington, Jr., 14
Johnston, Joseph E., 10, 29
Johnston, Lewis, 51
Jones, Alex, 276
Jordan, David S., 105
June Bug, 322

Kaminer, Bison, 262
Kaminer, Gus, 147
Karlson, Robert E., 198
Keck, Ray M. III, 265
Keith's Theatre, 86, 100, 355
Kennedy, Mrs. Edwin R., 135
Kennedy, John, 51, 187, 198, 358
Kennedy, Paca, 142f, 173
Kennedy, Robert, 188, 205
Kennedy, William Paca, 173
Kern, J.W., 264
Kern, J.W., III, 130
Kilpatrick, H.C., 130f
King, Caleb K., 271
King, F.D., Jr., 131
King, G.E., 306
King, Gator, 308, 343
King, Insect, 308
King, Martin Luther, 188, 204
King, No-Key, 308
King, Sunny, 308
Kinsolving, Arthur B. [ABK], xv, xx, 172, 351
Kinsolving, Arthur B. II (Big Tuie), xviii, 122, 125, 173, 270, 277, 291, 306f
Kinsolving, Arthur L. (Little Tui), 271, 301, 306
Kinsolving, Augustus B., 271
Kinsolving, Charles J., 38, 208
Kinsolving, Lester, 130, 301f
Kinsolving, Lucien, 122
Kinsolving, Lucien L., 270, 306
Klinefelter, Harry, 291f
Kloman, Felix, 134, 152, 270
Koonce, Lance, 214f
Kopper, Dick, 281
Kopper, S.K.C., 181
Kornberg, Grant C., 265
Kunkel, J.H., 82

Laird Acres, 160, 319
Laird, William W., 160
Lancaster, Dabney S., 270
Lane, J.T., 113–116, 237, 308
Lankford, Richard E., 181, 272
LaRoche, E.P., 130
Latham, Ella J., 169, 351
Latham, Robert E., xx, 147, 169, 252, 255, 275f, 302, 305, 321 Latin, 15, 18f, 93, 96, 127, 190–196, 296f
Lawson, Ewing, xvi, 243
Lay, Donald M., Jr., 270
Lea, Anthony A., 303

Lea, John W., 303
Lee, Agnes, 46
Lee, Cassius, 314ff
Lee, Fitzhugh, 314
Lee, Fitzhugh (another), 314
Lee, George B., 299
Lee, George Washington Custis, 54
Lee, L., Jr., 181
Lee, Light-horse Harry, 39
Lee, Mary Custis, 54
Lee, Peter James, 364
Lee, Robert E., 7f, 10, 16, 29, 31, 38f, 43f, 46, 48f, 54, 59, 67, 71, 80, 84, 10f, 110, 122f, 299, 302, 314ff
Lee, Robert Edmund, 271
Lee, Smith, 314
Lee, Susan Pendleton, xvii, 8–16
Leeper, Mary C.. 351f
Legends, 95, 297ff
Leigh, S.L., 176
Lemmon, F.T., Jr., 130
L'Engle, C.S., 335
Letters From Lee's Army, 89
Library, 102, 137, 148ff, 200, 218, 320, 352
Liggett, Emma C., 80
Liggett, Hiram S., 80
Lightning Bug, 322–326
Lincoln, Abraham, 27f, 48–53, 187
Lisanick, John J., 265
Lloyd, R.B., 130
Lowman, Gordon, 241
Lum, J. Brady, 288

McAlister Hospital, 119, 151
McCain, John S. III, 209–213, 272
McCandlish, Charles S., 281f
McClellan, E.L., 145
McClellan, George B., 46
McCreery, William W., 32
McCulloch, C.R., 82
McCullough, J.W., 128
McDaniel, Jamie, 348
McDaniel, Nelson, 265, 284
McGuire, Benjamin H., 32
McGuire, Hugh, 119
McGuire, Hunter, 131
McGuire, Hunter H., Jr., 131
McGuire, John P., 20–26, 32, 47f, 196, 232
McGuire, John P., Jr., 48, 271
McGuire, John P., III, 48
McGuire, Johnson, 103

McGuire, Judith B., xvii, xix, 23, 28, 30, 47f, 50, 351
McGuire's University School, 48
McKinley, William, 62, 187, 339
McLaughlin, Rosa, 351
McSwain, Jeffrey Y., 265
Mabley, J., 176
MacDonald, James R., 265
Macgill, C.P., 82
Machen, Lewis, 247, 264
Mack, Mr., 156, 161
Mackall, Charlie, 155
Mackall, L., Jr., 177
Mackall, William W., 169, 308
MacRae, G.D., 181
Magruder, John B., 10, 29
Magruder, John W., 22
Mahan, Milo, 15, 73, 312f
Male, Evan J., Jr., 265, 338
Mam' Peggy, 298
Mangham, Lance, 292, 329, 338f, 357f
Mars, 92, 122f, 188, 356
Marshall, James K., 32
Marshall, Thomas, 31
Marston, H.L., 177
Martin, Edward S., 183
Martin, Pete, 276
Mason, D.K., 181
Mason, J.S., 181
Mason, Roy, 120, 163
Mason, Saphead, 121, 308
Massey, E.T., 337
Massie, D.M., 130
Massie, Robert K., Jr., 273
Maulsby, D.L., 177
Maury, Richard L., 66
Meade, P.R., 337
Meade, William, 21, 77, 289
Meals, 137–140
Meem, James, 118, 120, 163, 172, 231, 234, 261, 267, 278ff, 286f, 292, 303, 349, 355
Memoirs of William Nelson Pendleton, xvii, 8–16
Menefee, R.M., 337
Menokin, 314
Merrimack, 30
Metz, J.D., 177
Meyers, J.H., 181
Meyers, T.E., Jr., 181
Michaux, William W., xvi
Micou, Richard W., 159
Military Academy, 8, 10, 16, 39, 174, 289

Miller, Henry J., 118, 165
Miller, John M., 265
Miller, Susan F., 265
Miller, W.C., Jr., 130
Mine Eyes Have Seen the Glory, 66, 293, 297f
Miracles, 300
Miscellanea, 301f
Missionary Society, 74, 141, 161f, 227
Misspellings, 302, 358
Mizell, Buddy, 119f
Mizell, Jack, 258f
Mobley, G.N., 130
Mobley, J.W., III, 130
Moncure, E. Conway, 119ff, 181, 252, 296, 336
Moncure, T.J., 176
Moncure, Thomas R., 303, 336
Moncure, W.A., 177
Monday holiday, 22, 85, 111, 165, 245f
Monthly Chronicle, 76f, 150, 190, 227, 260, 278, 289, 300
Monthly Record, 321
Moore, R. Walton, 71, 92, 272, 331f
Moore, W.P., Jr., 177
Morgan, H.J., Jr., 130
Morgan, Pida, 262
Morris, Mrs. Gouverneur, 37
Morris, J.C., Jr., 177
Morrison, F.M., 176
Morton, George, 155, 183
Morton, John S., 219
Moss, Charles G., 148
Moss, H.H., 176f
"Mr. Ball", 178
Mudtown, 98, 134f, 142, 161, 184, 234
Mueller, Bo, 163
Muhlenberg, William A., 312f
Maaller, G., 323
Murfee, James T., 169
Murph, D.S., Jr., 130
Murray, Heslett, 214
Murray, Lucy, 351
Music, 20, 111, 135, 145f, 158f, 218, 285, 355
Myers, Brent M., 265

Nalle, B.C., 337
Nalle, F.M., 335
Names, 304f
Naval Academy, 46, 64, 209
Nelson, Bruce, 159
Nelson, Kinloch (1858), 38, 270

Nelson, R.B., 159
Nelson, Robert, 15, 159, 182
Nelson, Rosalie, 121
Nelson, Seddon, 159
Nelson, Thomas Kinloch (1896), 111, 159, 166, 264, 270
Nevius, Chalmers, 115f
Newton, John B., 270
Nicknames, 102, 305–309
Nightingale, C.D., 181
Nobility, 309–312
"Nourishing Nora", 254f
Nugaeva, Natalya, 221ff
Nulsen, Greaseball, 308
Numbers, 312

Occupations, 358
Okie, Platt, 118f
Old, William W., Jr., 246f
Old Guard, xx, 96f, 355
On Hazardous Service, 40–46
Orrick, DeCourcy III, 200, 204, 207, 213, 230f, 234, 240, 252f, 261, 266f, 282, 287, 305, 320f, 328, 330, 336
Orton, Lawrence W., 40
Others, 312–317

P.S. Wilkinson, xvii
Packard, Joseph, 38, 77
Packard, Walter, 38, 122
Page, J.G., 176
Page, John, 15, 289
Page, R.B., 130
Page, Thomas Nelson, 15
Page, W.L., 130
Palmer, Allison, 99
Parker, Big Ace, 130, 262
Parrish, Honest Ned, 308
Parrish, Ike, 119, 121, 252
Paschall, Samuel, Jr., 207
Patterson, Douglass K., 354
Payne, John, 276
Paynter, Dick, 262
Peacock Alley, 162, 355
Pearl Harbor, 92, 356
Peebles, William S. IV, 271
Pelosi, Paul, 358
Pendleton, Susan—see Susan Lee
Pendleton, William Nelson, 8–16, 30f, 33, 38, 71, 196, 242, 274, 289, 333
Perry, F.S., 82
Peter, America P., 39
Peter, Britannia, 39

Peter, Columbia, 39
Peter, George W., 42
Peter, Walter G., 40–46
Peterkin, George W., 96, 270
Peterkin, Mrs. George W., 96
Philbrick, Harry, 107, 176, 308
Phillips, Allen, 218, 253, 263, 265, 290, 305, 321
Phillips, Jackie, 351
Phillips, Phil, 262
Phillips, W.C., Jr., 130
Pickett, George E., 66
Pinder, John B. III, 199f
Pinkerton, A.W., 176
Pithonian Society, 71f
Pleasance, A.C.E., 306
Pocahontas, 37, 309
Poe, Edgar Allan, 10, 18, 84, 232, 326
Poli's Theater, 162
Pomfret, J.D., 130
Population, 3f, 27f, 32, 53, 61, 90, 186, 229, 365
Pott, Possumtrot, 308
Pott, William S.A., 271
Potts, Eleanor, 14
Powell, Lewis T., 50
Pranks, 223—see also Fruits (Two)
Prevatt, P.L., 131
Price, J.W., 82
Prohibition, 91, 175, 184

Quaile, Birdie, 262
Quaile, G.R., 130
Quarles, Matt, 253f
Quin, Robert P., 118f, 151, 308

Radio, 118, 122, 176f, 281, 297, 355
Railroads, 5, 8, 27, 85, 104, 111f, 328, 349f
Randall, Blanchard, 219
Randall, C.C., 176
Randall, William, 135, 139
Randolph, A.G., 82
Randolph, B.M., 264, 337
Randolph, Cottontail, 308
Randolph, M.E., 176f
Randolph, Oscar deW., 247, 271, 335
Randolph, R.L., Jr., 130
Randolph, Thomas M., 37
Randolph, Virginia, 37
Randolph, W.H., 82, 264, 271, 335, 337
Rankin, E.S., 181

Rats (human), 21f, 99, 103, 115ff, 121, 268, 319, 327–333, 350
Rats (rodents), 57, 78, 221
Raven, The, 19, 84
Ravenel, Tis, 351
Ravenel, William B. III, 117, 198, 204f, 231, 240
Reade, Evelyn, 168
Reade, Frank R., 122, 168, 271
Reade, Mary R., 134, 145, 169, 351
Reade, Mary W., 134, 145, 169
Reade, Nan G., 169, 351
Reade, Stella, 145f, 169
Reade, Willoughby, xx, 96f, 125, 128, 134, 143, 145, 147, 158, 164ff, 168f, 180, 182, 185, 261, 264, 302, 306, 320
Reagan, Ronald, 189, 364
Reconstruction, 53, 83
Reid, Russian, 262
Revolution, 5, 27, 229
Reynolds, Ross, 348
Rhett, Albert M., 308
Rhett, R.G., Jr., 341
Rhodes Scholars, 104, 271
Rice, Edward A., 265
Richardson, Jelly, 342
Riddick, A.L., Jr., 130
Rinehart, Bill, 202
Rinehart, W.A., 341
Rixey, Eppa, 299, 339f
Robertson, E.W., 82, 337
Robertson, Harrison M., 273
Robinson, Carroll B., Jr., 265, 358
Robinson, Clarence W., Jr.,
Rodwell, Graham M., 231
Rogers, F.W., Jr., 130
Rogers, R.J., 130
Rogers, W.H., 128
Roosevelt, Eleanor, 93
Roosevelt, F.D., 92
Roosevelt, Quentin, 84, 108, 301f, 356f
Roosevelt, Theodore, 84, 121, 302
Roper, J.L., III, 130
Roper, Katherine E., 265
Round Hill School, 312
Rowe, Oran, 202
Rowe, Sandy, 281
Royall, Kenneth C., 272f
Runk, Dean, 284f
Rust, William F., Jr., 266, 281
Rutledge, F.R., 341

Salaries, 11, 13, 184, 244
Salisbury, R.C., 130

Salmon, Victoria N., 265
Sands, C.S., 181
Sasscer, L.G., Jr., 130f
Schley, R.L., Jr., 181
Seaman, Al, 178
Seamon, Alexander R., 108
Sebrell, J.N., 177
Seidule, Molly, 351
"The Seminary", 5, 7, 16, 20, 25f, 51, 56, 74, 98, 111, 113, 115, 123, 142, 144, 146f, 152, 158–161, 164–168, 170, 173f, 176, 184, 201, 242, 270, 279, 281, 293, 301, 314, 316
Semmes, D.H., 131
Semmes, George, 288
Semmes, John G., 305
Settle, Virginia, 265
Sexton, Speed, 308
Shackelford, Evelyn, 134, 169
Shackelford, Grigsby C., xx, 96f, 103, 134, 138, 144–147, 151, 167, 170, 176, 180, 263, 266, 274, 302, 309, 358ff
Shackelford, Jane B., 134, 167, 169
Shackelford, Kin, 134, 167ff, 184
Shackelford, Mabrey P., 134, 351
Shaia, Gregory J., 265
Shanks, W.F.G., 44
Shaver, Tony L. 265
Shelor, Bonnie, 351
Shelor, Joe, 253, 263, 265
Shepherd, Finley, 262
Shepherd, L.C., 128
Sherley, S., 181
Sherrill, Bits, 308
Shiers, Bill, 238f, 279ff, 296f
Shreve, Bill, 276
Six, Steve, 265
Skipper, Charles H., 265
Skoggard, Animal, 308
Smith, Billy, 357
Smith, Dean, 163
Smith, George A., 314
Smith, Jack, 215
Smith, Mr. Mom, 308
Smithsonian, 4, 62
Smoking—see Egypt
Snowden, Dane, 207f
Southall, Valentine W., 32
Spanish-American War, 51, 62
Sparrow, William, 316
Speidel, Fred C., 143, 170
Spinoza, Boche, 308
Sprigg, D. Francis, 270

St. Agnes School, 168
St. James School, 313
St. Paul's School, 313
Stabler, W. Brooke, 113, 271
Stalky and Co., 62
Stanton's store, 1
Steger, J.O., 337
Stewart, Misses, 96
Stires, Ernest M., 270, 274f
Stires, Louise H., 159
Stites, J.W., Jr., 131
Stocker, Brutey, 308
Stoney, Louise, 105
Stoney, Prunehead, 262
Story of a Southern School, xvf + [ABK]
Stowe, Harriet Beecher, 4
Stratton, Dick, 211
Streed, Jeffrey A., 265
Strider, I.H., 177
Strider, Jimmy, 177
Strider, Robert E.L. II, 271
Stringfellow, Franklin, 29, 48–52
Stuart, Albert R., 270
Stuart, Annie, 135f, 170, 284f
Stuart, George C., 100, 121, 135f, 142f, 146, 166, 172f, 264, 284
Stubbs, Richard M., 265, 357
Study hall, 154f, 166, 170, 199, 215, 277ff, 283
Styers, Skip, 281
Sulfanilamide, 93
Summer camp, 215, 284
Summer school, 179
Suthon, Walker J., Jr., 131, 273
Swan, Benjamin B., 265
Swift, E.W., Jr., 177
Swift, Henry W., 181, 336
Swimming pool, 151

Taliaferro, B.W., 176
Taliaferro, Robert C., 31
Tarbutton, Ben, 219
Tarzan of the Apes, 90
Tayloe, Edward D., 233f
Tayloe, James L., 30
Tayloe name, 303
Taylor, Archibald H., 59
Taylor, G.R., 177
Taylor, George, 137
Taylor, J.M., Jr., 176
Taylor, Stuart, 234f, 263
Taylor, W.H., 177

Taylor, W.H. IV, 176
Taylor, Walter, 156
Teeter, Mark, 218, 265
Telegraph, 4, 27
Telephone, 61, 141, 172, 304
Television, 140
Tennant, D.B., 82, 337
Thomas, Dick, 247
Thomas, G.C., 176
Thomas, J.W., 177
Thomas, John, 137
Thomas, Llewellyn, 129
Thomas, Suzanne F., 354
Thompson, R.C., 131
Thomsen, Betsy, 306, 351
Thomsen, Richard P., 76, 191, 193–202, 204, 206, 212, 244–250, 261f, 292, 300, 302, 305ff, 336, 350–354
Those Happy Years, xvii
Thur de Koos, Paul, 219
Thurman, A.G., 341
Tidwell, William A., 48
Tom Brown's School Days, 4
Tompkins, Charles V., xx, 117f, 120, 146f, 150, 169, 173, 178, 180, 198f, 266, 284, 292f, 303, 305, 346, 348
Tompkins, Margaret B., 146, 169, 326, 351
Tompkins, Peggy, 168, 266, 284, 292f
Tormentors Club, 158
Torrence, Clayton, 5, 39
Train, Robert, 121, 308
Transportation, 100, 346–350
Trapnell, Hall, 155
Trask, Son, 308
Treacle, 100, 249, 267
Treat, L.R., 335
Trenholm, Lee, 168
Trigg, J.G., 335
Tucker, H. St. George (Bishop), 152, 174, 299
Tucker, H. St. George (Professor), 288
Tucker, Richard D. III, 258ff
Tucker, W.M., 181
Tufts, J.R., 181
Tufts, Rutledge, 120
"Tuie," whence the nickname, 306
Tuition, 11, 15, 99, 151
Tyler, A., Jr., 176
Tyler, J.P., 177
Tyler, J.P., Jr., 176f
Tyler, John, 47
Typewriters, 61

Uncle Tom's Cabin, 4, 66, 92
"The University", 7f, 38, 56, 64, 66, 84, 93, 95, 122, 131, 173f, 190, 206, 213, 237f, 288f, 339f
Upshur, John, 46
Ut Sit Mens Sana . . ., 96

Vaill, F.S., Jr., 130f
Valz, E.V., 82
Varner, H.H., 128
Vest, George S., Jr., 272
Viet Nam, 3, 27, 188, 205, 209–213
Virginia Episcopal School, 216
Virginia Military Institute, 118f

Wafle, David, 219
Waiters, xx, 110f, 248
Walden, Ann, 351
Walden, Sydnor, 306, 342
Walke, R.A., 82
Walke, Roger A., Jr., 271
Walke, Rose, 351
Walker, Cornelius, 77, 270
Walker, D.S., Jr., 306
Walker, David, 128
Walker, John D., 276
Walker, John M., Jr., 265
Wall, 144
Wallace, George C., Jr., 273
Waller, John T., 47
Walsh, S.G., 128
Wannamaker, W.K., 130
Wanza, Joe, 135
Waples, J.B., 335
War of 1812, 3, 229
War of the Worlds, 92, 123
War Years with Jeb Stuart, 8, 88
Wardlaw, A.L., Jr., 130
Ware, J.W., 130
Warfield, Peter, 219
Warren, F.C., 181
Washington and Lee University, 8, 71, 84, 201, 216
Washington, city, *passim* + 354f
Washington College, 8, 67, 71
Washington, George, 7f, 51, 102, 228, 235, 297
Washington, S.L., 130
Waterman, A.B., 130
Waterman, Joe, 168
Waterman, Mrs. Joe, 168
Waters, B.W., 82
Waters, Todd, 361

Watkins, H.B.M., 82
Watkins, Louis D., 42
Watson, F.L., Jr., 181
Welch, Clem, 262
Welch, J.H., 130
Wertenbaker, Charles, xvii, 107, 276ff
Wetherill, W.C., Jr., 181
Whaley, Richard S., 272
Wheat, Roberdeau, 32–37, 39, 89, 274
Whispers, xx, 87, 150, 190, 227, 247f, 261, 266f, 306, 322–326
White, Addison, Jr., 271
White, Ben, 23
White, D.I., Jr., 82
White, David, 122
White, R.J., Jr., 181
White ties, 74, 117, 249f
Whittle, Francis M., 270
Whittle, Robert L., xx, 96f, 108, 120, 128, 138, 150f, 154, 175, 180, 249, 296, 306
Wickham, John, 237
Wickham, Littleton, 108, 235ff, 244
Wickham, Robert C., 28
Willard, Joseph E., 272
Willcox, Delsey, 262
Willcox, T.H., 128
Willett, J.A., Jr., 176
William and Mary College, 84
Williams, A.A., 176
Williams, Athlynn, 168
Williams College, 201
Williams, Dick, 168
Williams, F.C., 177
Williams, F.D., 181
Williams, Frank, 168f
Williams, Gertrude B., 168, 351
Williams, Kate, 46
Williams, Kevin, 219
Williams, Lawrence, 39
Williams, Marguerite, 168
Williams, Martha, 39, 44, 46
Williams, Richard P. [RPW], 77, 83, 96, 115, 138, 143, 146f, 168, 180, 190–193, 196, 245, 274, 296, 352
Williams, Weepy, 308
Williams, William G., 39
Williams, William Orton, 39–46, 51, 333
Wilmer, C.B., Jr., 176
Wilmer, Joseph P.B., 7, 73
Wilmer Literary Society, 73, 107, 145, 157, 172, 344
Wilson, E.E., Jr., 130
Wilson, R.C., 82

Wilson, Robert T., 260f
Wilson, Woodrow, 86, 91, 105
Winchester, James R., 57, 78, 270
Wires, John W., 265
Wollak, Chris, 251
Women, 25, 188, 350–354
Wong, Theodore, 276, 303f
Wood, J.M., 131
Wood, W.H., 177
Wood, W.H., Jr., 176
Woodall, Jeff, 219
Woodard, E.L., 176
Woodberry Forest School, 93, 111, 155ff, 167, 191, 208, 308, 317 Woodbury, Wilmington Flash, 308
Woodruff, Bumpsy, 308
World War I, 84, 86, 90, 105, 133f, 140, 150, 184, 191, 195, 252
World War II, 92, 125, 142, 191, 195f, 204f, 227, 276, 289
World War III ?, 274
Worthington, G.Y. III, 181

Worthington, Maria, 167
Worthington, Mary, 167
Worthington, Virginia, 167
Wright, Emmett, Jr., 364
Wright, Fred, 216
Wright, Ryvers, 213ff
Wroth, E. Pinkney, 121f
Wyatt, Rob, 219

Yale, 95, 156, 195, 201f
Yankees, 3f, 298, 314
Yarborough, R.F., Jr., 306, 265, 343
Yellott, John I., 271
Yen, Way C.W., 82, 272
Yonahnoka, Camp, 147
Young, John B., 118

Zabriskie, George, 113
Zabriskie, Philip T., 271
Zerkle, Zerk, 262
Zimmer, S.W., 335

About the Author

JOHN WHITE WAS BORN in Tarboro, "Queen City of the mighty Tar River in the Tarheel state of North Carolina." He graduated from EHS in 1930 and from Harvard College, and has an M.A. degree from George Washington University and a Ph.D. from the University of Edinburgh.

He worked for newspapers in Boston and Washington as a reporter-columnist, for the United States Information Service as a feature writer, and for the Smithsonian Astrophysical Observatory as Information Officer and observer at the SAO's satellite tracking stations in Florida, Curaçao and pre-Khomeini Iran (then called Persia). In 1965 he collaborated with astronomer Gerald Hawkins to produce the still-controversial book *Stonehenge Decoded,* and in 1982 he wrote a curious little paperback called *Rejection* which perhaps because of its glum title was resoundingly rejected. He has also written stories for magazines.

J.B. White

During World War II he navigated Marine Corps transport planes over the Pacific.

When he was a very little boy he saw very little eels swimming in the muddy waters of the Tar and was told that they had swum all the way from the great and wide Sargasso Sea, and he marvelled at Nature. Then, in the Philippines, where his father was a missionary, he saw what he still reckons was a dragon, and he marvelled even more at Un-Nature. Since then he has steadfastly pursued dragons and mermaids and unicorns and their fabulous-but-not-necessarily-false cousins through innumerable zoos, libraries and cathedrals (gargoyles are not the only stone monsters howling in those heights), and "one of these days—or decades" he hopes to finish his huge, definitive book of Unnatural History.

He lives in Cambridge, Massachusetts, in considerable content, thanks in large part, he supposes, to something the High School quietly put in him, or mercifully left in him, all those years ago.